SOA and Web Services
Interface Design

Morgan Kaufmann OMG Press

Morgan Kaufmann Publishers and the Object Management Group™ (OMG) have joined forces to publish a line of books addressing business and technical topics related to OMG's large suite of software standards.

OMG is an international, open membership, not-for-profit computer industry consortium that was founded in 1989. The OMG creates standards for software used in government and corporate environments to enable interoperability and to forge common development environments that encourage the adoption and evolution of new technology. OMG members and its board of directors consist of representatives from a majority of the organizations that shape enterprise and Internet computing today.

OMG's modeling standards, including the Unified Modeling Language™ (UML®), Model Driven Architecture® (MDA), and Systems Modeling Language (SysML) enable powerful visual design, execution and maintenance of software, and other processes—for example, IT Systems Modeling and Business Process Management. The middleware standards and profiles of the Object Management Group are based on the Common Object Request Broker Architecture® (CORBA) and support a wide variety of industries.

More information about OMG can be found at *http://www.omg.org/*.

Morgan Kaufmann OMG Press Titles

Distributed Systems Architecture: A Middleware Approach
Arno Puder, Kay Romer, and Frank Pilhofer

UML 2 Certification Guide: Fundamental and Intermediate Exams
Tim Weilkiens and Bernd Oestereich

Real-Life MDA: Solving Business Problems with Model Driven Architecture
Michael Guttman and John Parodi

Business Process Change: A Guide for Business Managers and BPM and Six Sigma Professionals
Paul Harmon

A Practical Guide to SysML: The Systems Modeling Language
Sanford Friedenthal, Alan Moore, and Rick Steiner

Master Data Management
David Loshin

Database Archiving: How to Keep Lots of Data for a Very Long Time
Jack Olson

SOA and Web Services Interface Design: Principles, Techniques, and Standards
Jim Bean

SOA and Web Services Interface Design
Principles, Techniques, and Standards

James Bean

AMSTERDAM • BOSTON • HEIDELBERG • LONDON • NEW YORK • OXFORD
PARIS • SAN DIEGO • SAN FRANCISCO • SINGAPORE • SYDNEY • TOKYO

Morgan Kaufmann is an imprint of Elsevier

Morgan Kaufmann Publishers is an imprint of Elsevier.
30 Corporate Drive, Suite 400, Burlington, MA 01803, USA

This book is printed on acid-free paper.

Notices
Knowledge and best practice in this field are constantly changing. As new research and experience broaden our understanding, changes in research methods, professional practices, or medical treatment may become necessary.

Practitioners and researchers must always rely on their own experience and knowledge in evaluating and using any information, methods, compounds, or experiments described herein. In using such information or methods they should be mindful of their own safety and the safety of others, including parties for whom they have a professional responsibility.

To the fullest extent of the law, neither the Publisher nor the authors, contributors, or editors, assume any liability for any injury and/or damage to persons or property as a matter of products liability, negligence or otherwise, or from any use or operation of any methods, products, instructions, or ideas contained in the material herein.

Library of Congress Cataloging-in-Publication Data
Application submitted

British Library Cataloguing-in-Publication Data
A catalogue record for this book is available from the British Library.

ISBN: 978-0-12-374891-1

For information on all Morgan Kaufmann publications, visit our
Web site at www.mkp.com or www.elsevierdirect.com

Printed in the United States of America

09 10 11 12 13   5 4 3 2 1

Contents

The companion website containing an image collection of all the figures in the text can be found at:

www.elsevierdirect.com/companions.jsp?ISBN=9780123748911

Acknowledgments

This book is largely a collection of my personal research, learning, experiences, and guidance that were shaped over time. Many people influenced the content and direction of this book, and I thank them for their wisdom and support. Special thanks goes to my family for their patience and support— Sue Bean, Lisa Clyde, Ron Clyde, Kimberly Bean (Bug), David Bean, Megan Bean and, of course, Connor.

I would like to thank Morgan Kaufmann publishers (Elsevier) and in particular Greg Chalson, Heather Scherer, Denise Penrose, Don Whitehead of MPS Content Services, and Anne McGee. I also want to thank the many subject-matter experts, contributors, reviewers, and others who influenced this book in some manner and patiently listened to me ramble on about the importance of XML, XML Schemas, SOA, Web services and data services: Bob Morgan; Shashikant Rao; Hitesh Seth; Todd Thompson; Kaustubh Mule; Mehmet Orun; VP Krishnan; Blair Kennedy; Jerome McEvoy; Brian Schween, Herb Adams Mark Reha; Bala Swaminathan; Donna Russell; Michael Sandberg; Hal Lavendar; Beth Ackerman; Neil Jarvis; Tony Shaw; Barb Wakefield; Dave Blidy; Jerry Blidy; Chris Dickson; Caren Shiozaki; Lara Tang; Marc Cantwell; Alexander Falk; Tara LeFave; Jackie Barkworth; Arka Muherjee, Ph.D.; Anne Marie Smith, Ph.D.; Peter Aiken, Ph.D.; Susan Urban, Ph.D.; Lori Gubernat, M.S.; John Gubernat; and many others (you know who you are).

I also think it is important to acknowledge the many contributions of the World Wide Web Consortium, OASIS Open, WS-I.org, IBM, Oracle, Sun, Microsoft, TIBCO, Altova, Sybase, The Open Group, and DAMA International. They have helped us to recognize SOA as a reality.

I truly hope you can benefit from this book, even if only in some small way.

Thank you!
James (Jim) Bean
SOA Lightning

SOA—A Common Sense Definition

1

To fully understand and implement a service-oriented architecture (SOA), it is critical to have a solid grounding in business and technology evolution. From this, we can describe a set of common sense analogies and then drive into practical examples. First and foremost is realizing that SOA is not exclusively a technology solution. Rather, SOA is an example of business and computing evolution. It is an architectural approach for business that includes and requires supporting technology capabilities. SOA enables business enterprises to become more dynamic, agile, and responsive to change.

1.1 ORIGINS OF SOA

Unfortunately, it is unclear exactly where the term "service-oriented architecture" originated. Rather than try to identify a specific individual or organization that coined the term, it is probably more important to describe what SOA is and how it has evolved to become a recommended approach to solving business challenges. IBM infers that SOA originated from several technologies and practices:

> The origin of SOA can be traced back to Remote Procedure Calls (RPCs), distributed object protocols such as CORBA and Java RMI, and component-based architecture such as J2EE/EJBs (Sun) and (D)COM/COM + /.Net (Microsoft).[1]

While this is a reasonable definition, it also implies a strong technical origin for SOA. While it is clear that SOA did evolve from technology origins, the reality is that SOA is also a business enabler. SOA begins to provide the long-awaited promises of rapid development, business agility, and reuse. To achieve these goals, SOA combines technology capabilities with the evolution and needs of the business enterprise.

To help explain the evolution of SOA, let's visualize a timeline of significant and related technology shifts (see Figure 1.1). Our starting point of interest is somewhere in the mid to late 1990s. This is the era where distributed computing, the Internet, e-commerce, and the Web started to become mainstream technologies for business. To keep a real-world focus, we'll extend our timeline to just beyond the present.

Along this timeline, we can see that there are three major shifts where technology takes on different roles in support of the business enterprise. These shifts in the role that technology plays are not limited to specific boundaries or time periods. We can visualize these shifts as "planes" that lie along

1

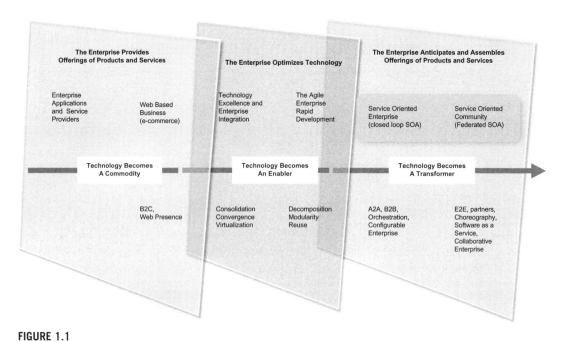

FIGURE 1.1

An Evolution of Business Technology

a timeline and overlap to some degree. As we can see, the three shifts become progressively impactful to the business enterprise:

1. Technology becomes a commodity.
2. Technology becomes an enabler.
3. Technology becomes a transformer.

1.1.1 Technology becomes a commodity

Initially and with the advent of the Internet, Web, and e-commerce, technology began to emerge as a commodity. That is, the technologies in this era began to take on less of a large scale and monolithic investment and began moving into lower cost and smaller scale, distributed platforms and shared infrastructures solutions. Processor performance and storage continued to scale upward, while costs stabilized, and, in many cases, costs even reduced.

What became obvious is that with distributed and Web computing, it became easier to develop and implement point solutions. The business enterprise was able to quickly onboard into the e-commerce space and to extend its Web presence. Along with this ability to rapidly implement lower cost commodity technology solutions, a number of challenges also resulted.

A proliferation of point applications and redundancy emerged as less desired outcomes. The business enterprise also realized that there were a number of other competitive, market, and economic pressures. With the low cost commoditization of technology, businesses of every type were able to enter into the fray. The business landscape was becoming one where competitive products and services were being rapidly offered to the market. Surprisingly, many of these competitive threats included small-scale startups and innovators that did not have the large organizations and processes to contend with. They could very quickly and easily penetrate the market at a modest cost. If your enterprise wanted to retain or improve its market position, it also needed to become more dynamic and responsive. This is often referred to as "business agility." To respond to these challenges and pressures, technology organizations became recognized as an equal partner at the business table.

1.1.2 Technology becomes an enabler

Addressing increased competitive threats required a new focus. The business looked to technologies for opportunities to optimize their delivery of solutions. This included a renewed emphasis on managing development, infrastructure, and operational cost, as well as a much-needed escalation in rapid delivery. The technology response to these business needs included a shift in focus to one of technical excellence, rapid development for solution delivery and including consolidation and virtualization for cost management, and integration to resolve the many disconnected point solutions. This is the plane along the timeline where technology became a business enabler. It is also when technology direction began to exhibit many of the basic characteristics of SOA.

Interestingly, the siloed and point solutions that resulted from rapid technology delivery during the Commodity phase also started to become painful to the enterprise. While a requirement of that period was to retain market share and to stay competitive, the overarching emphasis was on rapid delivery of commodity solutions, and this contributed to a proliferation of stand-alone technology applications. Operational and maintenance costs began to rise, and even more obvious was the degree of difficulty in connecting the various point systems and sharing of information.

The notion of a 360-degree view of a customer is perhaps the most common and obvious example of needed integration (e.g., a "360-degree view" that encompasses all customer data for a complete picture of the customer and customer relationships, across the enterprise). The value of a customer became more than the size of an order, and began to focus on the total relationship (both current and potential). However, having many different customer applications and methods of communicating and interacting with the business, the resulting customer information became disconnected and disparate. The ability to up-sell or cross-sell to a customer was difficult if not impossible. To resolve this new problem of disparate systems and data, "integration" in all of its various forms became another critical component of business enablement. We began to see Enterprise Application Integration (EAI) and Enterprise Information Integration (EII) gain momentum.

SOA emerged as a combination of an architectural approach and technology enabler for the enterprise. SOA introduced several new technologies with an emphasis on technical excellence, and including a number of new development practices. These new technologies became the technical capabilities that enable an SOA, and the development practices evolved to become a set of principles and governance. This is also the current state perspective of SOA for many business enterprises today. For those that have successfully led the SOA curve, it is almost a historical view.

1.1.3 Technology becomes a transformer

As the technology evolution continued, additional emphasis was placed on "transforming the enterprise." That is, transforming a business enterprise from reactive to proactive. The business enterprise is less focused on responding to the market (in this context, "responding is—after the fact"). Rather than being a follower of the market and competitive landscape, the enterprise begins to anticipate those demands. This is also where SOA becomes a transformational solution.

To some degree, this third plane in the technology evolution is unfinished. There continue to be new capabilities and enhancements to the SOA paradigm. One of which is a "closed loop SOA," where the technology orchestration of business processes not only enables the enterprise to offer new products and services, but with a feedback loop and simulation capabilities, the business can begin to reconfigure how it will do business. You'll learn more about this in Section 1.5, "Business Activity Monitoring."

As an enterprise transformer, there is also an emphasis on federated SOAs and extending into a service-oriented community. The most common service interaction is Application-to-Application (A2A), which is the foundation for all consumer-to-service interactions. While SOA-enabled federated servicing communities are still in their infancy, the expectation is that we will begin to see broader SOA-enabled collaboration that extends beyond A2A and into service collaborations between different enterprises (E2E). This model of collaboration includes enterprise relationships where business partners and competitors can play a role. Web 2.0 is another emerging area. There are some examples of currently available technology solutions classified as Web 2.0 today (such as mashups, wikis, and semantic tagging frameworks). However, there is some controversy as to an accurate definition of Web 2.0. Interestingly, while the definitions of SOA and of Web 2.0 vary, most industry perspectives are such that SOA and Web 2.0 exhibit a strong synergy and dependence. If you accept this perspective, SOA plays a fundamental role to underlay and support Web 2.0 technologies by delivering information with services.

No doubt, some industry practitioners would dispute this brief history of SOA. Others might argue that the technologies and pressures from which SOA originated, extend well beyond those described. Yet there are many definitions for SOA. Several are similar, while others are quite different. Some definitions emphasize SOA technology and others accentuate the business aspects of SOA. All of these views of SOA are to some degree accurate but lacking a concise definition that everyone has agreed or will agree to.

1.2 A DEFINITION FOR SOA

All of the various industry definitions for SOA are worthy of consideration. However, without a standard that everyone can agree upon, understanding the operational context becomes more important. Fundamentally, service-oriented architecture (SOA) is an evolution in technology that becomes a business enabler and eventually a business transformer. So how do we drive this statement into something that is more discrete and real world, and which can be easily understood without prescribing specific technology products?

Let's start with another, more explicit definition of SOA. The following definition is one that I have developed and refined while working on different SOA initiatives over of the past several years.

> *A service-oriented architecture (SOA) is a combination of consumers and services that collaborate, is supported by a managed set of capabilities, is guided by principles, and is governed by supporting standards.*[2]

The intent of this definition was to simply and carefully articulate all of the important characteristics and facets of an SOA. As you will notice, this definition does not call out a specific set of technologies. SOA is not something that you can just purchase as if it were a grocery item on a shelf. While technology capabilities are a requisite component of an SOA, SOA is not exclusively technology. Nor is this definition of SOA limited to Web services. While Web services are often recommended and are described in this book, this is not a specific limitation of SOA. The emphasis on Web services is from the perspective of standards-based interoperability. An effective SOA will allow participants and collaborators to interoperate. Web services simplify that interoperability by adding a standards perspective, where services and service consumers "speak" the same language. Interoperability is one of the SOA guiding principles that you will learn more about in Chapter 2, "Core SOA Principles."

To better understand this SOA definition, we can separate it into component parts. We can see that consumers, services, managed capabilities, principles, and standards all play a role. As we describe each of these definitional parts, it is important to remember that an effective SOA will have incorporated all of them in some manner.

1.3 CONSUMERS, SERVICES, AND INTERMEDIARIES

The first part of our SOA definition refers to consumers and services. Consumers and services are all participants and collaborators in an SOA. That is, they interact with one another to request services and resolve these requests. The context for these interactions is determined by the service interface and is typically expressed as a message that moves between the collaborators.

A consumer is a technology that in some manner interacts with, consumes, and exploits services. Typically and within the definition of an SOA, a consumer is an application or piece of software that will interact with another application or piece of software as a service or possibly as an intermediary. While SOA consumers are generally software, this is changing, and we'll begin to see more appliance and hardware SOA consumers.

The notion of a consumer is not unlike that of the similar analogy used from an economic perspective. A simple example of a consumer is the user of goods and services. We extend the analogy to that of an office supply customer. In this example, the office supply customer is interested in determining the current available inventory for a type of pen. After determining if the item is available and then ordering or purchasing one or more of the pens, the customer is then a consumer of the products and services provided by the office supply store.

Alternatively, a service is some form of encapsulated behavior that is exposed to consumers to resolve a request. With services, the notions of granularity and modularity also come into play. One example of a fine-grained service represents a single behavior or a limited set of related behaviors. Another example is a business service or an orchestrated service that includes combinations of behaviors, or defined interactions with other services to resolve a request.

From an SOA perspective, the service is generally some set of application functionality. The provider of the service may be a combination of the service behavior and the location at which it is identified and invoked. Again using the office supply analogy, the service being offered is that of returning the available inventory for an item. In this regard, the office supply store is known as the service provider. The interaction between the consumer and the service is enabled by a request for the available inventory position of an item and the inventory count returned in the reply. Similarly and using a simple request and response example, the SOA consumer requests something of the service, and in response, the service returns a reply (see Figure 1.2). It is important to note that SOA interactions are not limited to request and reply. There are other interactions that you'll learn more about in coming chapters.

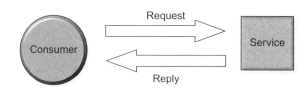

FIGURE 1.2

SOA Consumer and Service

FIGURE 1.3

SOA Consumer, Intermediary, and Service

An interesting extension of the consumer and service definition is that of an intermediary. As implied by the name, an intermediary is positioned somewhere between a consumer and a service. Note that this is a logical positioning, and the physical or network locations of the consumers, services, and intermediaries can vary. An intermediary may provide some form of service behavior, or it may just mediate between other consumers and services. If we carried our office supply analogy further, an example of an intermediary might be a discount retailer. The customer interacts directly with the discount retailer (in this case, as an intermediary), and the retailer then works with the office supply company on behalf of the consumer.

In a simple example, a consumer interacts with an intermediary rather than directly with the service. Depending upon the perspective and directionality of the interaction, an intermediary can hold similar roles of both a consumer and a service (see Figure 1.3). When following the interaction from the consumer to the intermediary, the intermediary can be thought of as the target of the interaction or even as a logical extension of the service. When following the interaction from the intermediary to the service, the intermediary can be thought of as an originator of the request or logically as a consumer of the service.

The need for an intermediary is optional. It will depend upon the granularity to which services have been defined, the type of interactions between consumers and services, how service behaviors and mediation are defined to the SOA, and the context in which the intermediary is defined. As one example, a previously implemented application system with a long history might provide valuable business behavior to the enterprise. However, this same application is considered as "legacy" or "historic" and might be platformed on a type of technology that does not allow for broad interoperability.

The functionality provided by this legacy application is critical to the business, but rebuilding the application as a more modular and interoperable SOA service might be cost prohibitive. There may be an alternative opportunity to develop a front end to the application that allows it to appear as if it were a functional and interoperable SOA service. This front end (e.g., a wrapper, façade, or mediation service) might be another separate application that does nothing but mediate the interactions between consumers and the existing application. In this example, the façade or mediation service acts as an intermediary between service consumers and the legacy application.

One very important point to remember is that with any interaction (consumer, intermediary, or service), the service interface is a critical component. It describes the rules by which the SOA participants and collaborators interact, and it also defines the context of that interaction as one or more messages.

1.4 MESSAGING—THE MEANS OF INTERACTION BETWEEN CONSUMER AND SERVICES

SOA participants and collaborators need to interact and communicate with each other. That interaction is enabled as a set of messages. A message contains content, which can represent a set of instructions or requests, a set of data elements and values, or it can contain information that is required to facilitate the interaction. The movement of messages between consumers and services follows a set of patterns (Message Exchange Pattern or MEP). The most common pattern is known as the request and reply pattern. With the request and reply pattern, the requester—usually a consumer—sends a message to a service. The service then responds with a reply message that is returned to the consumer.

The request message contains the instructions and potential content that the service requires in order to understand and then to execute against the request. Some practitioners might think of this as a set of parameters, an interface, or other means of communication between two applications. As you'll see later, there are more effective ways to structure a message than just a set of parameters. The reply message contains response content, an acknowledgement of success, or an acknowledgement of failure. This concept of a message to facilitate interactions between consumers and services is critical to SOA.

Since the request and reply message exchange pattern is largely conversational, we can use the analogy of human conversation and asking a question of someone. If we are looking for information about something, we might ask a simple question. In response, we should receive a reply that resolves our question, or if not, then a response to acknowledge that the question was not understood or the answer is unknown. If we are at the office supply store and curious about the available inventory for a blue pen, we might ask the sales clerk: "Do you have any blue pens on hand for item 1234?" In response, the sales clerk might say: "We have over 100 of those blue pens in stock right now." Let's break this example down further.

The example question is analogous to a request message sent to an SOA service. We specify a specific need, the question acts as the instruction to the service, and the information required for the sales clerk to understand our question and respond is included as content. The reply back from the sales clerk is direct and specific to our question. The response refers to our question about pens but does not refer to ink cartridges, rulers, or note pads. With this model of interaction, any customer can approach the office supply sales clerk and ask the same basic question. They will then get the same type of answer in response but reflecting an inventory position at that point in time. Alternatively, if we were not specific or we asked an irrelevant question, it is likely that the sales clerk would not understand the question and as a result, not be able to provide a meaningful reply.

This same model applies to SOA. We can extend the example to a consuming application that requires available inventory amounts for an office supply item, and an SOA service that provides the item catalog and inventory counts exposed by the office supply store. If the office supply store wants to provide a catalog and inventory service to any service consumer and regardless of the technology used, the store will need to rely upon a common message model (also known as a "canonical"). If not, then consumers of different technology platforms (COBOL, Java, .NET, or other) might unknowingly send a request message to the service in some form or format that it cannot understand. Using a canonical model from which to derive a common message scheme helps to resolve this potential problem. Although somewhat technical, another challenge is to resolve different methods for encoding the message. Extensible Markup Language (XML) has become the prevailing message form for SOA consumers and services.[3]

Unicode character encoding, which is common across many technology platforms, is the default encoding of choice for XML.[4] Unicode is largely platform agnostic, which simplifies the exchange of encoded data between many vendor technologies. XML also allows the user to define the names used for these element tags. That is, there is no single overriding or prescriptive naming scheme that applies to XML regardless of where or how it is used. In itself, this is of significant value, and the tag names can be highly descriptive and human readable as well as machine readable. Other forms of messaging and encoding can be used as well, but XML tends to be highly technology and platform agnostic, and it is widely supported.

In an SOA based on Web services, the message has a structure to allow for deeper integration and cross-platform collaboration. A key part of which is an enveloping scheme known as Simple Object Access Protocol (SOAP), which includes the message content, and is also encoded using XML. You'll learn more about SOAP in coming chapters. However, we'll start with a simple and more relaxed message format that still relies upon XML. The request message sent to the office supply Item Inventory Service contains the information that represents a request or a set of instructions (the example here uses what is sometimes referred to as "POX" or "plain old XML") (see Figure 1.4).

On receipt, the office supply Item Inventory Service accepts request messages and interrogates their content. If the content is information that it understands, it will then work to resolve the request and in response will send a reply back to the requesting consumer. The content of the reply message is based upon the interface definition.

We can see from the example reply that the Item Inventory Service was able to understand the request message and it then responded with a total inventory quantity value of "136" (see Figure 1.5). If the request message contained information that is irrelevant or inapplicable to the Item Inventory Service, the service would be unable to determine what was being requested and would most likely return a fault message. Fault messages provide information to a consumer when an error is encountered or the service cannot satisfy the request. The important concept here is that messaging enables the interaction between SOA participants and collaborators, regardless of their technology or platform.

As we might expect, another important aspect of the message is the set of rules that define what can be requested of a service, the required and allowable content of the message, the names of the elements that hold the content, the location of the elements within the message, and any metadata rules such as data type or length. This base set of information is described by the service interface. Simply put, the interface describes the contract for interaction between SOA participants, and a message is the execution of that contract. Without this interface definition and its rules, consumers and services would be unsure of what is expected or allowed in their interactions. This notion of the interface contract and the resulting message is perhaps the most important to enabling a true SOA.

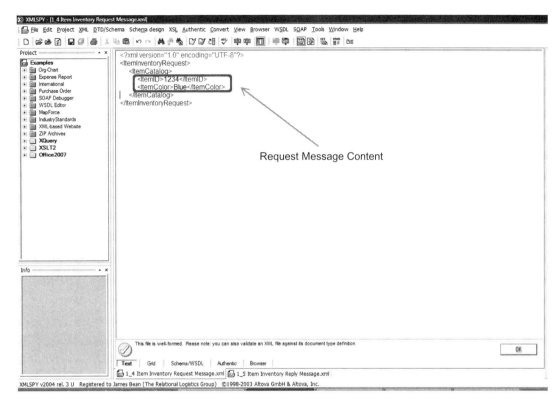

FIGURE 1.4

Item Inventory Request Message (Copyright 2003-2008 Altova GmbH, reprinted with permission of Altova)

Yet, collaboration between consumers and providers using messages is but one part of our SOA definition. In order to send and deliver messages between collaborators, a set of technology capabilities is also required.

1.5 SOA CAPABILITIES

Our earlier SOA definition also refers to "… a set of managed capabilities…." The intent of this statement is to address the supporting technologies that underlay an effective SOA. As you learned earlier, SOA is not specific to any one technology, vendor, or product. Rather, there is a combination of different technology capabilities that enable SOA functionality. As general classifications, the types of technology capabilities include

- Enterprise Service Bus (ESB)
- Service Registry and Repository (SRR)
- Business Process Management (BPM)
- Business Activity Monitoring (BAM)
- Web Services Management (WSM)

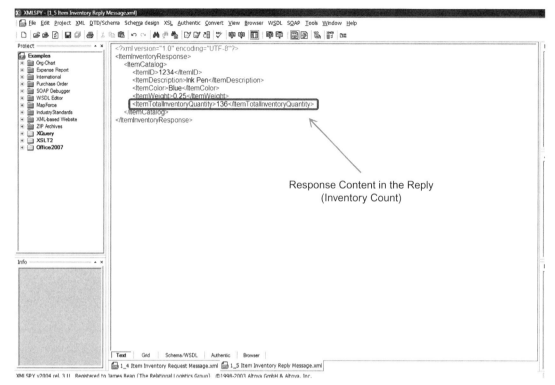

FIGURE 1.5

Item Inventory Reply Message (Copyright 2003-2008 Altova GmbH, reprinted with permission of Altova)

1.5.1 The Enterprise Service Bus—ESB

The Enterprise Service Bus (ESB) is a fundamental backbone technology that supports SOA. As implied by the name, the ESB is a "bus." That is, the bus is a technology capability that includes the network, transport, routing, delivery of messages and content, and supporting communication protocols (collectively referred to as the "service bus"), all of which are intended to be somewhat hidden or transparent to service consumers. For some grass-roots SOA efforts, the ESB could be a simple messaging technology or similar. However, simple messaging and middleware technologies are often more limited in their offered capabilities than an ESB.

Depending upon the vendor and the bus technology in question, a fully functional ESB can provide other supporting technical capabilities as well. When instructed, an ESB can reroute or redirect messages, transform a message from one format to another, and help to ensure a high degree of availability and assured delivery when combined with other SOA technologies, such as WSM.

SOA consumers and services are identified by address identifiers, more commonly known as "endpoints," which are attached to the bus. An endpoint is a logical address, identifier, or location where messages can be addressed, sent, and retrieved. As consumers interact with a service, they send a message to the defined endpoint for that service. The messages are then routed by the bus to the noted endpoint and ultimately to the service. When a service is intended to reply, it will send a response message back to the endpoint of the requesting consumer.

As a message is transported, a number of monitoring, delivery, and policy management activities take place along the way. The consumers do not require intricate knowledge of how the messages were transported or routed to the destination, as long as SLAs are met, and the collaboration is successful (see Figure 1.6). The ESB is an interesting concept that can be graphically represented in various ways. One graphic representation includes a circle with contact points for consumers and endpoints where information can move around, across, or between the contact points (endpoints) as needed. This graphical style for depicting an ESB is used throughout this book. However, it is important that this is not mistaken for a token ring network or other network topology.

To explain the function of an ESB with a more common sense definition, we'll use the analogy of a passenger bus within a public transportation system. Simply put, a passenger boards the bus at a bus stop and later exits at another bus stop. In this example, the bus stops are analogous to SOA consumer and service endpoints. Multiple and other passengers also board the bus and exit the bus along the route. Similarly, with an ESB, there may be many messages being routed between different endpoints (for multiple SOA consumers and services) at any time.

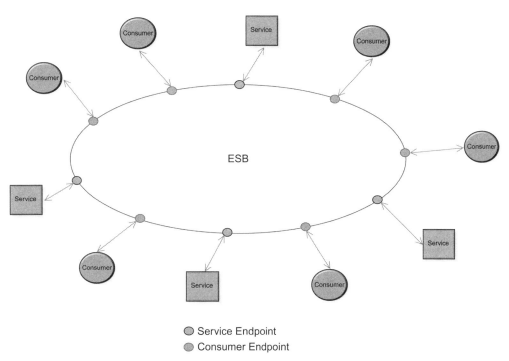

○ Service Endpoint
◉ Consumer Endpoint

The graphic representing an ESB is not intended to represent a "token ring" or any other network topology.

FIGURE 1.6

ESB—Enterprise Service Bus

With the transportation analogy, each passenger arrives safely and securely at his or her intended bus stop, within the expected timeframe, and at the expected cost of the bus ticket. However, the exact physical route taken, the horsepower of the bus, the type of fuel it consumes, the manufacturer of the bus, the exterior color of the bus, and so on are generally of little interest or concern to the passengers. Similar to the public transportation analogy, SOA collaborators are generally less interested in the underlying technical details of how a request message moved from the consumer to the service, or the response message returned from the service to consumer. When the passenger bus encounters road construction or traffic delays, the bus driver may elect to reroute to an alternative roadway. To optimize performance, the ESB can also reroute messages between different network nodes or find alternative routing schemes.

As previously described, endpoints are logical addresses or locations for an SOA consumer or service. That is, the endpoint for a service might not be the physical location for that service. Rather it might be a queue or a location from which messages are further redirected to the actual location of the service. This is not unlike the public transportation and passenger bus analogy. The passenger of the bus boards at a bus stop, which is similar to an endpoint. However, that passenger might live several blocks from there and walks to the bus stop. Similarly, when the passenger exits the bus at another bus stop (again similar to an endpoint), the passenger will typically continue on to the ultimate destination, which might be several blocks away.

Underlying our SOA can be a number of technologies. The SOA might rely upon message-oriented middleware, messaging, and queuing; might include other technologies such as event handlers and listeners; or might just transport messages using common protocols such as HTTP. The SOA architecture team determines the ESB product and technologies that represent the best fit for a specific purpose. However, what is important to understand is that an ESB capability is a core component of an SOA.

1.5.2 The Service Registry and Repository—SRR

So far, we have an understanding of the roles as participants and collaborators that consumers and services play, the importance of messages for enabling interaction between them, and the ESB as the technology capability for transporting messages. For an SOA with a limited number of consumers and services that are all well known to the organization, this model can work well as a foundation. However, as the number of consumers and services grows, remembering which service provides what functionality and the location of the service endpoints to send messages, quickly becomes unreasonable. The small-scale SOA model relies upon a high degree of human knowledge and interaction. For a growing or larger-scale SOA, there is a more effective approach.

If you were a technology analyst or developer for an order entry and processing application, you might want to know if there is an SOA service that can determine the on-hand inventory availability for an ordered item. In the small-scale enterprise, there might only be a small number of SOA services, and from talking to other technology developers or reading some documentation, you might be able to easily determine if such a service exists (see Figure 1.7). However, in the growing or larger-scale enterprise, this would be difficult if not impossible. Finding a specific service among several hundred or even several thousand services requires some type of catalog. The enabling SOA technology to help resolve this challenge is a service registry.

The service registry is similar to a catalog or a directory. It hosts published information about SOA services. Rather than seeking out people who might have developed services or reading large collections of documentation, you can search the service registry. As you find candidate services, you

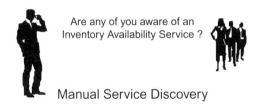

Manual Service Discovery

Service Registry Discovery

FIGURE 1.7

SRR—Service Registry

can then evaluate whether they can be used by your application. If they are applicable to your need, you can then acquire the necessary interface information that allows you to communicate and interact with the service from your consuming application. Continuing the earlier public transportation analogy, a service registry is similar to the passenger bus schedule. It describes bus and route numbers, bus stops, and similar information such as scheduling.

There is an industry standard and model for service registries known as Universal Description Discovery and Integration (UDDI).[5] This model provides a structure for hosting publications of descriptive and technical service metadata, as well as the definition of APIs for accessing and updating this information. There are several well-known and recognized UDDI-based service registry products available, and most SOA implementations will include a service registry capability for the reasons noted previously.

The model that is most often used to describe a UDDI registry is a telephone book. This analogy implies that like people and businesses found in a telephone book, services are described as entries in the registry and as part of an internal structure (including technical entities for the Business, the Service, Binding, and a more general classification entity known as the tModel) (see Figure 1.8). For our example, the business entity ("businessEntity") can be thought of as the publisher or owner of a service. A business entity may have published information in the service registry for zero, one, or more services. The service itself is represented by a business service entity ("businessService"). This entity contains some basic information such as a service name, description, and similar. The binding entity ("bindingTemplate") provides more technical information for a service. In the case of a Web service, the binding template describes some of the technical metadata that consumers of a service will require in order to bind to and interact with that service. The tModel is a more versatile entity in

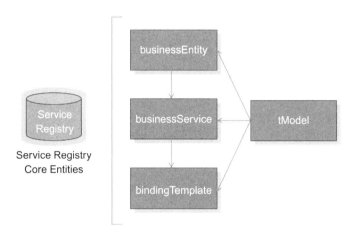

FIGURE 1.8

SRR—Service Registry Core Entities

the UDDI model. It can be attached to or associated with the other entities and can be used to describe categorization, identification, or even reference information.

Once a candidate service has been discovered and validated as meeting your needs, you can then begin the process of binding your consumer application to the service. The notion of binding is less constraining than might be implied from the name. Binding allows that a consumer will comply with, use, and understand the messages of a service as defined by the service interface. Currently, binding is usually resolved during consumer design and development (known as design-time or "static" binding). Binding can also be done more dynamically and at run-time. However, this "dynamic" binding is a more advanced capability. When we use messages derived from a well-defined interface to communicate between the consumer and service, we remain to a large degree independent or "decoupled." By decoupling consumers and services, we mitigate the impact from change and, in some cases, even the potential impact from events such as errors.

Interface artifacts are the sets of declarations and rules that define our interface. They are the artifacts from which messages are defined and created for consumer and service interactions. When using an SOA based on Web services, these are artifacts defined by a combination of Web Services Description Language (WSDL) and one or more XML Schemas (XSD). The WSDL for a service can be thought of as the overall technical interface specification. It serves as not only the definition of the interface but also contains technical information such as the allowable operations for a service and its endpoint address.[6] The WSDL is often the primary artifact used for publication of technical service information to a service registry.

From within the WSDL, one or more XML Schemas can then be incorporated or referenced (see Figure 1.9). These XML Schemas are in themselves almost a metadata language. That is, an XSD can describe the structure, types, and even some rules for the content of an XML message.[7]

An interesting observation of the UDDI registry model is that it is primarily responsible for hosting and exposing SOA service publication metadata. However, it is not usually the source for the actual WSDL and XSD service interface artifacts. The service artifact repository is another SOA technology

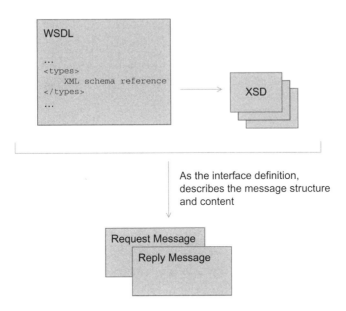

FIGURE 1.9

WSDL and XML Schemas as Service Interface Artifacts

capability that hosts the service interface artifacts. The second "R" from the "SRR" acronym describes the service artifact repository. The service artifact repository is complementary to the service registry and hosts the service interface artifacts (e.g., WSDL and XSD interface artifacts). When publishing information about the service to the service registry, the corresponding service interface artifacts are then also hosted in the service repository.

To retain the link between the service registry publication and the service interface artifacts in the service repository, the WSDL and XML Schemas (XSD) are assigned a URL or similar location and identifier. When using a UDDI-compliant service registry, the tModel can contain a reference or pointer to the location of the WSDL for that service publication (see Figure 1.10). Internal to the WSDL, an XML Schema "import" declaration can then reference or point to the XML Schema interface artifacts (XSDs) for that service. The relationships between the service registry to the WSDL and from the WSDL to the XML Schemas (via import) retain the linkage required for consumers to discover the service and bind to the service interface. The service artifact repository could be a robust commercial technology that includes governance functionality. However, a simple Web server, file management system, and Domain Name Server (DNS) may suffice. While an explicit service artifact repository technology may not be required, it is highly advantageous.

As you can see, the SRR represents critical SOA technology capabilities.

1.5.3 Business Process Management—BPM

So far, our definitions and examples have all focused on a simple consumer-to-service interaction. This is a powerful model, but it reflects an interaction that is almost like a fine-grained, peer-to-peer

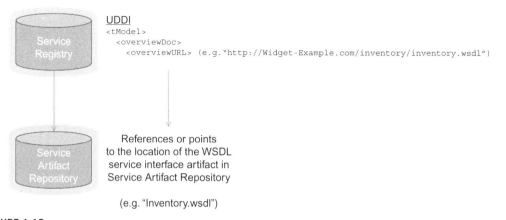

FIGURE 1.10

SRR—Service Registry and Repository

(consumer-to-service) interaction. In an SOA, a simple peer-to-peer analogy can be logically implemented. However, it is not a limitation of SOA or the ESB. A more appropriate use of the ESB also is to reroute messages or distribute them among several endpoints.

Another more effective model for consumer-to-service interaction is one where sets of services are referenced as complete business processes. Using our previous example of an inventory availability service, we could define an over arching assembly of services as a set of inventory update process steps. We might have an order entry system that not only needs to check available inventory for an ordered item but also needs to reserve or allocate that inventory for shipment. In this example, we might have another separate inventory allocation service. When combining the inventory availability and inventory allocation services, we now have the needed inventory processing for our order entry example (see Figure 1.11).

For our new inventory business process, we can create a service that first executes the inventory availability service to determine if the item being ordered is in fact available. If not, it can return a message to the order entry application (consumer) to let it know that the item must be backordered. If it is available, it can then allocate the ordered amount of inventory for later shipping against that order. This business service can be invoked by a consumer as a single business service interaction. Yet, the underlying and more fine-grained SOA services can be reused by reference, rather than recreating all of that functionality. In doing so, these services can also continue to independently resolve inventory availability and inventory allocation requests from other consumers.

This is a very powerful model. It not only allows us to reference, assemble, and reuse SOA services in many different ways, but it also allows us to retain a high degree of modularity. Our individual SOA services are the core building blocks of SOA. They are so modular and self-contained that even when referenced by a large business service, they can still be used independently by other business services and even by individual consumers. If we had a large inventory of SOA services available to us, and they covered a large set of required functionality for the enterprise, we might be able to assemble complete applications from these SOA services as building blocks, rather than developing new ones. Remember the earlier emphasis on business agility. The time to assemble and test these

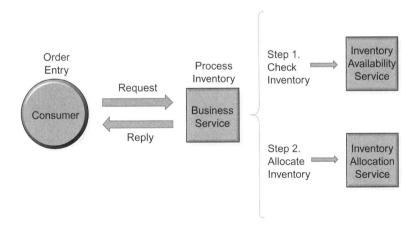

FIGURE 1.11

Business Service and SOA Services

higher-level business services is generally far less than with new development. As a result, we could deliver core business functionality much quicker.

The technology capability that enables this type of composite process and service interaction is known as Business Process Management (BPM). The BPM engine reads and executes process steps defined by a script. This script defines the process steps for the higher-level business service and associates them to the more fine-grained SOA services that will resolve the overall process. From a technical perspective, this script defines the set of steps to be invoked, the references to the named services for each step, and some patterns and behaviors for each of those subordinate service interactions.

The patterns and behaviors for each subordinate service interaction describe the information that must be passed between process steps, and also the actions to take when the information is not available or an error is encountered. The scripts that are understood by most BPM engines are based upon Business Process Execution Language (BPEL). This is another type of service artifact that references and exploits the standards, structures, and declarations of UDDI, WSDL, and XML Schemas that we described previously.[8]

An interesting challenge that faces most SOA adopters is when to define a business service, when to define an SOA service, and how to describe and formalize the notion of service granularity. In this context, a business service tends to be coarse-grained and represents a process (something generally understood by a business person as a business process with a set of steps and activities). Alternatively, an SOA service is more fine-grained and reflects the subordinate and more tactical process steps that underlay the business process. As you will learn in later chapters, not all services fit the definition of a coarse-grained composite or business service. Similarly, not all services fit well within the boundaries of a more fine-grained SOA service.

Our simple example of a composite business service that references and invokes more fine-grained SOA services for inventory availability and inventory allocation is described as an orchestration. An orchestration is a set of service interactions that are well defined, with clearly identified steps (usually ordered steps) that invoke a set of known services with known interactions. The rationale for the name "orchestration" is that the overall process is generally led, similar to an orchestra that is led by a conductor. All participants in the orchestration know their roles and their interactions, and they take their lead from the BPM engine and the script representing the steps of the business process.

Alternatively, there is another type of composite or business service that is more dynamic. This business process is known as a choreography. Like an orchestration, a choreography has a set of finer-grained steps and participating services. However, the degree of interaction can be broader and might include SOA services that are defined outside of the enterprise. In this case, the choreography drives a set of steps between collaborators, and they may invoke other services or functionality that is unknown to the original consumer. There may also be a more dynamic assembly of services and service interactions that reflect variations in response from the various SOA services involved as part of the process.

An analogy that is useful for choreography is a square dance. The "caller" at a square dance will decide what dance moves and configurations take place during the playing of music. The speed at which the participating dancers move and change position, can be driven by the caller or by the tempo of the music. While this may appear similar to that of an orchestra being led by a conductor, there is another difference. The scripting of the square dance is less well defined. The caller could change dance moves randomly during the music, and, in many cases, this will then change the dance partners. As you proceed through the square dance, one dancer may be paired with dancers other than those that he or she started with. With a choreography, the SOA services identified by the steps in the script might transition to other services or might interact with other services that were unknown to the original business service.

Choreography is not nearly as mature as orchestration. As choreography continues to evolve, the most common implementations will be Business-to-Business (B2B) and Enterprise-to-Enterprise (E2E). The definition of a collaborator will change as well. Rather than being limited to consumers and services that are developed and owned by the enterprise, the notion of a collaborator and SOA participant will extend to other third parties such as business partners and possibly even competitors. An example for the latter might be an opportunity to use a competitor's services as referenced within a choreography, rather than building one internally. Obviously, a competitive market will then require some form of mediation and possibly remuneration, but the potential scenarios are almost limitless.

The notion of choreography for SOA is a powerful one. When combined with other SOA capabilities such as Business Activity Monitoring (BAM), we can begin to envision a future where the business enterprise can reconfigure much of its business functionality to anticipate the market, rather than to react to it. To enable this future vision, our SOA needs to include a robust set of technology capabilities and an inventory of well-designed and functional SOA services. As we get deeper into this book, you will learn specific techniques for those SOA service designs, how to optimize your services, and most importantly the critical role of the service interface.

1.5.4 Business Activity Monitoring—BAM

In an SOA, there are a number of events that take place. These include the movement of messages between SOA participants and collaborators, the successful replies from services to consumers, and the errors or faults that are raised. Defining measures for each of these activities is critical for monitoring the health of the SOA as well as for presenting opportunities to optimize service interactions and avoid problems.

Business Activity Monitoring (BAM) is a technology that monitors the SOA infrastructure and reports on the noted activities as well as others. Although there are many different BAM technology products and offerings, most will include some form of monitoring or instrumentation that is attached to the ESB and extends out into the network at large. They will also include a reporting mechanism (usually visual and similar to a dashboard) that allows subject matter experts to define key measures they consider important to their enterprise and to then monitor against these measures.

Some BAM technologies are beginning to advance beyond visual reporting and alerting to a more interactive capability. Here, the subject matter experts can develop simulations as "what if" scenarios to compare monitoring feedback from the SOA. Dashboarding and other visualization capabilities provide an effective reporting and response mechanism. However, this is not the limit of BAM.

The future of BAM is yet to be determined. However, there is some thought that BAM will evolve to incorporate and attach business information to the more technical transaction information resulting from SOA events. Rather than just monitoring the number of successful and failed transactions for each service, BAM may evolve to compare transaction types with business data and to merge with the Business Intelligence space. As this future vision becomes a reality, the business will have the capability to simulate business activities that are based upon real-world and real-time transaction measures. They can make core business decisions and anticipate how the market will react. When combined with the ESB and BPM, they can also begin to inject changes back into the SOA that will be reflected as service behaviors. As a result, the business enterprise can begin to reconfigure the way it does business and how it interacts with collaborators. While this vision is not assured, and it may be some time before we could see tangible implementations of this type, it is a strong possibility.

1.5.5 Web Services Management—WSM

As part of the earlier ESB description, it was noted that an ESB can be instructed to redirect messages from one location or endpoint to another. The ESB could also be instructed to transform one message format to another. A Web Services Management layer (WSM) can facilitate those activities with policies. WSM is a technology that works with the ESB to trap events (usually at endpoints) and to either take action directly or to instruct the ESB to take action.

The emphasis of WSM is on the definition and the application of what are often described as policies. Policies are sets of behavior that can be defined to resolve a number of different activities. Policies can be defined for

- Identification of events
- Security
- Redirection
- Transformation
- Message validation
- Other custom policies

Once a policy is defined, it can be assigned to an endpoint in the ESB or to a group of endpoints. As a message or similar event reaches the endpoint, the policy will determine if it is an actionable event. If yes, it will then apply the policies assigned to the event and endpoint (see Figure 1.12).

Using our example of an inventory availability service, we can see how a message validation policy might be applied. There might be an authorized SOA consumer that is from outside the enterprise, and representing a B2B service interaction. This external consumer might be a business partner that is allowed to check availability of our inventory. When this external consumer sends a request message

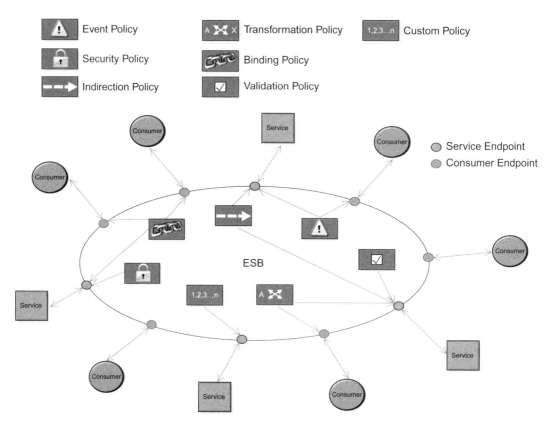

The graphic representing an ESB is not intended to represent a "token ring" or any other network topology.

FIGURE 1.12

Examples of Potential WSM Policy Types

to the inventory availability service, it is expected that like any other consumer, the message will conform to the structure and content expected by the inventory availability service. While this is usually the case, there may be an example where the external consumer has implemented an enhancement to its consuming application and that change has also introduced an unexpected data value to the item inventory request message. Rather than sending an identifying item number in the $<$ ItemID/ $>$ element of the request, the consumer now sends the item color in that element. If the inventory availability service is expecting a numeric item ID, and it receives an alpha string color description, it would fail with an error. Since this consumer is outside the enterprise, it is also outside of our direct control and testing.

Rather than waiting to receive messages and then fail with an error, a message validation policy could be assigned to the endpoint for the inventory availability service, where the message is validated by an XML parser (see Figure 1.13). When messages are received at that endpoint, the policy would be triggered, and the message would be validated (using an XML Schema and a validating parser). If validated

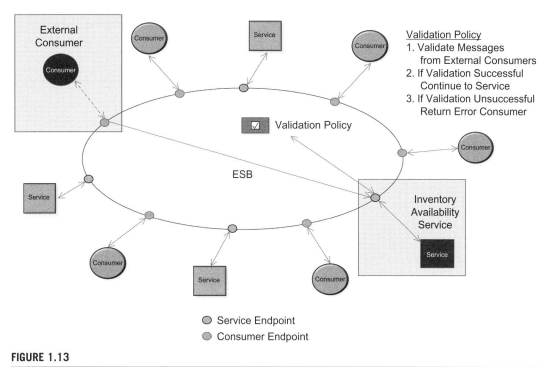

FIGURE 1.13

Message Validation Policy Assigned to an ESB Endpoint

successfully, the message could be sent on to the service for processing. If not, it could then be returned to the consumer with notification of a validation error. In this context, message validation assumes an XML-encoded message and an XML Schema (XSD) that describes the structure, types, and rules for the message. A validating XML parser is a technology that compares XML messages to their associated schemas. If an error or mismatch is encountered during validation, an error is then raised.

WSM products will typically tie into the ESB and published endpoints for application of policies. These products may include their own infrastructure for developing and managing the policies, while others may integrate with the SRR. Some WSM products can also incorporate run-time policies to identify and harvest "rogue" services, which have been deployed into the SOA without having been published to the SRR. By integrating with the SRR, the WSM technology can quickly match services to those that have been published and identify any mismatches or gaps. This capability of a WSM technology represents a form of run-time governance, which is something you'll learn more about in coming chapters.

1.5.6 Closing the SOA loop

You have been presented with a definition for SOA and learned about the various technical capabilities that support an SOA. The examples for each have so far been somewhat disconnected. However, there is a concept known as a "closed loop SOA," where all of the described SOA technologies are also connected. In this scenario, there is a conceptual feedback loop where the outcomes from a set of technology capabilities serve as the input for others.

As an example, BPM will invoke a set of SOA services as part of an orchestration or choreography from the Business Process Execution Language script (BPEL). The messages of those service interactions will be passed to endpoints on the ESB for routing to the target services. WSM policies will be applied to the endpoints and will help to administer and govern SOA interactions. BAM will monitor the SOA infrastructure and will provide metrics for SOA interactions. The outcomes from BAM can then be used to realign the services and service interactions in the SOA infrastructure. These configurations will be enabled by the BPM engine, and the loop will continue (see Figure 1.14)

Even with a closed-loop SOA, the expected future vision is that continued enhancements will allow BAM to incorporate business intelligence data in addition to SOA metrics. Dynamic service choreographies will emerge, and interactions will become more configurable. As a result, we'll begin to see the vision of a dynamic, agile, and configurable enterprise. With this future vision for BAM, business and technology leaders can monitor and measure combinations of technical and business events, and perform "what-if" simulations. Where a simulation produces more desirable results, the parameters and configuration data can be moved back into the service choreographies defined to BPM. Where these choreographed services are configurable and based upon the parameter changes, their behaviors and interactions can change. The business not only rapidly responds to change but can also simulate and even anticipate change.

As an example of this future vision, a choreographed process to accept inbound order quotes, price them, check inventory, and return a response, can be compared to the number and size of resulting orders placed. Using BAM, business leaders can monitor the quote transactions and simulate pricing

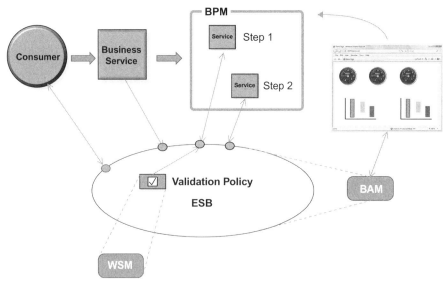

FIGURE 1.14

Closing the SOA Loop

and discount changes. Where an acceptable model is defined, it can be used to reconfigure the quote process by including new pricing parameter values for the service. This scenario is visionary and has a number of dependencies, but it is also a reasonable future expectation.

1.6 THE BENEFITS OF SOA

The obvious questions that arise with SOA are

- Why do we need all of this technology?
- Can't I just use my existing messaging infrastructure for the same thing?
- Isn't this somewhat complex?
- What do we gain from SOA?

All of these are valid questions and with an eye toward exploiting the existing technology capabilities of the enterprise. However, SOA goes much further than messaging and queuing, and it is far more than just a collection of expensive technologies. When implemented correctly and effectively, SOA can provide several potential benefits.

Perhaps one of the most often described benefits of SOA is enabling business agility. Every successful business enterprise realizes the importance of rapidly and effectively responding to customer and market demands. When an SOA has been implemented, the combination of enabling technologies, principles, and business processes allows the enterprise to rapidly and effectively change the way it does business. That is, the enterprise is able to rapidly offer products and services in response to customer demands and a changing marketplace.

Another potential benefit of SOA is an ability to leverage and exploit prior investments in technology. As you will learn, an effective SOA will be guided by several core principles. One of these is interoperability. The traditional business enterprise has evolved over many years. Along the way, there will have been significant investments in technology applications and software. Some will have been acquired as packaged applications. Others will have been internally developed. Yet, these same applications may have been developed on many different technologies and platforms. Even though these application platforms might not be considered as current state, they are still functional, they provide needed business capabilities, and the investment in them may have been considerable. Rather than always looking at large-scale application replacement and new development, an SOA implementation that supports broad interoperability can in some cases provide methods for integrating some of these same legacy applications and as a result extend their life.

Another benefit of SOA is in providing an architecture from which new business processes and functionality (what we will come to know as "services") can be developed and then reused by reference and assembly. Some technologists have disputed the notion of reuse. I contend that this is more of a misunderstanding of what reuse is. When an SOA service is designed, developed, and deployed while complying with SOA principles, patterns, and best practices, it exhibits characteristics of modularity, extension, and reuse. The ability to reuse an existing artifact then becomes common, and there is little need for large-scale refactoring to fit.

SOA can provide other potential benefits as well. Some will be obvious and measurable such as the ability to rapidly deliver business functionality, and some will be more intangible, subtle, and intrinsic to development processes and behaviors.

SUMMARY

Chapter 1 was specifically intended to resolve the industry impedance around SOA definitions and to make sure that we have the same basic understanding of SOA as we move forward. You will also learn more about the SOA principles in Chapter 2, "Core SOA Principles," which are just as critical to achieving an effective SOA as are the technology capabilities. In the chapters that follow, you'll learn more about types of services that SOA can support, and then we'll begin to dive deeply into tactical design patterns and techniques.

REFERENCES

1. IBM. Technology Options for Application Integration and Extended Enterprise Patterns. Redbooks Paper; 2004:10.

2. Bean J. SOA from A-to-Z. (presented at DAMA International and Wilshire Metadata conference Boston, 2007):8.

3. Bray T, Paoli J, Sperberg-McQueen CM, Maler E, Yergeau F, eds. Extensible Markup Language (XML) 1.0 (Fourth Edition) W3C Recommendation. (W3C, August 16, 2006). <http://www.w3.org/TR/2006/REC-xml-20060816/>.

4. The Unicode Consortium. *The Unicode Standard, Version 5.1.0.* Boston: Addison-Wesley; 2007 <http://www.unicode.org/versions/Unicode5.1.0/> (ISBN 0-321-48091-0, as amended by Unicode 5.1.0).

5. UDDI Version 3.0.2, UDDI Spec Technical Committee Draft (Copyright © OASIS Open 2002–2004). <http://uddi.org/pubs/uddi_v3.htm> (October 19, 2004).

6. Booth D, Liu CK, eds. Web Services Description Language (WSDL) Version 2.0 Part 0: Primer, (W3C, W3C Recommendation, June 26, 2007). <http://www.w3.org/TR/wsdl20-primer/>.

7. Fallside DC, Walmsley P, eds. XML Schema Part 0: Primer Second Edition (W3C, W3C Recommendation, October 28, 2004). <http://www.w3.org/TR/xmlschema-0/>.

8. Jordan D, Evdemon J, chairs. Web Services Business Process Execution Language Version 2.0, OASIS Standard, (Oasis, April 11, 2007). <http://docs.oasis-open.org/wsbpel/2.0/OS/wsbpel-v2.0-OS.html>.

Core SOA Principles

2

There is more to implementing a successful SOA than just technology capabilities. An effective SOA must also implement and embrace a number of important design, development, and management principles. In the context of SOA, a principle defines the framework in which consumers and services will collaborate and acts as general guidance for the design and development of services. There are numerous principles that can be applied to an SOA. However, in this chapter, we'll focus on the most fundamental. Minimally, these core SOA principles include

- Loose coupling
- Interoperability
- Reusability
- Discoverability
- Governance

An SOA implementation that is guided by these principles can exploit a number of advantages and benefits. Examples of these advantages can include mitigation of impact from change, cost avoidance for new development as the result of reuse, and an ability to exploit the prior investment in legacy technology assets.

2.1 LOOSE COUPLING

Loose coupling is a principle by which the consumer and service are insulated from changes in underlying technology and behavior. In some manner, the loose coupling principle describes a logical separation of concerns. That is, the consumers in our SOA are intentionally separated from direct or physical connection to services. The intent is to protect the individual integrity of each SOA consumer and SOA service and to avoid physical dependencies between them (see Figure 2.1).

When this principle is applied to the design of our services and the service interface, we can mitigate the impact of change. The most common example is an SOA service that has been previously implemented and deployed into the ESB. In this example, a number of consuming applications are successfully using the service. As new consumers find the service, they may also require additional functionality and data not defined to this service. If the service were tightly coupled with each of the

25

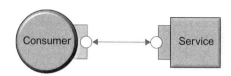

Tightly Coupled
(consumer interacts directly with the service)

Loosely Coupled
(consumer and service interact via messaging and the ESB)

FIGURE 2.1

Tight Coupling and Loose Coupling

previous consumers, the ability to add new functionality to the service would be significantly limited. When tightly coupled, those previously existing consumers would likely be affected by changes to the service. Alternatively, when consumers and services are loosely coupled, there are techniques that can be applied to help mitigate the impact of change to existing consumers of a service. Previous consumers are then unaware and generally unaffected by new additions to the service functionality.

To comply with the loose coupling principle, consumers and services do not communicate directly. As we learned in Chapter 1, consumers and services communicate via messaging. Using a message to exchange requests and replies avoids any direct technical connections between consumers and services. In addition to messaging, there are other service interface design techniques that can be applied to further limit the degree of coupling between consumers and the service.

Messages exchanged between consumers and services are realizations of the service interface. In the case of a Web service, the service interface is defined by the combination of a Web Service Definition Language artifact (WSDL) and an XML Schema definition (XSD) as its referenced metadata. These two types of interface artifacts (WSDL and XML Schemas) are the foundation of any Web service. The design and development of these two interface artifacts are a focus of the loose coupling principle. Other types of services can use other interface definitions and artifacts, but the same principle of loose coupling can still be applied.

The WSDL is the primary interface artifact for an SOA Web service (see Figure 2.2). It can be thought of as the overall and technical interface definition. Among other things, the WSDL exposes the functionality of the service as operations. Alternatively, an XML Schema defines the structure, the containers, and the types that are represented in the messages used for interacting with that service. This relationship between these two SOA Web service interface artifacts is very important.

The WSDL conforms to a widely recognized language from the World Wide Web Consortium.[1] Among other things, the WSDL exposes the functionality of the service as operations and the data that are required for each operation.

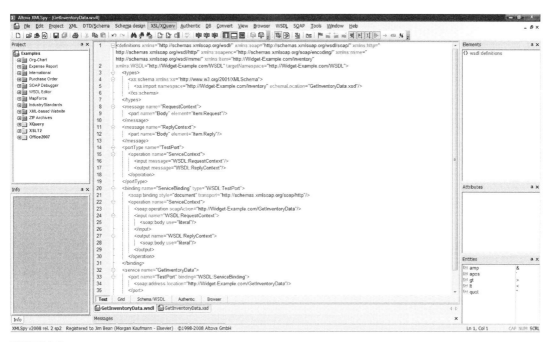

FIGURE 2.2

Example WSDL using XML Spy from Altova (Copyright 2003-2008 Altova GmbH, reprinted with permission of Altova)

While the WSDL represents the overall technical interface of a service, it lacks a defined message format for exchanging information between consumers and the service. This missing context is provided by an XML Schema definition. Syntactically, the WSDL can reference one or more XML Schema definitions, or it can also include embedded XML Schemas. The association of an XML Schema to a WSDL is specified within the WSDL "< types/ >" child element (see Figure 2.3).

XML Schema is also defined by a well-known language.[2] The declarative syntax of an XML Schema is similar to a set of structure and type definitions, and it can also include supporting rules. From a purist perspective, an XML Schema is a form of metadata that describes and constrains XML formatted data, such as a request or a response message (see Figure 2.4).

An operation defined to a WSDL is a functional capability of a service. The operation instructs the service to perform a needed function, such as "add" a new Inventory Item, or retrieve ("get") Inventory Details for an item. Each operation can also be defined with one or more parameters. The parameters of an operation describe a set of contextual information that is expected by the service and allows it to process the request. Design techniques can be applied to the definition of an operation and also to the structure of the message that will to a large degree determine how loosely or tightly coupled a consumer and a service are.

A common service interface design style known as RPC encoded (Remote Procedure Call) prescribes that each operation of a service is a discrete function of the service and has one or more parameters. When a consumer sends a message to a service using an RPC-encoded style of message,

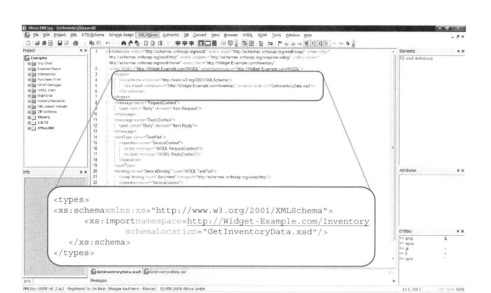

FIGURE 2.3

Example WSDL < types/ > Import Reference to an XML Schema using XML Spy from Altova (Copyright 2003-2008 Altova GmbH, reprinted with permission of Altova)

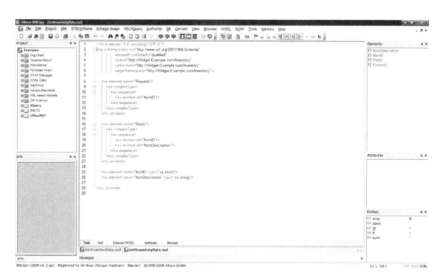

FIGURE 2.4

Example XML Schema using XML Spy from Altova (Copyright 2003-2008 Altova GmbH, reprinted with permission of Altova)

operations are usually named in the message, and parameters are filled with data values, including a prescriptive specification of the data type for each. Upon receiving the request message from the consumer, the service then extracts and processes the data values from each of the parameters. If the service determines that the parameter data values are correct and as expected, it can then process the request. Note that I have used the term "operation" in this description. Although there are differences from an object-oriented perspective, for the RPC example, you can think of an operation as being roughly analogous to a method.

A specific request to a service operation, and including its parameters, is often referred to as a method signature. A common analogy for parameters might be an explicitly defined list with item numbers, item names, colors, prices, sizes, and similar information. Each entry on the list occurs in a particular order and is defined with explicit data types (see Figure 2.5). The RPC-encoded design style works quite well when the type of interaction between consumers and the service is simple and rarely subject to change. However, when the service goes through eventual enhancement, such as adding new parameters, changing a parameter, or adding new content to a response message, those existing consumers of the service that have developed their messages to explicitly comply with the original operations and parameters will then have to also make corresponding changes. This is an example of tight coupling where a change to the service interface can impact and force residual change upon existing consumers.

Alternative to the RPC-encoded interface style, there are other design techniques and styles that can help to decouple consumers and services. With these other techniques, the consumers and services exchange more of a document context. We can think of this document style message exchange

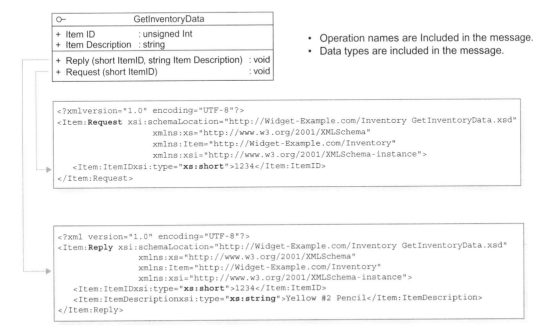

FIGURE 2.5

RPC Style Operations and Parameters

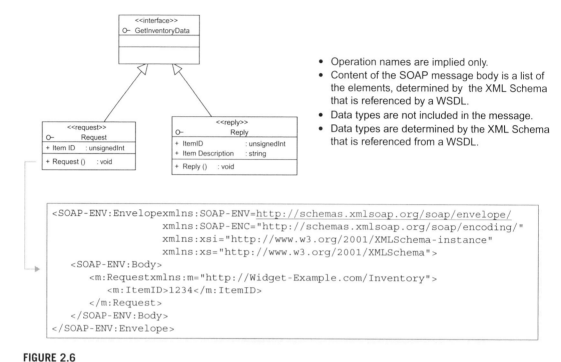

FIGURE 2.6

Document-Literal Style Operations

as being similar to a set of paragraphs that you would find on a printed letter or a page from a book. This technique is often referred to as document literal. Consumers are still required to include request message content that meets the expectations of the service, but they are not coupled to discrete technical characteristics of the service operation. As the service undergoes the addition of new data elements and similar enhancements, previously existing consumers of the service can be insulated from many of those changes. When combined with messaging as the method of interaction, the document-literal style interface is an example of implementing to the loose coupling principle (see Figure 2.6).

To further explain differences between the RPC-encoded and document-literal design styles, consider a simple inventory management service. As defined by its operations, the example inventory management service provides functionality for adding new office supply items to a database, reading data from the database, updating data in the database, and deleting records from the database. For each of the operations, the service expects a set of data values in the request message. With the RPC-encoded style, the interface might include a set of individual parameters for each operation, and where each of the parameters would have an order in which they need to occur in the message and an explicit data type. Alternatively, with the document-literal style, the interface would define a document context where the message contains a collection of elements and data values that are less dependent upon the technical specificity of the operations or the underlying behavior of the service. With a document-literal style interface, the XML Schema defines the structures and rules by

Table 2.1 List of Operations and Common Verbs

CRUD Operation	Common Verbs (use only one from the list)
Create	Create, Add, Insert
Read	Read, Get, Retrieve, Select
Update	Update, Modify, Maintain, Change
Delete	Delete, Remove, Kill, Eliminate

which the consumers and the service will define their messages. This technique externalizes and abstracts the message interaction and avoids specific technical constraints becoming part of the message content.

Another important consideration is consistency in our interface definitions. For the example inventory management service, there are four basic operations: Add, Get, Update, and Delete. The combination of these operations represents what is often described as CRUD (Create, Read, Update, and Delete). As defined to a service interface, operations are usually described in a manner where the intended function is also part of the operation name. The operation name is most often prefixed with a common language verb, such as "Get," "Add," "Update," or "Delete."

There is no single standard for naming operations or for prescribing specific verbs for the operation names. The choice of which verb to apply to an operation name is left to each individual enterprise. However, it is an enterprise best practice to standardize on a single, common set of verbs for each type of operation. This standard set of operations verbs will help to avoid ambiguity between different services and the functionality that they provide. It would not be advisable to have some services and their operations use "Read" as a prefix to the operation name (as in "ReadInventoryData"), while others use "Get" (as in "GetInventoryData"). In this case, the service operations and potentially the services are redundant. Table 2.1 lists somewhat common verbs used to prefix service operation names.

In Chapter 14, "Service Operations and Overloading," you'll learn more about other operations and verbs that extend beyond basic CRUD functionality.

For our example inventory management service, we'll focus on read functionality as a "Get" type of operation. To "Get" (as in, read) data from a database, we have to know which data instance or row is being requested. This might require lookup information such as an identifier or a primary key. The lookup information allows the database to find and return matching records. The concept of a database read is similar to a service operation of "Get." Similarly, lookup information such as an identifier or primary key is required to perform a database read and is analogous to the parameters of a service operation. To request a read of inventory data using the inventory management service, a consumer would have to specify the service operation that will "Get" data (as in, "GetInventoryData") and also include identifying or matching information used for the lookup. In the example, the read operation is similar to a SQL "select" statement for a relational database (see Figure 2.7).

Like the example, a service may invoke a set of database activities as part of its behavior. However, this is not a limitation. Through the service operations, a service could also provide computational, presentation, transformation, and other types of behavior as well. Regardless of the functionality provided by the service, the loose coupling principle must be applied.

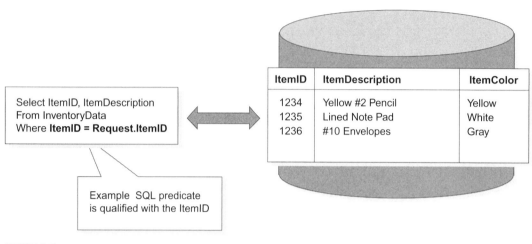

Select ItemID, ItemDescription
From InventoryData
Where **ItemID = Request.ItemID**

Example SQL predicate
is qualified with the ItemID

ItemID	ItemDescription	ItemColor
1234	Yellow #2 Pencil	Yellow
1235	Lined Note Pad	White
1236	#10 Envelopes	Gray

FIGURE 2.7

SQL Select Statement

2.2 INTEROPERABILITY

Like the loose coupling principle, interoperability is critical to implementing a successful SOA. Interoperability is a principle that eliminates technology specificity and constraints that may prohibit, restrict, or constrain the ability to collaborate in the SOA. Interoperability allows consumers and services that are developed and platformed on different technologies to exchange information and collaborate. That is, a service might be developed using Java, platformed on a server using the Linux operating system, and accessing an Oracle database. Consumers of this service might be developed using Visual C++ or even COBOL. They might run on Windows platforms or mainframe MVS platforms. The variations and possibilities are almost endless. A core tenet of SOA is to allow these consumers and services to collaborate, regardless of the technology on which they are based.

Similar to the loose coupling principle, messaging plays a significant role in supporting the interoperability principle. As an agreed-upon format, a message allows the participants of the SOA collaboration to interact with an interface abstraction that insulates consumers and services from the physical characteristics of their specific technologies. However, allowing poorly defined or unrestricted forms of messaging can thwart the interoperability principle. Rather, the encoding and structure of the message play a role. The interface functionality afforded by the service operations can also play a role.

As you learned in Chapter 1, Extensible Markup Language (XML) is a broadly accepted and supported form of message encoding. Almost all technology platforms provide some degree of support for XML. While the example can vary, when the platform supports an XML parser and Unicode, it can then consume and produce XML messages. Even in those cases where XML support might be limited, a transformation technology can be used to convert other message formats and encoding to and from XML.

For some legacy technologies such as COBOL, there may be other more subtle limitations to using XML messages. Some compilers require that COBOL File Definitions and Working Storage definitions

COBOL File Definition

```
05  Reply.
    10    Item-ID                PIC 9(4)  NOT NULL.
    10    Item-Description       PIC X(25).
```

XML Message

```
<SOAP-ENV:Envelope xmlns:SOAP-ENV="http://schemas.xmlsoap.org/soap/envelope/"
                   xmlns:SOAP-ENC="http://schemas.xmlsoap.org/soap/encoding/"
                   xmlns:xsi="http://www.w3.org/2001/XMLSchema-instance"
                   xmlns:xs="http://www.w3.org/2001/XMLSchema">
   <SOAP-ENV:Body>
     <m:Reply xmlns:m="http://Widget-Example.com/Inventory">
       <m:ItemID>1234</m:ItemID>
       <m:ItemDescription>Yellow #2 Pencil</m:ItemDescription>
     </m:Reply>
   </SOAP-ENV:Body>
</SOAP-ENV:Envelope>
```

FIGURE 2.8

COBOL Structure vs. XML Format

remain largely fixed positional. That is, data that are defined and referenced by declarations in these sections are expected to occur in a specific order and to start in a specific position. On the other hand, XML allows for a more flexible and dynamic structure (see Figure 2.8). As an example, a COBOL program might expect that a message includes Item Number data in positions 1 to 10, defined as an Integer, and followed by an Item Description in positions 11 to 30 as a String. If the Item Description were considered as optional to the XML message, yet required by the COBOL program (where it would be defined as NOT NULL), this may result in a mismatch, an anomaly or failure of the application.

It is important to note that some COBOL compilers have provided additional capabilities to help resolve the difficulties of this example. However, significant refactoring of an existing application may be required. Exploiting investments in previously developed legacy applications where a more positional message format is required can be of significant value. One technique to help resolve this data exchange impedance is to provide an option in the service interface that is resolved by service functionality, to preserve the sequence and modality (null or not null) of the message. With this technique, the consumer can specify whether all elements of the response message must be present, regardless if there were corresponding data values. In response from the service, elements that could not be populated with data values would include empty elements as placeholders (see Figure 2.9). This would allow the legacy consumer to retain the structural integrity of the message, similar to the expected positional format. Adding a "Preserve Empty Elements" option to the service interface and

XML Message

```
<SOAP-ENV:Envelope xmlns:SOAP-ENV="http://schemas.xmlsoap.org/soap/envelope/"
                   xmlns:SOAP-ENC="http://schemas.xmlsoap.org/soap/encoding/"
                   xmlns:xsi="http://www.w3.org/2001/XMLSchema-instance"
                   xmlns:xs="http://www.w3.org/2001/XMLSchema">-instance"
    <SOAP-ENV:Body>
      <m:Reply xmlns:m="http://Widget-Example.com/Inventory">
        <m:ItemID>1234</m:ItemID>
        <m:ItemDescription/>
      </m:Reply>
    </SOAP-ENV:Body>
</SOAP-ENV:Envelope>
```

In this example, the ItemDescription element does not contain any data. However, to preserve the structure of the message, it is still included as an empty element.

FIGURE 2.9

XML Message with Empty Element Containers

the supporting service behavior does require additional work and can add to the complexity of the service. This technique will need to be carefully evaluated to determine if it provides offsetting value.

Interestingly, techniques such as using a document-literal style of interface and using XML Schemas can also help to support the interoperability principle. When the technologies of consumers and a service vary, another area of mismatch is often the type system that is supported. A service might require an element of type, nonNegativeInteger. Yet, the consumer might only support integer types that can resolve to a positive, negative, or unsigned value. An RPC-encoded style interface might include an intrinsically declared type for the element in the message. However, if either participant in the collaboration cannot resolve to that type set, it may introduce problems.

Alternatively, a better approach might be to define a document-literal style interface for the service, where the XML Schema determines the type system for the message, and each participant in the collaboration maps to the type system. This may require type casting (mapping and abstracting types to a closest possible denominator) or some additional transformation behavior. It might also introduce a design requirement for the service, where the type system limitations of potential consumers are supported by mapped types in the service interface. As one example, Java EE 5 and JAXB binding maps Java types to a number of XML Schema types (see Table 2.2).[3]

There are other type mappings that may apply. The best practice design technique is to evaluate the type systems of potential service consumers, examine the degree of abstraction for type mappings, and exploit mapping classes and frameworks available to those technologies.

2.3 REUSABILITY

Reuse is an overused and often misunderstood concept. In the simplest sense, reuse is to use something more than once. Yet, this is an ambiguous statement and can add confusion to the notion of

Table 2.2 Example Subset of JAXB Java Types and XML Schema Data Types

Java Class Type	XML Data Type
java.lang.String	xs:string
java.math.BigInteger	xs:integer
java.math.BigDecimal	xs:decimal
java.util.Date	xs:dateTime

SOA. The principle of reusability is to design and develop with an emphasis on cost avoidance. A service that is designed and developed to support the loose coupling and the interoperability principles is likely a good candidate for reuse. That is, original consumers as well as new consumers can exploit the functionality of the service. As new consumers express their requirements and where those requirements can be met by the functionality of the existing service, they can avoid having to design and develop yet another new service.

This is also the case when a significant historic investment has been made in legacy applications and services, and where new development may not be cost effective. To a significant degree, a standard method of encoding and defining messages allows consumers and services to be loosely coupled. If the legacy applications can produce and consume XML messages, and the service interface design has avoided the inclusion of platform or technology specific technical characteristics, there is a greater opportunity to reuse those legacy applications.

To achieve service reuse there are dependencies on other principles and best practice techniques. The ability to find (discover) a service that meets the functional requirements of a consumer is critical and will be described in the next section. It is also important to note that not all services are completely reusable in their original form. Some services may provide much of the functionality required by a new consumer but not everything that is required. When this occurs, there may be an opportunity to extend the service beyond its original scope and functionality.

Extending the functional capabilities of a service might require the addition of new data to be contained in the response message or modification of an existing operation, or it might even include new service operations. Extension of an existing service is not a trivial task, and depending on how well the service and the interface comply with SOA principles, previously existing consumers might be impacted from the changes. Of critical importance is to mitigate or eliminate the impact of service changes to existing consumers, and yet to exploit the already developed capabilities of the service by reuse.

Usually, an extension to an existing service will also require some residual modification of the interface that defines the interaction of consumers with the service. Where possible, changes should be hidden from previously existing consumers of the service. A number of techniques can be exploited here. One of the most powerful is to use service interface extension points. These are areas of the service interface that can be redesigned later and hidden from existing consumers.

In the case of a Web service where WSDL, XML Schemas, and XML come into play, there are capabilities such as XML Schema wildcards that can often be exploited (see Figure 2.10). The wildcard is an optional area that references another separate XML Schema (sometimes referred to as a namespace). The declarative syntax and rules that define the reference can help to hide this extension from existing consumers. In this example, existing service consumers do not see nor enable the additional wildcard schema as an extension to the service interface, unless they specifically request it. However, new consumers have the option of referencing this additional schema and incorporating the content into their messages (see Figure 2.11).

The use of a wildcard to extend the service interface does not magically extend the functionality of the service or to build out its underlying behavior. These are still service development and refactoring activities that must take place. It also requires that new consumers of the service are fully WSDL, XML Schema, and XML capable.

Subset Wildcard Reference Extracted from XML Schema

```
...
  <xs:element name="ExtensionArea
      <xs:complexType>
          <xs:sequence>
              <xs:any namespace="http://Widget-Example.com/Inventory/ExtensionURI"
              processContents="strict"
               minOccurs="0" maxOccurs="unbounded"/>
          </xs:sequence>
      </xs:complexType>
  </xs:element>
...
```

FIGURE 2.10

XML Schema Reference to a Wildcard Extension

XML Message with Extension Area Content (as Defined by Wildcard)

```
<?xml version="1.0" encoding="UTF-8"?>
<Item:Replyxsi:schemaLocation="http://Widget-Example.com/Inventory GetInventoryData%20-
%20with%20Wildcard.xsd http://Widget-Example.com/Inventory/ExtensionURI
ItemInventoryExtensionV1.1.xsd"
             xmlns:Item="http://Widget-Example.com/Inventory"
             xmlns:ItemExt="http://Widget-Example.com/Inventory/ExtensionURI"
             xmlns:xsi="http://www.w3.org/2001/XMLSchema-instance">

   <Item:ItemID>4096</Item:ItemID>
   <Item:ItemDescription>String</Item:ItemDescription>
   <Item:ExtensionArea>
     <ItemExt:Version>
        <ItemExt:MajorVerNo>1</ItemExt:MajorVerNo>
        <ItemExt:MinorVerNo>1</ItemExt:MinorVerNo>
     </ItemExt:Version>
     <ItemExt:ItemWeight>4.26</ItemExt:ItemWeight>
     <ItemExt:ItemPackage>Carton of 144</ItemExt:ItemPackage>
   </Item:ExtensionArea>
</Item:Reply>
```

FIGURE 2.11

XML Message with a Wildcard Extension

Some SOA practitioners will dispute the need to extend a service. They may contend that developing another new service as a version of the original with the added functional capabilities is a better solution. This is a difficult challenge that needs deep consideration. Some SOA development tooling and technology has matured to the point where development is entirely model driven. This greatly simplifies and expedites service development and as a result, the cost of development is significantly reduced. However, this does not always provide a method of reuse for the original service, and multiple services with a subset of the same base functionality and code can result. This approach of continually creating new versions of a service will add to the number of deployed services and supporting service interface artifacts that have an operational cost and must be managed and maintained. Even though tooling might provide rapid development capabilities, deploying yet another new service with extended functionality is not always the best choice.

2.4 DISCOVERABILITY

As described within the context of the reuse principle, discovery is critical. Finding a service (discovery) is the first step to service reuse and consumption. Even though a service might provide extensive functionality, it is largely ineffective if the service cannot be discovered for later use. The typical solution to service discovery is a service registry. As described in Chapter 1, a service registry is similar to a catalog or inventory of services. It contains published information about a service. A typical commercial service registry technology also includes some form of search or find capability. This allows designers and developers to search for already developed services as candidates for reuse (see Figure 2.12).

However, to enable an effective search function, the service must have been published with a set of descriptive information that serves as the basis for later discovery. Service registries based upon the UDDI specification provide a classification capability via tModel and categoryBag taxonomy entries. In a simple sense, discovery of services from a registry requires that when published, it included some managed set of entries from a taxonomy. The taxonomy supported by a service registry is a list of terms that describes the service and its capabilities. In some cases, a search capability is available as an add-in or client to development tooling. This allows the developer to search a service registry from within his or her environment without having to open another application or session.

As candidate services are discovered, the developer can then evaluate whether the service functionality will meet the requirements of the consumers. If yes, the service can then be reused. If not, then the service might become a candidate for extension. In the case of extension, the service should provide a base set of functionality and content that resolves some requirements of the consumer. Additional content or a new operation can then be considered as extensions to the base service. This additional extension design and development generally requires less effort than developing an entirely new service. If the base functionality of the service does not meet the requirements of the consumers, then development of a completely new service might be the result.

2.5 GOVERNANCE

A successful SOA and services implementation will incorporate services and service artifacts that comply with the loosely coupled, interoperable, reusable, and discoverable principles. SOA governance will

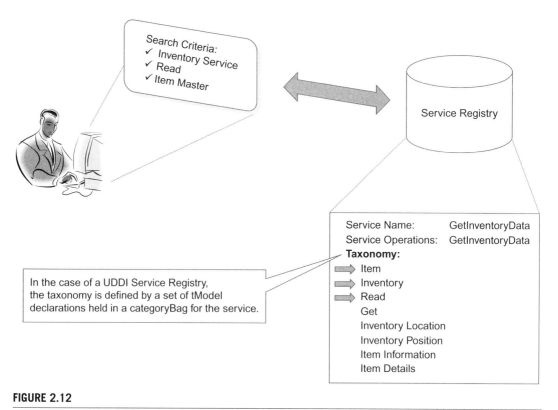

Search Criteria:
✓ Inventory Service
✓ Read
✓ Item Master

Service Registry

In the case of a UDDI Service Registry,
the taxonomy is defined by a set of tModel
declarations held in a categoryBag for the service.

| Service Name: | GetInventoryData |
| Service Operations: | GetInventoryData |

Taxonomy:
➡ Item
➡ Inventory
➡ Read
Get
Inventory Location
Inventory Position
Item Information
Item Details

FIGURE 2.12

Discovery of Service Publications Using a Service Registry

provide the rules and framework from which compliance to these principles can be measured and identify opportunities for appropriate remediation of noncompliance. Some SOA practitioners might argue
that governance is a process or a practice, rather than a principle. I contend that to implement an effective
SOA, governance is more fundamental and crosses the lifecycle of SOA. As an SOA principle, it is
pervasive throughout our service design and development practices and also is part of the operational
interactions between consumers and services with the ESB. In this regard, SOA governance should consider three different views:

- Design-time
- Bind-time
- Run-time

Using SOA governance to ensure compliance should not be taken lightly. At a minimum, there
should be well-defined guidance for the design and development of services and service interface artifacts. There should also be prescriptive guidance for developers in regards to the bind-time environment, which tends to be a more mechanical, process-driven set of governance activities. Additionally,

the run-time environment needs to be governed. This last is largely enabled by SOA technologies and infrastructure.

2.5.1 Design-time governance

Design-time governance includes a combination of different activities, and can be expressed as a set of design rules. An example of design-time guidance is the Web Services Interoperability Profile.[4] The WS-I Basic Profile is an example of well-defined and broadly accepted industry guidance for interoperability. It includes requirements specific to the different artifacts associated with a Web service that will help to assure a high degree of interoperability (one of our core SOA principles).

Other design-time guidance can include design patterns and best practices that will help to ensure that services and service interface artifacts are loosely coupled, reusable, and discoverable. All of which are also core SOA principles. The methods for measuring compliance and for enforcement can include governance reviews, such as checklists, peer reviews, and more formal review and compliance processes. Other methods for ensuring design-time guidance can be implemented as development technology, where rules are scripted and used by evaluation tooling to determine if an artifact is in compliance.

There are also complexities to design-time governance. Some environments will rely upon model driven development technology or development tooling, where there is limited opportunity to apply extrinsic patterns and best practices, or to refactor the generated service artifacts. This presents a challenge because there becomes a trade-off between the ability to very quickly generate and deliver services (as code), and the degree to which those delivered services can be reused and maintained. With the ability to quickly generate code, there may be less of an ability to evaluate and apply other patterns and best practices. With a refactoring approach, development time and cost may be higher. There are obvious advantages and disadvantages with either approach, and each enterprise will need to determine how best to exploit them.

2.5.2 Bind-time governance

Bind-time governance is often overlooked. It involves the mechanical steps of associating consuming applications with services. To enable a consuming application to invoke and interact with a service requires a form of "binding." The term binding is not a violation of the loose coupling principle. Rather, it is the technology reference between the consuming application and the interface of a service. Binding is typically done by a utility program, where the WSDL for the service and its referenced XML Schemas are used to map the service interface and messages to the internal behavior of the consumer. Upon completion, the consumer will be able to create and send request messages to the service and will also be able to receive and consume response messages from the service.

This binding activity is straightforward and familiar to most developers. However, there are some nuances that need to be governed. As one example, the typical SOA will include separate technology infrastructure environments for the purposes of development, testing, and production. As implied by the names, each environment hosts applications, consumers, services, and service artifacts of a particular lifecycle state. Those that are in the process of development will usually be positioned in the development environment. Those that are ready for broader-scale testing are positioned in the test environment, and those that have been accepted for deployment are in the production environment. The separation of environments is intended to avoid untested applications, consumers, and services from being accessed in production and potentially causing problems.

Bind-time governance enforces this separation of environments and helps to ensure that consumers respect the environment boundaries in which they reside. Consider the example of a consuming application that is currently in production. It might be disastrous if the consuming application were bound to a service that was deployed in the development environment. The service might be untested or at a very low level of maturity and could provide anomalous data in the response message back to the consumer.

Most developers will challenge the need for bind-time governance. The assumption is that consumers and services are application programs. The separation of environments in an enterprise is very clear, and the operations or change management processes will ensure that binding does not violate those boundaries. However, for SOA and Web services, the interface artifacts that are required for binding (WSDL and XML Schemas) are usually hosted in the service repository. If the repository does not provide a separation by lifecycle or by environment, the artifacts may be exposed for binding regardless of their state. To help avoid the problem, a Service Registry and Repository (SRR) is a strongly recommended SOA technology capability. Even with a service repository, the configuration and rules for binding must be clearly defined and governed.

2.5.3 Run-time Governance

Run-time governance is SOA technology driven and can include a number of different types. The most common examples of run-time governance include quality of service (QoS), validation, transformation, security, and endpoint indirection. As a run-time policy, QoS is a target measure where the availability and performance of a service for its consumers is monitored and managed. Run-time validation governance ensures that the structure and content of a message comply with the defined interface for the service. Run-time transformation governance can apply a message transformation (converting one message format to another) to ensure that the target for a message will receive a format it can interpret. Run-time security governance can help to enforce the authentication and authorization of consumers for services.

The enforcement of run-time governance is most often enabled by Web Services Management (WSM) technologies and will also often require a service repository to act as the source for governance policies (rules for compliance). The rules for governance are defined as policies and are maintained in the service repository. Policies are assigned to endpoints defined in the ESB. When a message is sent to an endpoint, or an event is trapped, the policies assigned to the endpoint are then invoked as a form of governance.

The service registry may also come into play for run-time governance. All services that are deployed into products should also be published to the service registry. However, there may be services that have been deployed in the SOA infrastructure and associated to an ESB endpoint, but they are not published to the service registry. As a result, messages are sent to and from the endpoint, but there is nothing available to describe what the service interaction is. This also requires a service registry to use as the source for published service information. These "rogue services" can then be trapped and appropriate action taken.

SUMMARY

SOA principles (i.e., loose coupling, interoperability, reusability, discoverability, and governance) provide critical guidance for the design and development of services and the service interface. Loose coupling helps to mitigate the impact of service changes to consumers. Interoperability helps to ensure that services can be used by consumers of almost any technology. Reusability optimizes the design and development process and helps to avoid new development costs. Discoverability supports reusability and requires that services are published in a manner that allows them to be easily found (discovered) for later reuse.

SOA principles also serve as a foundation for SOA governance. SOA governance should consider three different lifecycle states or views: design-time, bind-time, and run-time. Design-time governance can include industry guidance as well as internal principles, patterns, and best practices. Bind-time governance is largely mechanical and helps to reserve the separation of environment boundaries of development, test, and production. Run-time governance applies policies to ESB-defined endpoints and ensures that appropriate actions are taken.

The emphasis of this book is on SOA and Web services. However, in Chapter 3, "Web Services and Other Service Types and Styles," you'll learn more about other types of services that can be used in an SOA.

REFERENCES

1. Christensen E, Curbera F, Meredith G, Weerawarana S, eds. Web Services Description Language (WSDL) 1.1 (W3C, March 15, 2001). <http://www.w3.org/TR/wsdl>.
2. Fallside DC, Walmsley P. XML Schema Part 0: Primer Second Edition (W3C, October 28, 2004). <http://www.w3.org/TR/xmlschema-0/>.
3. Jendrock E, Ball J, Carson, D, Evans I, Fordin S, Haase K. Java EE 5 Tutorial, Binding XML Schemas, Part No: 819-3669-10, Table 17-2, (Sun Microsystems Inc., September 2007). <http://java.sun.com/javaee/5/docs/tutorial/doc/bnazq.html>.
4. Ballinger K, Ehnebuske D, Gudgin M, Nottingham M, Yendluri P. Basic Profile Version 1.0 (Web Services Interoperability Organization, April 16, 2004). <http://www.ws-i.org/Profiles/BasicProfile-1.0-2004-04-16.html>.

Web Services and Other Service Types and Styles

An SOA is not restricted to one type or style of service. Rather, the services exposed to consumers over the service bus can be a mix of different service types. The functional and nonfunctional capabilities of a service, and the degree to which it can comply with the core SOA principles, are criteria that drive the design of appropriate SOA service types. Some of the most common SOA service types typically include Web services, Representational State Transfer (ReST) style services, and Fixed Position (FP) API style services.

There has been ongoing industry debate regarding the choice of service styles, including Web services (those that comply with WSDL, XML Schemas, and SOAP) and those described as ReST style services. Each of the SOA service types has advantages and disadvantages. Web services rely upon a rigorous set of standards, while ReST style services are simpler and less prescriptive. Interestingly, in a mid- to large-scale enterprise, there may be multiple service types, including combinations of Web services, ReST style services, and—when legacy applications are involved in service collaborations—FP API services as well. The best way to resolve the service style controversy is more about understanding the differences among these service types and how they can provide value to your specific enterprise, and less about the preferences of the architect, technologist, or designer.

3.1 WEB SERVICES AND SOAP

The type of service emphasized in this book is a Web service, primarily due to the benefits of interoperability. A Web service will expose some core set of functionality to consumers. Depending upon the granularity of the service, this functionality may be described by one or more service operations. The reality is that most SOA Web services are designed to deliver information to a consumer, or depending upon the operation, will allow a consumer to request that the service manipulates underlying information. In addition to this more contextual definition, Web services also include compliance with several Web service standards (also referred to as WS-*, Web service stack, or SOAP stack standards). The topics of security, management, and communication protocols can extend the list of WS-* standards that define and support a Web service. When consumers and services adopt and comply with the WS-* stack of standards, there are relatively few issues with the exchange of messages and greater levels of interoperability (see Figure 3.1).

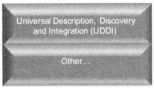

FIGURE 3.1

Web Services Standards Stack

However, there are four standards that are core to the definition of a Web service and its interface. These four core standards include

- Web Service Description Language (WSDL)
- XML Schemas Definition Language (XSD)
- Extensible Markup Language (XML)
- Simple Object Access Protocol (SOAP)

In context of a Web service, we can think of WSDL as the overall service interface definition. That is, the WSDL describes the name and location of the service, the operations exposed by the service, and the expected inputs and outputs defined by the interface. WSDL is defined by a specification from the World Wide Web Consortium. At present, there are two primary WSDL specifications in play. The first (WSDL 1.1) is broadly recognized and implemented across tooling and technologies.[1] The second, WSDL 2.0, is a more recent revision to the WSDL 1.1 specification and includes a number of valuable enhancements and extensions.[2] At the time of writing, WSDL 1.1 is implemented and used by most organizations for their Web services. WSDL 1.1 will be used for many of the examples in this book, with additional clarification and examples of WSDL 2.0 where appropriate.

The WSDL defined for a service can also reference or intrinsically define the more fine-grained interface content using XML Schema within the WSDL < types/ > child element (see Figure 3.2).

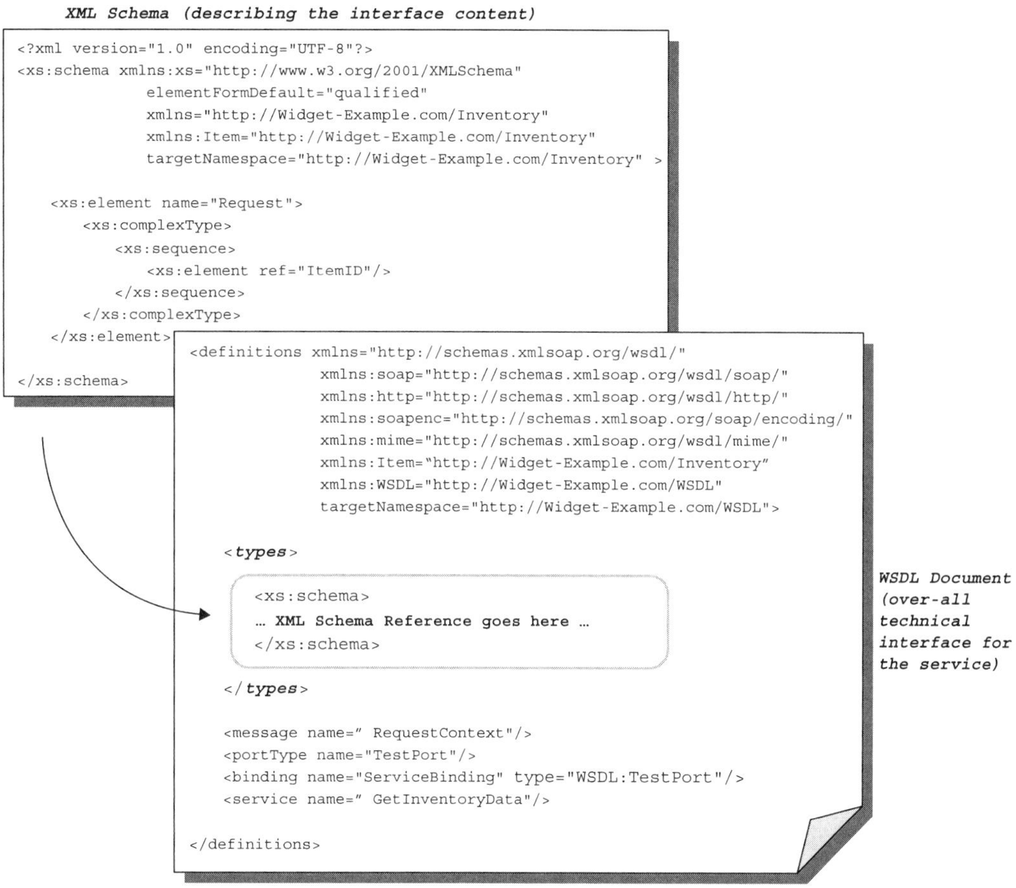

XML Schema (describing the interface content)

```
<?xml version="1.0" encoding="UTF-8"?>
<xs:schema xmlns:xs="http://www.w3.org/2001/XMLSchema"
           elementFormDefault="qualified"
           xmlns="http://Widget-Example.com/Inventory"
           xmlns:Item="http://Widget-Example.com/Inventory"
           targetNamespace="http://Widget-Example.com/Inventory" >

    <xs:element name="Request">
        <xs:complexType>
            <xs:sequence>
                <xs:element ref="ItemID"/>
            </xs:sequence>
        </xs:complexType>
    </xs:element>

</xs:schema>
```

```
<definitions xmlns="http://schemas.xmlsoap.org/wsdl/"
             xmlns:soap="http://schemas.xmlsoap.org/wsdl/soap/"
             xmlns:http="http://schemas.xmlsoap.org/wsdl/http/"
             xmlns:soapenc="http://schemas.xmlsoap.org/soap/encoding/"
             xmlns:mime="http://schemas.xmlsoap.org/wsdl/mime/"
             xmlns:Item="http://Widget-Example.com/Inventory"
             xmlns:WSDL="http://Widget-Example.com/WSDL"
             targetNamespace="http://Widget-Example.com/WSDL">

    <types>

        <xs:schema>
        … XML Schema Reference goes here …
        </xs:schema>

    </types>

    <message name=" RequestContext"/>
    <portType name="TestPort"/>
    <binding name="ServiceBinding" type="WSDL:TestPort"/>
    <service name=" GetInventoryData"/>

</definitions>
```

WSDL Document (over-all technical interface for the service)

FIGURE 3.2

WSDL and XML Schema

While definitions vary, a good way to think of XML Schema is as a constraining metadata language for XML. As a part of the Web services standards stack, an XML Schema is used to define and constrain the content of an XML document. XML Schema Definition Language (XSD) is also a broadly recognized and implemented specification of the W3C.[3]

The message that is moved or exchanged between SOA collaborators (e.g., collaborators as consumers and services) is derived from the service interface definitions of the XML Schema. For a Web service, the XML Schema that defines those messages is referenced by or embedded within a WSDL (see Figure 3.3). XML is the encoding scheme, as well as the structural representation of a message instance.[4] As you have already learned, XML is largely platform agnostic and can exploit Unicode, which allows service consumers and services to communicate, regardless of the technology on which they are developed.

SOAP is really more of a combination protocol and message framework.[5] Interestingly, the original name of Simple Object Access Protocol implied an overly prescriptive object paradigm and has

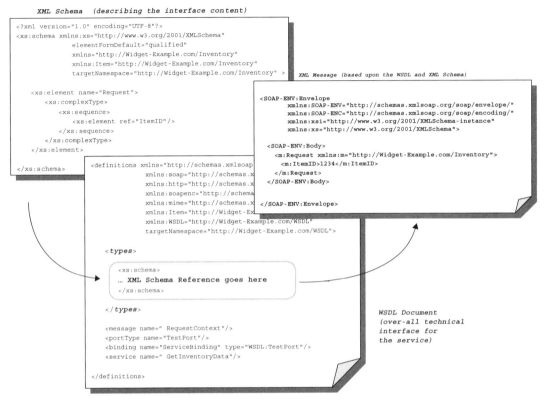

FIGURE 3.3

WSDL, XML Schema, and the XML Message

since been used less, with the acronym of "SOAP" being the more well-known and accepted name. SOAP follows an envelope paradigm that is roughly analogous to that of the paper envelope in which you might send a letter using the postal service.

Continuing the postal service analogy, the postal envelope includes the address of the intended destination (similar to a service endpoint) for the recipient, and usually a type of postage to determine what delivery mechanism is to take place: normal, air, expedited delivery, and so on (analogous to the service protocol and binding). Internal to the envelope is the letter or document being mailed, which is analogous to the message being sent as a request or a reply.

The SOAP envelope has a header ($<$ soap:header/ $>$) that can contain descriptive addressing and delivery information, and a body ($<$ soap:body/ $>$) that contains the XML encoded message. In the case of an error, SOAP also has an optional fault area ($<$ soap:fault/ $>$), which can contain information about the error and is returned to the consumer. The content of the SOAP body is also referred to in the abstract sense as containing the message "payload" (see Figure 3.4).

Fundamentally, a Web service can be thought of as providing functionality to deliver, manipulate, and exchange data of a given context. Data values are encapsulated in the message by XML tags, which

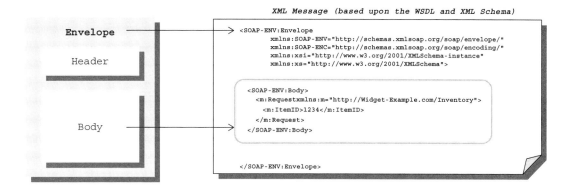

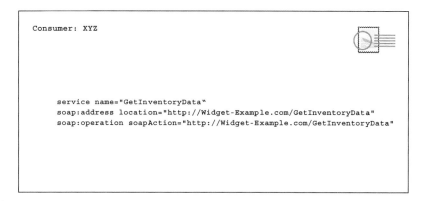

FIGURE 3.4

The SOAP Envelope

are then encapsulated in a SOAP body and within the SOAP envelope that is moved between service collaborators. In the simplest sense, we can think of a Web service as resolving one or more requests for delivering information or resolving requests to manipulate information at some underlying source.

In an SOA context, Web services tend to prevail as a service type for integration and discretely defined information delivery. A declared need of almost any business is to provide information completeness as the 360-degree view of customers, the product catalog, and other core enterprise data. When the enterprise has evolved over many years, including a variety of technologies and application packages, this desire for "information completeness" is obviously complicated by the vertical technology solutions that enable its day-to-day operations. While SOA is not analogous to an Enterprise Application Integration (EAI) solution, when used for this purpose and combined with Web services, it can provide tremendous value. The typical enterprise integration problem is a combination of siloed applications, parochial data structures, and technology-specific platforms. All of which can be resolved by core SOA capabilities and, to a great degree, by supporting Web services.

Web services standards help to ensure a high degree of interoperability (all participants speak the same technology language when communicating with other participants). Also, the context in which these SOA participants communicate is defined by a consistent service interface. Last, the use of XML as an encoding scheme allows these participants to produce and consume messages and content that can be understood across their various technology platforms. In large part, all of this is enabled by compliance with Web services standards ("WS-*"). An SOA Web service consumer will form a request for information based upon the interface specifications of that service.

Web services can also be designed to hide the underlying structural and technology uniqueness of their implementation. This additional capability of SOA and Web services helps to resolve the integration problem. Consuming applications do not require explicit knowledge of the information sources or technical implementations that sit behind the service. They request information that they need and consume the content of the response.

Another advantage of Web services is information delivery. Information delivery refers to acquiring data from one or more systems, rationalizing that data into a single view, transforming the data into a consistent form, and delivering that data to one or more consumers. Not only does this definition of information delivery help to further solve the earlier described information completeness need, but it can also deliver information to standards-based and semantically linked aggregation technologies, such as Web 2.0 mashups.

From these two examples (EAI and information delivery), we can see that the advantages of Web services are primarily a combination of interoperability resulting from WS-* standards compliance and broad-scale technology support. It is the Web services standards stack that provides a high degree of interoperability. Further, Web services are largely ubiquitous in that almost all major technology vendors have in some manner provided support for Web services and WS-* standards.

Some may argue that the sheer complexity of the Web services standards stack and the potential for resulting operational latency will negate (or at least reduce) the value of Web services. While this argument is worthy of consideration, like any technology there are advantages and disadvantages. It is more important to understand the value of Web services and then map core SOA principles to functional and nonfunctional requirements of the enterprise. In turn, these characteristics can then help to determine which service type or what combination of service types will best enable the enterprise.

3.2 REST STYLE SERVICES

Representational State Transfer (ReST) style services are largely attributed to the PhD dissertation by Dr. Roy Fielding.[6] A common interpretation of Dr. Fielding's description of ReST style services is one that closely mimics the basic operation of the World Wide Web and relies upon communication protocols such as HTTP (Hypertext Transfer Protocol). ReST services focus on identifying and providing resources, rather than exchanging individual transactions. An HTML Web page is one easily understood example of a resource in this context.

An analogy that describes ReST style services is similar to a browser request for a Web page. The user types a Uniform Resource Locator (URL) in the address bar of the browser. The URL is a type of identifier that refers to a location on the Internet. Similarly, a Uniform Resource Identifier (URI) is an identifier for a specific resource on the Internet (such as a Web page). If the user is seeking a specific Web page rather than whatever resource is located at that URL, the URL is appended with a specific resource identifier and a resource type (HTML, in this example). When the user presses Enter or clicks Send, the browser issues an HTTP GET to the resource located at the specified URL.

If the identified resource is found, it is then returned to the browser, and based upon the type, is rendered for the user (see Figure 3.5).

The ReST model is quite powerful and proven by millions of Web users and Web pages. It relies heavily upon the notion of an identified resource, the resource type, and the core HTTP command set. These HTTP commands are also similar to CRUD activities (Create, Read, Update, and Delete) (see Table 3.1). ReST also defines the notion of state as being transferred from one participant to another. In this example, state is transferred from the requester of the HTML page to the server. Everything required to complete the interaction is provided in the request, and the result is exposed in the response.

HTTP supports other commands as well such as HEAD, CONNECT, and so on, but they are not in scope of this discussion.

To further explain the browser analogy, in the ReST model, the HTTP GET command is similar to a database "read," where the database is the location of the requested resource. If the requested data resource is not found at the identified location, an HTTP "not found" message is returned to the browser (typically as a "404" error). Using an extension of the Item Inventory Service example from previous chapters, this is similar to having an HTML-based inventory Web page for an item defined as a URL/URI to a server. The user specifies the desired inventory item and Web page as a URL in the browser, most likely including something like the Item ID as the URL resource included in the address. Upon pressing Enter or clicking Send, the browser then sends an HTTP GET to that server and for that specific resource. If found, the Web page is then returned to the browser.

The example of an HTML page as a resource also follows quite well with Dr. Fielding's paper, where he describes that the "REST interface is designed to be efficient for large-grain hypermedia data transfer, optimizing for the common case of the Web...."[7] As we can see, with the ReST model, there is no need for a WSDL, XML Schema, or a SOAP protocol. The minimal set of standards required to request, acquire, return, and render the information is already built into the underlying infrastructure of the browser, HTTP, and the Web. The interaction is quite simple and easy to understand. Yet for a SOA, the ReST model is not without limitations. As one example, Dr. Fielding describes the importance of a "uniform interface." However, Dr. Fielding further describes: "The trade-off, though, is that a uniform interface degrades efficiency, since information is transferred in a standardized form rather than one which is specific to an application's needs."[8] With any consumer-to-service interaction, the interface plays a critical role. The ability to maintain consistency is actually of value to service interactions and further enables the SOA principle of interoperability. However, there may be restrictions on easily extending the interface to accommodate change. The examples are not criticisms but rather observations that should also be taken into account when exploiting the value of ReST style services in your SOA.

Table 3.1 HTTP Commands vs. CRUD Activities

HTTP Command	CRUD Activities
POST	Create
GET	Read
PUT	Update (write in place, overlay)
DELETE	Delete

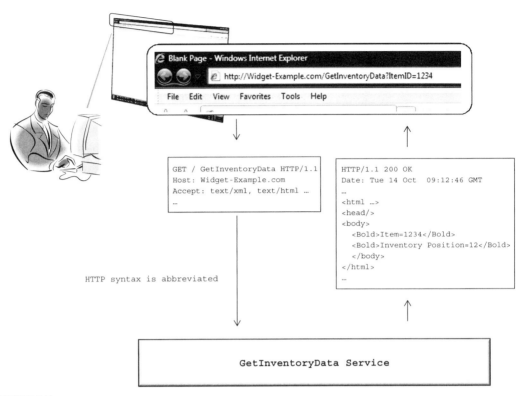

FIGURE 3.5

A Simple ReST Interaction

Several Web sites and supporting e-businesses use ReST style services with great success. This is typically true for B2C and browser-based interactions. This is also true with some B2B interactions as well. Yet, there are some questions as to the impact of change. When the ReST style service is modified and must include new data as part of the resource or more importantly change the resource identifier, there may be residual changes required of all consumers using that service. There are some techniques that can be applied to help mitigate the impact of change, but it takes a carefully thought out architecture and strict compliance with the service contract.

Some might say this is of little concern, and the provider will just create a new version of the service that represents the new resource content and identifier. Those consumers that are using the original version 1 of the service would continue without impact, and new consumers would use the new version 2 of the service. That is all well and good, but this scenario now results in multiple services having to be managed by the provider, and there may be some confusion for new consumers as to which service they should be using and why there are different versions (service version 1 or version 2). This example is not necessarily catastrophic. However, it is brittle. When there are many services and a potential for frequent change, the result can become an operational challenge.

Regardless, ReST is a simple, clean, and well-proven model. It doesn't require a significant set of complex standards. As a result, it may also have some performance advantages over Web services.

3.3 LEGACY SERVICES AND APIs

One challenge that faces SOAs, especially when there are significant past investments in existing applications and data, is exploiting those legacy systems as SOA services. Often, these applications were developed using technologies with an expectation of proprietary file and record processing. Most often, the format of the data input to and output from these applications is positional, where each character of data is allocated a specific linear position in the file. With the advent of XML, fixed position interfaces have become an integration complexity. There have also been some advances with XML translators and parsers for these older technologies. While these advances help to remove much of the complexity related to encoding, there are still some difficulties to overcome.

The challenge is in recognizing that unless your business enterprise is less than 15 or 20 years old, there will no doubt be several operational legacy applications, many of which will be developed with older technologies such as COBOL. In many cases, these applications are reasonably well-designed (within the bounds of their technology capabilities) and still provide important operational functionality to the business. Attempting to redesign and redevelop all of these applications would be both a monumental and unreasonably expensive task. However, SOA can also allow for the onboarding and exploitation of some legacy technologies.

There are several technical solutions and patterns that can be applied. One is to develop a translator that acts as an SOA intermediary and sits between these legacy consumers and services. The translator would intercept messages moving between the SOA participants and then translate (and transform) them into a fixed-position API structure that could be understood by the legacy application. Another technique is to "wrap" legacy consumers and services with a Web service like façade. This façade would enable a similar capability to that of the translator but would be specific to each legacy application.

Regardless of the technology solution, it is important to understand some of the complexities and important design considerations that may come into play. As one example, a COBOL application that consumes and produces file and record data may have specific expectations as to what data will occur in what position (see Figure 3.6). Many of the new COBOL and XML parsers will map the XML tagged content to the corresponding COBOL fields. However, XML is quite flexible. Some messages may accommodate data that is of optional modality; that is, an element defined to an XML message might be optional or not required. If empty, the element is not required to appear in the message. This can leave a gap in the sequence of message elements and potentially a mismatch when mapping to the COBOL file definition.

Interface impedance between fixed position and the more flexible message encoding supported by XML can be resolved. However, it requires analysis and additional design techniques for the translator or service façade. One pattern for resolving this specific challenge is allowing legacy consumers of a service the option of requesting that all data elements of a response from the service must appear in the message, and regardless of whether they contain data values or not. This pattern will result in a size increase for the over-the-wire message, since the empty XML element tags will still be populated in the message and the tag names included in the overall character count. Alternatively, nonlegacy service consumers do not require the empty tags in the message, and they can set the request value off.

The messages are still encoded as XML and can be either encapsulated within a SOAP body (as with a Web service), or within the request message string of a ReST style service. As these legacy applications are targeted for enhancement or more importantly replacement, they can then be redesigned to exploit current SOA capabilities.

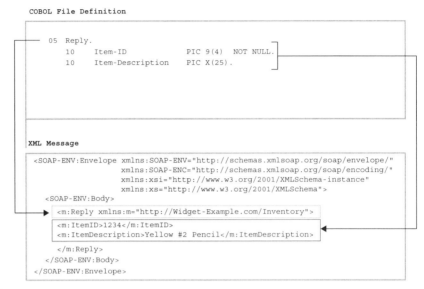

FIGURE 3.6

XML to COBOL Mapping

Table 3.2 Comparison of SOA Principles to Service Types

SOA Principles	Web Service	ReST	Fixed Position API
Interoperability	Excellent	Good	Poor
Loose coupling	Excellent	Excellent	Poor
Reusability	Excellent	Good	Fair
Discoverability	Excellent	Fair	Poor

SUMMARY

As we have seen, there may be valid rationale for including any of the described service types or even combinations of service types in the enterprise SOA. Yet, the debate over which service type and style is best will no doubt continue. This debate will be further complicated with continued advances in the SOA and servicing space, such as adding Web 2.0 technologies as consumers of SOA services. The challenge for any architect is to remove personal bias and to classify the service styles according to their best fit against SOA principles, nonfunctional requirements, functional capabilities, and interaction patterns.

Tables 3.2 through 3.5 are examples of such a technique. The classifications valued in these tables are based upon personal experience. The needs of any enterprise can vary, and should be used to revise the tables and to make SOA service type and style choices of value.

In Chapter 2, "Core SOA Principles," you learned several guiding principles that help to ensure the SOA is effective as a technology solution to the enterprise. The degree to which a service type can

Table 3.3 Comparison of SOA Nonfunctional Requirements to Service Types

SOA Nonfunctional Requirements	Web Service	ReST	Fixed Position API
Simplicity	Fair	Excellent	Poor
Maintainability	Good	Good	Poor
Extensibility	Excellent	Fair	Poor
Performance	Good	Excellent	Good
Scale	Good	Fair	Poor

Table 3.4 Comparison of SOA Functional Capabilities to Service Types

SOA Functional Capabilities	Web Service	ReST	Fixed Position API
Information delivery	Excellent	Good	Poor
Enterprise integration	Excellent	Fair	Poor
Resource delivery	Fair	Excellent	Poor
Security	Excellent	Good	Fair
Legacy application support	Fair	Fair	Excellent

help to meet these core principles can also be used to determine whether a service type or style would be advantageous to the enterprise (see Table 3.2).

Nonfunctional requirements are often described as the technical qualities or "...ilities" that help a technology solution add value. While there are many different nonfunctional requirements that may be of importance to the enterprise (the reader is encouraged to extend the table as necessary), a few of the more common are included in Table 3.3.

Functional requirements are more difficult to define, as they will vary tremendously from enterprise to enterprise. However, some of the more common applications of SOA are for information delivery, integration, resource delivery, security, and legacy applications support. Table 3.4 describes how the different service types align and support each of these criteria.

Another consideration for determining which service types will be of value is the set of interaction patterns in which SOA will facilitate participants. The most common interaction patterns include Application-to-Application (A2A), Business-to-Business (B2B), and Business-to-Consumer (B2C). A2A interactions tend to be somewhat fine-grained. That is they are transactional and often describe the interactions that support integration and information delivery between applications. B2B interactions are more about collaboration between different businesses or business units. These businesses can be of the same enterprise or can include external partners. B2C interactions will often include a user interface and are typically customer facing. They can be very dynamic and include variable requests for information. Table 3.5 shows these interaction patterns.

Table 3.5 Comparison of SOA Interaction Patterns to Service Types

SOA Interaction Patterns	Web Service	ReST	Fixed Position API
A2A	Excellent	Fair	Good
B2B	Excellent	Good	Poor
B2C	Fair	Excellent	Poor

REFERENCES

1. Christensen E, Curbera F, Meredith G, Weerawarana S, eds. Web Services Description Language (WSDL) 1.1, (W3C, March 15, 2001). <http://www.w3.org/TR/wsdl/>.

2. Chinnici R, Moreau J-J, Ryman A, Weerawarana S, eds. Web Services Description Language (WSDL) Version 2.0 Part 1: Core Language (W3C, June 26, 2007). <http://www.w3.org/TR/wsdl20/>.

3. Fallside DC, Walmsley P, eds. XML Schema Part 0: Primer. 2nd ed. (W3C, October 28, 2004). <http://www.w3.org/TR/xmlschema-0/>.

4. Bray T, Paoli J, Sperberg-McQueen CM, Maler E, Yergeau F, eds. Extensible Markup Language (XML) 1.0 (Fourth Edition) (W3C, September 29, 2006). <http://www.w3.org/TR/REC-xml/>.

5. Mitra N, Lafon Y, eds. SOAP Version 1.2 Part 0: Primer. 2nd ed. (W3C, April 27, 2007). <http://www.w3.org/TR/soap12-part0/>.

6. Fielding RT. Architectural Styles and the Design of Network-Based Software Architectures (University of California, Irvine, Dissertation, 2000). <http://www.ics.uci.edu/~fielding/pubs/dissertation/top.htm/>.

7. Fielding RT. Architectural Styles and the Design of Network-based Software Architectures, Section 5.1.5, "Uniform Interface" (University of California, Irvine, Dissertation, 2000). <http://www.ics.uci.edu/~fielding/pubs/dissertation/top.htm/>.

8. Fielding RT. Architectural Styles and the Design of Network-based Software Architectures, Section 5.1.5, "Uniform Interface" (University of California, Irvine, Dissertation, 2000). <http://www.ics.uci.edu/~fielding/pubs/dissertation/top.htm/>.

Data, the Missing Link

Any number and types of services can be enabled within the SOA architecture. These services, their definitions, and their interactions can vary. Those that are most common include business services, functional services (which can include behavioral and utility services), and data services. The general notion of a service often appears to be application centric. However, data sits at the core of most services and is critical to SOA. These services can also be exposed as Web services, which provide a number of interoperability and loose coupling advantages. The key to which is the Web service interface.

Business services sit at the highest level of interaction in an SOA and represent a common business process, such as "add a new item to the product catalog (see Figure 4.1)." A business service is typically enabled by a business process that includes an aggregate set of more fine-grained service steps and can be described technically by the Business Process Execution Language (BPEL).[1] The name "business process" can also imply a human interaction, including a user interface or a workflow. However, human interaction is not an explicit requirement of a business service or its enabling business process, and BPEL support for human interaction is a somewhat recent trend. A business service could also be implemented as an Application-to-Application (A2A) interaction without a user interface or human interaction.

The value of a business service is to present a simple, composite point of interaction to consumers that incorporate an aggregate set of process steps and service interactions. The consumer of a business service is also shielded from the technical complexity of the underlying process steps and services. An example business service might be something like "AddNewProduct," where there are several underlying steps required to add a new product to the product catalog. However, it is not necessary to expose these more fine-grained details to the consuming application. Rather, it is much simpler for the consumer to interact with the business service and let the business process manage the more fine-grained interactions and steps.

A functional service tends to be more fine-grained than a business service. Like a business service, a functional service can also be enabled by a supporting business process. However, a rule of thumb is to limit the scope and functionality to a well-defined and closely related set of interactions. In some manner, this supports the ability to modularize, assemble, and reuse functional services as participants in other business services. Functional services are also sometimes referred to as utility or behavioral services. Most often, they perform some explicit set of application of logic and apply business rules or behavior. An example of a behavioral service might include "Compute Tax Amount." The example Compute Tax Amount service might perform a couple of steps, including lookup from a tax table and applying a set of business rules for taxation to the data received in the request message

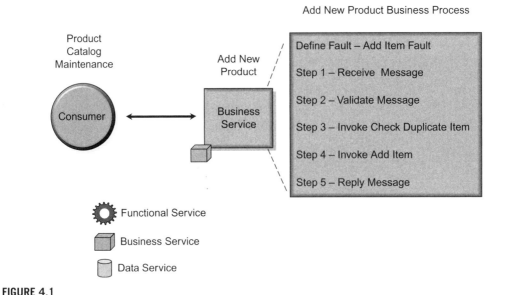

FIGURE 4.1

Add New Product-Business Service

(such as an item identifier, purchase location, and item price). As another type of functional service, a utility service invokes a well-defined and utilized set of capabilities (see Figure 4.2). Most often, a utility type of functional service will invoke a commercially available software utility or similar application. A common example of a utility service is the XML parser validation of an input message, that is, XML validation to compare the structure and content of an XML-encoded message with the rules and constraints defined to a corresponding XML Schema. This type of utility service might invoke a separate and stand-alone XML parser as the primary process step.

As a way to automate the day-to-day business of the enterprise, the value of business services and functional services within an SOA is obvious. Unfortunately, the critical roles that data and data services play in an SOA are often overlooked and misinterpreted. The reality is that SOA, like most other technology architectures, is largely about the acquisition, delivery, manipulation, management, and consumption of data. The sources of information that underlay many of these SOA activities are data that reside in databases, files, tables, documents, and so on. The ability to expose, manipulate, and move this data to and from consumers is core to many SOA services. This is not to say that an SOA is exclusively a data architecture, but that data is a significant capability among the SOA service types.

Even with the prior example business service of "Add New Product," a product catalog database is required and is the data source that enables that service. Without a product catalog or similar data repository of some type, adding a new product is not possible. The new product that is being added as a result of the service must have a place to reside. The service-specific activity to add the new product into the product catalog is, in this example, an Add Item data service. Further, before the new product data can be inserted in the product catalog, an additional step to check for duplicates is required. This check duplicates data service and interrogates the product database to determine if the item already exists (see Figure 4.3). Again, the need for data and data services becomes apparent.

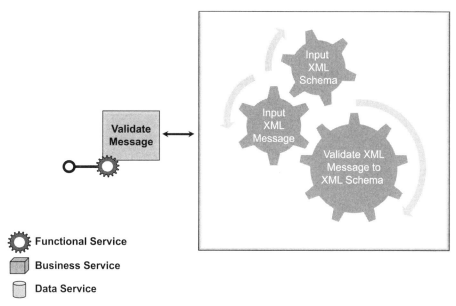

FIGURE 4.2

Validate Message—Utility Service

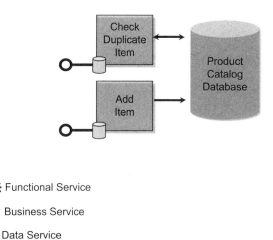

FIGURE 4.3

Check for Duplicates and Add Item—Data Services

When we look at the total end-to-end process and set of interactions that enable the example Add New Product business service, we find that all three types of services are involved: a business service as the primary interaction point for the consumer, a functional service (utility) to validate the accuracy of the request message, and data services to check for duplicate items and to add the new item to the

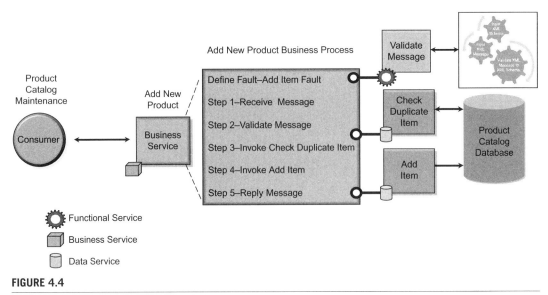

FIGURE 4.4

End-to-End Process for Add New Product

product catalog (see Figure 4.4). Although the example functional utility service and the two data services are represented as process steps invoked by the Add New Product service example, they can also be invoked independently and can be executed by other business services as well (as a form of reuse).

The product data repository (a database in this example) is not exclusive to the example Add New Product business service or even to an SOA servicing paradigm. In fact, this product data store can be accessed and used by other SOA services, as well as by traditional applications. As we'll see in coming chapters, the ability to search for, acquire, and deliver information to consumers, regardless of the data source technology involved, is a significant part of the SOA value proposition. This fundamental need for data in an SOA servicing paradigm is the "missing link" that is all too often overlooked.

4.1 DATA AT REST—PERSISTENCE

The classification of data as "data at rest" has become widely recognized. Data at rest reflects a traditional view of data, where data activities are applied to data that resides in a data repository (see Figure 4.5). For our purposes, we can generalize a data repository as a collection of data instances and values that are persisted in some type of data structure, file, database, or document. The types of technologies that host such data structures are many; the most common include relational databases, object-relational databases, object databases, XML databases, file systems, and content management systems.

The long-standing practices associated with data architecture disciplines are founded in the description, definition, and specification of data as it exists in a data repository. Some of the more recognized data architecture roles include data modeler, data administrator, data architect, and database administrator. Some tasks, activities, and responsibilities for each of these roles may overlap, whereas others are more specific to the level of abstraction, interaction with business partners, and technical specialization.

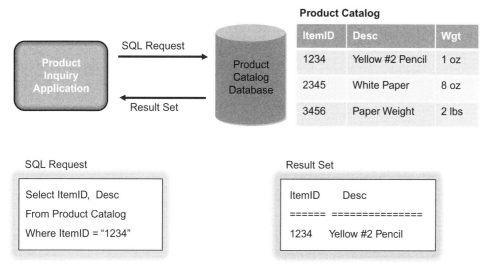

Product Catalog

ItemID	Desc	Wgt
1234	Yellow #2 Pencil	1 oz
2345	White Paper	8 oz
3456	Paper Weight	2 lbs

SQL Request

```
Select ItemID,  Desc
From Product Catalog
Where ItemID = "1234"
```

Result Set

```
ItemID     Desc
======  ================
1234     Yellow #2 Pencil
```

FIGURE 4.5

Data at Rest, Traditional Database Access

With each of these data repository types and also with the roles that define and manage them, there is the concept of persistence. As an abstract definition, "persistence" refers to something that is first created and then remains afterward. Extending this definition of persistence to data, we can infer that once data instances and values are placed into a data repository, they remain through a lifecycle. This explanation becomes analogous to the notion of "data at rest." The more fine-grained activities that operate on data in the repository are part of the lifecycle. As might be expected, data are first instantiated. That is, the data are "created." Once created, the data are then available for access by application and service consumers. The data at rest can be viewed, modified, and potentially deleted at end of life.

This description of data at rest should be rudimentary for any technologist. Where classification of data at rest applies in an SOA is specific to the earlier example of a business service. Even though the example Add New Product business service includes a number of nondata activities, it also involves a data store (the product catalog database). Also important is to recognize that the example data store is not exclusive or limited to the SOA or services. The same data store can also be accessed by more traditional applications, some of which might be local to that system or from many other systems. As an at rest data repository, the data instance and values remain to be accessed and manipulated by any authorized application.

Metadata is another important consideration for data at rest (and, as you will see later, for data in motion). Some refer to metadata as data about data. However, this is a somewhat ambiguous definition. Perhaps a more specific definition of metadata is the descriptive and structural characteristics of, and the rules that apply to, data. A subset of metadata from the Add New Product example would include characteristics of the product catalog database and the data at rest that are persisted within it.

A subset of example metadata might include

- Database Type
- Database Location
- Database Name
- Table Name
- Column Name (or field name) for each of the data values
- Column Data Type
- Column Length
- Column Null or Mandatory/Optional Rule

To correctly access and interpret the data instances and values within the product catalog, the consuming application or service must have some knowledge of its metadata. When the consuming application will request a modification to data, the data type, length, and the mandatory/optional rules become critical. If the data do not comply with these metadata rules, the data modification will be prohibited, will fail, or, in a poorly designed service, will introduce anomalous data into the data repository. As we'll see with data in motion, metadata also plays a critical role in the Web service interface design process.

4.2 DATA IN MOTION—MESSAGED CONTEXT

Data in motion extends that data analogy to consider a more transactional scenario. Data that has been positioned within a message and moved from one service interaction participant to another is defined as "data in motion," rather than "data at rest." The message that contains the data is the context of an interaction between service collaborators. In a simple request and response interaction, the consumer will insert some type of data into a request message. That message is then sent to the endpoint representing the service. When routed over the enterprise service bus to the service, the message is then received and the data extracted by the service. Depending upon the service type, granularity, and operation being requested, the service will then perform some type of processing. The result of that processing is then inserted as data into a response message, which is returned to the consumer. As we can see from the example, the data within those messages are "in motion", rather than sitting in a data repository such as a database (see Figure 4.6).

The data contained in the example request and response messages are specific to the service type, offered functionality, and operations. This is an interesting situation, in that the data in motion have often originated from a data at rest data source. Further, the service (especially a data service) will often abstract some of this data from the at rest source before returning it to the requesting consumer. The intent is to insulate the consumer as much as possible from the underlying technology or even the potential disparity between different data source implementations.

With an established enterprise, there are often multiple data at rest sources for data of the same basic context. As an example, the enterprise might have developed and implemented an order entry system, and within that system, product catalog data are managed and maintained. Separately, the enterprise may have also purchased and implemented a commercial software package for managing the development and manufacturing of products, where product master data are again managed and maintained. While both of these examples have data of the same basic context (products), the underlying data source implementations can be quite different. These differences are often reflected

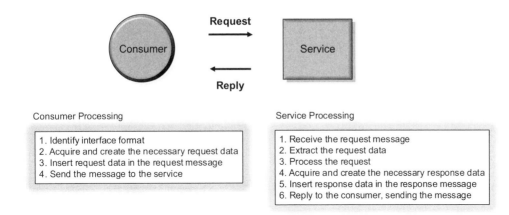

FIGURE 4.6

Data in Motion, Request and Response

by variations of metadata (the descriptive and structural characteristics of data and the rules that apply to data that we learned about earlier).

A service that exposes or operates on this product data from both data at rest sources will have to resolve the differences and present a consistent response to a requesting consumer, or there may be a requirement for two different services that limit their processing to a single source of product data. In either scenario, the Web service interface defines the context of the service capabilities and resolves to a representative abstraction that, in turn, becomes the data in motion (see Figure 4.7). Regardless, there are one or more data at rest data sources that sit behind the example service.

The example can also be reversed to consider the consumer of the service. While the data being requested might originate from a data at rest source that sits behind the service, once the response is received, the data of that response might be inserted into yet another data at rest source local to the consumer. Some data practitioners will view this as a replication of source data, which is usually not a recommended practice. However, replication of data acquired from a service is not always the case, nor the intent. In many scenarios, the consumer will acquire the data for further enrichment or to present the data to a person via a human user interface.

The data instance or values extracted and returned as data in motion content of the response message represent a core design consideration for the service. There are a number of complex patterns that will need to be evaluated and potentially applied to the Web service interface. As one example, the data at rest source might include a very large number of related structures such as database tables. Within each of these structures might be tens or even hundreds of individual fields or database columns. On a request from a consumer, having to navigate these many relationships and collect the data from all of the possible structures and fields quickly becomes unmanageable. Another important pattern is the granularity of the service. Will the service provide a read-only inquiry into the data, or will it also expose operations for adding new data, updating existing data, or deleting data? There are also more technical characteristics of the service, such as the volume of data returned in a response message, the number of requests for data from consumers, and the frequency that requests from consumers will be received. Then, there are also patterns to rationalize the data at rest source data into

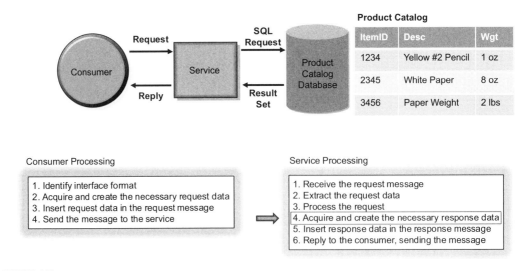

FIGURE 4.7

Data in Motion, Data at Rest Source

a common context, allowing all consumers to rely upon a well-defined and consistent expression of the data in the response message. Complicating these patterns are the technical considerations and enabling capabilities of the environment. Depending upon how well each of these patterns apply and where they might conflict, the result begins to drive the Web service interface design.

The service requirements, technical characteristics, and patterns described in Table 4.1 are selected and then used to drive an appropriate service and service interface design. The design process starts at this high level and then drives deeper into the service capabilities and operations, all of which represent the scope of the service. Once the scope has been formalized, the best fit for purpose design patterns can be determined.

The metadata for data in motion is also a critical design consideration that will result in one or more Web service interface artifacts. Much of the metadata for data in motion is derived from the data at rest (name, data type, length, null rules, etc.). The importance of data consistency becomes obvious when considering that consumers from any originating system, application, or technology will need to interact with the service and consume the data exposed by the service. Rather than forcing the complexities of different data source implementations on the consumer, the service will need to expose data in a more consistent way. The metadata that describes the data at rest sources are used for mapping to a standard representation of the data described by the Web service interface. In this example, the metadata of importance to service consumers are the XML Schemas that describe and constrain the request and response messages (see Figure 4.8).

Given the importance of data and metadata to the Web service interface, there is a need for technology tools that allow the architect or practitioner to develop and maintain the Web service interface artifacts. Some SOA and Web service integrated development environments (IDEs) include their own tools for this purpose. Other technologies provide a more model-driven approach where the Web service interface artifacts are generated from models. Still others do not provide supporting technologies and assume that the Web service interface designer will rely upon code editors or other similar tooling.

Table 4.1 Service Requirements, Characteristics, and Design Patterns

Service Requirements	Technical Characteristics	Service Design Patterns
High volume of data involved	Performance, latency	Coarse Grained Service, Crossing Multiple Data Contexts
Moderate volume of data involved	Availability	Coarse Grained Service, Crossing Multiple Data Structures
Low volume of data involved	Scalability	Coarse Grained Service, Scoped to a Single Data Context
Read-only inquiry	Transaction completeness	Coarse Grained Service, Multiple Operations
Add new data	Transaction correctness	Coarse Grained Service, Overloaded Operations
Modify existing data	Transaction consistency	Fine-Grained Service, Single Operation
Delete existing data		
	Complexity of the source data relationships and structures	Rationalized Data Context
High number of consumer requests	Multiple data sources for the same basic context	
Moderate number of consumer requests	Quality and reliability of the data	Consumer Directed Data Context Selection
Low number of consumer requests		Consumer Directed Data Structure Selection
	Technology limitations of consumers (legacy consumer)	Consumer Directed Update Correlation
High frequency of consumer requests		Consumer Directed Empty Elements
Moderate number of consumer requests	Consumer authentication	
Low number of consumer requests	Consumer authorization (to the service and the operations)	
	Secure message content	
Service consumers will interact with the service		
Service consumers and traditional, nonservice applications will interact with the service		

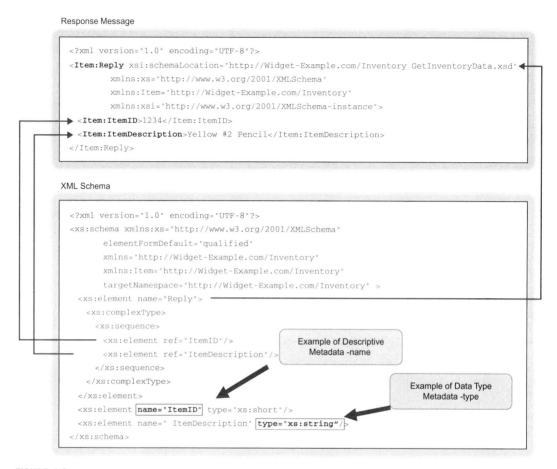

FIGURE 4.8

Data in Motion, XML Schema as Metadata

While this book is not about tool usage, the need for appropriate tooling is important to consider. The service interface artifacts are complex enough that the right tooling can make a significant difference. The primary tools used to create the example Web service interface artifacts for this book include XML Spy and MapForce, both from Altova (Copyright 2003-2008 Altova GmbH, reprinted with permission of Altova) (see Figure 4.9). There are other similar tools in the marketplace, and the syntactical edit, validation, and generation capabilities specific to WSDL, XML Schemas, and XSLT are important for evaluating and selecting your own tooling.

SUMMARY

While SOA and services are often interpreted as process centric, this is not always the case. Processes are in fact a core part of any SOA, and they facilitate the interaction of SOA service collaborators.

FIGURE 4.9

XML Schema using XML Spy (Copyright 2003-2008 Altova GmbH, reprinted with permission of Altova)

However, underlying most SOA services are one or more data sources. This raises the importance of data in the SOA paradigm and emphasizes the need for data and metadata in the process of Web service interface design. Yet, this emphasis on data is not limited to traditional data architecture. Rather, there are two important views of data to consider in your SOA. One is "data at rest," where data instances and values are persisted in some form of data repository, and the other is "data in motion," as the data contained in messages that are moved between service participants and defined by the Web service interface.

The disciplines for exploiting and optimizing data at rest sources and structures are supported by the roles of Data Modeler, Data Administrator, Data Architect, and Database Architect, all of which are all reasonably well-known and accepted. These data at rest structures are most often supported by some type of database. However, this is not a restriction. The data sources could be flat files, documents, or almost any other type of data repository. Metadata plays a critical role in defining not only the characteristics and rules for data at rest sources but also those of data in motion as messages. This metadata can be quite extensive and, in some cases, complex. Metadata tooling to help create, edit, and manage metadata (especially for data in motion, as with Web services interface artifacts such as WSDL and XML Schemas) is recommended. As you'll learn in Chapter 5, "Data Services," the ability to extract data from multiple data at rest sources and resolve to a consistent expression of that data in a Web service response message is the key to enterprise integration.

REFERENCE

1. Jordan D, Evdemon J, chairs, Web Services Business Process Execution Language Version 2.0, OASIS Standard (April 11, 2007). <http://docs.oasis-open.org/wsbpel/2.0/OS/wsbpel-v2.0-OS.html/>.

Data Services

5

Data services deliver and manipulate information from data at rest implementations (data at rest are persisted in a database, file management system, document, or similar). In a simple sense, data services access the databases, files, documents, and similar implementations that serve traditional business applications. As a result, data services help to unlock the information held by line of business and application-specific systems, and provide a solution to enterprise application and information integration challenges. As data values are extracted from these data source structures, they are placed into messages to become data in motion (data in motion is the movement of data in messages between two or more collaborators), which can be transported, shared, distributed, and replatformed for use by other consumers and applications.

Composite data services are exposed to the SOA architecture as coarse-grained business services that are supported by an underlying orchestrated business process. A composite data service exposes data-specific functionality and includes a number of subordinate and more fine-grained data service interactions. By hiding the underlying and fine-grained processing, composite data services also simplify consumer interactions and data operations. Data service consumers can specify a number of options in the service interface that allow the response to be somewhat customized to their specific needs and limitations. Consumers are also insulated from data service subprocesses, such as message validation, data existence checking, and error handling.

Underlying composite data services are more fine-grained data services that deliver and manipulate data from data at rest implementations. However, these fine-grained data services are tightly scoped to one data source, application, or system each, and they usually do not have another underlying orchestrated business process. Fine-grained data services also include an explicit and limited set of data operations. A single fine-grained data service might perform a data value quality check, or a single CRUD operation, such as "Add". However, they will rarely combine functional activities and are generally positioned as a very narrow data capability in the SOA. Consumers can be designed to also exploit these fine-grained data services directly, but their interaction becomes somewhat complex and "chatty" (as in, frequent back and forth message interactions). Most often, they are invoked as individual steps from within a higher level, composite service.

As an example, the Add New Product service of the previous chapter ("AddNewProduct") is a coarse-grained, composite data service that resolves consumer requests to add new products to the Product Catalog Database. As a composite service, consumers provide the requisite data in the request message (defined according to the Web service interface definition), and message to the exposed endpoint for the service. On receipt, the Add New Product service invokes an orchestrated business process, which in turn messages to other subordinate and fine-grained services. The business process resolves a number of functional interactions such as validating the original consumer request message and verifying that the requested addition is not a duplicate of a product already found in the database. These business process steps are required to ensure a high degree of data integrity and consistency. However, by including them as process steps under the composite Add New Product data service, the consumer is insulated from all of this complexity. In a conceptual sense, the consumer's role in the interaction is to comply with the Add New Product service interface, provide the data to be added in the request message, send the message to the service for processing, and await a reply.

This composite data servicing pattern is very effective and provides a high degree of reuse at two levels. By encapsulating (hiding) the various fine-grained processing steps from the consumer and abstracting (simplifying) the consumer-to-service interaction, the composite data service becomes a self-contained data processing engine. Designers and developers of consuming applications have a simpler service interaction to consider and, as a result, can deliver needed functionality quicker. This capability segues into a higher degree of data service reuse. Additionally, the more fine-grained services that are referenced and invoked by the composite data service are not limited only to that business process. Rather, these fine-grained services (including fine-grained data services) can be reused by reference from across almost any number and type of other composite services. Another benefit of composite data services is the resolution of data impedance from across applications. With a moderate to large enterprise, data sources for the same basic context will have been implemented in multiple data at rest implementations. Composite data services can resolve the mapping and transformation of data from these varied data sources. As a result, composite data service consumers are exposed to an abstracted standard for data, helping to resolve the enterprise and information integration problem.

5.1 A SINGLE DATA AT REST DATA SOURCE

The example Add New Product data service is simple in operation. It is limited to performing a single CRUD operation ("Add") and also to a single data source (the "Product Catalog Database"). The classification of a composite data service is analogous to that of a business service, but with a functional scoping that is specific to data. As a composite, the service is supported by an underlying business process. The business process for the example Add New Product service includes an orchestrated set of steps to ensure the request message is complete and accurate, to ensure the new product item does not already exist in the Product Catalog Database, and to add the new item to the same database. Each of these steps reference and invoke other fine-grained services. Two of the business process steps refer to fine-grained data services. The fine-grained "Check Duplicate Item" and "Add Item" data services operate on a single data at rest implementation (see Figure 5.1).

The Add New Product service is implemented as a Web service. The request and reply messages are encoded as XML and are included in a SOAP envelope. The structure and context of the messages are defined by an XML Schema, and a WSDL represents the overall service interface. Consumers provide product data in a request message and send it to the Add New Product data

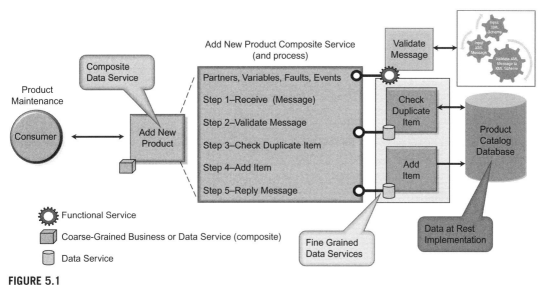

FIGURE 5.1

Add New Product Service

service, where it is then processed. The request message content, including the new product data, is an example of data in motion. To resolve a request, the Add New Product service invokes an orchestrated set of several finer-grained services as part of its supporting business process. As described in Chapter 1, "SOA—A Common Sense Definition," an orchestration is a set of service interactions that are well defined, with clearly identified steps (usually ordered steps), each of which invokes a set of known services with known interactions. Following are the steps defined to the Add New Product service orchestration:

1. Receive (receive the request message from a consumer)
2. Validate Message (invoke a fine-grained utility service to validate the request message)
3. Check Duplicate Item (invoke a fine-grained data service to check for duplicates)
4. Add Item (invoke a fine-grained data service to insert the item into the database)
5. Reply (develop a reply message with success or fail and return to the consumer)

The example Add New Product service relies upon a BPEL process to define each of the steps, and an SOA platform that has implemented a Business Process Management engine (BPM) to invoke and coordinate the subordinate service interactions (see Example 5.1).[1] When the BPEL process has successfully completed, the new product requested by the consumer will be added to the product catalog database, and a response is returned (with the reply message representing an example of "data in motion"). Unless an individual step of the process fails, the requesting consumer is unaware of the underlying processing and retains a simpler, coarse-grained interaction. However, the responsibility for completing the overall process remains with the Add New Product service, and each of the detail process steps becomes critically important.

Example 5.1

Add New Product BPEL Process (abbreviated)

```xml
<?xml version="1.0" encoding="UTF-8" ?>
- <process name="AddNewProduct" targetNamespace="http://Widget-Example.com/
Inventory" xmlns:tns="http://Widget-Example.com/Inventory" xmlns="http://docs.oasis-open.
org/wsbpel/2.0/process/executable">
- <partnerLinks>
<partnerLink name="Consumer" partnerLinkType="tns:AddNewProductRequest" myRole="AddNewProdduct
Service" partnerRole="Consumer"/>
<partnerLink name="ValidateMessage" partnerLinkType="tns:ValidationLink" myRole="ValidationServiceRe
quester" partnerRole="ValidationService"/>
<partnerLink name="CheckDuplicateItem" partnerLinkType="tns:CheckDuplicateItemLink" myRole="Duplic
ateItemServiceRequester" partnerRole="DuplicateItemService"/>
<partnerLink name="AddItem" partnerLinkType="tns:AddItemLink" myRole="AddItemServiceRequester"
partnerRole="AddItemService"/>
</partnerLinks>
- <variables>
<variable name="AddNewProductRequest" messageType="tns:AddNewProductRequestMessage"/>
<variable name="ValidationRequest" messageType="tns:AddNewProductRequestMessage"/>
<variable name="ValidationResponse" messageType="tns:AddNewProductResponseMessage"/>
<variable name="ValidationFault" messageType="tns:AddNewProductFaultMessage"/>
<variable name="CheckDuplicateItemRequest" messageType="tns:AddNewProductRequestMessage"/>
<variable name="CheckDuplicateItemResponse" messageType="tns:AddNewProductResponseMessage"/>
<variable name="CheckDuplicateItemFault" messageType="tns:AddNewProductFaultMessage"/>
<variable name="AddItemRequest" messageType="tns:AddNewProductRequestMessage"/>
<variable name="AddItemResponse" messageType="tns:AddNewProductResponseMessage"/>
<variable name="AddItemFailure" messageType="tns:AddNewProductFaultMessage"/>
<variable name="AddNewProductResponse" messageType="tns:AddNewProductResponseMessage"/>
<variable name="AddNewProductFault" messageType="tns:AddNewProductFaultMessage"/>
</variables>
- <faultHandlers>
- <catch faultName="tns:ValidationFault" faultVariable="ValidationFault" faultMessageType="tns:
AddNewProductFaultMessage">
<reply partnerLink="Consumer" portType="tns:AddNewProductPort" operation="Add" variable="AddNewPro
ductFault" faultName="ValidationFault"/>
</catch>
- <catch faultName="tns:CheckDuplicateItemFault" faultVariable="CheckDuplicateItemFault"
faultMessageType="tns:AddNewProductFaultMessage">
<reply partnerLink="Consumer" portType="tns:AddNewProductPort" operation="Add" variable="AddNewPro
ductFault" faultName="CheckDuplicateItemFault"/>
</catch>
- <catch faultName="tns:AddItemFault" faultVariable="AddItemFailure" faultMessageType="tns:
AddNewProductFaultMessage">
```

```
<reply partnerLink="Consumer" portType="tns:AddNewProductPort" operation="Add" variable="AddNewPro
ductFault" faultName="AddItemFault"/>
</catch>
- <catchAll>
- <sequence>
- <assign>
- <copy>
<from expression="string('ProcessFault')"/>
<to variable="AddNewProductFault" part="FaultMessage"/>
</copy>
</assign>
<reply partnerLink="Consumer" portType="tns:AddNewProductPort" operation="Add" variable="AddNewPro
ductFault" faultName="ProcessFault"/>
</sequence>
</catchAll>
</faultHandlers>
- <eventHandlers>
– <onMessage partnerLink="ValidateMessage" portType="tns:ValidateMessagePort" operation="Validate"
variable="ValidationFault">
<throw faultName="tns:ValidationFault" faultVariable="ValidationFault"/>
</onMessage>
– <onMessage partnerLink="CheckDuplicateItem" portType="tns:CheckDuplicateItemPort"
operation="Check" variable="CheckDuplicateItemFault">
<throw faultName="tns:CheckDuplicateItemFault" faultVariable="CheckDuplicateItemFault"/>
</onMessage>
– <onMessage partnerLink="AddItem" portType="tns:AddItemPort" operation="Add"
variable="AddItemFault">
<throw faultName="tns:AddItemFailure" faultVariable="AddItemFailure"/>
</onMessage>
</eventHandlers>
– <sequence name="AddNewProductProcess">
<receive partnerLink="Consumer" portType="tns:AddNewProductPort" operation="Add" variable="AddNe
wProductRequest" createInstance="yes"/>
- <assign>
- <copy>
<from variable="AddNewProductRequest" part="RequestMessage"/>
<to variable="ValidationRequest" part="RequestMessage"/>
</copy>
</assign>
<invoke partnerLink="ValidateMessage" portType="tns:ValidateMessagePort" operation="Validate" inputVa
riable="ValidationRequest" outputVariable="ValidationResponse"
faultVariable="ValidationFault"/>
– <assign>
– <copy>
```

```
<from variable="ValidationResponse" part="ResponseMessage"/>
<to variable="AddNewProductResponse" part="ValidationResponseMessage"/>
</copy>
</assign>
– <assign>
– <copy>
<from variable="ValidationFault" part="FaultMessage"/>
<to variable="AddNewProductFault" part="ValidationFaultMessage"/>
</copy>
</assign>
– <assign>
– <copy>
<from variable="AddNewProductRequest" part="RequestMessage"/>
<to variable="CheckDuplicateItemRequest" part="RequestMessage"/>
</copy>
</assign>
<invoke partnerLink="CheckDuplicateItem" portType="tns:CheckDuplicateItemPort"
operation="Check" inputVariable="CheckDuplicateItemRequest" outputVariable="CheckDuplicateItemRespo
nse" faultVariable="CheckDuplicateItemFault"/>
- <assign>
- <copy>
<from variable="CheckDuplicateItemResponse" part="ResponseMessage"/>
<to variable="AddNewProductResponse" part="CheckDuplicateResponseMessage"/>
</copy>
</assign>
- <assign>
- <copy>
<from variable="CheckDuplicateItemFault" part="FaultMessage"/>
<to variable="AddNewProductFault" part="CheckDuplicateFaultMessage"/>
</copy>
</assign>
– <assign>
– <copy>
<from variable="AddNewProductRequest" part="RequestMessage"/>
<to variable="AddItemRequest" part="RequestMessage"/>
</copy>
</assign>
<invoke partnerLink="AddItem" portType="tns:AddNewItemPort" operation="Add" inputVariable="AddItemRe
quest" outputVariable="AddItemResponse" faultVariable="AddItemFault"/>
– <assign>
– <copy>
<from variable="AddItemResponse" part="ResponseMessage"/>
<to variable="AddNewProductResponse" part="AddItemResponseMessage"/>
</copy>
```

```
</assign>
– <assign>
- <copy>
<from variable="AddItemFault" part="FaultMessage"/>
<to variable="AddNewProductFault" part="AddItemFaultMessage"/>
</copy>
</assign>
<reply partnerLink="Consumer" portType="tns:AddNewProductPort" operation="Add"
variable="AddNewProductResponse"/>
</sequence>
</process>
```

A BPEL for a composite data service (as with the example Add New Product data service) will generally include partner link definitions as the references to subordinate fine-grained services. When a referenced fine-grained service is also a Web service, the property attributes of the partner link definitions and also of the various interactions (e.g., receive, invoke, and reply) will map to WSDL interface definitions for those services. The BPEL can implement a synchronous request-reply message exchange pattern, or it can also implement a more synchronous fire-and-forget message exchange pattern. The example Add New Product service follows a request-reply pattern.

Step 1 of the business process as described in Figure 5.1, "Add New Product Service," receives the request message from a consumer. With a SOAP-based Web service,[2] this step includes the following:

1. Receive the SOAP envelope (e.g., "<ns:Envelope/>" where "ns" is the namespace qualifier).

2. Extract the request message content from the SOAP body (e.g., "<ns:Body/>" where "ns" is the namespace qualifier).

The request message and data values contained in the SOAP body are the context of the service interaction (see Figure 5.2). There are several possible techniques for extracting the message body content from the SOAP envelope. For example, when the service is developed using Java, the getSOAP-Body method of the SOAPMessage class can expose the body of the envelope.[3] Another technique includes writing an XPath expression to navigate the SOAP envelope and extracting the SOAP body contents. A third and less optimal technique is to develop application behavior natively to navigate, parse, and extract the body contents as a subset XML document.

Step 2 of the business process as described in Figure 5.1, "Add New Product Service," validates that the structure, content, and typing of the request message match what is expected by the Add New Product service (see Figure 5.3). This is both a fundamental and critical step for Web service interactions. This step invokes a separate functional service ("Validate Message" service) to validate the request message. This validation service passes the request message as extracted in the previous step from the SOAP envelope body to a utility known as a validating XML Parser. XML Schemas express the rules and constraints for the XML message defined by the service interface. These schema-defined rules include the naming of the elements that contain data values of the request (tags), the location and order of those elements within the message structure, and—in a well-defined Web service interface—the semantics and typing for the data values.

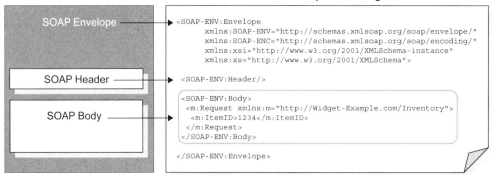

FIGURE 5.2

SOAP Envelope, SOAP Body, and the Request Message

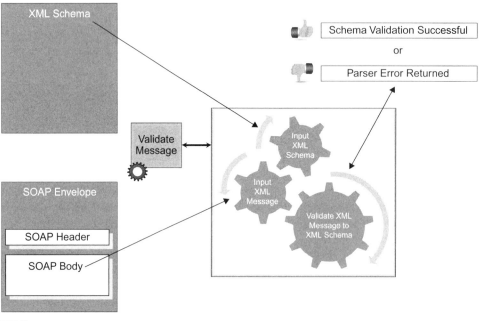

FIGURE 5.3

Validating XML Parser

A validating XML Parser compares an XML-encoded message to one or more XML Schemas of the service interface and identifies any evidence of noncompliance. If the message is determined to comply with the rules and constraints of the service interface schema, step 3 is then processed. Alternatively, if the message is determined not to be "valid," an error is thrown, and the process advances to step 5 where a fault message is returned to the consumer.

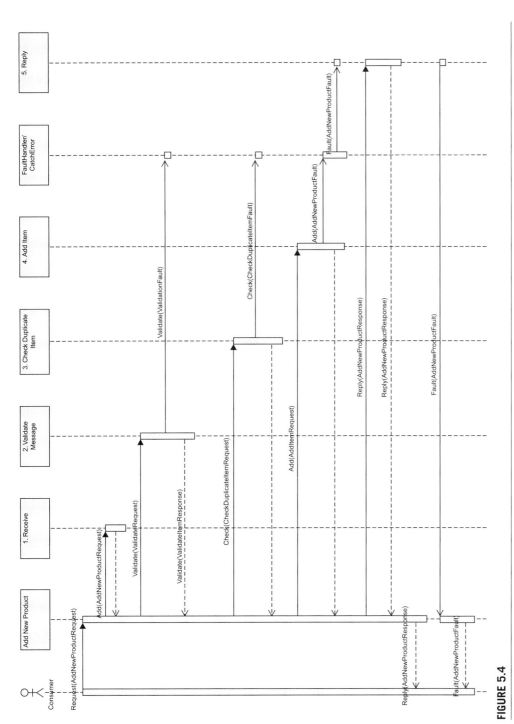

FIGURE 5.4

Add New Product Sequence Diagram

Step 3 of the business process as described in Figure 5.1, "Add New Product Service," verifies that the requested item does not already exist ("Check Duplicate Item" service). The Check Duplicate Item service is a fine-grained data service that extracts the Item ID data value from the request message ("<ItemID/>"), inserts the Item ID into a SQL data query, submits the query to the Product Catalog Database, and then interprets the result from the database. The Check Duplicate Item service has only one discretely defined "Check" operation and, in this example, acts upon only a single data source (the Product Catalog Database).

The message passed to the Check Duplicate Item service from the overall Add New Product business process is still encoded as an XML message. A process known as unmarshaling is used by the Check Duplicate Item service to extract the content and to retrieve the Item ID. Once the data values are extracted, they are also mapped to the object model of that service. In this case, the object model is an internally defined object structure that includes the objects and relationships from the class definitions of the application. This allows the Check Duplicate Item service to process the data values natively and to build a query with the Item ID data value in the SQL predicate.

For the example, the Product Catalog Database is implemented as a relational architecture, and the Check Duplicate Item query will be submitted as SQL. The success or failure of the query determines whether the requested product (Item ID) already exists in the database or not. Relational databases and database APIs compliant with X/Open provide a SQL Status or similar SQL Error code for communicating the success of a SQL query.[4] Some relational database products have also implemented extensions to provide additional information.

The DB2 Universal Database exposes a SQL Communication Area (SQLCA), and includes a SQLCODE and SQLSTATE to report the query processing result.[5] Procedural languages such as COBOL have historically used the SQLCA to acquire processing status and error codes (note that the SQLCA has been deprecated in the most recent X/Open specification). In the DB2 example, the SQLCA includes a processing response code (SQLCODE, sqlCode, or sqlcode). If the Item ID value as included in the SQL query already exists in the database, the query result would produce a successful SQLCODE (something like a "0"). The returned SQLCODE value is similar to a SQLSTATE where a value of "00000" (or "00") also notes success. Alternatively, a SQLSTATE value of "01000" (or "01") is a warning, and a value of "02000" (or "02") is a "No Data" response. If the Item ID does not exist, which in the example is also the desired result, the query should result in a SQLSTATE or SQLCODE value of something other than "0" (usually a SQLCODE value of "100" or a positive or negative integer value that corresponds to "no rows found" or "no rows qualified").

In the case of Java, JDBC, and some persistence frameworks, a SQL Exception class is exposed, and with the getSQLState and getErrorCode methods, provides visibility into the result of a database query. Depending upon the implementation, a "getSqlca" method[6] or a "getErrorCode" method can be used to acquire the SQL State and is similar to the SQLCA SQLCODE previously described.[7] The Microsoft .NET framework also includes a SqlException class that exposes a number of properties for determining a database state and SQL error.[8]

Regardless of the specific exception or error implementation, if, during this step, the query returns a successful read where the item ID value is already found in the database, the product requested for add is then considered to be a duplicate, and the process advances to step 5 with a fault message returned informing the consumer that the item already exists. Faults can be raised in the BPEL process as the result of triggering events, or they can also be raised when directed by conditional case logic, where return variables (output variables) are evaluated. If the query returns a not found or similar condition signifying that the item does not already exist, the process successfully advances to step 4.

Step 4 of the business process as described in Figure 5.1, "Add New Product Service," adds the item to the database. Since processing has advanced from the prior Check Duplicate Item step without error, this step assumes that the requested product (Item ID) does not already exist in the database and invokes another fine-grained data service to add the requested item ("Add Item" service). The Add Item data service takes the content from the original request message, forms a SQL statement to add the item, and submits a SQL insert to the Product Catalog Database. Similar to step 3, the query will result in a SQLException, SQLSTATE, or SQLCA and SQLCODE. Although unexpected, if the example SQL insert were to fail, the appropriate error data are collected, and the process then advances to step 5 as a fault. If the SQL insert is successful, the data are collected, and the process also advances to step 5.

Step 5 of the process returns a message to the requesting consumer. If any step of the Add New Product service process failed, the offending error data is returned as a SOAP fault message. If all steps of the process were successful, a reply message with the Item ID and a "success" notification (contained in the SOAP Body) is returned to the requesting consumer (see Figure 5.4).

Even if the requesting consumer were to access the database directly rather than using a data service, each of the steps defined by the example business process would be required to ensure a high degree of integrity and completeness. However, the requesting consumer would then need to include all of the internal logic for each of these same process steps. The obvious advantages of using the Add New Product service allow that the consumer is insulated from the complexity of these individual steps, and the Add New Product service is largely reusable by any number of consumers. Yet the example Add New product data service is limited to a single data at rest source. Significant complexities arise when multiple data at rest sources are required.

5.2 MULTIPLE AND DISPARATE DATA AT REST SOURCES

With its current scope, the Add New Product example is a somewhat simple composite data service. Although it is supported by several underlying process steps and subordinate services, there is only one data at rest source used in the process (the Product Catalog Database). Unfortunately, in a moderate to large enterprise, this is rarely the case. Rather, there are separate and vertical applications, with each managing their own data at rest implemented version of the same basic data. This is also an example of the enterprise integration problem that plagues many organizations.

As any enterprise evolves and matures, there are many business and technology decisions that come into play, each of which can have significant implications to data at rest implementations. During periods of growth, some organizations will focus on business acquisition. Often, an acquired business will also have its own enabling technologies, applications, and data. It may be deemed too costly or complex to extract and migrate the data of the acquired business into the operational systems of the enterprise. Yet, the value of that new data is obvious and may have even been part of the acquisition rationale.

Another common example is the use of packaged software applications (sometimes referred to as COTS, i.e., Commercial Off The Shelf applications). While most software packages provide APIs for accessing the underlying data stores, the API functionality may have technology-specific limitations. Since the data at rest implementations and the supporting context of these COTS solutions are parochial to the application, it is rare that the data are structured in the exact same manner as other data at rest implementations of the enterprise.

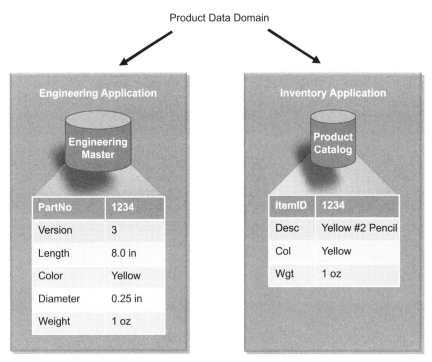

FIGURE 5.5

A Core Data Concept Implemented Across Multiple Data at Rest Sources

Another and possibly the most common example is organic growth. As the enterprise has continued to grow, the need for rapid technology solutioning may unfortunately take precedence over more effective architectural patterns and design best practices. Often, this will result in development of vertical and disjoint solutions with significant data replication. As the enterprise continues to evolve, each of these solutions and additional data replications will often shift further away in structure and semantics from their originating sources.

All of these examples and many others have contributed to the integration problems that plague today's typical enterprise. SOA, Web services, and, more importantly, data services can provide a largely enabling technology set to help address the challenge. However, these same technology enablers are not exclusively the answer. Data is an enterprise asset. It is largely harvested, acquired, manipulated, enriched, and consumed by business constituents. They are the subject matter experts who understand the business value and semantics of enterprise data. Identifying the applications and data at rest sources of roughly analogous data, and aligning on consistent and cross organization definitions for this data are requisite business activities. These important tasks are also part of the SOA governance, where the SOA architects and service designers look to converge and rationalize data at rest sources, rather than create further redundancy (see Figure 5.5).

Enterprise integration is not the only value of SOA and Web services, but it is an obvious one. Attaining a cross-line of business and cross-application view of enterprise data is a long desired goal of many an enterprise. While each vertical application is largely functional there is a significant missed opportunity when data of the same context is locked in separate data at rest implementations. A carefully designed data service can provide a potential solution.

Before developing a data service, the architect or designer must determine the scope of data that will be involved. Data scope describes a context or focal subject and can be referred to as a data domain. Subject matter experts from the business community are critical to defining the data domains of the enterprise and determining which applications host data that should participate in those domains. The data domain for the example Add New Product service is specifically Product data, and the current implementation is limited to a single data at rest source. The Add New Product service can be extended to also consider additional and similar data from the Engineering system. The resulting service will provide a 360-degree view of products for the enterprise.

Data practitioners will often apply an architecture pattern described as the data of record. The data of record for a specific data domain is the authoritative and recognized source of information crossing all lines of business and applications. When the scenario includes multiple data at rest implementations that are also of different structural and semantic definitions, identifying or developing a single data of record can be a significant challenge. However, a data service can hide those complexities and, in many cases, resolve the impedance between data at rest sources of the same domain. The result is a logical data of record.

This approach can have tremendous value to the enterprise. The historic investment in the individual operational systems and data can often be preserved. Disruption to the vertical systems and the business operations they support is minimized. Further, the logical data service can be designed in a manner where the service interface provides options to consumers that allow them to selectively request service functionality (a Web service interface in this example). As with the single data source example, a composite data service is defined above the data sources and hides the complexity of access from consumers. Depending upon the operation exposed by the service, consumers can predetermine if they want to act upon one of the data at rest sources or the entire set of data that has been defined. This is most common with a read-only "Get" service but can also apply to some other service operations.

To enhance the Add New Product data service by adding a second data at rest implementation requires some specific technical information. The designer must have identified the type of data persistence technology in use and the connection methods for accessing the new data at rest source. The designer must also have harvested metadata that describes the specific structures, semantics, and types for the data. Sources of the necessary metadata will usually include data models, process models (for business rules), file layouts, and the system catalog or similar structural descriptors for data at rest implementations. Once this metadata information has been harvested, it must be reviewed by subject matter experts from the business community to help determine which parts of the data should be exposed to service consumers, any business rules that might apply, and the standard by which the data will be returned as data in motion to consumers. This standard also serves as the common canonical for mapping the different data sources to resolve any impedance between the data at rest implementations. Predefined industry canonicals can also be acquired from industry groups or vendors and can help to jump-start the mapping process.

The Add New Product process orchestration will also require modification and extension. Each of the steps will be evaluated to determine whether it is still required and if it needs to be revised or extended. New process steps will also be required to access the additional data at rest implementations. Within the scope of the operations exposed by the service, any potential options will need to be

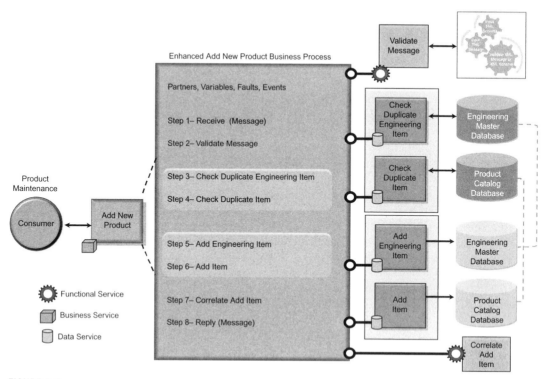

FIGURE 5.6

Enhanced Add New Product Service

considered. When included in the design of the service, the interface will be revised to include them as request options for consumers (see Figure 5.6).

The data domain that defines the scope of data for the revised Add New Product service is determined to include the already implemented Product Catalog Database. However, the data service will also need to include data from the Engineering Master Database. The existing steps of the orchestrated business process are still required. However, there also are several new process steps and subordinate fine-grained services that will be added. The most obvious include Check Duplicate Engineering Item and Add Engineering Item services.

The designer might consider adding this additional functionality to the existing process steps and supporting services. However, adding this functionality expands the processing of the subordinate fine-grained services and makes them less isolated and reusable. This is an important decision that could have longer term implications to the SOA architecture.

As an example, if the Check Duplicate Items data service is designed to now check both the Product Catalog Database and the Engineering Master Database, depending upon the degree to which the logic is coupled to the data source layer, other composite data services might not be able to reuse it. There are also some important operational design considerations. At the lowest layer of the SOA and data servicing architecture are the database implementations. Using the example of a database, there are a number of operational characteristics that can influence performance, latency, availability, and other technical qualities of the systems in which they reside. While it might initially seem advantageous to localize the database insert behavior for both the Product Catalog Database and the Engineering Master Database into a single service, the resulting database operations can be impacted. If the overall Add New Product data service begins to experience a high volume of requests, the resulting Add Item service will also incur a similar increase in requests. Depending upon the database access methods, structure of the SQL insert, the defined unit of work at the database level, and the locking schemes of the database implementations, the Add Item service might experience increased latency. Further, the operational applications in the separate engineering and product systems continue to operate on the same databases, and they might also experience latency as a result of locking and contention with the requests from the data services. Although a database analyst (DBA) might be able to address some of the problems in each database, being able to easily identify specific areas of opportunity and to address the root cause of the latency can become complicated. Alternatively, if the Add Item process activities are designed into separate services, and each is limited to operations on their specific database implementations, there is a greater potential to avoid problems and, when they occur, to identify the root cause and resolve them.

As with the Add New Product example, when the service operation is not read only, there is yet another design complexity. Separating the process steps to access each data at rest source independently requires some form of correlation. Anomalies that might be encountered when a Check Duplicate Engineering Items service returns an "Item Found" result (the item already exists), but the Check Duplicate Items service returns an "Item Not Found" result, mean a processing decision must be made. Either the responses from the two services need to be correlated, or a fail on condition event for either service needs to be defined. This might seem trivial at first, but the consistency and integrity of the underlying data at rest sources will rely upon an effective correlation scheme. Depending upon the data at rest database implementations, APIs, and query languages, a recommendation would be to resolve this complexity with a commercial federated query and transaction management solution. The importance of correlating a complete unit of work across federated databases requires support for distributed transactions. The final commit transaction needs to be implemented as the result of transaction coordination across the data at rest sources, or rolled back if the transaction for any one of the participating data at rest sources fails. This example extends to other process steps as well (as with Add Engineering Item and Add Item process steps). As potential design decision examples:

- On any duplicate item found condition, return a fault message to the consumer and end the process.

- If one item is determined to already exist, but the other does not, ignore the existing item and insert only the new item.

- If one item is determined to already exist, but the other does not, interrogate the existing item to determine if it is in fact the same, and, if yes, insert the new item. Otherwise, return a fault message to the consumer and end the process.

Correlation behavior can in some cases be developed and implemented either as a process step and service to invoke a federated database transaction server, or intrinsically to the overall BPEL orchestrated process as a flow where the steps are invoked in parallel. However, determining which design approach is best should not be exclusive to a technology pattern or approach. This is another example of needed SOA governance and an area where business subject matter experts can help.

The Add New Product service will be revised to include new process steps in the orchestrated business process with data access for both the Product Catalog and the Engineering Master Databases. Rather than introducing complex correlation processing for the check duplicate items processing, the unit of work processing will include an "all or nothing" pattern. The duplicate check will be defined to execute in parallel, but a found condition in either database will trigger a fault response to the consumer.

A final correlation is required before committing the inserts to the separate Product Catalog and Engineering Master Databases. Since the final steps are specific to an Add operation, the end result data for both databases must be in a logically consistent state. That is, the Add (insert) of the new items into both the Engineering Master Database and the Product Catalog Database must be successful. There are a number of commercial transaction management products that can help to correlate federated database transactions and distributed queries as a single unit of work. These technologies can also mediate individual transaction failure and rollback. For the Add New Product service example, a similar, but fictitious technology will be implemented as a process step and messaged as a subordinate service (see Figure 5.7).

The previously existing Add New Product process steps will remain as originally defined. The Receive Message step is fundamental and required. This is the step that receives the request message from consumers of the service. The validation step is also requisite and verifies that the received message conforms to the service interface context as defined by an XML Schema.

A new Check Duplicate Engineering Item process step and a service are added to the BPEL definition. This step is analogous to the already defined Check Duplicate Item step. However, the Engineering Master Database is the additional data at rest source used for checking. The original Check Duplicate Item step and service remain as part of the process. A BPEL flow ("<flow/>") will be added to execute both of the check duplicate process steps in parallel.

The intent is to check both the Engineering Master Database and the Product Catalog Database to determine if the requested item already exists. If the item exists in either database, the overall Add New Product service will return a fault message to the consumer and terminate processing. The metadata that describes the item identifier differs between these two databases. The Engineering Master Database refers to a "PartNo", while the Product Catalog Database refers to an "ItemID". This is a common scenario when multiple data at rest implementations are included in the scope of a data service, and it requires that the requested product is expressed in a manner that can be used by each database. Resolution for the enhanced Add New Product data service assumes that the appropriate translations are included in the process.

Assuming the check for duplicates processing is successful, the process will advance to add processing. Similar to the check duplicates process, a new step to Add Engineering Item will be added to the process. The process is similar to the previously existing Add Item step, where a SQL instruction to "insert" the data will be created. This new SQL statement will then be submitted to the Engineering Master Database for processing. The original Add Item process step and service all remain. These two Add steps will be included in a BPEL flow to run in parallel. However, correlation is critical at this point in the process. In order for the databases to be consistent, the Add operation (insert) into each database must be successful. To help accomplish this, new Correlate Add Item process step and service will be added. The Correlate Add Item step will assume that a federated database server and distributed query processor will be invoked. Note that the specific implementation of database correlation will depend upon the technology employed. As one scenario, the federated database technology may be implemented as a background listener and transaction manager, and a single distributed SQL

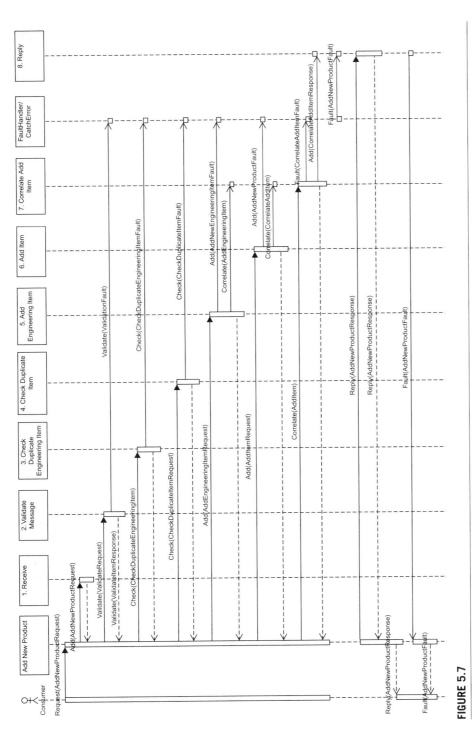

FIGURE 5.7

Enhanced Add New Product Sequence Diagram

statement will declare a unit of work and include the database insert statements for both databases. If this were the case, the BPEL steps and referenced services would be declared differently. It might be necessary for the BPEL to include only a single Add Item step and a referenced data service that includes the noted unit of work and distributed SQL statement (see Example 5.2).

Upon successful insert of the data to both the Engineering Master Database and the Product Catalog Database, and correlation of the database transactions, a reply will be returned to the requesting consumer.

Example 5.2
Enhanced New Product BPEL Process

```
>?xml version="1.0" encoding="UTF-8" ?>
- <process name="AddNewProduct" targetNamespace="http://Widget-Example.com/
Inventory" xmlns:tns="http://Widget-Example.com/Inventory" xmlns="http://docs.oasis-open.
org/wsbpel/2.0/process/executable">
- <partnerLinks>
<partnerLink name="Consumer" partnerLinkType="tns:AddNewProductRequest" myRole="AddNewProdduct
Service" partnerRole="Consumer"/>
<partnerLink name="ValidateMessage" partnerLinkType="tns:ValidationLink" myRole="ValidationServiceRe
quester" partnerRole="ValidationService"/>
<partnerLink name="CheckDuplicateItem" partnerLinkType="tns:CheckDuplicateItemLink" myRole="Duplic
ateItemServiceRequester" partnerRole="DuplicateItemService"/>
<partnerLink name="CheckDuplicateEngineeringItem" partnerLinkType="tns:
CheckDuplicateEngineeringItemLink" myRole="DuplicateEngineeringItemServiceRequester"
partnerRole="DuplicateEngineeringItemService"/>
<partnerLink name="AddItem" partnerLinkType="tns:AddItemLink" myRole="AddItemServiceRequester"
partnerRole="AddItemService"/>
<partnerLink name="AddEngineeringItem" partnerLinkType="tns:AddEngineeringItemLink" myRole="AddEn
gineeringItemServiceRequester" partnerRole="AddEngineeringItemService"/>
<partnerLink name="CorrelateAddItems" partnerLinkType="tns:CorrelateAddItemsLink" myRole="CorrelateA
ddItemsServiceRequester" partnerRole="CorrelateAddItemsService"/>
</partnerLinks>
- <variables>
<variable name="AddNewProductRequest" messageType="tns:
AddNewProductRequestMessage"/>
<variable name="ValidationRequest" messageType="tns:AddNewProductRequestMessage"/>
<variable name="ValidationResponse" messageType="tns:AddNewProductResponseMessage"/>
<variable name="ValidationFault" messageType="tns:AddNewProductFaultMessage"/>
<variable name="CheckDuplicateItemRequest" messageType="tns:
AddNewProductRequestMessage"/>
<variable name="CheckDuplicateItemResponse" messageType="tns:
AddNewProductResponseMessage"/>
<variable name="CheckDuplicateItemFault" messageType="tns:AddNewProductFaultMessage"/>
```

```
<variable name="CheckDuplicateEngineeringItemRequest" messageType="tns:
AddNewProductRequestMessage"/>
<variable name="CheckDuplicateEngineeringItemResponse" messageType="tns:
AddNewProductResponseMessage"/>
<variable name="CheckDuplicateEngineeringItemFault" messageType="tns:
AddNewProductFaultMessage"/>
<variable name="AddItemRequest" messageType="tns:
AddNewProductRequestMessage"/>
<variable name="AddItemResponse" messageType="tns:
AddNewProductResponseMessage"/>
<variable name="AddItemFailure" messageType="tns:AddNewProductFaultMessage"/>
<variable name="AddEngineeringItemRequest" messageType="tns:
AddNewProductRequestMessage"/>
<variable name="AddEngineeeringItemResponse" messageType="tns:
AddNewProductResponseMessage"/>
<variable name="AddEngineeringItemFailure" messageType="tns:
AddNewProductFaultMessage"/>
<variable name="CorrrelateAddItemsRequest" messageType="tns:
AddNewProductRequestMessage"/>
<variable name="CorrelateAddItemsResponse" messageType="tns:
AddNewProductResponseMessage"/>
<variable name="CorrelateDuplicateItemsFault" messageType="tns:
AddNewProductFaultMessage"/>
<variable name="AddNewProductResponse" messageType="tns:
AddNewProductResponseMessage"/>
<variable name="AddNewProductFault" messageType="tns:AddNewProductFaultMessage"/>
</variables>
- <faultHandlers>
- <catch faultName="tns:ValidationFault" faultVariable="ValidationFault" faultMessageType="tns:
AddNewProductFaultMessage">
<reply partnerLink="Consumer" portType="tns:AddNewProductPort" operation="Add" variable="AddNewPro
ductFault" faultName="ValidationFault"/>
</catch>
- <catch faultName="tns:CheckDuplicateEngineeringItemFault" faultVariable=
"CheckDuplicateEngineeringItemFault" faultMessageType="tns:
AddNewProductFaultMessage">
<reply partnerLink="Consumer" portType="tns:AddNewProductPort" operation="Add" variable="AddNewPro
ductFault" faultName="CheckDuplicateEngineeringItemFault"/>
</catch>
- <catch faultName="tns:CheckDuplicateItemFault" faultVariable="CheckDuplicateItemFault"
faultMessageType="tns:AddNewProductFaultMessage">
<reply partnerLink="Consumer" portType="tns:AddNewProductPort" operation="Add" variable="AddNewPro
ductFault" faultName="CheckDuplicateItemFault"/>
</catch>
```

```
- <catch faultName="tns:AddEngineeringItemFault" faultVariable="AddEngineeringItemFailure"
faultMessageType="tns:AddNewProductFaultMessage">
<reply partnerLink="Consumer" portType="tns:AddNewProductPort" operation="Add" variable="AddNewPro
ductFault" faultName="AddEngineeringItemFault"/>
</catch>
- <catch faultName="tns:AddItemFault" faultVariable="AddItemFailure" faultMessageType="tns:
AddNewProductFaultMessage">
<reply partnerLink="Consumer" portType="tns:AddNewProductPort" operation="Add" variable="AddNewPro
ductFault" faultName="AddItemFault"/>
</catch>
- <catch faultName="tns:CorrelateAddItemFault" faultVariable="CorrelateAddItemFailure"
faultMessageType="tns:AddNewProductFaultMessage">
<reply partnerLink="Consumer" portType="tns:AddNewProductPort" operation="Add" variable="AddNewPro
ductFault" faultName="CorrelateAddItemFault"/>
</catch>
- <catchAll>
- <sequence>
- <assign>
- <copy>
<from expression="string('ProcessFault')"/>
<to variable="AddNewProductFault" part="FaultMessage"/>
</copy>
</assign>
<reply partnerLink="Consumer" portType="tns:AddNewProductPort" operation="Add" variable="AddNewPro
ductFault" faultName="ProcessFault"/>
</sequence>
</catchAll>
</faultHandlers>
- <eventHandlers>
- <onMessage partnerLink="ValidateMessage" portType="tns:ValidateMessagePort" operation="Validate"
variable="ValidationFault">
<throw faultName="tns:ValidationFault" faultVariable="ValidationFault"/>
</onMessage>
- <onMessage partnerLink="CheckEngineeringDuplicateItem" portType="tns:
CheckEngineeringDuplicateItemPort" operation="Check" variable="CheckDuplicateEngineeringItemFault">
<throw faultName="tns:CheckDuplicateEngineeringItemFault"
faultVariable="CheckDuplicateEngineeringItemFault"/>
</onMessage>
- <onMessage partnerLink="CheckDuplicateItem" portType="tns:CheckDuplicateItemPort"
operation="Check" variable="CheckDuplicateItemFault">
<throw faultName="tns:CheckDuplicateItemFault" faultVariable="Check
DuplicateItemFault"/>
</onMessage>
```

```
- <onMessage partnerLink="AddEngineeringItem" portType="tns:AddEngineeringItemPort" operation="Add"
variable="AddEngineeringItemFault">
<throw faultName="tns:AddEngineeringItemFailure" faultVariable="AddEngineeringItemFailure"/>
</onMessage>
- <onMessage partnerLink="AddItem" portType="tns:AddItemPort" operation="Add"
variable="AddItemFault">
<throw faultName="tns:AddItemFailure" faultVariable="AddItemFailure"/>
</onMessage>
- <onMessage partnerLink="CorrelateAddItem" portType="tns:CorrelateAddItemPort" operation="Correlate"
variable="CorrelateAddItemFault">
<throw faultName="tns:CorrelateAddItemFailure" faultVariable="CorrelateAddItemFailure"/>
</onMessage>
</eventHandlers>
- <sequence name="AddNewProductProcess">
<receive partnerLink="Consumer" portType="tns:AddNewProductPort" operation="Add" variable="AddNew
ProductRequest" createInstance="yes"/>
- <assign>
- <copy>
<from variable="AddNewProductRequest" part="RequestMessage"/>
<to variable="ValidationRequest" part="RequestMessage"/>
</copy>
</assign>
<invoke partnerLink="ValidateMessage" portType="tns:ValidateMessagePort"
operation="Validate" inputVariable="ValidationRequest" outputVariable="ValidationResponse"
faultVariable="ValidationFault"/>
- <assign>
- <copy>
<from variable="ValidationResponse" part="ResponseMessage"/>
<to variable="AddNewProductResponse" part="ValidationResponseMessage"/>
</copy>
</assign>
- <assign>
- <copy>
<from variable="ValidationFault" part="FaultMessage"/>
<to variable="AddNewProductFault" part="ValidationFaultMessage"/>
</copy>
</assign>
- <flow>
- <sequence>
- <assign>
- <copy>
<from variable="AddNewProductRequest" part="RequestMessage"/>
<to variable="CheckDuplicateEngineeringItemRequest" part="RequestMessage"/>
```

```
</copy>
</assign>
<invoke partnerLink="CheckDuplicateEngineeringItem"
portType="tns:CheckDuplicateEngineeringItemPort" operation="Check" inputVariable="Check
DuplicateEngineeringItemRequest" outputVariable="CheckDuplicateEngineeringItemResponse"
faultVariable="CheckDuplicateEngineeringItemFault"/>
- <assign>
- <copy>
<from variable="CheckDuplicateEngineeringItemResponse" part="ResponseMessage"/>
<to variable="AddNewProductResponse" part="CheckDuplicateEngineeringResponseMessage"/>
</copy>
</assign>
- <assign>
- <copy>
<from variable="CheckDuplicateEngineeringItemFault" part="FaultMessage"/>
<to variable="AddNewProductFault" part="CheckDuplicateEngineeringFaultMessage"/>
</copy>
</assign>
- <assign>
- <copy>
<from variable="AddNewProductRequest" part="RequestMessage"/>
<to variable="CheckDuplicateItemRequest" part="RequestMessage"/>
</copy>
</assign>
<invoke partnerLink="CheckDuplicateItem" portType="tns:CheckDuplicateItemPort" operation="Check"
inputVariable="CheckDuplicateItemRequest" outputVariable="CheckDuplicateItemResponse"
faultVariable="CheckDuplicateItemFault"/>
- <assign>
- <copy>
<from variable="CheckDuplicateItemResponse" part="ResponseMessage"/>
<to variable="AddNewProductResponse" part="AddEngineeringItem"/>
</copy>
</assign>
- <assign>
- <copy>
<from variable="CheckDuplicateEngineeringItemFault" part="FaultMessage"/>
<to variable="AddNewProductFault" part="CheckDuplicateEngineeringFaultMessage"/>
</copy>
</assign>
</sequence>
</flow>
- <flow>
- <sequence>
- <assign>
```

```
- <copy>
<from variable="AddNewProductRequest" part="RequestMessage"/>
<to variable="AddEngineeringItemRequest" part ="RequestMessage"/>
</copy>
</assign>
<invoke partnerLink="AddEngineeringItem" portType="tns:AddNewEngineeringItemPort" operation= "Add"
inputVariable="AddEngineeringItemRequest" outputVariable="AddEngineeringItemResponse"
faultVariable="AddEngineeringItemFault"/>
-  <assign>
- <copy>
<from variable="AddEngineeringItemFault" part="FaultMessage"/>
<to variable="AddNewProductFault" part="AddEngineeringItemFaultMessage"/>
</copy>
</assign>
- <assign>
- <copy>
<from variable="AddNewProductRequest" part="RequestMessage"/>
<to variable="AddItemRequest" part="RequestMessage"/>
</copy>
</assign>
<invoke partnerLink="AddItem" portType="tns:AddNewItemPort" operation="Add" inputVariable="AddItemR
equest" outputVariable="AddItemResponse"
faultVariable="AddtemFault"/>
- <assign>
- <copy>
<from variable="AddItemFault" part="FaultMessage"/>
<to variable="AddNewProductFault" part="AddItemFaultMessage"/>
</copy>
</assign>
</sequence>
</flow>
- <assign>
- <copy>
<from variable="AddEngineeringItemResponse" part="ResponseMessage"/>
<to variable="AddNewProductResponse"
part="CorrelateAddItemRequestMessage"/>
</copy>
</assign>
- <assign>
- <copy>
<from variable="AddItemResponse" part="ResponseMessage"/>
<to variable="AddNewProductResponse" part="CorrelateAddItemRequestMessage"/>
</copy>
</assign>
```

```
<invoke partnerLink="CorrelateAddItem" portType="tns:CorrelateAddNewItemPort" operation="Correlate"
inputVariable="CorrelateAddItemRequest" outputVariable="CorrelateAddItemResponse"
faultVariable="CorrelateAddtemFault"/>
- <assign>
- <copy>
<from variable="CorrelateAddItemRequest" part="ResponseMessage"/>
<to variable="AddNewProductResponse" part="ResponseMessage"/>
</copy>
</assign>
<reply partnerLink="Consumer" portType="tns:AddNewProductPort" operation="Add"
variable="AddNewProductResponse"/>
</sequence>
</process>
```

The Add New Product service design and BPEL do not yet take into account other technical complexities such as availability of the two data at rest sources, latency between the services and transactions, and a need for wait states. Further, there might be a need for correlation among sets of process steps (flows), case logic to identify conditional branching, and more advanced exception handling—all of which would be additional design optimizations.

5.3 RESOLVING IMPEDANCE WITH DATA SERVICES

The Add New Product data service helps to explain the necessary design considerations, process interactions, and the relationship between a composite data service and subordinate services. It can also serve as an example for resolving the impedance that exists between different data at rest implementations. While there are distinct element level differences between the Engineering Item Database and Product Catalog Database examples, there are also several common synergies (see Figure 5.8).

Between the two database implementations, there are three elements of a common context. However, each of the elements is named differently. This poses a challenge for the Add New Product composite service. The SQL queries required to check for duplicates and to add (insert) the new item data will have to incorporate unique naming constructs. Further, the consumer is at a disadvantage. The service will need to interpret the consumer request message and map the requested item data to the appropriate database elements. Forcing this complexity on the consumer is unreasonable from a design perspective, and it introduces significant potential for anomaly. The solution to this problem is to develop a single common canonicalized expression of the product data that can be used by any consumer and a set of mappings from that common canonical to the structural and semantic metadata for each of the underlying databases (see Figure 5.9).

Elements that are specific to the Engineering Master are mapped in to the canonical, and those elements specific to the Product Catalog are also mapped. Also, there are elements that are common in context and content between the two databases but are different in naming. To resolve the example of database element impedance, these elements have to be resolved to a single representation. A set of common elements is then included in the canonical model that is used as the standard for consumer-to-service interactions going forward.

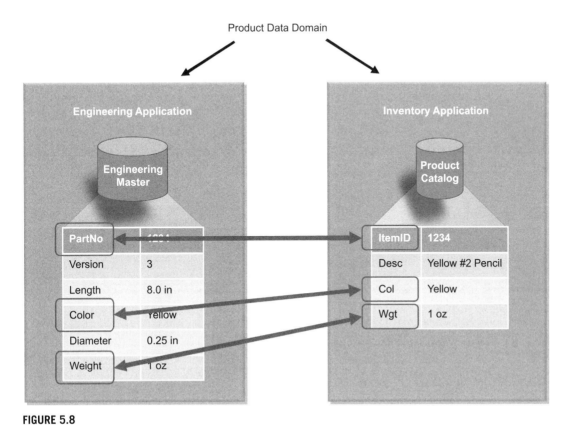

FIGURE 5.8

Data Element Impedance between Data Sources

The design of the canonical will often include a sampling of data values from the various data sources to validate the context and content of an element. This helps to ensure that a misnamed element does not mistakenly lead to a mapping anomaly. Identifying representative data value samples and validation of those samples is another area where business subject matter experts can provide assistance.

The common canonical is then used to design the content of the service interface. When the request is created by the consumer, the elements of the canonical will be declared in the message (see Figure 5.10). Since the Add New Product example is also a Web service, the message will be encoded as XML and will be contained within a SOAP message envelope. As noted, the Validate Message step of the underlying process will extract the SOAP Body content from the SOAP message.

Similarly, the response from the service to the consumer will also include the canonical elements. The reply message will also include completion status to inform the consumer whether the request was fully completed or terminated. Abnormal termination is noted by a SOAP fault, which is carried in the SOAP envelope and returned to the consumer.

Similarly, the reply message sent in response from the service to the consumer can optionally include the elements that were used for the Add of the new product as a form of validation for the service

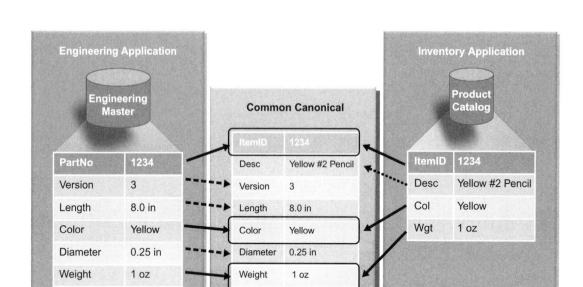

FIGURE 5.9

Common Canonical Model and Database Mappings

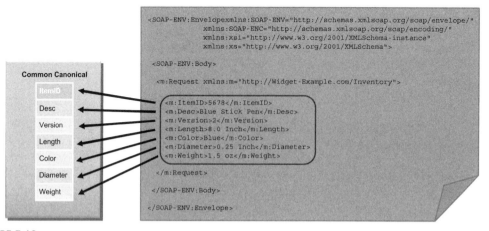

FIGURE 5.10

Example XML Request Message Based on the Canonical

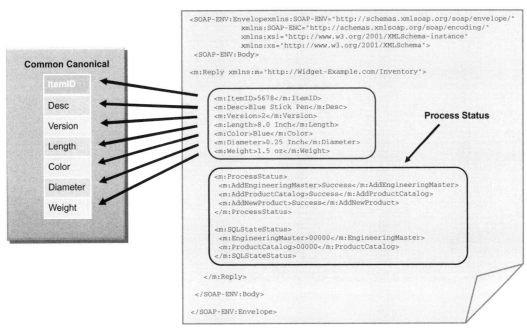

```
<SOAP-ENV:Envelopexmlns:SOAP-ENV="http://schemas.xmlsoap.org/soap/envelope/'
            xmlns:SOAP-ENC="http://schemas.xmlsoap.org/soap/encoding/"
            xmlns:xsi="http://www.w3.org/2001/XMLSchema-instance"
            xmlns:xs="http://www.w3.org/2001/XMLSchema">
  <SOAP-ENV:Body>

<m:Reply xmlns:m="http://Widget-Example.com/Inventory">

      <m:ItemID>5678</m:ItemID>
      <m:Desc>Blue Stick Pen</m:Desc>
      <m:Version>2</m:Version>
      <m:Length>8.0 Inch</m:Length>
      <m:Color>Blue</m:Color>
      <m:Diameter>0.25 Inch</m:Diameter>
      <m:Weight>1.5 oz</m:Weight>

    <m:ProcessStatus>
      <m:AddEngineeringMaster>Success</m:AddEngineeringMaster>
      <m:AddProductCatalog>Success</m:AddProductCatalog>
      <m:AddNewProduct>Success</m:AddNewProduct>
    </m:ProcessStatus>

    <m:SQLStateStatus>
      <m:EngineeringMaster>00000</m:EngineeringMaster>
      <m:ProductCatalog>00000</m:ProductCatalog>
    </m:SQLStateStatus>

  </m:Reply>

  </SOAP-ENV:Body>

</SOAP-ENV:Envelope>
```

FIGURE 5.11

Example XML Reply Message Based on the Canonical

request. These elements are also mapped to common canonical elements. The reply message will also include completion status to inform the consumer whether the request was fully completed or terminated (see Figure 5.11). Abnormal termination is noted by a SOAP fault, which is carried in the SOAP envelope and returned to the consumer.

The example reply message includes two sections for response information. Neither of these sections is required, nor are they based upon a standard. Rather, they are implementation defined and "optional," and provided in the reply message only when requested by the consumer. This approach of providing additional options in the request is sometimes referred to as overloading. That is, the basic operations exposed by the service can be extended to provide additional functionality on request.

5.4 CRUD-BASED DATA SERVICES

The example Add New Product service exposes only a single operation: "Add". As implied by the operation, a new instance of product data is to be added to one or more databases. A Web service can expose multiple operations. However, a recommended best practice is to keep the scope of a data service narrow, that is, to limit the functionality of a service on a single Create, Read, Update, or Delete operation (CRUD). When additional functionality is required to extend the capabilities of the service, options can be added to the Web service interface and request message. However, any options that

Table 5.1 List of Extended Operations and Common Verbs

CRUD Operation	Common Verbs (use only one from the list)
Create	Add, Create, Insert, Maintain
Read	Get, Read, Retrieve, Select
Update	Update, Modify, Change, Maintain
Delete	Delete, Remove, Kill, Eliminate
Check	Check, Check Exists, Check Duplicates
Correlate	Correlate, Synchronize
List	List, Set
Metadata	Info, About, Metadata
Ad Hoc Query	Query, Select
Search	Search, Find, Seek
Validate	Validate, Verify, Parse
Replicate	Copy, Replicate
Move	Move, Transport, Relocate

extend a CRUD operation require that the service can interpret the additional request information and appropriately resolve the request. A few examples of extended options include the following:

- Provide before and after images for an update service.
- Provide service completion status.
- Provide SQL database status for an update service.
- Provide the descriptive metadata with a reply message.

The scoping of a data service to CRUD operations has significant value to the overall SOA architecture. When a data service is limited in scope to a single CRUD operation, it provides the ability to tune and optimize the process steps that support the service, as well as the data at rest implementations that are the focus of the service. When multiple CRUD operations are exposed by a single data service, the supporting processes and services are no longer isolated and can result in operational complexity.

The notion of CRUD is based on traditional data at rest practices. However, as application and data architectures have continued to evolve when combined with an SOA servicing analogy, a simple set of four CRUD operations has become a limitation. The CRUD analogy has since been extended and includes several other operations. Each operation is described by a verb.

The list of extended operations includes such additions as List, Query, Correlate, and several others (see Table 5.1). A design best practice is to develop a list of standard operation verbs for the enterprise. Compliance with this practice would prohibit a single operation from having more than one verb declaration. This avoids the potential for duplication of services and service operations. Using the example Add New Product service, there is a single operation and verb that is exposed to consuming applications. If multiple verbs were allowed to describe the Add operation, a service designer might not realize that the Add New Product service has already been implemented and, as a result, might develop a new "Create New Product" service that performs that same operation. If this new and redundant service were implemented, the architects and designers of consuming applications might not understand which service can resolve their needs.

The first step to implementing the service operation and verb naming best practice is to identify which operations from the list in Table 5.1 will be supported by the enterprise. Next, a commonly recognized and easily understood verb naming convention must be developed. Only a single verb should be allowed for any one operation. The list of standard operations and verbs is then published as the enterprise standard for all service design and development.

SUMMARY

In an SOA paradigm, data services are a core and fundamental enabler of the enterprise. A data service can help to insulate consuming applications from the complexities of a data at rest implementation. Data services can also help to resolve the application and data integration challenge that plagues today's enterprises. When properly designed and implemented, data services also exhibit a significant degree of reuse and as a result reduce service development costs, consumer development costs, and time-to-market delivery of business enabling technologies.

The examples from this chapter represent the difference between coarse-grained data services, which are orchestrated (typically using a BPEL-based process), and more fine-grained data services, which can serve to support and are reused by other service interactions. Composite data services can even begin to act in the role of logical data of record sources. This also helps to resolve the enterprise integration challenge, while exploiting existing investment in operational systems and data.

However, SOA and data services are not exclusively technology. Business subject matter expertise is required to help identify the data scoping and domains of interest for service development. Business subject matter experts are typically responsible for the acquisition, harvesting, manipulation, enrichment and consumption of enterprise data, and they will have knowledge of the metadata and business rules that are requisite to a data service implementation. The development of a standard canonical data expression that crosses applications and lines of business is also a critical activity. Here again, business subject matter experts can provide much needed guidance as to what common data semantics will be easily understood by the entire enterprise.

The service interface and more importantly the capabilities of Web services can be exploited to advantage. Data services that are exposed to consumers are aligned to a narrow set of standard operations and verbs. XML-encoded request messages can be designed to include other options that extend a supported service operation. This allows consumers to exploit the standard capabilities of a data service, while also tailoring the request and response to their own processing.

This chapter also focused on an internal development approach to data services. However, there are many commercial data integration and data servicing technologies that can help to simplify the development process. Some of these data servicing technology platforms can also provide more advanced capabilities in support of technical system qualities such as performance and availability. When combined with the SOA architecture, features such as data caching, data virtualization, and federated transaction management can serve as a significant enterprise enabler.

The combination of SOA, Web services, and data servicing can help resolve these challenges and at the same time exploit previous investment in each of these vertical applications and their data at rest implementations.

REFERENCES

1. Jordan D, Evdemon J. chairs, Web Services Business Process Execution Language Version 2.0, OASIS Standard (April 11, 2007). <http://docs.oasis-open.org/wsbpel/2.0/OS/wsbpel-v2.0-OS.html/>.

2. Mitra N, Lafon Y, eds. "SOAP Version 1.2 Part 0: Primer. 2nd ed." (W3C, April 27, 2007). <http://www.w3.org/TR/soap12-part0/>.

3. Java2 Platform Enterprise Edition, J2EE v1.4, SOAPMessage Class, Copyright 2003 Sun Microsystems, Inc. <http://java.sun.com/j2ee/1.4/docs/api/javax/xml/soap/SOAPMessage.html/>.

4. *X/Open CAE Specification, Data Management: Structured Query Language (SQL)*, Version 2, X/Open Document Number: C449 (Reading, UK: X/Open Company Ltd.).

5. DB2 Version 9 Database for Linux, Unix and Windows, Declaring the SQLCA for Error Handling, © IBM Corporation 1993, 2008. <http://publib.boulder.ibm.com/infocenter/db2luw/v9/index.jsp?topic=/com.ibm.db2.udb.apdv.embed.doc/doc/t0004664.htm/>.

6. DB2 Universal Database, Handling an SQLException under the DB2 Universal JDBC Driver, © IBM Corporation 1993, 2006. <http://publib.boulder.ibm.com/infocenter/db2luw/v8/index.jsp?topic=/com.ibm.db2.udb.doc/ad/tjvjcerr.htm/>.

7. "The Java Tutorials, Creating Complete JDBC Applications, Retrieving Exceptions" (Sun Microsystems, Inc., 1995-2008). <http://java.sun.com/docs/books/tutorial/>.

8. MSDN Microsoft Developer Network. NET Framework Developer Center, SqlException Class, © 2008 Microsoft Corporation. <http://msdn.microsoft.com/en-us/library/system.data.sqlclient.sqlexception.aspx/>.

Transformation to Resolve Data Impedance

SOA and Web services rely upon the service interface to define "what" is being requested as a set of data values and operations, and also "what" is returned as the result of service processing. However, complexity arises when SOA and Web service consumers are from different applications and with varied data value definitions. This becomes clearly evident with different requests for data services that collect or act upon data that may originate from across many different data at rest implementations.

As described in Chapter 5, data services can help to access, manipulate, and expose data from these varied sources, but the problem of data impedance remains. For the more established enterprise, a myriad of applications and data sources will have evolved over years of evolution and change. Even though the same basic data context extends across these data sources, the definitions and implemented data structures can vary widely. As one example, the general context of a manufactured item that is inventoried and eventually sold might be described as combinations of a Product, an Item, and an Inventory Item, each with a different set of supporting data structures, elements, and element names. If left to each individual application designer, the solutions will often result in multiple and varied implementations of proprietary services, and each requiring some type of conversion logic.

In an SOA and Web services environment, impedance between implemented data sources and structures can extend into the service interface and messaging. A parochial and fine-grained Engineering Product data service will return data in a structure that is representative of that specific system. Similarly, a fine-grained data service that exposes Inventory Item data will return a different set of data structures and elements that are specific to inventory management. This complicates processing for consuming applications that require data from both systems. As with a composite data service, the consumer should be shielded from those disparate data at rest implementations, and the service interface should represent a consistent way of returning data back to the consumer, rather than a disparate mix of structures and representations. Refactoring each service and implemented data at rest source to follow a standard is the desired solution. However, a large scale, en masse refactoring and development for applications and services is generally not a reasonable approach or cost effective. Alternatively, transformation of messaged data (as data in motion) is an approach that can help to resolve data impedance.

In the context of SOA and Web services, messages are defined by the service interface, and transformation converts a source message format to a target message format. To accomplish this task, the transformation process requires a mapping from the source to the target, and a set of metadata definitions and rules. Even with the transformation process, the resolution of data impedance is not simple. If the servicing paradigm were to include many different data sources (rather than just a single source and target), there could be numerous transformations and variations between transformed target results. The transformation is no longer limited to simple A to B scenarios but rather several combinations such as A to B to C to D, A to C, A to D, and so on. While this approach would eventually resolve data impedance, the number of needed transformations contributes to the problem and each transformation requires a mapping, metadata definitions, and transformation rules. Each of which must be developed and also maintained. With this scenario, there is also a continued lack of consistency for service consumers.

A more optimal approach to transformation relies upon a canonical model to serve as the baseline for all transformations. A canonical is a type of standard or common representation that serves as the benchmark for all data expressions. It can be developed for a specific set of data, a subject area, or all data across the entire enterprise. The overriding emphasis of the canonical is consistency in naming, structure, and definition. In this manner, each transformation only refers to one source and one target (represented by the canonical). This helps to reduce the number of other unique or "one-off" transformations that would follow. As a new data service is developed, the Web service interface exposed to service consumers is designed in compliance with the canonical and regardless of the data source structures or other services it might interact with (see Figure 6.1).

The canonical might be expressed graphically as a data model or an extended UML class model, or it might be a collection of textually described metadata characteristics. Obviously, a robust set of metadata resulting in a more rich canonical will be of greater value to the enterprise and can be used to derive interface definitions and to support development of message transformation logic. For the simplest example of a canonical, an element might be defined by a limited set of metadata such as the data type and length. A more extensive example might include a set of rich metadata with a description, element name derivatives, and business rules. Examples of rich metadata can include the following:

- Element Name
- Element Name Derivatives (as with Abbreviations, Acronyms, Synonyms)
- Element Name Context (as with a general context in which the element applies)
- Element Type (as with Parent, Child, or Standalone)
- Parent Element Reference (when the element is defined as a Child)
- Element Realization (as with Abstract, Concrete)
- Element Description
- Element Data Type
- Element Minimum Length
- Element Maximum Length
- Element Total Required Length
- Element Non-Fractional Positions (as with a decimalized value)
- Element Fractional Positions (as with a decimalized value)
- Element Modality (as with Mandatory/Required, Optional)
- Individual Element Security (as with Open, Sensitive, Protected)
- List of Example Values
- List of Allowable Values
- List of Excluded Values
- Minimum Allowable Value (as with the lower end of a range)

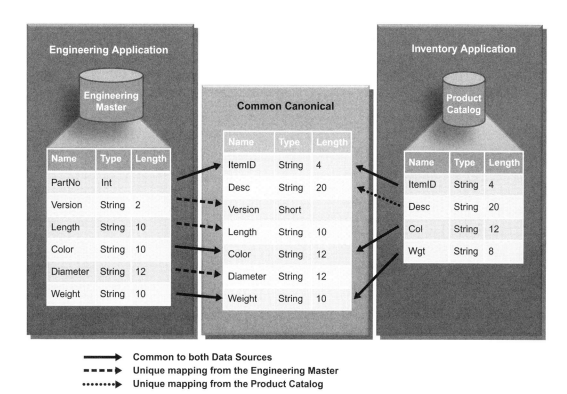

FIGURE 6.1

Common Canonical Model and Data Source Impedance

- Maximum Allowable Value (as with the upper end of a range)
- Default Value
- Fixed Value
- External Reference Structure (as with a separate table of Allowable Values)
- List of Allowable Characters
- List of Excluded Characters
- Data of Record System (as with the recognized single source of the truth and owning system for this element)
- Reference to a Data Standard (as with an international or industry data standard)
- Contained Pattern or Expression (as with a Regular Expression)
- Computational Business Rules

Each element of the canonical would require similar metadata (see Table 6.1). The structures or logical groupings of elements and relationships between those structures would also be described by similar metadata. Data at rest sources would be mapped to the canonical allowing data services to then map the canonical structures and elements to their service interface. This helps to simplify the mapping of service interfaces to and from the canonical.

Table 6.1 Example of Rich Canonical Metadata for an Element

Element Name	Element Description		
ItemID	Primary identifier for an Item. An Item is a product or service unit that is manufactured, inventoried, offered, sold, and shipped to customers.		
Element Name Derivatives	**Element Name Context**		
	ProdNo	Product	
	ItemNo	Item	
	PartNo	Part	
	PartNum	Service	
	PartID	Offering	
Element Type	Standalone		
Parent Element Reference	None		
Element Realization	Concrete		
Element Modality	Required		
Individual Element Security	Protected		
Element Data Type	**Min Length**	**Max Length**	**Fixed Length**
String	4	4	4
	Non-Fractional Numeric Positions	**Fractional Numeric Positions**	
	N/A	N/A	
List of Example Values	0001, 1234, 5678, 9999		
List of Allowable Values	N/A		
List of Excluded Values	0000		
Minimum Allowable Value	0001		
Maximum Allowable Value	9999		
Default Value	N/A		
Fixed Value	N/A		
External Reference Structure	N/A		
Allowable Characters	0,1,2,3,4,5,6,7,8,9		
Excluded Characters	a-z, A-Z, !,@,#,$,%,^,&,*,(,),_, + , = ,?,/,\		
Data of Record System	Engineering Master		
Reference to Data Standard	N/A		
Contained Pattern or Expression	[0-9]{4}		
Computational Business Rules	Unique value for each assigned instance		
	Centralized autogeneration to avoid duplicates No implicit, explicit, or embedded intelligence to the data value		

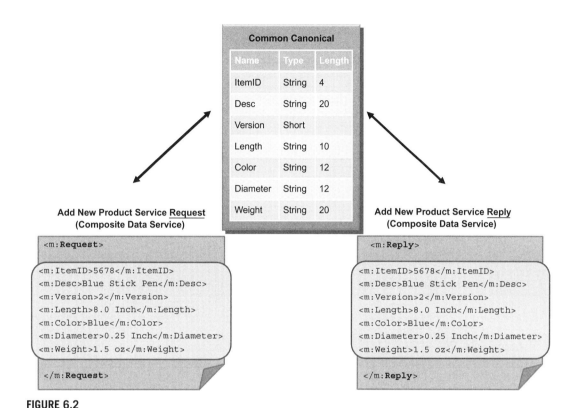

FIGURE 6.2

Request and Reply Mapped to the Common Canonical

As the standard to resolve differences between other services and data sources, the canonical model abstracts away from different implementations as a common point of reference that can be used by any consumer or service. From a conceptual vantage, compliance with the canonical will ensure that a service consumer "speaks" the recognized interface metadata and language of a service, and the service will respond in the same language when returning a reply (see Figure 6.2).

The canonical model can be specific to a single subject area or set of needed data. However, a common implementation of a canonical is more of an overall enterprise scope, and is then partitioned or subclassed to represent functional areas of the business and common data concepts such as Items, Customers, Invoices, Orders, Reference Data, and so on. When defined by the canonical, these common data concepts provide consistency across lines of business, systems, applications, and operational functions. Unique or parochial definitions are avoided for new application and service development, while the sources and targets of existing implementations are mapped to the canonical allowing for transformation as needed.

A canonical can be developed internally and specific to an individual enterprise, or in many industries, it may be acquired from an external source such as an industry consortium or even a commercial technology vendor. When developed internal to the enterprise, the canonical tends to be more specific to existing processes and data, allowing for an easier transition to implementation. When obtained from an external source, the defined processes and data are more of a common vocabulary or language that has been synthesized from common processes across other organizations of the same industry. The externally acquired or "industry canonical" can often include a more extended set of processes and data than the enterprise was aware of and can also simplify the Business-to-Business (B2B) service interactions with other external organizations and partners. Most often, the enterprise will also customize or extend the industry canonical to include items that are unique to their own organization and exclude those items that might be irrelevant.

Alternative to using an acquired industry canonical, the internally developed canonical takes on a more enterprise-specific perspective. Development of the internal enterprise canonical can be a significant and costly effort, and most are approached incrementally while focusing on common subject areas. This helps to avoid long-term and costly development. In this manner, development of the internal enterprise canonical is prioritized according to those processes and data of greatest importance, or those that are shared across the broadest number of applications. Another advantage of an internally developed enterprise canonical is that the existing business taxonomy and vocabulary is largely retained. The naming of processes and data tends to reflect long-standing and commonly used business language, rather than having to re-educate the enterprise with a potentially different industry-aligned vocabulary. Regardless of whether the canonical is externally acquired or internally developed, ensuring accuracy and real-world context will also require combinations of technology, and business subject matter experts are required participants during development of the canonical. The end result will be the standard or benchmark to which services and service interfaces will map and transform.

6.1 TRANSFORMATION

The technical definition for transformation tends to rely upon specific transformation technologies and syntactical languages such as XML Stylesheet Language Transformations (XSLT).[1] However, and as a general definition, transformation can be thought of as a process for converting a source message format to a target message format. This definition also fits well in an SOA and Web services context, given that messages are XML-encoded artifacts.

XSLT is a well-known and well-documented technology that supports XML. This is not a strict limitation, however, as XSLT can also be applied to other types of artifacts. For a Web service message, an XSLT document is a language that describes the navigation of the XML message, and the matching and selecting of structures and elements. This process relies in part on XPath, which is another related technology.[2]

Basically, the XSLT describes a navigational path through a source XML message with the matching of elements. Some elements are then selected for processing, and a resulting output message is created. The processing can include a number of functional capabilities such as simple replication of the element and moving any contained data to an analogous element in the output or target message, or there can be more complex processing where the target has a different structure, different naming, and even significant derivation from that of the source.

The functionality afforded by XSLT is quite robust, and, similar to other technology languages, XSLT can be structured in different ways and optimized to fit a particular process. While expertise with XSLT is a desirable skill for Web services design, and a handcrafted XSLT artifact can be developed for most Web service message transformations, it is not always requisite. A number of mapping

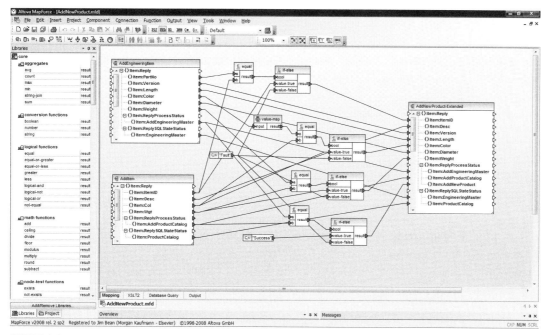

FIGURE 6.3

Mapping Between Source and Target Using MapForce from Altova (Copyright 2003-2008 Altova GmbH, reprinted with permission of Altova)

and transformation tools have been developed that provide a graphical user interface with simple drag-and-drop mapping and transformation capabilities. These tools have tremendously simplified the transformation process.

MapForce from Altova (Copyright 2003-2008 Altova GmbH, reprinted with permission of Altova) is one example of mapping and transformation technology that can generate a resulting XSLT, as well as other types of transformation artifacts (see Figure 6.3). This helps to avoid the handcrafting of XSLT or similar transformation syntax. The graphical transformation and the XSLT transform can also be harvested, reused, and refactored to meet other message transformation needs (see Example 6.1).

Example 6.1

Source to Target Mapping Generated XSLT

```
<?xml version="1.0" encoding="UTF-8" ?>
- <!--
This file was generated by Altova MapForce 2008r2sp2
YOU SHOULD NOT MODIFY THIS FILE, BECAUSE IT WILL BE
OVERWRITTEN WHEN YOU RE-RUN CODE GENERATION.
```

Refer to the Altova MapForce Documentation for further details.
http://www.altova.com/mapforce
-->

```
- <xsl:stylesheet version="2.0" xmlns:xsl="http://www.w3.org/1999/XSL/Transform" xmlns:xsi="http://www.
w3.org/2001/XMLSchema-instance" xmlns:n="http://Widget-Example.com/Inventory" xmlns:xs="http://www.
w3.org/2001/XMLSchema" xmlns:vmf="http://www.altova.com/MapForce/UDF/vmf" xmlns:fn="http://www.
w3.org/2005/xpath-functions" exclude-result-prefixes="fn vmf xs xsi xsl" xmlns="http://Widget-Example.
com/Inventory">
- <xsl:template name="vmf:inputtoresult">
<xsl:param name="input" select="()" />
- <xsl:choose>
- <xsl:when test="$input='B-252'">
<xsl:value-of select="'Blue'" />
</xsl:when>
- <xsl:when test="$input='Blue'">
<xsl:value-of select="'Blue'" />
</xsl:when>
</xsl:choose>
</xsl:template>
<xsl:namespace-alias stylesheet-prefix="n" result-prefix="#default" />
<xsl:output method="xml" encoding="UTF-8" indent="yes" />
<xsl:param name="AddEngineeringItemExampleReplyInstance" select="'C:/Data and Documents/
Books/SOA Service and Interface Design/Chapter 6/Chapter 6 Examples/AddEngineeringItem-
ExampleReply.xml'" />
- <xsl:template match="/n:Reply">
- <n:Reply>
- <xsl:attribute name="xsi:schemaLocation" separator="">
<xsl:sequence select="'http://Widget-Example.com/Inventory C:/DATAAN~1/Books/SOASER~1/CHD8CD~1/
CHAPTE~1/AddNewProduct-Extended.xsd'" />
</xsl:attribute>
<xsl:variable name="Vvar1_firstSource" select="." />
- <xsl:for-each select="doc($AddEngineeringItemExampleReplyInstance)/n:Reply">
- <xsl:for-each select="n:PartNo">
<xsl:variable name="Vvar156_PartNo_string" as="xs:string" select="xs:string(.)" />
- <xsl:for-each select="$Vvar1_firstSource/n:ItemID">
<xsl:variable name="Vvar170_ItemID_string" as="xs:string" select="xs:string(.)" />
<xsl:variable name="Vvar172_result_equal" as="xs:Boolean" select="($Vvar156_PartNo_string) =
($Vvar170_ItemID_string)" />
- <xsl:variable name="Vvar173_cond" as="xs:string">
- <xsl:choose>
- <xsl:when test="($Vvar172_result_equal)=true()">
- <xsl:variable name="Vvar172_result_equal_when" as="xs:string*">
<xsl:sequence select="$Vvar170_ItemID_string" />
</xsl:variable>
```

```
<xsl:sequence select="xs:string(fn:string-join(for $i in $Vvar172_result_equal_when return fn:string($i),''))"
/>
</xsl:when>
- <xsl:otherwise>
- <xsl:variable name="Vvar172_result_equal_otherwise" as="xs:string*">
<xsl:sequence select="'Fault'" />
</xsl:variable>
<xsl:sequence select="xs:string(fn:string-join(for $i in $Vvar172_result_equal_otherwise return fn:
string($i),''))" />
</xsl:otherwise>
</xsl:choose>
</xsl:variable>
- <n:ItemID>
<xsl:sequence select="$Vvar173_cond" />
</n:ItemID>
</xsl:for-each>
</xsl:for-each>
</xsl:for-each>
- <xsl:for-each select="n:Desc">
<xsl:variable name="Vvar180_Desc_string" as="xs:string" select="xs:string(.)" />
- <n:Desc>
<xsl:sequence select="$Vvar180_Desc_string" />
</n:Desc>
</xsl:for-each>
- <xsl:for-each select="doc($AddEngineeringItemExampleReplyInstance)/n:Reply">
- <xsl:for-each select="n:Version">
<xsl:variable name="Vvar185_Version_short" as="xs:short" select="xs:short(.)" />
- <n:Version>
<xsl:sequence select="$Vvar185_Version_short" />
</n:Version>
</xsl:for-each>
</xsl:for-each>
- <xsl:for-each select="doc($AddEngineeringItemExampleReplyInstance)/n:Reply">
- <xsl:for-each select="n:Length">
<xsl:variable name="Vvar190_Length_string" as="xs:string" select="xs:string(.)" />
- <n:Length>
<xsl:sequence select="$Vvar190_Length_string" />
</n:Length>
</xsl:for-each>
</xsl:for-each>
- <xsl:for-each select="doc($AddEngineeringItemExampleReplyInstance)/n:Reply">
- <xsl:for-each select="n:Color">
<xsl:variable name="Vvar193_Color_string" as="xs:string" select="xs:string(.)" />
- <xsl:variable name="Vvar195_result" as="xs:string?">
```

```
- <xsl:call-template name="vmf:inputtoresult">
<xsl:with-param name="input" select="$Vvar193_Color_string" />
</xsl:call-template>
</xsl:variable>
- <xsl:if test="fn:exists(fn:data($Vvar195_result))">
- <xsl:for-each select="$Vvar1_firstSource/n:Col">
<xsl:variable name="Vvar208_Col_string" as="xs:string" select="xs:string(.)" />
<xsl:variable name="Vvar210_result_equal" as="xs:boolean" select="($Vvar195_result) = ($Vvar208_Col_
string)" />
- <xsl:variable name="Vvar211_cond" as="xs:string">
- <xsl:choose>
- <xsl:when test="($Vvar210_result_equal)=true()">
- <xsl:variable name="Vvar210_result_equal_when" as="xs:string*">
<xsl:sequence select="$Vvar208_Col_string" />
</xsl:variable>
<xsl:sequence select="xs:string(fn:string-join(for $i in $Vvar210_result_equal_when return fn:string($i),"))"
/>
</xsl:when>
- <xsl:otherwise>
- <xsl:variable name="Vvar210_result_equal_otherwise" as="xs:string*">
<xsl:sequence select="'Fault'" />
</xsl:variable>
<xsl:sequence select="xs:string(fn:string-join(for $i in $Vvar210_result_equal_otherwise return fn:
string($i),"))" />
</xsl:otherwise>
</xsl:choose>
</xsl:variable>
- <n:Color>
<xsl:sequence select="$Vvar211_cond" />
</n:Color>
</xsl:for-each>
</xsl:if>
</xsl:for-each>
</xsl:for-each>
- <xsl:for-each select="doc($AddEngineeringItemExampleReplyInstance)/n:Reply">
- <xsl:for-each select="n:Diameter">
<xsl:variable name="Vvar218_Diameter_string" as="xs:string" select="xs:string(.)" />
- <n:Diameter>
<xsl:sequence select="$Vvar218_Diameter_string" />
</n:Diameter>
</xsl:for-each>
</xsl:for-each>
- <xsl:for-each select="doc($AddEngineeringItemExampleReplyInstance)/n:Reply">
- <xsl:for-each select="n:Weight">
```

```
<xsl:variable name="Vvar221_Weight_string" as="xs:string" select="xs:string(.)" />
- <xsl:for-each select="$Vvar1_firstSource/n:Wgt">
<xsl:variable name="Vvar235_Wgt_string" as="xs:string" select="xs:string(.)" />
<xsl:variable name="Vvar237_result_equal" as="xs:Boolean" select="($Vvar221_Weight_string) =
($Vvar235_Wgt_string)" />
- <xsl:variable name="Vvar238_cond" as="xs:string">
- <xsl:choose>
- <xsl:when test="($Vvar237_result_equal)=true()">
- <xsl:variable name="Vvar237_result_equal_when" as="xs:string*">
<xsl:sequence select="$Vvar235_Wgt_string" />
</xsl:variable>
<xsl:sequence select="xs:string(fn:string-join(for $i in $Vvar237_result_equal_when return fn:
string($i),"))" />
</xsl:when>
- <xsl:otherwise>
- <xsl:variable name="Vvar237_result_equal_otherwise" as="xs:string*">
<xsl:sequence select="'Fault'" />
</xsl:variable>
<xsl:sequence select="xs:string(fn:string-join(for $i in $Vvar237_result_equal_otherwise return fn:
string($i),"))" />
</xsl:otherwise>
</xsl:choose>
</xsl:variable>
- <n:Weight>
<xsl:sequence select="$Vvar238_cond" />
</n:Weight>
</xsl:for-each>
</xsl:for-each>
</xsl:for-each>
- <n:ReplyProcessStatus>
- <xsl:for-each select="doc($AddEngineeringItemExampleReplyInstance)/n:Reply">
- <xsl:for-each select="n:ReplyProcessStatus">
- <xsl:for-each select="n:AddEngineeringMaster">
<xsl:variable name="Vvar247_AddEngineeringMaster_string" as="xs:
string" select="xs:string(.)" />
- <n:AddEngineeringMaster>
<xsl:sequence select="$Vvar247_AddEngineeringMaster_string" />
</n:AddEngineeringMaster>
</xsl:for-each>
</xsl:for-each>
</xsl:for-each>
- <xsl:for-each select="n:ReplyProcessStatus">
- <xsl:for-each select="n:AddProductCatalog">
<xsl:variable name="Vvar254_AddProductCatalog_string" as="xs:string" select="xs:string(.)" />
```

```
- <n:AddProductCatalog>
<xsl:sequence select="$Vvar254_AddProductCatalog_string" />
</n:AddProductCatalog>
</xsl:for-each>
</xsl:for-each>
- <xsl:for-each select="doc($AddEngineeringItemExampleReplyInstance)/n:Reply">
- <xsl:for-each select="n:ReplyProcessStatus">
- <xsl:for-each select="n:AddEngineeringMaster">
<xsl:variable name="Vvar259_AddEngineeringMaster_string" as="xs:string" select="xs:string(.)" />
- <xsl:for-each select="$Vvar1_firstSource/n:ReplyProcessStatus">
- <xsl:for-each select="n:AddProductCatalog">
<xsl:variable name="Vvar278_AddProductCatalog_string" as="xs:string" select="xs:string(.)" />
<xsl:variable name="Vvar280_result_equal" as="xs:Boolean" select="($Vvar259_AddEngineeringMaster_
string) = ($Vvar278_AddProductCatalog_string)" />
- <xsl:variable name="Vvar281_cond" as="xs:string">
- <xsl:choose>
- <xsl:when test="($Vvar280_result_equal)=true()">
- <xsl:variable name="Vvar280_result_equal_when" as="xs:string*">
<xsl:sequence select="'Success'" />
</xsl:variable>
<xsl:sequence select="xs:string(fn:string-join(for $i in $Vvar280_result_equal_when return fn:string($i),''))"
/>
</xsl:when>
- <xsl:otherwise>
- <xsl:variable name="Vvar280_result_equal_otherwise" as="xs:string*">
<xsl:sequence select="'Fault'" />
</xsl:variable>
<xsl:sequence select="xs:string(fn:string-join(for $i in $Vvar280_result_equal_otherwise return fn:
string($i),''))" />
</xsl:otherwise>
</xsl:choose>
</xsl:variable>
- <n:AddNewProduct>
<xsl:sequence select="$Vvar281_cond" />
</n:AddNewProduct>
</xsl:for-each>
</xsl:for-each>
</xsl:for-each>
</xsl:for-each>
</xsl:for-each>
</n:ReplyProcessStatus>
- <n:ReplySQLStateStatus>
- <xsl:for-each select="doc($AddEngineeringItemExampleReplyInstance)/n:Reply">
- <xsl:for-each select="n:ReplySQLStateStatus">
```

```
- <xsl:for-each select="n:EngineeringMaster">
<xsl:variable name="Vvar291_EngineeringMaster_string" as="xs:string" select="xs:string(.)" />
- <n:EngineeringMaster>
<xsl:sequence select="$Vvar291_EngineeringMaster_string" />
</n:EngineeringMaster>
</xsl:for-each>
</xsl:for-each>
</xsl:for-each>
- <xsl:for-each select="n:ReplySQLStateStatus">
- <xsl:for-each select="n:ProductCatalog">
<xsl:variable name="Vvar298_ProductCatalog_string" as="xs:string" select="xs:string(.)" />
- <n:ProductCatalog>
<xsl:sequence select="$Vvar298_ProductCatalog_string" />
</n:ProductCatalog>
</xsl:for-each>
</xsl:for-each>
</n:ReplySQLStateStatus>
</n:Reply>
</xsl:template>
</xsl:stylesheet>
```

In the typical enterprise, service consumers originate from applications with unique data definitions. These same consumers may require data from many other applications and those unique data at rest implementations. Resolving the impedance between these many different data definitions with multiple service interfaces and messages would result in a proliferation of one-off servicing solutions and defeat the core SOA principles of interoperability and loose coupling. An alternative approach is to develop a composite data service that relies upon a canonical to provide a common enterprise definition for this same data.

The example composite data service will include an orchestrated BPEL process that invokes other services to access the varied data source implementations. As these fine-grained services are invoked, they will return data in reply messages that are of varied structure and content. The differences might simply be how element names are spelled (e.g., "PartNo" vs "ItemID", "Weight" vs "Wgt", or "Color" vs "Col"), or there might be other differences such as missing elements (e.g., a missing "Description" from one reply message, and missing "Version" and "Diameter" elements from another message). To provide a single, consistent reply back to the originating consumer, it becomes necessary to transform these different messages into a common message format as the response (see Figure 6.4).

The canonical serves an important purpose to transformation. It provides the common metadata, vocabulary, and structure to define the transformed target message. Each of the unique reply messages from the individual data services invoked by the composite service will be mapped to the metadata definitions of the canonical. These separate and unique reply messages will then be transformed to a single, common message structure and combined into one reply message that is returned to the originating consumer (see Figure 6.5).

The resulting "canonicalized" reply message avoids ambiguity and represents a standard data definition, a side effect of which is compliance with the loose coupling SOA principle. The service consumers

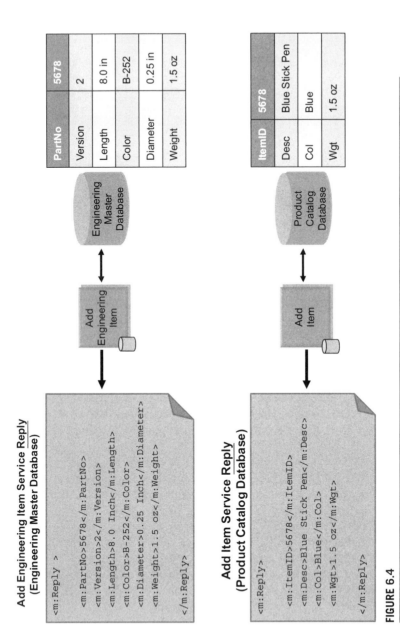

Add Engineering Item Service Reply
(Engineering Master Database)

```
<m:Reply >

    <m:PartNo>5678</m:PartNo>
    <m:Version>2</m:Version>
    <m:Length>8.0 Inch</m:Length>
    <m:Color>B-252</m:Color>
    <m:Diameter>0.25 Inch</m:Diameter>
    <m:Weight>1.5 oz</m:Weight>

</m:Reply>
```

PartNo	5678
Version	2
Length	8.0 in
Color	B-252
Diameter	0.25 in
Weight	1.5 oz

Engineering Master Database

Add Engineering Item

Add Item Service Reply
(Product Catalog Database)

```
<m:Reply>

    <m:ItemID>5678</m:ItemID>
    <m:Desc>Blue Stick Pen</m:Desc>
    <m:Col>Blue</m:Col>
    <m:Wgt>1.5 oz</m:Wgt>

</m:Reply>
```

ItemID	5678
Desc	Blue Stick Pen
Col	Blue
Wgt	1.5 oz

Product Catalog Database

Add Item

FIGURE 6.4

Separate Reply Messages with Different Data Representations

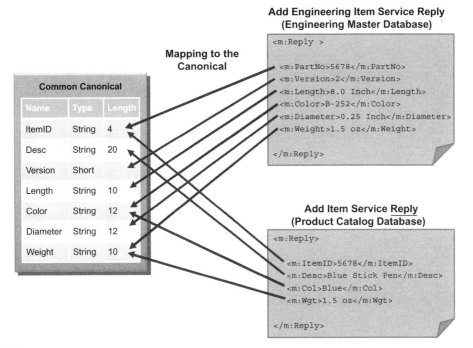

FIGURE 6.5

Mapping Separate XML Messages to the Canonical for Transformation

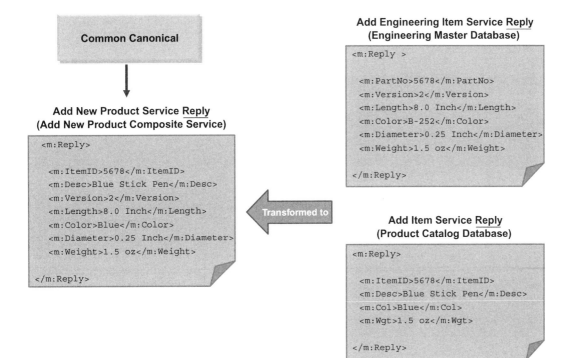

FIGURE 6.6

Single Canonicalized and Transformed Reply Message

are not explicitly coupled to the varied and underlying data sources of the service. Rather, the composite data service combined with the canonicalized interface and reply message act as an intermediary (see Figure 6.6). Changes to the underlying data sources are not propagated to the consumers. Rather, any changes to those data sources are mapped to the canonical and added as extensions to the interface.

To this point, the examples of transformation have been specific to the structural representation and naming of elements within that structure. However, another perspective of transformation is also required to resolve data impedance. In addition to differences between message structures, there can be differences between the data values contained by the elements of those structures.

6.2 TRANSLATION

Another capability of transformation deals with the manipulation of data values contained within a structure and its elements. While opinion varies, a way to describe this more content-focused form of transformation is data "translation." With this separation, transformation is more specific to the conversion of message structures, whereas translation addresses the content of those structures. Addressing both types of transformation are critical to effective service interface design.

Describing data translation separate from transformation might invoke a cry of foul from some practitioners. However, this is less of a physical separation and more of a different focus or emphasis.

An element of a message might already be structurally aligned with an element of the target, but the data values of those elements might not be consistent. As examples, two source messages and a target message might already include a common and canonicalized element specific to Color ("< Color/ >"). However, the data value contained by the Color element of one source message might be "B-252", while the data value of the Color element in the other source message might be "Blue". The process of transforming the message elements is not required, but a translation of the two different Color data values is required (see Figure 6.7).

As an example specific to element transformation, the Product Number element from the Add Engineering Item service reply message ("< PartNo/ >") would be "transformed" to a corresponding Item ID element defined by the canonical ("< ItemID/ >"). Once the transformation process has resulted in a structure and elements that match the intended target, the data values contained by those resulting elements must also be acceptable to the canonical.

With translation, the depth of metadata and richness of the canonical begins to take on even more importance. Using the previous example of a color element, the element name implies that a contained data value will represent a color, but there is no explicit description of the allowable values or types that is evident from the name. Without the requisite canonical metadata and a translation process, the potential for misinterpretation by consuming applications and resulting data anomalies becomes obvious. If a color code data value is returned in a reply message, and the requesting consumer is unaware of the color codes implemented by the different source systems, an error will result. Even with simple translations such as "Yes" to "Y" and "No" to "N", the additional process of data translation is sometimes overlooked (see Table 6.2).

The example of a canonical can be represented as a graphic with a set of supporting metadata. However, in an operational context, Web services rely upon XML Schemas for the service interface and message definition but not on a reference to a separate canonical model artifact. For the Web service interface, XML Schemas can be considered as a form of metadata language that describe and constrain

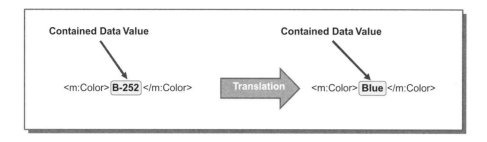

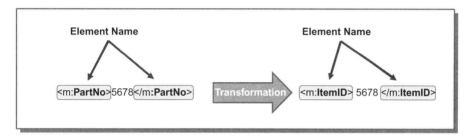

FIGURE 6.7

Transformation vs Translation

XML-encoded messages. They have a rich syntax that includes a number of possible declarations and rules (something that will be further described in Chapter 10, "XML Schema Basics"). A strong synergy exists between the canonical metadata and the metadata defined by an XML Schema. This synergy allows that much of the metadata from the canonical can also be expressed by the XML Schemas of a service interface. Tools such as MapForce (Copyright 2003-2008 Altova GmbH, reprinted with permission of Altova) can import the metadata required for mapping and transformation from service interface schemas, as well as metadata from data at rest sources. As a result, the request and reply messages defined by the service interface can also be mapped to the imported metadata of the canonical.

An alternative method to visual drag-and-drop transformation mapping tools is to manually map and align the names of message structures and elements. A set of example XML request and reply messages with sample data will usually suffice. Messages encoded in XML have visible tag names, but they do not include rich metadata or declarative constraints. The message elements can be matched to determine where equivalent elements might exist between message formats. Rather than handcrafting the example XML messages, XML Editing tools such as XML Spy (Copyright 2003-2008 Altova GmbH, reprinted with permission of Altova) can automatically generate a sample XML message from an XML Schema (see Figure 6.8).

The generated sample XML message can also be defined to include example data values. If the XML Schema was defined with a strongly typed set of metadata and including a list of allowable values from enumerations, the resulting XML messages will have a reasonable "look," but further enhancement of the sample data values to be more real world is recommended. While these data values are not used to define the transformation process, they allow the designer of the service to visualize the source and target messages (see Example 6.2).

Table 6.2 Canonical Metadata Used for Translation

Element Name	Element Description			
Color	A visual property of an Item based upon the spectrum of light. An Item is not available in all possible color variations. While Black and White may not be colors, they are allowable values.			
Element Name Derivatives	Color	**Element Name Context**	Color	
	Col		Hue	
			Saturation	
			Brightness	
			Gloss	
Element Type	Standalone			
Parent Element Reference	None			
Element Realization	Concrete			
Element Modality	Required			
Individual Element Security	Open			
Element Data Type	**Min Length**	**Max Length**	**Fixed Length**	
String	1	12	0	
	Non-Fractional Numeric Positions	**Fractional Numeric Positions**		
	N/A	N/A		
List of Example Values	Blue, Red, Green, Yellow, Orange, Violet, Brown, Gray, Black, White			
List of Allowable Values	Blue, Red, Green, Yellow, Orange, Violet, Brown, Gray, Black, White			
List of Excluded Values	N/A			
Minimum Allowable Value	N/A			
Maximum Allowable Value	N/A			
Default Value	N/A			
Fixed Value	N/A			
External Reference Structure	Color Code Reference (Color_Code_Ref)			
Allowable Characters	a-z, A-Z, Whitespace			
Excluded Characters	N/A			
Data of Record System	Product Catalog			
Reference to Data Standard	N/A			
Contained Pattern or Expression	*[a-zA-Z]*			
Computational Business Rules	Translate all values to standard using External Reference Structure.			

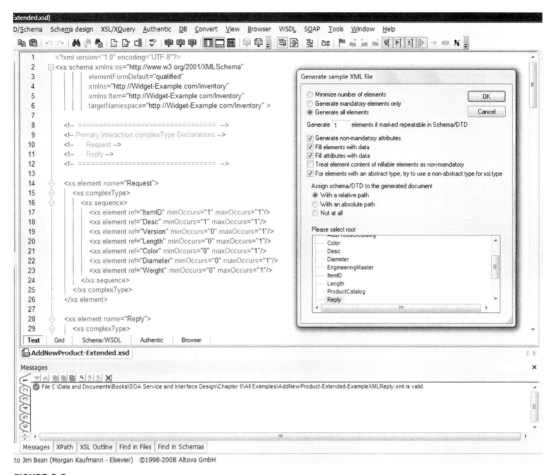

FIGURE 6.8

Generating a Sample XML Message from XML Spy (Copyright 2003-2008 Altova GmbH, reprinted with permission of Altova)

Example 6.2
Generated and Manually Enhanced Sample XML Message

```
<?xml version = "1.0" encoding = "UTF-8" ?>
- <!--
Sample XML file generated by XML Spy v2008 rel. 2 sp2 (http://www.altova.com)
-->
- <Item:Reply xsi:schemaLocation = "http://Widget-Example.com/Inventory AddNewProduct-
Extended.xswd" xmlns:Item = "http://Widget-Example.com/Inventory" xmlns:xsi = "http://www.
w3.org/2001/XMLSchema-instance">
```

```
<Item:ItemID>5678</Item:ItemID>
<Item:Desc>Blue Stick Pen</Item:Desc>
<Item:Version>2</Item:Version>
<Item:Length>8.0 Inch</Item:Length>
<Item:Color>Blue</Item:Color>
<Item:Diameter>0.25 Inch</Item:Diameter>
<Item:Weight>1.5 oz</Item:Weight>
- <Item:ReplyProcessStatus>
<Item:AddEngineeringMaster>Success</Item:AddEngineeringMaster>
<Item:AddProductCatalog>Success</Item:AddProductCatalog>
<Item:AddNewProduct>Success</Item:AddNewProduct>
</Item:ReplyProcessStatus>
- <Item:ReplySQLStateStatus>
<Item:EngineeringMaster>00000</Item:EngineeringMaster>
<Item:ProductCatalog>00000</Item:ProductCatalog>
</Item:ReplySQLStateStatus>
</Item:Reply>
```

Mapping of XML messages to a canonical usually begins with the taxonomy and naming of structures and elements. When the names are syntactically equivalent (i.e., the character by character spelling of one element name matches that of another), the mapping is intuitive and often accurate. However, and even in this case, the full equivalence of elements is still subjective. The metadata that describes each element and its allowable contents is not always implicit in the element's name. This is another example where the richness of metadata from the canonical becomes important (see Figure 6.9).

Using the previous example figure Color element ("< Color/ >"), the element name is common between the two XML messages. While syntactical element name mapping is generally the most common and easiest to resolve, it is sometimes imperfect. As can be seen from the example, syntactical matching of element names does not guarantee the semantic equivalence of allowed or contained data values. The Engineering Item "Color" element carries a data value of "B-252", while the identically named Canonical Item "Color" element carries a different value of "Blue". The mapping of elements in preparation for transformation will need to also take into account the impedance between data values and include data translation (see Figure 6.10).

Other more complex variations and examples are often encountered, such as implied syntactical equivalence. Implied syntactical equivalence occurs when the spelling of different elements is

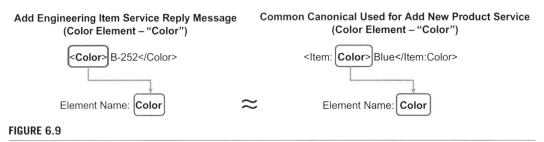

FIGURE 6.9

Example of Syntactical Element Name Equivalence

closely analogous but not identical. Continuing the previous color example, one message might contain an element named as "Color" ("< Color/ >"), while another message might contain an element named as "Col" ("< Col/ >"). This type of implied syntactical equivalence is also quite common with abbreviations, acronyms, and synonyms. Ensuring that the mapping is accurate often requires a combination of element tag name matching, sampling and comparison of data values (from real-world data sources), and evaluation by a business subject matter expert (see Figure 6.11).

In each of the prior examples, the mapping of elements was a "1 to 1" match (e.g., one Color element mapped to another Color element, etc.). A "1 to 1" mapping is the most common and easiest to identify and resolve. However, there are other examples where one element might map to multiple elements.

6.3 AGGREGATION

Aggregation is a more complex type of transformation that includes a combination of transformation and translation. It combines two or more elements and their contained data values into a single aggregate element. The opposite form of aggregation is decomposition, which is also a complex transformation and requires not only the separation of data to two or more elements but a parsing of the contained data for separation.

The requirement for an aggregation type of transformation is quite common and can apply to examples such as a person's name. The reply message structure from a customer profile data service might include multiple elements, with each representing part of a person's name (e.g., "< GivenName/ >",

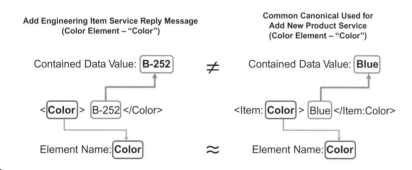

FIGURE 6.10

Example of Semantic Mismatch

FIGURE 6.11

Example of Implied Syntactical Equivalence

"< MiddleName/ >", and "< FamilyName/ >"). However, an additional requirement of the customer profile service design might be to include a full name element ("< PersonName/ >"), where the person's name would be used by service consumers for marketing, mailing, personal contact, or similar purposes.

While the Person Name example can be resolved quite easily with transformation by inserting a new Person Name element, it does not provide a simple way to also combine the contained data values of the three source elements. For some examples, a simple concatenation of the separate data values as one data value might suffice, but with a Person Name there is an implicit need to preserve a whitespace character as a delimiter between the name parts. Without this properly located delimiter, a consumer of the service would receive a jumble of characters in the Person Name element of the reply message (e.g., "JohnMSmith") (see Figure 6.12).

Aggregation of a full person name such as described requires the data values from the individual name part elements to be concatenated, and a constant representing a whitespace character (a blank space) is inserted between the individual name part values. The MapForce tool from Altova (Copyright 2003-2008 Altova GmbH, reprinted with permission of Altova) simplifies this capability by providing a library of built-in functions, such as concatenation, equality, and if-then-else conditions. To resolve this

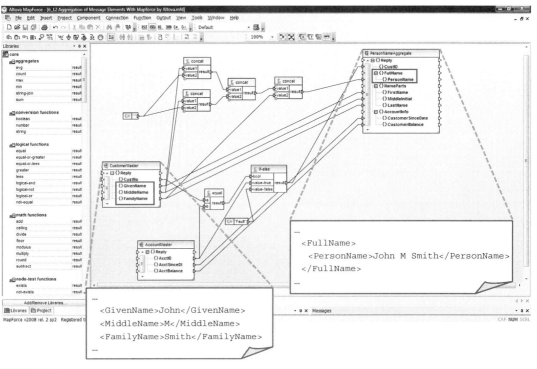

FIGURE 6.12

Aggregation of Message Elements with MapForce by Altova (Copyright 2003-2008 Altova GmbH, reprinted with permission of Altova)

particular example, a graphical mapping between elements is done by linking the elements to a concatenation function and inserting the constant where needed. The generated XSLT from the mapping also includes the appropriate concatenation function, as well as the whitespace constant (see Figure 6.13).

Other forms of aggregation can apply to quantitative data values, and will require mathematical functions to sum or otherwise derive a result from the source elements and the data values. This example would be common in an inventory management scenario, where a composite data service exposes the total on-hand inventory for an item from across all regional storage locations. Individual data services might be defined to each of the regional inventory locations and return the on-hand inventory quantity for the item specific to that location. The composite service would then invoke these separate inventory location services and sum the resulting on-hand inventory for inclusion in the reply message back to the consumer (see Figure 6.14).

The mapping for the aggregate inventory data service and reply message back to the originating service consumer also includes the individual on-hand quantity elements from each location in addition to the total. An add function is applied to the individual inventory On Hand Quantity elements resulting in a total On Hand Quantity. Since the add function is primarily for adding two values, multiple add functions are required to incrementally develop the total across the three example locations. Some data practitioners will notice that this technique results in a somewhat denormalized message structure and may argue that the consumer of the on-hand inventory service should only be provided with the individual location on-hand quantities and not the total. If normalized, the consumers would then be able to perform whatever aggregate logic they need to determine the total on-hand across all locations and separate from the service. While normalization is a common technique for data at rest implementations, it is important to recognize that data in motion has a different set of complexities.

XSLT "fragment"

```
…
<FullName>
   <xsl:for-each select="doc($CustomerMasterReplyInstance)/Reply">
      <xsl:variable name="Vvar20_CustomerMaster" select=".">
       <xsl:for-each select="GivenName">
        <xsl:variable name="Vvar105_GivenName_string" as="xs:string"select="xs:string(.)"/>
        <xsl:for-each select="$Vvar20_CustomerMaster/MiddleName">
         <xsl:variable name="Vvar110_MiddleName_string" as="xs:string"select="xs:string(.)"/>
          <xsl:for-each select="$Vvar20_CustomerMaster/FamilyName">
             <xsl:variablename="Vvar115_FamilyName_string" as="xs:string"select="xs:string(.)"/>
             <PersonName>
               <xsl:sequence select="fn:concat(fn:concat(fn:concat ($Vvar105_GivenName_string, $Vvar107_const),
                              fn:concat($Vvar110_MiddleName_string, $Vvar107_const)),
                              $Vvar115_FamilyName_string)"/>
             </PersonName>
          </xsl:for-each>
         </xsl:for-each>
       </xsl:for-each>
   </xsl:for-each>
</FullName>
…
```

FIGURE 6.13

MapForce Generated XSLT for Aggregate Person Name (Copyright 2003-2008 Altova GmbH, reprinted with permission of Altova)

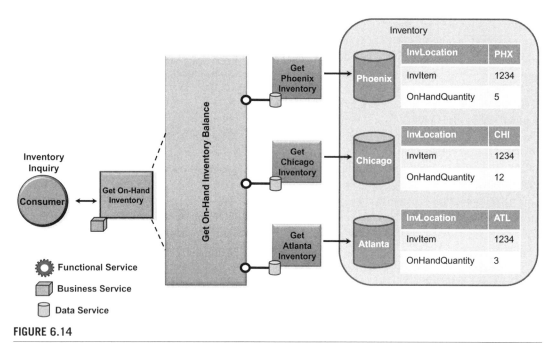

FIGURE 6.14

Aggregate On-Hand Inventory Service

The need to simplify the consumer's interaction with the service, as well as reducing the amount of individual one-off consumer logic to develop totals, will often override the process of normalization for a service and data in motion scenario (see Figure 6.15).

Decomposition is the opposite of aggregation and is also a common transformation. Decomposition parses the contents of a single element into individual data values and moves them to separate elements in the target. Decomposition is another complex type of transformation that also includes data translation. The decomposition function can include string functions or possibly mathematical functions for quantitative data values. Inverting the earlier person name example, the decomposition of Person Name ("< PersonName/ >") to separate name part elements (e.g., "< GivenName/ >", "< MiddleName/ >", and "< FamilyName/ >") would require a substring function to parse the data value, and a method of detecting the whitespace that separates each name part. The substring would be positioned either before or after the whitespace (see Figure 6.16).

Another type of transformation provides a method of abstraction. This allows multiple types of a structure to be substituted for each other.

6.4 ABSTRACTION

Abstraction removes implementation specificity and resolves a mapping across disparate structures. The realization of an abstraction is sometimes referred to as a generalization hierarchy, where subtypes

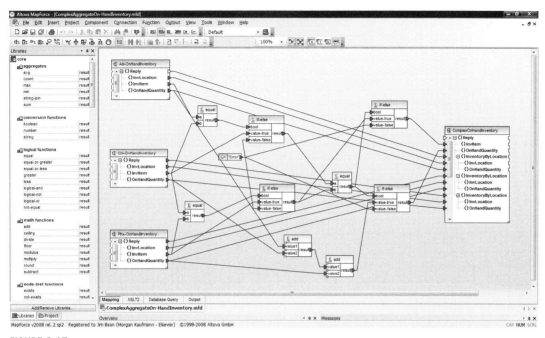

FIGURE 6.15

Aggregate On-Hand Inventory Mapping with MapForce by Altova (Copyright 2003-2008 Altova GmbH, reprinted with permission of Altova)

can inherit and replace the structure of a parent supertype. In the case of abstraction, the parent supertype is never realized in a physical sense, and only the subtypes exist to replace it in the message.

A common example of abstraction is associated with different address types. An address is a form of location for someone or something. It may represent the locator for a physical place such as a residence address, or it may represent a more virtual location such as a telephone number or an e-mail address. Some service consumers might need to acquire the location of a person as a method of initiating contact and without constraint as to which type of address it is. For some customers, the residence or postal address might be available, while for others only a telephone number might be available. A Customer Contact data service would expose whatever contact information is available for the customer regardless of type. The challenge for transformation technologies such as XSLT is resolving the concept of polymorphism. Polymorphism implements a variable outcome where any one of a set of possible outcomes can be instantiated. The complexity lies with identifying and resolving the existence of a particular element over another. While abstraction can be resolved, the transformation functionality required to accomplish a polymorphic type of transformation will usually include multiple transformation steps and possibly a combination of XSLT and other transformation technologies.

Some practitioners avoid polymorphic interfaces. However, it is a powerful method for resolving abstraction requirements. Interestingly, XML Schemas support abstraction and polymorphism in the service interface as a combination of an abstract "head" element declaration and referencing

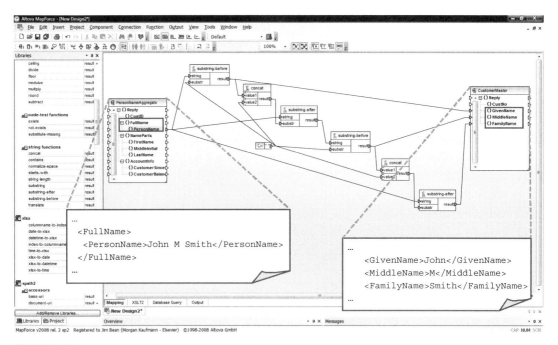

FIGURE 6.16

Decomposition of Aggregate Person Name with MapForce by Altova (Copyright 2003-2008 Altova GmbH, reprinted with permission of Altova)

"substitutionGroup" element declarations. The type differences between substitutionGroup elements can sometimes introduce type casting complexity, and a general recommendation is to define the head element as "anyType" (see Figure 6.17).

Abstraction is a valuable Web service interface design technique. However, it can introduce some complexity to transformation. Effective service design requires an understanding of advantages and limitations and ensuring that the service, service interface XML Schemas, and any requisite transformation are well-defined.

6.5 RATIONALIZATION

Rationalization combines data from different source messages into one but also allows the service consumer to optionally request the elements that were used in the rationalization process. This is not unlike the Person Name example, where the canonical might specify three discrete name part elements to describe a person's name. However, a significant number of consumers might also have an additional servicing requirement for a fully concatenated person name as a single element.

Some service consumers might require only the three person name parts as defined by the canonical. However, other consumers might also require the aggregate fully concatenated person name element.

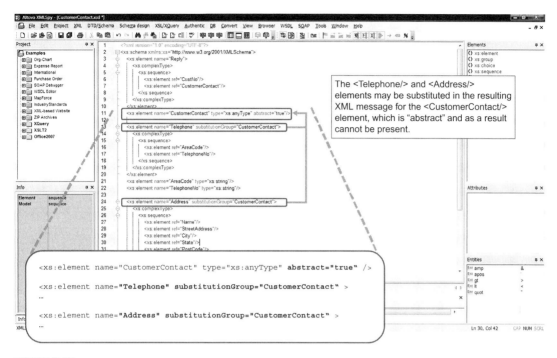

FIGURE 6.17

XML Schema substitutionGroup References with XML Spy by Altova (Copyright 2003-2008 Altova GmbH, reprinted with permission of Altova)

This is a common practice that extends into the service interface and message transformation processes. Leaving the choice to the consumers is the recommended approach for resolving this need. As described previously, transformation tools such as MapForce from Altova (Copyright 2003-2008 Altova GmbH, reprinted with permission of Altova) can simplify the mapping of multiple elements to an aggregate, and the generated XSLT can resolve the transformation.

The service can be designed to include options in the request message, where each consumer specifies if he or she will need the complete person name in the reply, the individual name part elements, or both. The service interface XML Schema can define all of these name elements as optional, which leaves the consumer with some flexibility. The processing required to determine which of the Person Name elements are being requested then becomes the responsibility of the service. The service will need to interpret the options set in the consumer's request message and appropriately acquire and position the resulting data in the reply message (see Figure 6.18).

Providing consumer-driven options as request message content in the service interface can resolve a variety of complexities and position the service for broad utility and reuse. This technique can also introduce processing complexity if overused or poorly designed. The interface and supported functionality of the service should be a well-defined and deterministic set. That is, for most services, the available options and format of the response message should be reasonably stable. An unmanaged

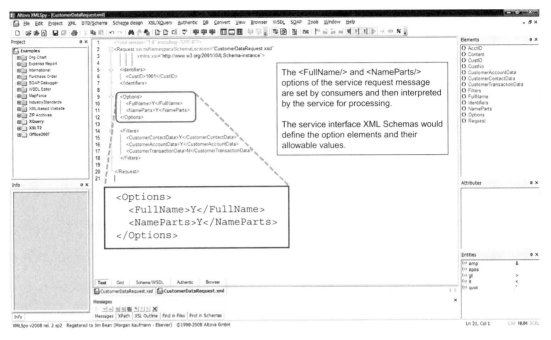

FIGURE 6.18

Request Message Options for Rationalization of Elements with XML Spy by Altova (Copyright 2003-2008 Altova GmbH, reprinted with permission of Altova)

service that allows for significant variation or ad-hoc consumer-driven functionality can result in maintenance complexity and also the potential for poor operational performance (resulting from processing latency). The emphasis with resolving rationalization requirements should be on broad reuse, a deterministic set of options, and a well-defined interface (for both the request and reply messages).

SUMMARY

Transformation can be used to resolve data impedance that transitions from multiple and disparate data at rest sources into data in motion messages. Defining the service interface that results in these messages is a core activity of the service design process. An effective service interface design also requires a deep understanding of metadata, and the use of a canonical as the standard or benchmark used for transformation. This avoids a proliferation of one-off and proprietary transformations and presents a potential solution to help resolve enterprise integration challenges.

In an SOA and Web services context, transformation is a capability that converts one XML-encoded message structure to another. While not limited to message structures and elements, it is a common use of transformation technology such as XSLT. Translation is another view of transformation that emphasizes the data values contained within the XML message elements. Even though a message structure might be transformed into another, this does not always resolve the impedance that exists between the contained data values. In addition to transformation, data values must be translated to values acceptable to the target.

Aggregation is another form of transformation that focuses on combining separate elements and data values into a one structure or element. Alternatively, decomposition separates one element into multiples and parses the data content into separate data values. Abstraction allows one or more replaceable structures to be positioned within a reply message (roughly analogous to polymorphism). While abstraction is a powerful interface design technique, it should be approached with care, as some transformation technologies may have limited capabilities.

Rationalization is another interface design technique that provides reply options to the consumer. Consumers might require a canonicalized expression of data, an aggregation, or a combination. Request message options defined to the service interface allow the consumer to select the rationalized data that will be included in the reply message.

Transformation will typically require a set of supporting technologies such as XSLT. While this is a common approach, and XSLT is rich in transformation functionality, it is similar to a programming language and can be complex. Mapping and transformation tools such as MapForce and XML Editors such as XML Spy from Altova (Copyright 2003-2008 Altova GmbH, reprinted with permission of Altova) can be used to advantage. These tools provide graphical mapping and robust XML editing capabilities and can generate artifacts such as XSLT transforms or sample XML messages. Although these tools can provide extensive service interface design and message transformation capabilities, design best practices are still required. An unmanaged proliferation of XSLTs, XML Schemas, and sample XML messages is not always a good solution.

REFERENCES

1. Kay M, eds. "XSL Transformations (XSLT) Version 2.0" (W3C, January 23, 2007). < http://www.w3.org/TR/xslt20/ >

2. Chamberlin D, Berglund A, Boag S, et. al, eds. "XML Path Language (XPath) Version 2.0" (W3C, January 23, 2007). < http://www.w3.org/TR/xpath20/ >

The Service Interface—Contract

Every SOA service interaction involves some form of consumer request and usually an exchange of information. Consumers will send a request and specify a service operation, and the service will resolve that request. The Message Exchange Patterns (MEPs) can vary from request-reply to an asynchronous fire-and-forget, but the interaction and exchange of information is constant. The consumer request is expressed in the body of a request message, and the service response is expressed in a reply message (assuming a request-reply MEP). In either case, the content of the message is described as "data in motion" and must be structured according to the service interface definition.

Ensuring that these service collaborators understand and comply with the expectations of the service is paramount to success. If the consumer of a service submits a message that cannot be understood by the service provider, the request for servicing will not be resolved. Fundamentally, consumers of a service must comply with the expectations of that service as defined by the service interface.

Similarly, functionality of the service should have been designed to provide resolution to some set of consumer requirements. The service should be designed in a manner that promotes the SOA principles of loose coupling and interoperability. However, most enterprise SOA implementations include consumers of many types and technologies. There may be sufficient rationale to incorporate a set of options that simplify the consumer-to-service interaction and that help to optimize the technology. When included as part of the service behavior, these options are also defined to the service interface and can be specified by consumers in their request messages.

The resolution of a consumer request can be a disconnected and asynchronous process, where the service performs some process but does not reply back to the consumer. Resolution of a request more commonly is reflected as a servicing response, including some information being returned to the consumer as part of a reply message. Regardless, the service has a responsibility to either reject the incoming consumer request message (if incorrect or it cannot be understood), and to resolve a consumer request when the request complies with the service interface.

In a simple sense, this set of interactions, roles, and responsibilities is roughly analogous to a legal contract such as for purchasing real estate. In a typical real estate contract, there is a buyer and a seller. Each plays a specific role, and there are responsibilities for each that are set out in the contract. In an SOA and servicing paradigm, the consumer can be thought of as the buyer, and the service can be thought of as the seller. The consumer is buying point in time, service functionality. The service is providing that functionality to the consumer.

127

Extending the contract analogy, there are also terms and conditions. There might be some set of individual responsibilities that is expected of either or both the consumer and the service (see Figure 7.1). The consumer might be expected to provide data in several elements of the request message, and as an option, might also include other elements. Similarly and depending upon the content of the request message, the service is expected to perform some operation and, if a response is needed, will be required to return data in the reply message. Also similar to a legal contract, the service might be required to provide notification of contract violations or what is sometimes described as "default" against the contract. If the service cannot process the request or there is some underlying error, a fault message must be returned to the consumer.

Each of the responsibilities and supporting processes are described by the service interface and designed into the service operations and behavior. For SOA and Web services, the consumer and service interactions and the requisite responsibilities are defined by the service interface and, more specifically, by a set of service interface artifacts. The WSDL (Web Service Description Language) describes a service as a combination of type references, ports, operations, and bindings. When combined with XML Schemas for the types, the WSDL can be thought of as the overall service interface and contract. To invoke and collaborate with a Web service, the consumer must comply with its intrinsic and referenced definitions.

Recently, a new WSDL specification was approved as a recommendation by the W3C.[1] While many vendors have begun to include support for WSDL 2.0, the previous incarnation of the WSDL specification (actually a "note" rather than a more formal specification) is still broadly used and supported.[2]

The WSDL can either implicitly incorporate, or can reference an externally defined set of message structures and type definitions. These structures and types are specified by an XML Schema.[3] XML Schema Definition Language (sometimes referred to as XSD) is a set of syntactical metadata declarations that prescribe the structure, types (element definitions), and constraints for XML-encoded artifacts, such as request and reply messages. These metadata definitions for a Web service interface can be defined by a single XML Schema or by multiple XML Schemas that are referenced and assembled together. As one service interface design technique, separate XML Schemas can be defined for each of the request message, the reply message, and the content of a fault message. In a Web

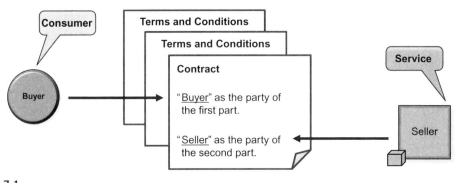

FIGURE 7.1

Legal Contract Analogy

service interface, XML Schemas are one of the most important parts and are referenced as WSDL types ("< types/ >"). Using the contract analogy, the XML Schema declarations specify the terms and conditions of the contract. Combined, the WSDL and XML Schemas are the Web service interface definition, and they represent the service contract. As an SOA technology, WSM (Web Services Management) can further extend the service contract with policies to for things like tracking service level agreements and enforcing security.

In a Web services contract, the request and reply messages are formatted as XML (Extensible Markup Language).[4] The messages must conform to the context and content declarations described by the XML Schemas as the WSDL < types/ >. Taking the analogy a step further, the messages are encapsulated in the body of a SOAP envelope.[5] Using the contract analogy, the SOAP envelope and XML-encoded messages represent the "execution" of the service contract (see Figure 7.2).

Before engaging in a service interaction or "executing the service contract," the consumer requires copies of the WSDL and the < types/ > referenced XML Schemas that represent the Web service interface. These artifacts are acquired from a service artifact repository or file system, after the service has been published and deployed for use. The consumer then "binds" to the service interface, using the WSDL and XML Schemas artifacts. Binding to the service interface is a somewhat technical function and exploits a binding utility or software with the result being an object model or object mapping. The object model allows the consumer to create and populate XML request messages with the data expected by the service and to receive, extract data, and process response messages from the service.

If the service consumer is not in compliance with the service contract (e.g., the Web service interface), the service interaction cannot be successfully completed. In most cases, this means the service

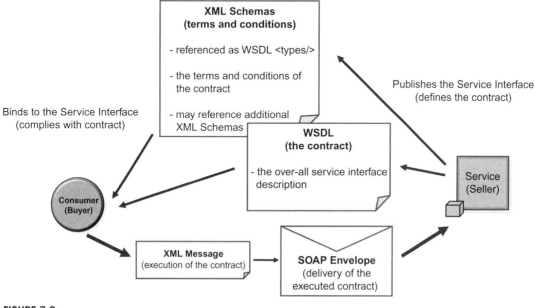

FIGURE 7.2

The Web Service Interface Contract

will not be able to understand or interpret a consumer request and will either reject the message outright or will immediately respond to a request with a fault message. Even when the consumer has complied with the structural definition of the service interface for the request message, if the content of the elements in that message do not meet the requirements and constraints of the XML Schemas, the service will return a fault message. The service contract obligations of the consumer and of the service are clear, and these obligations are set out by the Web service interface definition.

7.1 WEB SERVICES DESCRIPTION LANGUAGE—WSDL

Web Services Description Language (WSDL) is an XML-encoded artifact. This is not to confuse WSDL with an XML-encoded message but purely as the encoding used for specifying the syntax of the WSDL language. At present, WSDL 1.1 is a broadly implemented and supported WSDL "note," and WSDL 2.0 was recently defined as a "recommendation" of the World Wide Web Consortium. While there are declarative and syntactical differences between the two WSDL specifications, the general purpose of WSDL and its role in describing a Web service interface are analogous. That is, WSDL serves as the overall service description and the overall service interface contract.

Other types of SOA services, such as ReST style service or other types of non-Web services, do not require WSDL to define the service interface. However, interactions between the consumer and the non-Web service still require some form of interface-driven contractual agreement. When properly defined, the Web service interface is represented by a collection of referenced artifacts and declarations. When the Web service is also a coarse-grained, BPEL-managed orchestration, the interface is more of an assembly of artifacts than a single, monolithic artifact. Where a BPEL orchestration refers to other subordinate and fine-grained services, the Web service interface includes WSDL, XML Schemas, BPEL, and from BPEL, references to WSDLs and XML Schemas for those services as well. Some Business Process Management technologies (BPM) will use an optimized form of the BPEL (as in a complied or run-time format) (see Figure 7.3).

The WSDL artifact is identified by an external file name (something like "AddItem.wsdl") and an internally defined namespace. Although definitions vary, think of a namespace as a method of providing uniqueness to XML declarations, such as those in WSDL. WSDL can reference or include declarations for other Web services artifacts, such as XML Schemas, and even SOAP references for binding. Collisions between like-named or duplicate declarations within WSDL can result in an anomaly. Assigning declarations to a namespace helps to avoid collision when element declarations are of the same name.

The types of namespaces include default, target, and user defined (or qualified). While the example described here is specific to WSDL, all namespaces are XML declarations and comply with the XML Namespaces specification.[6] Namespace declarations are typically identified by an "xmlns" or a "targetNamespace" attribute. The attribute name is followed by an equal sign ("="), and then by the namespace (as a string or name, but most often declared as a URI [Uniform Resource Identifier] to provide uniqueness). The default namespace applies to declarations that are not already assigned to another namespace by name or prefix. WSDL, XML Schemas, SOAP, and XSLT all have their own predefined default namespaces. Only one default namespace is allowed per artifact.

The target namespace ("targetNamespace") applies to declarations that are not already assigned to another namespace and can be used to reference and assemble an artifact like WSDL or an XML Schema from multiple component parts. The individual parts will all have a defined targetNamespace,

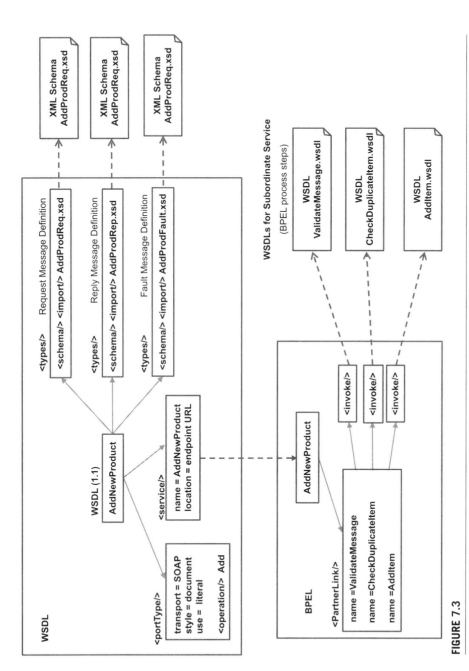

FIGURE 7.3

Relationship Between Service Interface Artifacts

and an "import" element will make reference to the target namespaces of those component parts. The notion of component part assembly is a powerful method of reuse and interface management. It is especially important that XML Schemas are referenced and assembled from component schemas. Only one targetNamespace is allowed per artifact.

A user-defined or "qualified" namespace applies to any declaration or name where the same prefix is used to qualify a declaration or a name (in this example, "Item"). Multiple user-defined and qualified namespaces are allowed within an artifact, but the prefix for each must be unique. For example, from a WSDL: < part name="Body" element="Item:Request"/ >, where the element name of "Request" is qualified by the "Item" prefix and therefore participates in the "Item" namespace.

Avoiding potential collisions becomes even more important with coarse-grained services that are defined by a BPEL-orchestrated process. Subordinate Web services defined as a process step from within that BPEL will also have a service interface defined by WSDL. Having unique WSDL namespace declarations avoids potential collision or unintended overlap between those Web service interactions (see Figure 7.4).

Like other XML-formatted artifacts, the structure of WSDL is hierarchical. There is a highest-level parent or "root" element for WSDL and then child elements nested below it. These child elements can also have their own nested children, and so on. As an XML-encoded artifact, a WSDL also supports attributes, which are another type of data container associated with elements. Attributes and

Namespaces taken from a WSDL 1.1 example

```
<definitionsxmlns=http://schemas.xmlsoap.org/wsdl/
            xmlns:soap="http://schemas.xmlsoap.org/wsdl/soap/"
            xmlns:http="http://schemas.xmlsoap.org/wsdl/http/"
            xmlns:soapenc=http://schemas.xmlsoap.org/soap/encoding/
            xmlns:mime="http://schemas.xmlsoap.org/wsdl/mime/"
            xmlns:Item="http://Widget-Example.com/Inventory"
            xmlns:WSDL="http://Widget-Example.com/WSDL"
            targetNamespace="http://Widget-Example.com/WSDL">
```

xmlns=http://schemas.xmlsoap.org/wsdl/

Default Namespace (for WSDL 1.1). This namespace will be applied to WSDL declarations that are not already assigned to another namespace by name or prefix. Generally applies to WSDL specific syntax. XML Schema has its own default namespace, as does SOAP, and XSLT. Only one default namespace is allowed per artifact.

targetNamespace="http://Widget-Example.com/WSDL"

Target Namespace. This namespace will be applied to WSDL declarations that are not already assigned to another namespace. Conceptually, the targetNamespace refers to the WSDL itself, and is used in a reference when the WSDL is composed of multiple component parts and must then be assembled. The individual parts will all have a targetNamespace, and the WSDL "import" element will make reference to the namespaces of those component parts. A similar example applies to XML Schemas that are referenced and assembled from component schemas. Only one targetNamespace is allowed per artifact.

xmlns:Item="http://Widget-Example.com/Inventory"

Prefixed or qualified namespace. This namespace is user-defined and applies to any declaration or name where the same prefix is used to qualify a declaration or a name (in this example "Item"). Multiple user-defined and qualified namespaces are allowed, but the prefix must be unique. As an example: <part name="Body" element="Item:Request"/>, where the element name of "Request" is qualified by the "Item" prefix and participates in the "Item" namespace.

FIGURE 7.4

Namespace Declarations

elements can both contain data values, but an attribute can only be declared to an element. A simple analogy is to think of an attribute as a "property" of an element.

Both WSDL 1.1 and WSDL 2.0 include a highest-level root element. The root element of WSDL 1.1 is < definitions/ >, while the root element of WSDL 2.0 is < description/ >. Both WSDL 1.1 and WSDL 2.0 allow for forms of assembly, where WSDL can be defined by sets of component WSDL declarations that are then assembled by reference to represent the complete WSDL. However, the WSDL 1.1 component assembly was more abstract and relies upon the WSDL interpreter technology, whereas WSDL 2.0 has specific import and include declarations for component references.

As child element declarations, both WSDL 1.1 and WSDL 2.0 allow for a < types/ > element. The < types/ > element plays a critical role for either referencing or embedding the XML Schema definitions (also known as "in-lining"). Regardless of whether the XML Schemas are referenced or intrinsically declared, strict compliance with the XML Schema syntax is required. WSDL 1.1 then associates message definitions ("< message/ >") to the XML Schemas content that is defined to the WSDL < types/ > element. A child element of the WSDL < message/ > element allows for specific reference to a structure or element declared within the XML Schemas. WSDL 2.0 also relies upon the < types/ > declarations for XML Schemas but has deprecated the < message/ > element and referenced the XML Schemas within an < interface/ > element.

WSDL 1.1 includes a < portType/ > child element declaration that has been replaced in WSDL 2.0 with an < interface/ > child element. WSDL 2.0 references the < types/ > declared XML Schemas using an < interface/ > and child < operation/ > element, and then an < input/ > or < output/ > or < infault/ > or < outfault/ > element reference within the operation. From a conceptual vantage, the XML Schema definitions referenced by the types define the request messages to be created by the service consumers and the reply and fault messages returned by the service.

Both WSDL 1.1 and WSDL 2.0 include a < binding/ > element. The binding element associates the interface types and context as message specifications, with operations of the service. The protocol is also defined in the binding element, such as SOAP over HTTP. However, unlike WSDL 1.1, WSDL 2.0 allows for multiple interface and binding definitions, as well as interface inheritance (where one interface definition can be inherited and extended by another). WSDL 2.0 also provides for explicit Message Exchange Patterns (MEPs) in the "pattern" attribute of the < interface/ >, child < operation/ > element.

WSDL 1.1 identifies the endpoint for the service using a named < service/ > element and child < address/ > element. In an SOA, this is the endpoint defined to the Enterprise Service Bus (ESB), where request messages are sent by service consumers. WSDL 2.0 also includes a named < service/ > element and has added a child < endpoint/ > element with an "address" attribute (see Figure 7.5).

Faults encountered by the service with data returned in a fault message are handled somewhat differently between WSDL 1.1 and WSDL 2.0. In WSDL 1.1, fault message type content is declared to the < portType/ > element and then specifically referenced by name from the < binding/ >, child < operation/ >, and child < fault/ > element. WSDL 2.0 defines faults more explicitly in the < interface/ > and < binding/ > and allows a fault to be defined to replace the usual reply message. The fault can also be reused across interactions. This WSDL 2.0 technique aligns more closely with common MEPs.

When the binding specifies SOAP, the message content is carried in the < body/ > element of the SOAP envelope, and the entire SOAP envelope is messaged to the service endpoint. SOAP also supports a < header/ > element where other information can be declared, such as routing and security

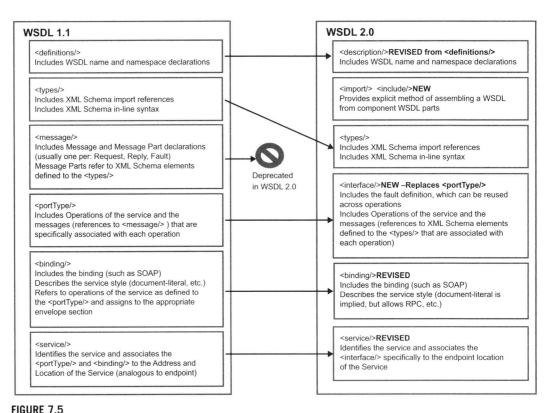

FIGURE 7.5

Comparing WSDL 1.1 and WSDL 2.0 Structures

information. This additional header information is not part of the message context or payload and is usually ignored by endpoint service behavior to resolve the service request. However, header information can be used for administrative functions such as logging, security, and audit. WSDL 1.1 allows SOAP < header/ > content to be defined by an XML Schema and then referenced by the < binding/ > and child < input/ > element. WSDL 2.0 provides for a SOAP extension in the < binding/ > and child < input/ >, < output/ >, and < fault/ > elements as a < soap:header/ > element. While SOAP < header/ > information is not used as context or payload information, it can be defined and inserted by service intermediaries and by Web Services Management (WSM) policies. This allows for additional SOA functionality such as the application of a policy or to provide further routing information (see Figure 7.6).

As described in Chapter 2, "Core SOA Principles," a technique for implementing the "loose coupling" principle is designing the service interface to be "document literal," as opposed to a more RPC-style interface, avoiding message declared types and explicit operations parameters. WSDL 1.1 describes the interface style (RPC, doc-lit, other) as content of the < binding/ > element and "style" attribute, combined with the "use" attribute of the < binding/ > child < input/ > and < binding/ > child < output/ > elements. A recommended implementation of WSDL 2.0 implies a "document-literal"

Subset Fragment of WSDL

```
<binding name="ServiceBinding" type="WSDL:TestPort">
  <soap:bindingstyle="document" transport="http://schemas.xmlsoap.org/soap/http"/>
  <operation name="ServiceContext">
    <soap:operationsoapAction="http://Widget-Example.com/GetInventoryData"/>
    <input name="Request">
      <soap:header message="WSDL:HEADER" part="Header" use="literal"/>
      <soap:bodyuse="literal"/>
    </input>
                            Content of the HEADER is defined by an XML
  </binding>                Schema declared to the WSDL <types/>
```

Subset Fragment of SOAP Message (Request Message)

```
<SOAP-ENV:Envelopexmlns:SOAP-ENV="http://schemas.xmlsoap.org/soap/envelope/"
          xmlns:SOAP-ENC="http://schemas.xmlsoap.org/soap/encoding/"
          xmlns:xsi="http://www.w3.org/2001/XMLSchema-instance"
          xmlns:xsd="http://www.w3.org/2001/XMLSchema">
<SOAP-ENV:Header>
  <m:Header xmlns:m="http://Widget-Example.com/Inventory/Header"
          role="http://Widget-Example.com/Inventory/Header/Actor/Actor-1"
          mustUnderstand="1"/>
</SOAP-ENV:Header>

  <SOAP-ENV:Body/>
</SOAP-ENV:Envelope>
```

FIGURE 7.6

SOAP Header Example

style of operations. However, RPC and other styles can be specified using the < interface/ > and child < operation/ > element, with a value for the "style" attribute.

While WSDL is the overall service interface description, the XML Schemas that are referenced or intrinsically declared in WSDL are critical to the service contract.

7.2 XML SCHEMAS—XSD

XML Schemas are a syntactical language that describe and constrain a referencing XML-encoded document or message. In a Web service interface context, the structure and elements of the request and reply messages are defined by XML Schemas. These schemas are referenced by the < types/ > element of WSDL. As a part of the Web service interface, XML Schemas can be thought of as describing the terms and conditions of the contract.

When designing the Web service interface, the architect will determine what functionality is required of the service and what data is required by consumers. The service functionality is then used to define service operations, and the required data is used as context for designing the service reply message. The architect then rationalizes the service operations and reply message content to determine the data that is required in the consumer request message. A highly effective and recommended technique is to conceptualize the request and reply messages as sample instances, and then to craft the XML Schemas that describe those messages, elements, and any constraining rules.

With a data service, there is a correlation between the consumer request and the information that is returned by the service in the reply. As an example, the consumer might request Item Master data for a particular Item ID. The corresponding reply message would then include data for that requested Item in the elements of the reply message. In this simple scenario, it is critical that the consumer specify the request message and content in a manner that can be fully understood by the service. If not, the service will return a fault.

XML Schema supports a number of syntactical declarations. The schema can define individual elements, structures (e.g., grouped collections of elements that may be nested as children of a parent element), and strong typing to include data types and constraining facets (such as length, precision, enumerations, etc.). Elements can also be defined to support cardinality, where a single element can be repeated a specified number of times within the message. These metadata-like capabilities play a critical role in ensuring that the service interface (contract) is well-defined. Further information on XML Schemas syntax and capabilities is described in Chapter 10, "XML Schema Basics."

When a consumer sends a request message to a service, compliance of the message structure and content with the service contract is implied but not guaranteed. A poorly designed and engineered consumer application might incorrectly map or bind to a service interface definition and produce a message that is not understood by the service. This can result in a service anomaly and a fault message being returned back to the consumer. Similarly, a poorly designed service interface that does not provide adequate metadata for the contract can be the cause. The latter is an important service design consideration, and XML Schemas can provide a number of effective syntactical capabilities. Although there are advantages and disadvantages to consider, XML Schema declarations such as specifying default values and a list of allowable values (as enumerations) can help (see Figure 7.7).

A separate and optional process can be invoked as part of the consumer-to-service interaction to check for compliance of a request message with the service interface contract. This process is known as schema validation and requires a technology known as a validating parser. The validating parser compares an XML-encoded message to a referenced XML Schema and reports any errors. In a Web service interaction, the XML Schemas are referenced by WSDL for the service and are a core part of the service interface and contract. With very rare exceptions, a validating parser does not modify or otherwise correct the XML message, and any resulting corrections are left to the application that created the message. Typically, remediation of a noncompliant XML message requires further analysis that may also include a redesign of the consuming application and a rebinding to the service interface.

7.3 EXTENSIBLE MARKUP LANGUAGE

Extensible Markup Language (XML) is the method of structuring and encoding a message for a Web service interaction. Other types of SOA services might use a more proprietary format such as a positional or delimited messages, which are somewhat common for legacy consumers and services. Advantages of using XML over other types of message formats are a combination of the following:

- XML is generally platform agnostic.
- XML is self-describing and extensible.
- XML enforces the notion of a structural hierarchy.

XML Schemas, second edition

<schema/> Includes schema name and namespace declarations.	**<any/>** References another namespace (XML Schema) and may be used to extend an existing schema dynamically. The referenced "wildcard" namespace is correlated in the XML instance document (such as a message) with the XML Schema namespace and location/name combination.
<import/>, <include/>, <redefine/> References another, separate component XML Schema. Generally used to assemble multiple component schemas into a larger schema context.	
<element/> Elements are data containers. They may be defined to hold data values, or other nested, child elements.	**<group/>** A structure that is similar to <complexType/>. However, a <group/> of elements is specifically intended to be further referenced within the schema as a form of reuse.
<simpleType/> Defines a strong type that may be applied to an <element/> or an attribute as a data container. Optionally, allows extension and derivation such as enumerations, length, decimal scale and precision, regular expression formatting, etc.	**attribute** A data container that is roughly analogous to an <element/>. However, an attribute follows the syntax of attribute-value-pair (e.g., Name="test"), whereas an <element/> follows the syntax of an open and close tag (e.g., <Name>test</Name>). Elements may be named and defined globally to a schema and also repeat. An attribute cannot repeat by name and is defined to the context of an already defined element.
<complexType/> Generally a complex structure that may describe multiple elements, multiple complexTypes.	
<sequence/>, <choice/>, <all/> Compositor that defines how child elements are defined to a <complexType/> structure.	

FIGURE 7.7

Subset List of Important XML Schemas Declarations

As a platform-agnostic encoding format, XML relies heavily on the Unicode standard.[7] Unicode is a standard that includes a set of codes to describe text characters. As one example, the ASCII character codes are recognized by the Unicode standard as part of the "C0 Controls and Basic Latin" code set. Most technology platforms either directly support Unicode encoded characters, or a method of transforming between character codes is available.

XML is self-describing. Within an XML-encoded artifact, such as a message, the element and attribute tags that describe the message content are user-defined. That is, the designer of the service interface defines the element and attribute tag names. This allows the service designer to apply a degree of intelligence and semantic context to elements and attributes. Rather than some abstract naming convention, or system-assigned and nonintelligent names, the service interface designer has tremendous latitude in specifying names. While XML messages are typically run-time generated and consumed, the template from which the messages are generated is an XML Schema. That XML Schema contains declarations for all of the elements and attributes in the message, including

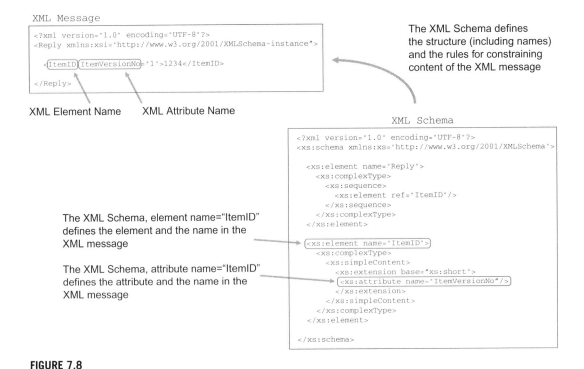

FIGURE 7.8

XML Element Names

the requisite names that will be applied. Also, design-time activities and mapping of message content between dissimilar applications is more intuitive and greatly simplified when the message element names are self-describing (see Figure 7.8).

XML is also case sensitive. That is, the user-defined element and attribute names can be specified using uppercase characters, lowercase characters, or combinations. The character case used in a tag name does imply a degree of uniqueness. A tag name of < ItemID/ > is different from < itemid/ >. This capability further enhances the readability of the service messages and simplifies design and mapping of the service. Since the element and attribute names are user-defined, XML is also naturally extensible. That is, the implementer may decide to add new elements later. As long as the syntactical and structural rules of XML are complied with (sometimes referred to as being "well formed"), the new elements can be added. However, even with XML, the addition of new content to an XML message must consider the service interface contract. Participants in a service collaboration must be able to understand and consume the XML elements as defined by the contract. If not, then the contract is "broken."

XML elements are also described by a combination of an "open" tag and a "close" tag. Any representative data is placed between the open and close tags. XML also allows for an abbreviated tag syntax when there is no data for the element, and the element is allowed to remain empty. XML

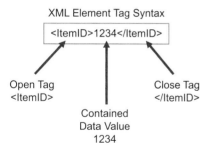
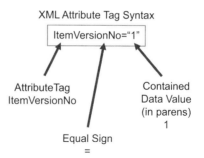

FIGURE 7.9

XML Element and Attribute Tag Syntax

elements can also be defined to repeat by name with a parent element, which is often described as cardinality. XML attributes are defined in context of an element (they cannot be defined to stand alone in the XML structure), and they follow a simple attribute-value-pair format. While multiple attributes can be defined to a single element declaration, they are not allowed to repeat with the same name (see Figure 7.9).

XML also enforces a structural hierarchy to a message. As a hierarchy, there is a single "root" element to any XML-encoded artifact. Child elements can be defined to a parent and represent a form of nesting. These elements can have siblings at the same level of the hierarchy, as well as their own children. The depth of element nesting is unlimited. The hierarchical message structure is also closely aligned with an object hierarchy and, as a result, provides a method of mapping from the message definition to the consumer and service behavior (see Figure 7.10).

Interestingly, XML is also the syntactical encoding for most other Web services artifacts, including WSDL, XML Schemas, and SOAP. The advantages of using XML for encoding other artifacts are the same for using XML generally. The content models for these artifacts (WSDL, XSD, etc.) are user-defined and extensible, and the artifacts are generally platform agnostic.

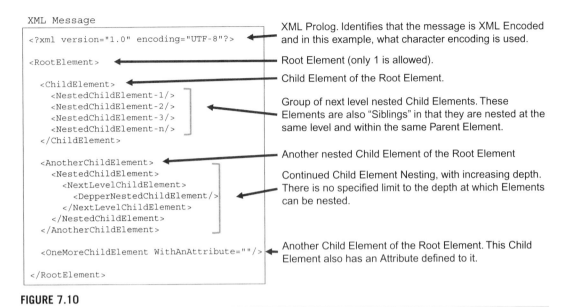

XML Message
```
<?xml version="1.0" encoding="UTF-8"?>

<RootElement>

  <ChildElement>
    <NestedChildElement-1/>
    <NestedChildElement-2/>
    <NestedChildElement-3/>
    <NestedChildElement-n/>
  </ChildElement>

  <AnotherChildElement>
    <NestedChildElement>
      <NextLevelChildElement>
        <DepperNestedChildElement/>
      </NextLevelChildElement>
    </NestedChildElement>
  </AnotherChildElement>

  <OneMoreChildElement WithAnAttribute=""/>

</RootElement>
```

XML Prolog. Identifies that the message is XML Encoded and in this example, what character encoding is used.

Root Element (only 1 is allowed).

Child Element of the Root Element.

Group of next level nested Child Elements. These Elements are also "Siblings" in that they are nested at the same level and within the same Parent Element.

Another nested Child Element of the Root Element

Continued Child Element Nesting, with increasing depth. There is no specified limit to the depth at which Elements can be nested.

Another Child Element of the Root Element. This Child Element also has an Attribute defined to it.

FIGURE 7.10

Structure of an XML Message Instance

SUMMARY

To facilitate a service interaction, an agreement must exist. This agreement (often referred to as the "contract") is defined by the service interface, and noncompliance will result in an inability to process a request and possibly a fault message returned to consumers. The service interface follows legal contract analogy, with a buyer (the consumer) and a seller (the service). The contract (WSDL) also includes terms and conditions (XML Schemas). As the consumer and service execute in compliance with the contract, they exchange messages (XML).

The design of the Web service interface is possibly the single most important activity for service design. The designer or architect will need to identify the type of service interaction and MEPs, determine the needed service functionality as service operations, and then formalize the result of those operations as message content. Once the service interface has been designed, design of the service behavior can be matched to the service interface.

REFERENCES

1. Chinnici R, Moreau J-J, Ryman A, Weerawarana S, eds. "Web Services Description Language (WSDL) Version 2.0 Part 1: Core Language" (W3C, June 26, 2007). <http://www.w3.org/TR/wsdl20/>.

2. Christensen E, Curbera F, Meredith G, Weerawarana S, eds. "Web Services Description Language (WSDL) 1.1" (W3C, March 15, 2001). <http://www.w3.org/TR/wsdl/>.

3. Fallside DC, Walmsley P, eds. "XML Schema Part 0: Primer 2nd ed." (W3C, October 28, 2004). <http://www.w3.org/TR/xmlschema-0/>.

4. Bray T, Paoli J, Sperberg-McQueen CM, Maler E, Yergeau F, eds. "Extensible Markup Language (XML) 1.0. 4th ed." (W3C, August 16, 2006, edited in place September 29, 2006). <http://www.w3.org/TR/REC-xml/>.

5. Mitra N, Lafon Y, eds. "SOAP Version 1.2 Part 0: Primer. 2nd ed." (W3C, April 27, 2007). <http://www.w3.org/TR/soap12-part0/>.

6. Bray T, Hollander D, Layman A, Tobin R, eds. "Namespaces in XML 1.0. 2nd ed." (W3C, August 16, 2006). <http://www.w3.org/TR/REC-xml-names/>.

7. The Unicode Consortium. *The Unicode Standard, Version 5.1.0, defined by: The Unicode Standard, Version 5.0 as amended by Unicode 5.1.0*. Boston: Addison-Wesley; 2007 <http://www.unicode.org/versions/Unicode5.1.0/>.

Canonical Message Design

8

Service interface design is where the SOA principles, resolution of impedance, data at rest sources, and other important SOA concepts begin to converge. There are several approaches that can be followed for service and service interface design. For a Web service, the design process can include different working artifacts, all of which fall into the Web services standards described in previous chapters (including WSDL, XML Schemas, XML, and SOAP). A recommended approach is to focus on a top-down design and development of the Web service interface and then derive the required service behavior based upon that service interface.

This top-down approach to service design can proceed by either designing the XML Schemas that will describe and constrain the Web service interface or by modeling example messages using XML. Either of these approaches can work quite well, and there are advantages and disadvantages to each. Starting with creation of XML Schemas tends to result in a more fine-grained set of service interface artifacts with much greater detail and more explicit syntactical declarations and constraints. This often allows the Web service interface to be developed more rapidly and with fewer intermediate design steps. However, it also requires a significant degree of expertise with XML Schemas syntax.

As the alternative, starting with examples of XML request and reply messages is somewhat more visual (although still using XML syntax). The example messages are almost a prototype that reflects the intended message structures and content that will be exchanged between consumers and services (often referred to as a "canonical message design"). The example messages include elements and sample data that are self-describing and intuitive, and they can be easily understood by technical and business subject matter experts during reviews (see Figure 8.1). The service designer can then quickly refine the examples based upon reviewer feedback. Once a reasonable final state is reached, the example XML messages can then be used as a baseline or template to create or—depending upon tooling capabilities—to "generate" the XML Schemas.

As described in Chapter 5, "Data Services," and also in Chapter 6, "Transformation to Resolve Data Impedance," the enterprise canonical model describes a standard expression for enterprise data. That is, the enterprise canonical is a model for the common information (and processes) that can be reused across the enterprise. Although it is a different type of canonical model, a "canonical message design" also serves as a standard. The canonical message design is the standard expression for the information exchanged between consumers and services. Some service developers might initially question the need to standardize service interfaces or even to derive them from a model or design effort. The rationale being that development tools can easily generate the interface and even some of the core operations behavior from a simple object model or even from a database catalog (in the case of a data service).

143

```
<?xml version="1.0" encoding="UTF?8"?>
<Reply>


    <ContentSection>

      <ItemDetailSection>
        <ItemID>5678</ItemID>
        <Desc>Blue Stick Pen</Desc>
        <Version>2</Version>
        <Length>8.0 in</Length>
        <Color>Blue</Color>
        <Diameter>0.25 in</Diameter>
        <Weight>1.5 oz</Weight>
      </ItemDetailSection>


    </ContentSection>

</Reply>
```

FIGURE 8.1

Example XML Message

While it is difficult to dispute the simplicity by which service code and service interface artifacts can be generated from tooling, taking a narrow development approach that is limited to a single system, or insular set of data, can

- Add to the enterprise integration problem by deploying more and more unique data definitions within each service interface
- Result in artifacts that tend not to be reusable
- Result in artifacts that cannot easily be extended later without impact to already existing consumers
- Result in an increasing number of artifacts, code, and so on that must then be managed and later maintained or enhanced
- Result in services that may not be optimized to support varied consumer types
- Result in service interfaces and messages that carry an excessive payload

Signs of success with SOA include an increase in the number of highly reusable cross-platform and cross-application services, a reduction in the development of unique and vertical system or line of business applications, and a reduction in the number and complexity of transformations between systems. Representing data in motion, the messages exchanged between services are one source of measurement data that contributes to SOA success. An emphasis on service interface standardization and consistency in the service interface will result in fewer transformations and will promote higher levels of reuse. An additional benefit of canonical message design, rather than tooling-based service development, is a consideration for future and as of yet unknown service enhancements. Incorporating extension points to later extend a service while mitigating impact from change to previously existing consumers of the service is also of tremendous value.

Relying exclusively on service and object modeling and development tooling may not always be the most effective approach. Unfortunately, not all service development tooling is at a point of maturity where these complexities and challenges are resolved. However, there is tremendous value to model-driven development and service development and generation technologies. Where the technology environment is heavily reliant upon service tooling, a recommended and possibly more effective approach is to model and generate the service artifacts, and then to further review, refine, optimize and refactor those tooling-generated artifacts.

8.1 THE MESSAGE IS A HIERARCHY

With user-defined and self-describing tag names, XML serves well for designing message. As described in Chapter 7, "The Service Interface—Contract," XML is self-describing (i.e., the element and attribute tag names are included in the message). This allows the service designer to craft an example or prototype message with elements that are intuitive to humans (both technology and business subject matter experts). Through a process of refinement, these example messages become the canonical message design and serve as the base for the service interface.

XML messages are a hierarchy. That is, the first and topmost element of the message is the root element, and all other elements are defined to and encapsulated within that root element. As described in the previous chapter, only one root element is allowed per XML document. This well-formedness rule of XML applies to all XML documents, messages, and generally to XML as syntax. The single root element rule also applies to a message contained as payload in a SOAP envelope, where the SOAP envelope also provides the root element ("< SOAP:Envelope/ >").

Web services also rely on SOAP for the protocol and envelope.[1] This means that the over-the-wire format of the XML message will also include a higher level set of predefined SOAP elements (also as XML) carried message. This should not be a concern during canonical message design, as the basic enforcement of a single root element is implicit. From the perspective of SOAP, the top-level and overall root element of the message sent across-the-wire is the SOAP "Envelope" element ("< SOAP:Envelope/ >"), and all other message elements are carried within it. Nested within the SOAP envelope, there are other SOAP elements such as the SOAP Header (an optional element, as "< SOAP:Header/ >") and the SOAP Body ("< SOAP:Body/ >"). The content and context of a request or reply message is carried in the SOAP "Body" element (see Figure 8.2).

Canonical message design is less concerned with the SOAP envelope structure, which is assumed to be the overall message envelope for Web services, and more with the content and context of the information that will be contained within the SOAP Body. The root element of the canonical message design will be the first and only direct child within the SOAP Body, which complies with the single root element rule of XML.

The root element of the canonical message design should be representative of the service interaction as a message exchange type. This will help to distinguish between messages and will also simplify the later definition of the WSDL. There are four primary types of Web services Message Exchange Patterns (MEPs). The MEPs have been further extended with WSDL 2.0 interfaces[2] to include combinations of explicit fault interactions, but the primary message types of any service rely upon one or more of three basic message types:

- Request (corresponding to the WSDL < input/ > message type)
- Reply (corresponding to the WSDL < output/ > message type)
- Fault (corresponding to the WSDL < fault/ > message type)

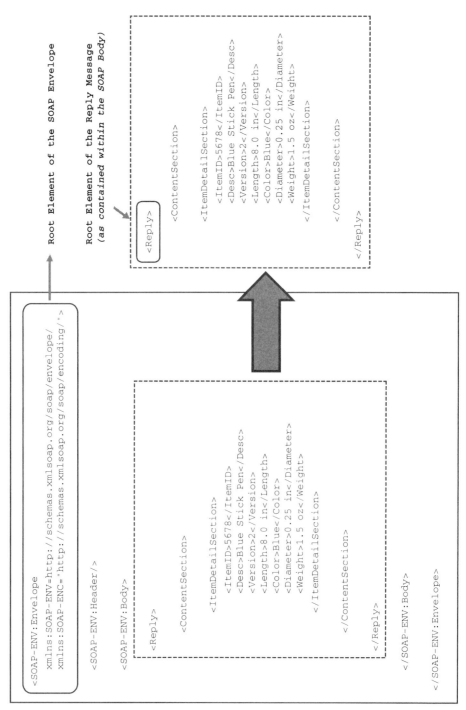

```
<SOAP-ENV:Envelope
    xmlns:SOAP-ENV=http://schemas.xmlsoap.org/soap/envelope/
    xmlns:SOAP-ENC="http://schemas.xmlsoap.org/soap/encoding/">

<SOAP-ENV:Header/>

<SOAP-ENV:Body>

    <Reply>

        <ContentSection>

            <ItemDetailSection>
                <ItemID>5678</ItemID>
                <Desc>Blue Stick Pen</Desc>
                <Version>2</Version>
                <Length>8.0 in</Length>
                <Color>Blue</Color>
                <Diameter>0.25 in</Diameter>
                <Weight>1.5 oz</Weight>
            </ItemDetailSection>

        </ContentSection>

    </Reply>

</SOAP-ENV:Body>

</SOAP-ENV:Envelope>
```

Root Element of the SOAP Envelope

Root Element of the Reply Message
(as contained within the SOAP Body)

```
    <Reply>

        <ContentSection>

            <ItemDetailSection>
                <ItemID>5678</ItemID>
                <Desc>Blue Stick Pen</Desc>
                <Version>2</Version>
                <Length>8.0 in</Length>
                <Color>Blue</Color>
                <Diameter>0.25 in</Diameter>
                <Weight>1.5 oz</Weight>
            </ItemDetailSection>

        </ContentSection>

    </Reply>
```

FIGURE 8.2

The Root Element of the SOAP Envelope and of the Message

Complex Type with Nested Child Elements

Complex Type with Mixed Content and Nested Child Elements
("<ItemID/>" has a data value and child elements)

```
<?xml version="1.0" encoding="UTF-8"?>
<Reply>

    <ContentSection>

        <ItemDetailSection>
            <ItemID>5678</ItemID>
            <Desc>Blue Stick Pen</Desc>
            <Version>2</Version>
            <Length>8.0 in</Length>
            <Color>Blue</Color>
            <Diameter>0.25 in</Diameter>
            <Weight>1.5 oz</Weight>

        </ItemDetailSection>

    </ContentSection>

</Reply>
```

```
<?xml version="1.0" encoding="UTF-8"?>
<Reply>

    <ContentSection>

        <ItemDetailSection>
            <ItemID>5678

                <Desc>Blue Stick Pen</Desc>
                <Version>2</Version>
                <Length>8.0 in</Length>
                <Color>Blue</Color>
                <Diameter>0.25 in</Diameter>
                <Weight>1.5 oz</Weight>

            </ItemID>

        </ItemDetailSection>

    </ContentSection>

</Reply>
```

FIGURE 8.3

Parent Element Complex Type and Mixed Content

A reply message type is generally a good standard from which to begin the canonical message design process. The rationale is that the reply message from a service in return to a consumer can contain a full representation of the expected business data as a response from the service. In addition to the business data of the reply message, a good service design will also allow for an optional service processing status, an echoed image of the request message, and similar information. For most services, this makes the reply message an ideal artifact to prototype and model, and a Reply element ("< Reply/ >") should be the root element and immediate child of the SOAP Body element. As the canonical message design process progresses, the other message types (Request and Fault) will also be considered and later designed.

Following the Reply element, the canonical message design continues with the analogy of a hierarchy, and other more contextual parent, child, and sibling elements can be included as appropriate. A parent element includes or encapsulates other elements within. A parent element is sometimes referred to as a "complex type." Interestingly, a parent element can also include data values of its own in addition to encapsulated child elements. This is referred to as "mixed content" and is not recommended (see Figure 8.3).

A child element is encapsulated by and nested within a parent element. That is, the child element is located between the open tag and the close tag of the parent element. Each element, regardless of whether a parent element or a child element, must be defined by a named open tag and a corresponding close tag (or using an abbreviated empty tag syntax when the element has no contained data value). These tag names are critical to the canonical message design and are recommended to have been derived from the enterprise canonical model names or some other recognized standard for the enterprise. These names should be intuitive to either a business or technology person and will add semantic richness to the canonical message design.

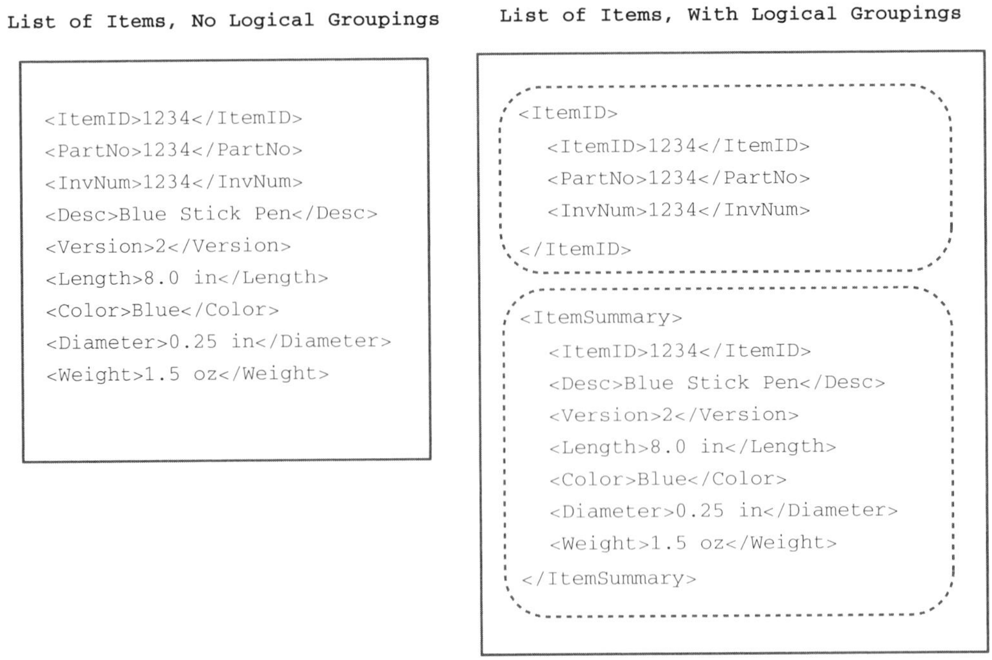

List of Items, No Logical Groupings   List of Items, With Logical Groupings

```
<ItemID>1234</ItemID>
<PartNo>1234</PartNo>
<InvNum>1234</InvNum>
<Desc>Blue Stick Pen</Desc>
<Version>2</Version>
<Length>8.0 in</Length>
<Color>Blue</Color>
<Diameter>0.25 in</Diameter>
<Weight>1.5 oz</Weight>
```

```
<ItemID>
    <ItemID>1234</ItemID>
    <PartNo>1234</PartNo>
    <InvNum>1234</InvNum>
</ItemID>
```

```
<ItemSummary>
    <ItemID>1234</ItemID>
    <Desc>Blue Stick Pen</Desc>
    <Version>2</Version>
    <Length>8.0 in</Length>
    <Color>Blue</Color>
    <Diameter>0.25 in</Diameter>
    <Weight>1.5 oz</Weight>
</ItemSummary>
```

FIGURE 8.4

List of Elements vs Logical Groupings of Elements

A parent element might contain one child element, multiple and repeating occurrences of a child element, multiple and uniquely named elements, or no elements at all. When multiple child elements are encapsulated by the same parent element, and they are placed at the same level of "nesting," they are considered to be siblings. Each child element can also define another hierarchy that includes its own child elements, and so on. This capability of XML allows for different logical groupings of elements and potentially each with their own structures and substructures. There is no specified limit to the number of elements or the depth at which elements can be nested in an XML message. However, there may be advantages to setting a reasonable limit to the depth of nesting, which is described in Chapter 19, "Performance Analysis and Optimization Techniques."

Another message design consideration is that a data service might acquire data values of the same basic context but from different data sources (e.g., < ItemID >1234< /ItemID >, < PartNo >1234< /PartNo >, and < InvNum >1234< /InvNum >). Each of these elements can be carried in the same reply message, or the designer might decide to only carry one standard element. For the latter example, the single standard element should be derived from the enterprise canonical model. The data service will then need to invoke or include some type of transformation behavior to resolve among the different element names. Alternatively, the service designer may decide to carry all of the elements in the message. Carrying all of these elements in the message as one list of same-level children with the Reply element creates a confusing message and complicates navigation of those message elements for consumers. A more effective approach is to logically group and nest related elements as children under other parent elements.

While designing a hierarchical message is not the same as creating a relational data model or designing a data at rest source, there are a few synergies. A modeled data entity is also a logical grouping of attributes that help to describe and characterize the entity. A parent XML element with a logical collection of nested child elements can be thought of as roughly analogous. The child elements that are nested within the parent element are usually related or of some conceptually similar context. For the example where all of the elements are carried in the message, the service designer might design a parent element of name Item ID ("< ItemID/ >") and then nest the different elements as children within it (e.g., < ItemID >1234< /ItemID >, < PartNo >1234< /PartNo >, and < InvNum >1234 < /InvNum >). It is important to note that in a relational data model, the assignment of attributes to an entity and the relationships between entities comply with a set of rules, whereas XML parent and nested child elements are not explicit data modeling constructs and comply only with the syntactical rules of XML and of any referenced and constraining XML Schemas (see Figure 8.4).

As an alternative to elements, another type of XML container is the attribute, not to be confused with data modeling attributes. Attributes are similar to elements in that they can contain data values, and several of the constraints that apply to XML elements also apply to XML attributes. However, attributes are not defined as standalone containers. That is, an attribute must be defined specifically to an element (not nested as a child within a parent element). Attributes also follow the "attribute-value-pair" syntax ("attributeA="123"), where elements follow the open and close tag syntax ("< elementA >123< /elementA >").

XML elements are hierarchical and result in a more intuitive message structure. The open and close tags around each data value are also intuitive and, from a more technical perspective, help to simplify the over-the-wire representation of the message. As a result, XML elements should be exploited as the primary data containers for a Web service message.

Beginning the service interface design process with XML-encoded prototype canonical messages is a powerful and recommended approach. However, it is not a trivial exercise. A good Web service interface design will require compliance with core SOA principles (interoperability and loose coupling) and a consideration for resolving and avoiding data impedance.

8.2 TOP-DOWN CANONICAL MESSAGE DESIGN

SOA and Web services can be designed using several different approaches. One is to begin the service design process by developing the service behavior (object classes and code), and then to later generate the service interface from that code. A similar design technique can be applied when wrapping existing or legacy applications for use as a service. This is often referred to as bottom-up service design. While the bottom-up approach can be effective, it tends to be more focused on a specific and intended service deployment and does not consider the exchange or sharing of standardized information between consumers and services, and across systems and applications. Since the bottom-up approach starts with service behavior, it also does not easily recognize nor address future and unknown requirements for additional data in the service interface.

Alternative to the bottom-up design approach is the top-down approach (also known as design by contract). With the top-down design approach, service design starts with a focus on the service interface and the information contained in the request and reply messages that will move between consumers and services. The rationale for the top-down approach is that for the message information exchanged between service collaborators, the operations on that information represent a more real-world view of the servicing requirements and behavior. The top-down design approach also recognizes that over time, there will be new and as of yet unknown information that is required by consumers. The ability to later add information can be designed into the service interface and messages (known as extension points).

As described earlier, top-down design can begin with either the crafting of XML Schemas that will describe and constrain the Web service interface or with the design of prototype messages that will then be used to create the XML Schemas. For the seasoned practitioner, starting with design of the XML Schemas for the interface can be an effective approach. However, these XML Schemas are not as intuitive as an example XML message, and validation to requirements with the business subject matter experts can be difficult. A more intuitive approach is to start with an example XML message and then when the design is complete, either generate or craft the representative XML Schemas.

The canonical message design process is one of progressive refinement (see Figure 8.5). With each step, business and technical subject matter experts review the design artifacts and provide feedback. The service designer then enhances the canonical message examples and drives into a more technical and optimized design. Additional context is added along the way, and the example reply message is also refactored to reflect the service MEP (which may also include request and fault message designs).

Once the canonical message design has reached its final state, it becomes the model for creating the XML Schemas of the Web service interface. It is this final set of artifacts (canonical message design and representative XML Schemas) that are used to develop the WSDL and the service behavior.

8.2.1 Design requirements

Before starting development of an ad-hoc message as the example, the service designer will need to capture some basic service requirements. These requirements can be represented as use case models, data models, class models, message content lists, extractions from enterprise canonical models, or similar requirements and design artifacts. As long as the scope, content, context, and intent of the service are described, the canonical message design process can begin. In addition to basic requirements, there are several other important inputs to the process (see Figure 8.6).

Also, canonical message design is not exclusively an exercise in describing data content of a message. While that message content is absolutely critical, the design process also needs to consider the types of consumers that might invoke the service, the types of consumer and service interactions (MEPs), naming and metadata to help resolve impedance, and guidance to comply with core SOA principles. The basic service requirements (the representative need or problem to be resolved) is combined with this additional design criteria (design constraints and guidance), as the input to the canonical message design process.

The information requirements for the service are often associated with the intended service operations. Together, they serve as the scope for the service, and both are used as input to the design process. The intended service operations reflect the behavior that will be applied to the information content of the message, or as a result will produce the information content. The service operations may be specified by a verb or reflect an action to be taken. The most basic operations are classified as CRUD (Create, Read, Update, and Delete). These verbs are common across data services and may apply to business services and, in some cases, even to utility services as well (see Table 8.1). The CRUD analogy can also be extended to include a more specific set of operations, including extensions

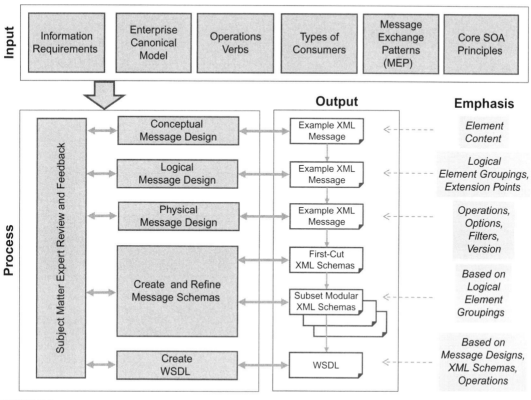

FIGURE 8.5

The Canonical Message Design Process

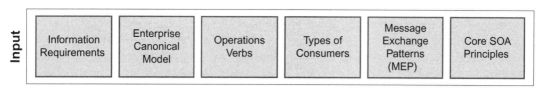

FIGURE 8.6

Canonical Message Design Process Requirements and Input

to "Read" such as "List" (where list results in multiple instances of information in the response) and "Search" (allowing for varied find criteria). Operations verbs should not be selected at random. They should be derived from a standard list, and all services should then exploit that standard list of verbs.

During development of the canonical message design, named elements will be added to an example message and populated with sample data. The intent is to represent a working example of a message that will move between the consumer and service. Similar to the operations verbs, element names

Table 8.1 List of Extended Operations and Common Verbs

CRUD Operation	Common Verbs (use only one from the list)
Create	Add, Create, Insert, Maintain
Read	Get, Read, Retrieve, Select
Update	Update, Modify, Change, Maintain
Delete	Delete, Remove, Kill, Eliminate
Check	Check, Check Exists, Check Duplicates
Correlate	Correlate, Synchronize
List	List, Set
Metadata	Info, About, Metadata
Ad Hoc Query	Query, Select
Search	Search, Find, Seek
Validate	Validate, Verify, Parse
Replicate	Copy, Replicate
Move	Move, Transport, Relocate

should be derived from a standard and easily recognized by business and technical subject matter experts. Reusing element names and metadata from the enterprise canonical model also provides consistency and avoids proliferation of enterprise integration problems from one-off data definitions.

Also of importance is the metadata that describes and constrains the data values for each element of the message. Basic examples of element metadata include the data type, length, and allowable values for each element. To represent real-world examples, the sample data values used to populate the canonical message design must comply with this metadata. The enterprise canonical model should serve as the source for those standard element names and the representative metadata.

The potential types of consumers will also influence the canonical message design. If the consumer is a new, object-oriented application that was specifically engineered to comply with core SOA principles, the canonical message design will be less complex. However, already existing or legacy consumers and those with limited support for Web service interactions will introduce complexity to the service design and the service interface. The canonical message design might need to account for these complexities and include technical elements as processing options to allow a broad base of consumers to interact with the service. Recognizing the consumer types as input to the process can play a significant role during the physical message design step.

The intended interaction between consumers and the service also serve as part of the requirements input to the canonical message design process. This interaction is described by an MEP with the most common example being request-reply. With a request-reply MEP, two separate messages will be designed (the request and the reply). With an asynchronous fire-and-forget MEP, only a request message is required. Error behavior and the resulting fault message will also be important but can be addressed after the canonical message design has been completed. If the type of consumer and service interaction is unknown at the outset of the design process, a recommendation is to assume a request-reply MEP, and to start with the reply message. Message types (request, reply, and fault) also map to intrinsic WSDL declarations, which is a last step in the canonical message design process.

Although not directly reflected as element content, the core SOA principles are critical guidance that should be considered throughout the design process. Compliance with these principles will help to ensure that the service and the service interface are optimized. Of significant importance are the interoperability and the loose-coupling principles. The canonical message design should always consider that multiple consumers from different systems and platforms and potentially using different technology will invoke the service. Compliance with Web services standards provides significant support for interoperability, but design techniques such as allowing for unique requirements of legacy consumers will also extend the interoperability principle. However, incorporating design elements into the message and interface for unique requirements that might be specific to only one or two consumers might impact the ability of other consumers to use the service. The canonical message design should avoid anything that would specifically couple a consumer to the service or that will prohibit the service from use by other consumers or being extended later.

8.2.2 Conceptual message design

The first attempt at developing a canonical message design will be conceptual with a focus on the information content of the message, rather than technical elements. Although the canonical message design contains only the information content of the message, it should be a syntactically correct and "well-formed" XML message. That is, it should comply with the syntactical and structural rules of XML. The canonical message design will also require review by business and technology subject matter experts, and may result in enhancement.

The prototype XML message that represents the canonical message design can be handcrafted using a simple text editor. However, the ability to check for syntactical correctness as the message design proceeds can become complex, and the example message will be prone to error. A more effective approach is to use an XML Editor tool such as XML Spy from Altova (Copyright 2003-2008 Altova GmbH, reprinted with permission of Altova). The XML Spy tool not only allows the designer to check the message for syntactical well-formedness, but also provides "helpers" and editor capabilities such as tabbed indenting of nested child elements that can enhance the visual layout of the example message (see Figure 8.7).

To start the conceptual message design process, the service designer will acquire the consumer information requirements. These information elements might be explicit element definitions, a list of element names, an attributed data model, or some other representation. Once collected, the information requirements are mapped and aligned with the enterprise canonical model. The service designer will identify existing elements and reuse those element names and metadata. This avoids adding variations of already defined data and metadata. The service designer might also identify other information elements from the canonical model that are required dependencies of an information element. In this case, the service designer will capture and reuse those additional elements and include them in the conceptual message design. Where a required information element might not exist in the enterprise canonical model, the service designer will validate the definition and then add it to the enterprise canonical model for later reuse by other services. Adding the new element to the enterprise canonical model will also require governance to avoid redundancy and ensure a high level of data quality.

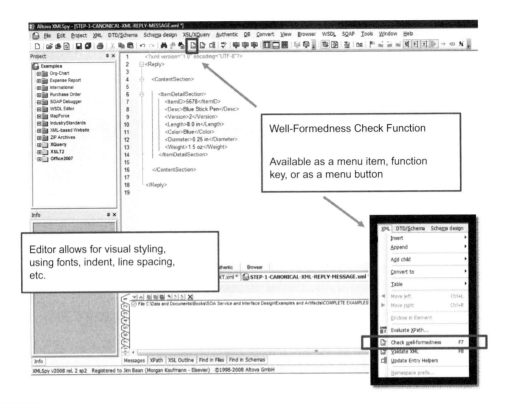

FIGURE 8.7

Well-Formedness Checking with XML Spy from Altova (Copyright 2003-2008 Altova GmbH, reprinted with permission of Altova)

To simplify later message design steps, elements that exhibit affinity or dependency can be collected into some initial groupings that are intuitive and obvious. During this step of the canonical message design process, these groupings are purely conceptual and for convenience. They will be subject to change in later steps.

The individual information elements will then be represented in the canonical message as syntactical XML elements, with open and close element tags. Element names derived from the enterprise canonical model will be reused. To further clarify the information elements of the message, example data values should also be included. The data values should also comply with the metadata rules and constraints defined to the enterprise canonical model. The combination of XML message elements and example data values will enrich the message design and further support review and validation by subject matter experts. The example data values can also be used in later steps to create XML Schemas and verify correctness.

Another important consideration is the need to repeat an element in the message (referred to as "cardinality" or from an object-oriented perspective as "multiplicity"). Some data and metadata practices will dictate that every element of the message must be uniquely named. This can avoid ambiguity of message content and also defines a static number of repeating elements. An alternative, more

```
        Uniquely Named, Multiple Elements                 Same Named, Repeating Elements

  <PostalAddress>                                 <PostalAddress>
     <AddressLine1>123 Main St.</AddressLine1>       <StreetAddress>123 Main St.</StreetAddress>
     <AddressLine2>Unit 12</AddressLine2>            <StreetAddress>Unit 12</StreetAddress>
     <AddressLine3>Mail Stop 6</AddressLine3>        <StreetAddress>Mail Stop 6</StreetAddress>
  </PostalAddress>                                </PostalAddress>
```

Each child element of <PostalAddress/> is a   *<StreetAddress/> element is allowed to repeat 3*
separate and uniquely named element in this   *times with parent <PostalAddress/> element, in*
example   *this example*

FIGURE 8.8

Repeating Message Elements

effective, approach is to carefully evaluate and allow a named element to repeat (with the same name). This capability of XML is only supported with elements and not allowed for attributes. The required and the maximum allowed number of repeating element occurrences are syntactically declared in the XML Schema, which is created in a later design step. A common example of repeating message elements is for a postal address (see Figure 8.8). The street address lines of the address can be defined as individual and uniquely named elements, or as repeating same named elements of the message. Where appropriate, repeating elements of the same name is a more flexible and powerful design pattern that exploits the capabilities of XML and XML Schemas. However, either technique will work.

The resulting XML message design should be a reasonable example of the information elements carried in a reply message. The use of XML as the medium for expressing the canonical message design provides a visual representation that can be easily reviewed and validated with both business and technology subject matter experts. The conceptual message design can also be refined and easily extended as the process continues (see Figure 8.9).

8.2.3 Logical message design

The emphasis of logical message design moves from a conceptual view of the message information items to a more structural view of the message that reflects variations between consumers. Some message interactions can involve a significant number of information elements being returned in the message. The number of message elements is not limited by Web services, the service interface, or XML. However, a large number of elements can result in a complex message and difficulty in validating the design. After implementation and during run-time, a complex message with a large number of elements can also impact performance and scalability of the service. During the logical message design process, the conceptual message design is further enhanced and potentially reorganized. The service designer will evaluate the conceptual message design and message elements. Groupings of elements might be evident and there might be other opportunities for further grouping. The service operations and the types of service consumers play a role in determining what groupings are required.

When the intended service operation type is a "read" of data, there are one or more data at rest sources where the underlying data will originate. The elements of the reply message will reflect the consumer requested information elements and the data values from those data sources as values of the corresponding message elements. The data values may have been acquired from several different

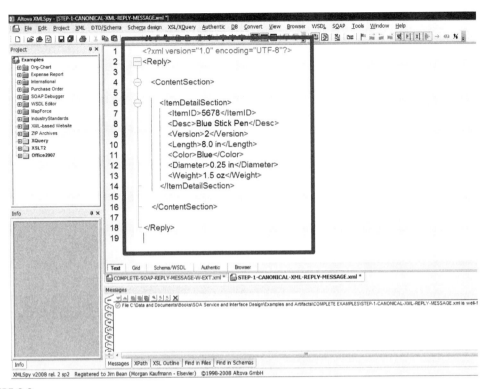

FIGURE 8.9

Conceptual Message Design (Copyright 2003-2008 Altova GmbH, reprinted with permission of Altova)

databases, tables, and columns. When collected together in one message, the reply represents a context. Effectively navigating that context might require different views of the returned message data.

Using an Item Master analogy, the returned message for a read type of operation will include several elements and data values related to an item. Depending upon the type, not all consumers will always require all elements of the reply message. Forcing all consumers to always receive and navigate the entire list of message elements is more of an anti-pattern. As an alternative, the reply message could be reorganized with element groupings of some contextual affinity, which helps to address the navigational requirements for different types of consumers.

A grouping of elements based upon contextual affinity would be similar to grouping measured dimensions of an item or product together (e.g., Item Length, Item Diameter, and Item Weight). Other examples of contextual groupings would be a summary collection of Item elements (e.g., Item ID and Item Description) and also a separate detail collection of Item elements (e.g., Item ID, Item Description, Item Version, Item Length, Item Color, Item Diameter, and Item Weight). Where logical groupings are defined, the conceptual message design from the previous process step will be extended to include parent elements (one for each required grouping). The elements of those groups are then repositioned and nested as child elements (see Figure 8.10).

Contextual Grouping of Elements   Navigational Groupings of Elements

```
<?xml version="1.0" encoding="UTF-8"?>
<Reply>

  <ContentSection>

    <ItemDetailSection>
      <ItemID>5678</ItemID>
      <Desc>Blue Stick Pen</Desc>
      <Version>2</Version>
      <Color>Blue</Color>

      <MeasuredDimensions>
        <Length>8.0 in</Length>
        <Diameter>0.25 in</Diameter>
        <Weight>1.5 oz</Weight>
      </MeasuredDimensions>

    </ItemDetailSection>

  </ContentSection>

</Reply>
```

```
<?xml version="1.0" encoding="UTF-8"?>
<Reply>

  <ContentSection>

    <ItemSummarySection>
      <ItemID>5678</ItemID>
      <Desc>Blue Stick Pen</Desc>
    </ItemSummarySection>

    <ItemDetailSection>
      <ItemID>5678</ItemID>
      <Desc>Blue Stick Pen</Desc>
      <Version>2</Version>
      <Length>8.0 in</Length>
      <Color>Blue</Color>
      <Diameter>0.25 in</Diameter>
      <Weight>1.5 oz</Weight>
    </ItemDetailSection>

  </ContentSection>

</Reply>
```

FIGURE 8.10

Logical Element Groupings

Not all services or all service messages will require both summary and detail element groupings. Also, the service designer should comply with the SOA loose-coupling principle and not define a message with every possible grouping of elements for each possible consumer. Rather, there will be obvious and common sense patterns that reflect real-world affinities and also navigational element groups that can be used by many different types of service consumers. Also, while caution is advised, some elements can be located within multiple groups. As an example, the Item ID element is an identifier for each Item and roughly analogous to a primary key of a database table. This element is a good candidate to repeat in all logical element groupings of the example message.

Another important logical message design activity is to anticipate future requirements and allow for as of yet unknown elements being added to the message. This activity is subjective and requires more of an architectural perspective. The service designer will need to balance between known and discretely defined requirements and the potential for new elements that might be required later.

The intent of this activity is not to blindly guess at elements that might be of future interest and to include them in the message design. Rather, the service designer should acknowledge that change and future additions are inevitable, and identify where such including those additions might make sense in context of the logical element groupings. If the service designer cannot conceptualize where such additions might be needed, information elements added to the overall message context should be allowed.

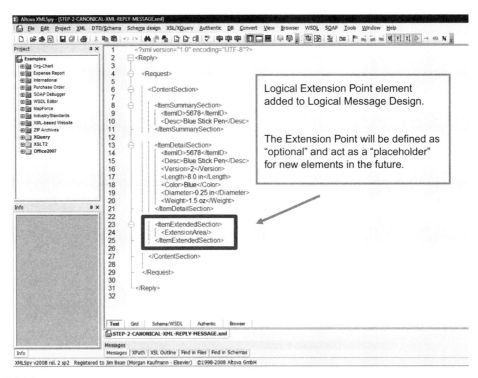

FIGURE 8.11

Logical Extension Point Element (Copyright 2003-2008 Altova GmbH, reprinted with permission of Altova)

Where such additions are anticipated, a new element to represent an "extension point" should be added to the message (see Figure 8.11). The extension point elements will also be parent elements for logical groupings, but additional content of each extension point will remain undefined and empty. As the XML Schemas are defined in later steps, these extension points will be defined as "optional" and not required to be included or appear in the message. They act as more of a future placeholder and can be later extended with a design pattern known as wildcard extension. Wildcard extension is described in Chapter 13, "The Interface and Change."

Like the conceptual message design, the logical design also requires review by business and technology subject matter experts. They might identify additional logical element groupings or extension points, and they might recommend additional information elements that were not originally included in the service requirements. The example XML message should again be checked for well-formedness and the result representing a completed logical message design.

8.2.4 Physical message design

Conceptual and logical message design emphasizes more of the business context of the message, whereas physical message design extends into the more technical aspects of the service interface. For the logical groupings of elements that have been defined and validated, consumers will need a method of specifying which are being requested in the reply. The service will also need a method of identifying what element data the consumer is requesting. While the conceptual and logical message designs have focused on the reply message, this same content serves to guide the request message.

For a consumer to inform the service of what is being requested, it will need to include some contextual information in the request. Using an example of a service to read and return Item Master data, the consumer will need to specify the operation ("Get") and also any identifying data that are required to find the desired Item. The consumer-requested operation will be included as new request message elements, while the identifying data elements will be reused from the previously defined reply message content (elements such as "< ItemID/ >"). The granularity of the service scope can also play a role with requested operations. Some services will be defined as a low level of granularity where each operation is supported by a separate and unique service. In this case, adding requested operation elements is not necessary. However, for other services the service granularity might be mixed or coarse-grained, where multiple operations are supported. Operations can also be supported by WSDL declarations and service ports. These are explicit operations, and the consumer does not need to include the operation verb in the message. Rather, the target endpoint location of the request message and port address will identify which service operation is being requested. Alternatively, if multiple service operations are supported as internal service behavior and yet defined to a single endpoint and port, the requested operation is data value that is incorporated within the message context. This is also referred to as "operations overloading" as described in Chapter 14, "Service Operations and Overloading."

As a recommendation, the service interface design should allow for multiple service operations to be specified as message content (operations overloading). Each operation element can be further described or classified, which acts as a service design requirement and clarifies the operation types. The consumer-requested operations will later be transitioned to service behavior and logic and may be used to determine the granularity of the service (e.g., one operation per service, or a single service that allows multiple operations).

The consumer will also need a method of requesting which of the logical element groupings defined in the previous message design step, should be returned in the reply message. The requested element groupings will be by request message information "filters." Some consumers might require multiple element groupings returned in the reply message, and each will be requested by a separate filter element (such as "< IncludeItemSummary/ > and < IncludeItemDetail/ >").

While considering the potential types of consumers and variations for processing data from the service, there will also be several technical requirements that can be resolved with request message options. As an example, some types of legacy consumers might have limitations for processing XML messages. These types of legacy consumers might be implemented with procedural languages such as COBOL and are then only able to process a positional list of XML message elements. This type of processing can require that all elements of the reply must be included and present in the message, even when a message element is empty of any data value. This scenario is further complicated when elements of the reply message are defined as optional. For these legacy types of consumers, this requires that the service must be aware of the consumer's processing limitation and force empty elements to be populated in the reply message. Having an option to force empty elements in a reply message can also help with testing the service by allowing for consistent message content in the reply, whereas object-oriented applications can map to and process XML messages that are more flexible, where optional and empty elements are not required in the reply message. For the latter example, this results in a more optimized and "lean" reply message.

Other types of request options allow consumers to correlate updates across data at rest sources (typically limited to Create, Update, and Delete operations) and to include pre-update and post-update images as elements in the reply message. Another type of option allows the consumer to request the technical processing status in the reply, such as the SQL State for a data service. Still other options can allow the original request message data to be echoed back in the reply message and to include metadata for each data element of the reply, such as its data type, length, and—if defined to an array—the data value location in the array.

A superset of suggested request message options includes the following:

- Include Processing Status in the Reply
- Include Empty Containers
- Fix the Length of Data Values
- Synchronize Updates Using Supplied Correlation ID
- Echo All Request Content in the Reply
- Include Pre-Update Image in the Reply
- Include Post-Update Image in the Reply
- Include Element Metadata in the Reply

As a general design recommendation, request message options (see Figure 8.12) should be intuitively named and valued only with a binary response (e.g., Yes, No – or – True, False). Depending upon the supported service operations and MEP, not all options will apply. It is also important to note

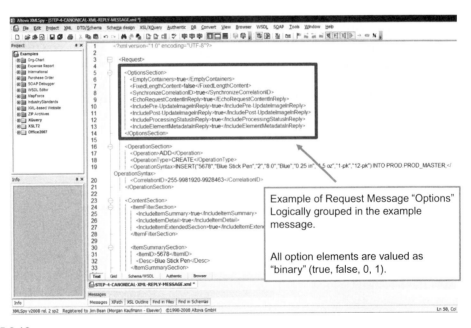

FIGURE 8.12

Example Message Options (Copyright 2003-2008 Altova GmbH, reprinted with permission of Altova)

that designing for these operations, options, and filters in the service interface still requires service behavior and processing logic. The service implementation for these options might require implementation of helper classes to assist with the service behavior. Depending upon the types of options, these helper classes would then also be candidates for reuse across other services.

A read operation is the simplest and easily understood example. A more complex servicing scenario such as a "Create" (Add) operation will extend the message design and, depending upon the options allowed in the request, the reply message design might need to include pre-update and post-update images of the data elements. Once the request options have been defined, reviewed, and validated, the representative elements are included in the canonical message design (see Example 8.1). The service interface designer will then separate the canonical message design into two separate request and reply message designs. Portions of the two resulting message designs will be similar and will borrow from many of the same elements. As the interface schemas are developed and the service behavior is realized as classes, the common element definitions, subset schemas, and object classes become reuse candidates. The consumer-requested operations, options, navigational filters, and processing status elements should be logically grouped and nested within parent elements of the canonical request message design. Similar to the previous reply message design, example data values should also be provided for all request message elements (see Example 8.2).

Example 8.1
Canonical Request Message Design

```
<?xml version="1.0"encoding="UTF-8"?>
-<REQUEST:Request xsi:schemaLocation="http://Widget-Example.com/Inventory/Product/Add/
REQUEST AddNewProductRequestMessage.xsd http://Widget-Example.com/Inventory/ExtensionURI
ItemInventoryExtensionV1.1.xsd">
<xmlns:REQUEST="http://Widget-Example.com/Inventory/Product/Add/REQUEST" xmlns:VERSION="http://
Widget-Example.com/Version" xmlns:OPTIONS="http://Widget-Example.com/Options" xmlns:
OPERATIONS="http://Widget-Example.com/Operations" xmlns:FILTER="http://Widget-Example.
com/Inventory/Product/Add/Filter" xmlns:CONTENT="http://Widget-Example.com/Inventory/Product/
Add/Content" xmlns:EXT="http://Widget-Example.com/Inventory/ExtensionURI" xmlns:xsi="http://www.
w3.org/2001/XMLSchema-instance">
- <VERSION:VersionSection>
 <VERSION:RequestMajorVersion>1</VERSION:RequestMajorVersion>
 <VERSION:RequestMinorVersion>0</VERSION:RequestMinorVersion>
 </VERSION:VersionSection>
- <OPTIONS:OptionsSection>
 <OPTIONS:EmptyContainers>true</OPTIONS:EmptyContainers>
 <OPTIONS:FixedLengthContent>false</OPTIONS:FixedLengthContent>
 <OPTIONS:SynchronizeCorrelationID>true</OPTIONS:SynchronizeCorrelationID>
 <OPTIONS:EchoRequestContentInReply>true</OPTIONS:EchoRequestContentInReply>
 <OPTIONS:IncludePre-UpdateImageInReply>true</OPTIONS:IncludePre-UpdateImageInReply>
 <OPTIONS:IncludePost-UpdateImageInReply>true</OPTIONS:
IncludePost-UpdateImageInReply>
```

```
<OPTIONS:IncludeProcessingStatusInReply>true</OPTIONS:IncludeProcessingStatusInReply>
<OPTIONS:IncludeElementMetadataInReply<true</OPTIONS:IncludeElementMetadataInReply>
</OPTIONS:OptionsSection>
- <OPERATIONS:OperationSection>
<OPERATIONS:Operation>ADD</OPERATIONS:Operation>
<OPERATIONS:OperationType>CREATE</OPERATIONS:OperationType>
<OPERATIONS:OperationSyntax>INSERT("5678","Blue Stick Pen","2","8.0","Blue","0.25 in","1.5 oz","1-
pk","12-pk") INTO PROD.PROD_MASTER;</OPERATIONS:OperationSyntax>
<OPERATIONS:CorrelationID>255-9981920-9928463</OPERATIONS:CorrelationID>
</OPERATIONS:OperationSection>
- <CONTENT:ContentSection>
- <FILTER:ItemFilterSection>
<FILTER:IncludeItemSummary>true</FILTER:IncludeItemSummary>
<FILTER:IncludeItemDetail>true</FILTER:IncludeItemDetail>
<FILTER:IncludeItemExtendedSection>true</FILTER:IncludeItemExtendedSection>
</FILTER:ItemFilterSection>
- <CONTENT:ItemSummarySection>
<CONTENT:ItemID>5678</CONTENT:ItemID>
<CONTENT:Desc>Blue Stick Pen</CONTENT:Desc>
</CONTENT:ItemSummarySection>
- <CONTENT:ItemDetailSection>
<CONTENT:ItemID>5678</CONTENT:ItemID>
<CONTENT:Desc>Blue Stick Pen</CONTENT:Desc>
<CONTENT:Version>2</CONTENT:Version>
<CONTENT:Length>8.0 in</CONTENT:Length>
<CONTENT:Color>Blue</CONTENT:Color>
<CONTENT:Diameter>0.25 in</CONTENT:Diameter>
<CONTENT:Weight>1.5 oz</CONTENT:Weight>
</CONTENT:ItemDetailSection>
- <!--
==================================================
====
-->
- <!--
The following example message content is illustrative only
-->
- <!--
The content of the extension area is undefined and unknown
-->
- <!--
==================================================
====
-->
- <CONTENT:ItemExtendedSection>
```

- <CONTENT:ExtensionArea>
- <EXT:Version>
<EXT:MajorVerNo>**1**</EXT:MajorVerNo>
<EXT:MinorVerNo>**1**</EXT:MinorVerNo>
</EXT:Version>
<EXT:BasePackagingUnit>**1–pk**</EXT:BasePackagingUnit>
<EXT:BulkPackagingUnit>**12–pk**</EXT:BulkPackagingUnit>
</CONTENT:ExtensionArea>
</CONTENT:ItemExtendedSection>
</CONTENT:ContentSection>
</REQUEST:Request

Example 8.2
Canonical Reply Message Design
 <?xml version="1.0" encoding="UTF-8" ?>
 − <REPLY:Reply xsi:schemaLocation="**http://Widget-Example.com/Inventory/Product/Add/REPLY
AddNewProductReplyMessage.xsd http://Widget-Example.com/Inventory/ExtensionURI ItemInventoryExtension
V1.1.xsd**" xmlns:REPLY="**http://Widget-Example.com/Inventory/Product/Add/REPLY**" xmlns:STATUS="**http://
Widget-Example.com/Status**" xmlns:REQUEST="**http://Widget-Example.com/Inventory/Product/Add/REQUEST**"
xmlns:VERSION="**http://Widget-Example.com/Version**" xmlns:OPTIONS="**http://Widget-Example.com/
Options**" xmlns:OPERATIONS="**http://Widget-Example.com/Operations**" xmlns:FILTER="**http://Widget-
Example.com/Inventory/Product/Add/Filter**" xmlns:CONTENT="**http://Widget-Example.com/Inventory/Product/
Add/Content**" xmlns:METADATA="**http://Widget-Example.com/Metadata**" xmlns:EXT="**http://Widget-Example.
com/Inventory/ExtensionURI**" xmlns:xsi="**http://www.w3.org/2001/XMLSchema-instance**">
- <STATUS:Status>
- <STATUS:ReplyProcessStatus>
<STATUS:AddEngineeringMaster>**Success**</STATUS:AddEngineeringMaster>
<STATUS:AddProductCatalog>**Success**</STATUS:AddProductCatalog>
<STATUS:AddNewProduct>**Success**</STATUS:AddNewProduct>
</STATUS:ReplyProcessStatus>
- <STATUS:ReplySQLStateStatus>
<STATUS:EngineeringMaster>**00000**</STATUS:EngineeringMaster>
<STATUS:ProductCatalog>**00000**</STATUS:ProductCatalog>
</STATUS:ReplySQLStateStatus>
</STATUS:Status>
- <REQUEST:Request>
- <VERSION:VersionSection>
<VERSION:RequestMajorVersion>**1**</VERSION:RequestMajorVersion>
<VERSION:RequestMinorVersion>**0**</VERSION:RequestMinorVersion>
</VERSION:VersionSection>
- <OPTIONS:OptionsSection>
<OPTIONS:EmptyContainers>**true**</OPTIONS:EmptyContainers>

```
<OPTIONS:FixedLengthContent>false</OPTIONS:FixedLengthContent>
<OPTIONS:SynchronizeCorrelationID>true</OPTIONS:SynchronizeCorrelationID>
<OPTIONS:EchoRequestContentInReply>true</OPTIONS:EchoRequestContentInReply>
<OPTIONS:IncludePre-UpdateImageInReply>true</OPTIONS:
IncludePre-UpdateImageInReply>
<OPTIONS:IncludePost-UpdateImageInReply>true</OPTIONS:
IncludePost-UpdateImageInReply>
<OPTIONS:IncludeProcessingStatusInReply>true</OPTIONS:IncludeProcessingStatusInReply>
<OPTIONS:IncludeElementMetadataInReply>true</OPTIONS:IncludeElementMetadataInReply>
</OPTIONS:OptionsSection>
- <OPERATIONS:OperationSection>
<OPERATIONS:Operation>ADD</OPERATIONS:Operation>
<OPERATIONS:OperationType>CREATE</OPERATIONS:OperationType>
<OPERATIONS:OperationSyntax>INSERT("5678","Blue Stick Pen","2","8.0","Blue","0.25 in","1.5 oz","1-
pk","12-pk") INTO PROD.PROD_MASTER;</OPERATIONS:OperationSyntax>
<OPERATIONS:CorrelationID>255-9981920-9928463</OPERATIONS:CorrelationID>
</OPERATIONS:OperationSection>
- <CONTENT:ContentSection>
- <FILTER:ItemFilterSection>
<FILTER:IncludeItemSummary>true</FILTER:IncludeItemSummary>
<FILTER:IncludeItemDetail>true</FILTER:IncludeItemDetail>
<FILTER:IncludeItemExtendedSection>true</FILTER:IncludeItemExtendedSection>
</FILTER:ItemFilterSection>
- <CONTENT:ItemSummarySection>
<CONTENT:ItemID>5678</CONTENT:ItemID>
<CONTENT:Desc>Blue Stick Pen</CONTENT:Desc>
</CONTENT:ItemSummarySection>
- <CONTENT:ItemDetailSection>
<CONTENT:ItemID>5678</CONTENT:ItemID>
<CONTENT:Desc>Blue Stick Pen</CONTENT:Desc>
<CONTENT:Version>2</CONTENT:Version>
<CONTENT:Length>8.0 in</CONTENT:Length>
<CONTENT:Color>Blue</CONTENT:Color>
<CONTENT:Diameter>0.25 in</CONTENT:Diameter>
<CONTENT:Weight>1.5 oz</CONTENT:Weight>
</CONTENT:ItemDetailSection>
- <!--
============================================================
====
-->
- <!--
The following example message content is illustrative only
-->
- <!--
```

The content of the extension area is undefined and unknown
-->
- <!--
 =
 = = = =
-->
- <CONTENT:ItemExtendedSection>
- <CONTENT:ExtensionArea>
- <EXT:Version>
 <EXT:MajorVerNo>**1**</EXT:MajorVerNo>
 <EXT:MinorVerNo>**1**</EXT:MinorVerNo>
 </EXT:Version>
 <EXT:BasePackagingUnit>**1–pk**</EXT:BasePackagingUnit>
 <EXT:BulkPackagingUnit>**12–pk**</EXT:BulkPackagingUnit>
 </CONTENT:ExtensionArea>
 </CONTENT:ItemExtendedSection>
 </CONTENT:ContentSection>
 </REQUEST:Request>
- <REPLY:ReplyContent>
- <REPLY:ReplyPre-UpdateImage>
- <CONTENT:ContentSection>
- <CONTENT:ItemSummarySection>
 <CONTENT:ItemID>**0000**</CONTENT:ItemID>
 <CONTENT:Desc />
 </CONTENT:ItemSummarySection>
- <CONTENT:ItemDetailSection>
 <CONTENT:ItemID>**0000**</CONTENT:ItemID>
 <CONTENT:Desc />
 <CONTENT:Version>**0**</CONTENT:Version>
 <CONTENT:Length>**0**</CONTENT:Length>
 <CONTENT:Color />
 <CONTENT:Diameter>**0**</CONTENT:Diameter>
 <CONTENT:Weight>**0**</CONTENT:Weight>
 </CONTENT:ItemDetailSection>
- <!--
 =
 = = = =
-->
- <!--
The following example message content is illustrative only
-->
- <!--
The content of the extension area is undefined and unknown
-->

```
- <!--
============================================================
====
-->
- <CONTENT:ItemExtendedSection>
  <CONTENT:ExtensionArea />
  </CONTENT:ItemExtendedSection>
  </CONTENT:ContentSection>
  </REPLY:ReplyPre-UpdateImage>
- <REPLY:ReplyPost-UpdateImage>
- <CONTENT:ContentSection>
- <CONTENT:ItemSummarySection>
  <CONTENT:ItemID>5678</CONTENT:ItemID>
  <CONTENT:Desc>Blue Stick Pen</CONTENT:Desc>
  </CONTENT:ItemSummarySection>
- <CONTENT:ItemDetailSection>
  <CONTENT:ItemID>5678</CONTENT:ItemID>
  <CONTENT:Desc>Blue Stick Pen</CONTENT:Desc>
  <CONTENT:Version>2</CONTENT:Version>
  <CONTENT:Length>8.0 in</CONTENT:Length>
  <CONTENT:Color>Blue</CONTENT:Color>
  <CONTENT:Diameter>0.25 in</CONTENT:Diameter>
  <CONTENT:Weight>1.5 oz</CONTENT:Weight>
  </CONTENT:ItemDetailSection>
- <!--
============================================================
====
-->
- <!--
The following example message content is illustrative only
-->
- <!--
The content of the extension area is undefined and unknown
-->
- <!--
============================================================
====
-->
- <CONTENT:ItemExtendedSection>
- <CONTENT:ExtensionArea>
- <EXT:Version>
  <EXT:MajorVerNo>1</EXT:MajorVerNo>
  <EXT:MinorVerNo>1</EXT:MinorVerNo>
  </EXT:Version>
```

```
<EXT:BasePackagingUnit>1–pk</EXT:BasePackagingUnit>
<EXT:BulkPackagingUnit>12–pk</EXT:BulkPackagingUnit>
</CONTENT:ExtensionArea>
</CONTENT:ItemExtendedSection>
</CONTENT:ContentSection>
</REPLY:ReplyPost-UpdateImage>
- <REPLY:ReplyElementMetadata>
- <METADATA:MetadataSection>
<METADATA:ElementName>ItemID</METADATA:ElementName>
<METADATA:ElementStructureType>Atomic Element</METADATA:ElementStructureType>
<METADATA:ParentElementName />
<METADATA:ElementDataType>Integer</METADATA:ElementDataType>
<METADATA:ElementLength>4</METADATA:ElementLength>
<METADATA:ElementScale>0</METADATA:ElementScale>
<METADATA:ElementPrecision>0</METADATA:ElementPrecision>
<METADATA:ElementSensitivity>Public</METADATA:ElementSensitivity>
<METADATA:ElementArrayDimensionXCount>0</METADATA:ElementArrayDimensionXCount>
<METADATA:ElementArrayDimensionYCount>0</METADATA:ElementArrayDimensionYCount>
<METADATA:ElementArrayDimensionZCount>0</METADATA:ElementArrayDimensionZCount>
<METADATA:ElementArrayMaxEntriesCount>0</METADATA:ElementArrayMaxEntriesCount>
</METADATA:MetadataSection>
</REPLY:ReplyElementMetadata>
</REPLY:ReplyContent>
</REPLY:Reply
```

In addition to a request and reply MEP interface, a fault message should also be designed (see Example 8.3). The fault message design will describe the potential outcome of service errors. Web service protocols such as SOAP[3] have a predefined message structure to ensure that participants in the service collaboration have the same understanding of an error. Additionally, the SOAP fault structure allows for service-specific and implementation-specific error reporting as well. These service-specific fault elements can include error codes and descriptions that are unique to the enterprise.

Example 8.3
Canonical Fault Message Design

```
<?xml version="1.0" encoding="UTF-8" ?>
- <FAULT:Fault xsi:schemaLocation="http://Widget-Example.com/Fault AddNewProductFault.xsd" xmlns:
FAULT="http://Widget-Example.com/Fault" xmlns:xsi="http://www.w3.org/2001/XMLSchema-instance">
- <!--
=================================================
-->
```

```
- <!--
The structure of this Fault message design, includes the
-->
- <!--
predefined structure of a SOAP Fault message as context
-->
- <!--
================================================
-->
- <FAULT:Code>
 <FAULT:Value>Receiver</FAULT:Value>
- <FAULT:Subcode>
 <FAULT:Value />
 </FAULT:Subcode>
 </FAULT:Code>
- <FAULT:Reason>
 <FAULT:Text>Data Service was unable find the requested ItemID</FAULT:Text>
 </FAULT:Reason>
 <FAULT:Node>text</FAULT:Node>
 <FAULT:Role>text</FAULT:Role>
- <FAULT:Detail>
 <FAULT:ItemIDFault>5678</FAULT:ItemIDFault>
 <FAULT:FaultCode>02000</FAULT:FaultCode>
 <FAULT:FaultType>No Data</FAULT:FaultType>
 <FAULT:FaultDesc>ItemID Not Found</FAULT:FaultDesc>
 </FAULT:Detail>
 </FAULT:Fault>
```

The final canonical message designs should continue through a final review with business stakeholders (to verify the business data elements and logical groupings) and technical subject matter experts (to verify the request options, navigational filters, and operations elements). The canonical message designs should also again be checked for syntactical compliance with XML. This will become important when creating the corresponding XML Schemas.

8.2.5 Create and refine message schemas

The completed and syntactically verified XML messages now serve as the final canonical message designs. These messages can also be used to begin the creation of service interface XML Schemas, which are the "terms and conditions" of the service contract, and the context of the service interface. To simplify the schema creation process, tools such as XML Spy (Copyright 2003-2008 Altova GmbH, reprinted with permission of Altova) can be used to automatically generate a first-cut XML Schema, using each of the canonical message designs as input (see Figure 8.13).

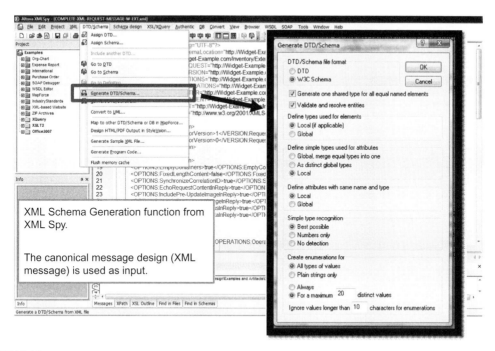

FIGURE 8.13

Generating an XML Schema with XML Spy from Altova (Copyright 2003-2008 Altova GmbH, reprinted with permission of Altova)

Each of the resulting XML Schemas for a canonical message design will be a representative set of metadata and constraints for the XML message. While many XML edit tools can tremendously simplify this part of the process and generate much of the needed schema syntax, these XML Schemas should be considered as a first-cut or initial draft. Additional clean-up and revision will be necessary to further streamline and optimize the resulting schemas.

The clean-up process can include reorganizing the schema declarations to follow whatever standard or template has been implemented by the enterprise. Some organizations have elected to organize the XML Schemas element and complexType declarations alphabetically by name, while others organize and group declarations by granularity. Taking the additional time to reorganize the generated schema syntax will simplify later interface maintenance and extension. A lengthy XML Schema that is maintained by someone other than the original designer can be a complex exercise. Reorganizing the schema can help to avoid that complexity.

Once the generated XML schemas have been reviewed and refined to more accurately reflect the canonical message designs, there is another opportunity for enhancement. The logical groupings message elements defined in the earlier logical message design process step will also serve as candidates to modularize as component XML Schemas. The rationale for this activity is that these separate component XML Schemas will become largely reusable in the development of other services.

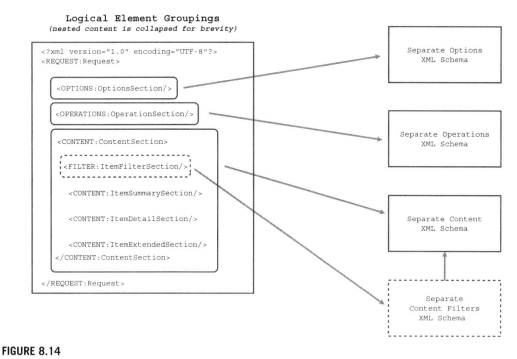

FIGURE 8.14

Logical Element Groupings as Separate XML Schemas

Once the schema declarations are extracted and reformatted as separate component XML Schemas, they are then referenced by an XML Schema "include" ($<$ xs:include/ $>$") or "import" ("$<$ xs:import/ $>$") declaration from the original or main schema. This allows the declarations of the separate schemas to be referenced as subsets and reused by the main schema. It also allows each of the separate subset schemas to become candidates for "reuse by reference and assembly" in other service interfaces. Several techniques for XML Schemas reuse are described in Chapter 12, "Schema Assembly and Reuse."

Not all logical groupings of elements are good candidates to extract and define as separate XML Schemas. Performing an assessment for potential reuse is recommended (see Figure 8.14). As an example, it might make sense to redefine the logical grouping of Item Master Elements as a separate XML Schema, but it might be suboptimal to separate some of more fine-grained groupings of elements such as item color and weight. The balance between granularity and reuse, and the selection of logical element groupings can be somewhat experiential and subjective. The service designer can use the canonical message model to identify the candidate logical element groupings, and then to validate them with business and technology subject matter experts.

8.2.6 Create WSDL

The refined and enhanced XML Schemas represent the terms and conditions of the service contract, and the context of the service interface. However, the technical interface artifact representing the over-all contract is still required. For a Web service, that artifact is a WSDL. The WSDL references or has embedded the XML Schemas of the interface. The structures, elements, and declarations of those schemas are used during run-time to instantiate and to consume the message content. The WSDL also defines the operations supported by the service, and exposed to consumers as MEPs. The service designer can exploit the canonical message designs and harvest much of the information required to create the WSDL.

Like the XML Schemas, a WSDL can often be generated from tooling. However, this will usually require a model of the service behavior as well as the XML Schemas as input. Alternatively, the service designer can craft the WSDL syntax by starting with a template, using an editor such as XML Spy (Copyright 2003-2008 Altova GmbH, reprinted with permission of Altova), and selecting the "new" types of document as "wsdl, Web Services Description Language." The designer can then add the requisite WSDL content.

The WSDL also describes other service interface information such as the protocol and binding (SOAP in the case of a Web service) and the document style (document-literal is recommended for WSDL 1.1 and is the assumed style for WSDL 2.0). The WSDL also includes other more technical information such as the operations URL and service address or endpoint. This information is usually derived as part of the service configuration and deployment process and may be added later.

The outcome of this process is a complete and syntactically correct set of canonical message designs (as prototype XML message examples), a set of XML Schemas, and the overall WSDL representing the service interface. These artifacts are the foundation for continued top-down service design and are then used to derive the service behavior.

8.3 MODEL-DRIVEN INTERFACE DESIGN

So far, canonical message design has relied upon a combination of designer (architect or designer or developer), service interface tooling (such as an XML editor), and a design to interface contract process (design the interface first and then the service behavior). An alternative service design process is one where a set of enterprise canonical models is used to extract content and then generate all of the service interface artifacts with tooling and technology (including the XML Schemas and WSDL). This alternative process is often referred to as model-driven interface design and is derived from similar model-driven development processes. The rational for this model-driven process is rapid delivery since the models already contain and define the context as attributed metadata for the service interface.

Using an enterprise canonical model for model-driven development is also a top-down design process. However, rather than starting with example XML messages, the service designer uses models and tooling to select the required interface content and then to forward-engineer or generate the service interface artifacts (WSDL and XML Schemas). Given the graphical simplicity and intuitiveness of a model, this approach is very effective. It also allows business and technology representatives to actively participate throughout the process. However, there are also some challenges and potential complexities.

Depending upon the type of model used to generate the interface and the tooling, the resulting service interface artifacts may not be optimized. The model-driven development generation process will rarely take into account different types of consumers and their unique requirements such as allowing for options and filters. The service interface generated from the canonical model might include a significant amount of message content that is not required by many consumers. Without the ability of a consumer to specify an option or filter, this can result in significant message size as payload sent across the wire and potentially resulting in latency.

Another potential area of concern with model-driven development is the ability to later modify and extend a service to accommodate new message elements. As later requirements and changes are introduced, the model must be modified and updated and then restart the process from the beginning with tasks for change assessment, model analysis, content extraction, and artifact generation process. While the refined models and use of tooling can help with the process, the result is often another new service interface and service (e.g., an additional, new version of the previously defined service). With this scenario, previously existing consumers may need to revise their internal logic as well as rebind to the interface in order to accommodate these changes.

This is not criticism of enterprise canonical models or of model-driven development. Rather, it is a set of observations and experiences. Disputing the value of an enterprise canonical model for service design is unwarranted. Rather, a canonical model is of tremendous value to any service interface and service design process. The challenges are in service interface and message optimization and also in the ability to extend a service while mitigating impact to already-existing service consumers. One recommendation that exploits the value of the canonical model and also allows for more optimized services is to use the model-driven and generated service interface artifacts as an initial baseline, template or reference. This approach is similar to the canonical message design process already described and allows the initial design steps to exploit the more graphical models of the enterprise canonical.

The graphical nature of the enterprise canonical models (visually represented as boxes, lines, and similar) allows the designer to rapidly select content for the service interface, and without the need to create a syntactical XML representation. The model-driven development process will then generate the XML Schema artifacts from that selected model content. However, rather than relying on these artifacts as deployment ready, these artifacts serve as a baseline or initial first cut and are then reviewed, refactored, and optimized using an XML edit tool. The resulting XML Schemas then vary from their original model generated state, but they will also be highly optimized. Similar to the canonical message design process, the service designer can also then include extension points and standard options and filters and incorporate them into the service behavior and processing. The value from model-driven development and delivery is retained, the process is rapid, the enterprise canonical models are exploited, content is reused, and the service and service interface are optimized.

SUMMARY

Canonical message design relies upon and exploits the structural, semantic, and intuitive characteristics of XML. Prototype message examples are crafted, reviewed, and refined to reflect combinations of information content requirements, operations, MEPs, and core SOA principles as design guidance. A number of best practice recommendations can help to enhance the process:

- Begin with a fully populated reply message as a prototype example.
- Use XML elements over that of XML attributes as the primary type of data container.
- Rely on repeating elements of the same name (cardinality) rather than multiple and uniquely named elements for the same type of data.
- Apply a standardized set of operations verbs.

The example messages and element content also take advantage of the metadata already defined to the enterprise canonical model. These example messages are reviewed throughout the process by combinations of business and technology subject matter experts, with continuous feedback and enhancement. With each step of the canonical message design process, the messages are refined and begin to reflect technical aspects of the service interface.

The resulting message examples (request, reply, and fault) are in combination the canonical message design for the service interface. They also serve as the basis from which the XML Schemas are initially generated and then further refactored. They also serve as criteria to guide decomposition into more modular and reusable schemas that can be referenced and assembled for the interface and reused by other services as well. The combination of the canonical message designs and the XML Schemas is then used to drive the creation of the service interface WSDL, which completes the design of service interface artifacts.

An alternative to canonical message design is model-driven development. With this approach, an enterprise canonical model (usually with a graphic representation of some type) is used to visually select the required information items from the model and rapidly forward-engineer the service interface with tooling (including the XML Schemas and WSDL). Model-driven development is becoming a somewhat common approach to service development. However, there are resulting challenges and also opportunities to improve and optimize the result. Rather than solely relying on the generated artifacts as end-state deployable, these same artifacts can be further enhanced and optimized, similar to the process described for canonical message design. With this hybrid approach, the enterprise canonical models are exploited, content is reused, and the service and service interface are optimized.

REFERENCES

1. Mitra N, Lafon Y, eds. "SOAP Version 1.2 Part 0: Primer. 2nd ed." (W3C, April 27, 2007). <http://www.w3.org/TR/soap12-part0/>.

2. Chinnici R, Moreau J-J, Ryman A, Weerawarana S, eds. "Web Services Description Language (WSDL) Version 2.0 Part 1: Core Language" (W3C, June 26, 2007). <http://www.w3.org/TR/wsdl20/>.

3. Mitra N, Lafon Y, eds. "SOAP Version 1.2 Part 0: Primer. 2nd ed." (W3C, April 27, 2007). <http://www.w3.org/TR/soap12-part0/>.

The Enterprise Taxonomy

One important measure of SOA effectiveness is evidenced by the simplicity in which services are discovered and then reused to resolve a new servicing requirement. Prior to initiating a new service design effort, the service designer should first seek out other existing services to determine if they might resolve their new requirements. When an already existing service has been found, it is then validated to the new requirements, and, if acceptable, it is then reused, rather than designing and developing a new service.

As SOA and servicing gain momentum in the enterprise, the number of available services can grow quite quickly. Attempting to find a service among many can become a daunting exercise. A potential failure of SOA and service design is a proliferation of new services that are the same as or closely similar to those that already exist. This failure can be attributed to an inability to describe a service when implemented and published, in a manner that supports rapid discovery as a candidate service of interest.

Prerequisites to discovering an already existing service are a Service Registry and Service Repository (SRR). As described in Chapter 1, "SOA – A Common Sense Definition," the service registry is similar to a directory or listing of available services. Once a service has been developed, information about that service is published to the service registry (see Figure 9.1). The service interface artifacts for that service are also persisted in a corresponding service artifact repository (in a Web Service analogy, the artifacts are the WSDL and XML Schemas). The ability to later discover a published service relies upon a taxonomy that effectively describes it.

A simple definition of taxonomy is "a listing of words or phrases that classify and describe something." However, this definition might be somewhat ambiguous, as a simple name can describe something. A more formal definition of taxonomy is "Taxonomy is the practice and science of classification. The word comes from the Greek *taxis* (meaning 'order,' 'arrangement') and *nomos* ('law' or 'science'). Taxonomies, or taxonomic schemes, are composed of taxonomic units known as taxa (singular taxon), or kinds of things that are arranged frequently in a hierarchical structure."[1] Perhaps the most common example of an applied taxonomy is that of "Linnean" taxonomy, which is used to describe species of organisms. This technique is a hierarchy of classifications that describe Kingdom, Phylum, Class, and so on. Each progressively lower level of the taxonomy becomes more specific and differentiates from the parent level above.

An example service that adds new products can be classified in several different ways. First the service has a name (such as "AddNewProduct"). While this name is descriptive and represents the

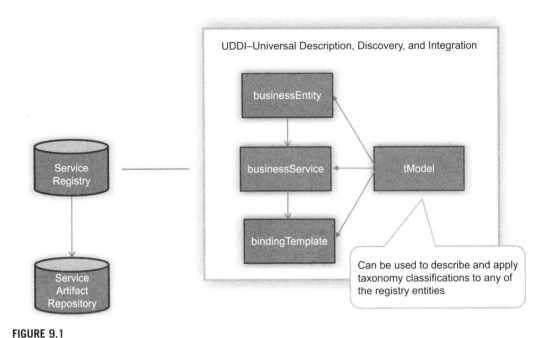

FIGURE 9.1

SRR – Service Registry and Repository

function of the service, it might not be sufficient to support later discovery. In addition to the service name, it can also be classified by the data on which it acts ("Product"), and it can also be classified based on the action taken (the service operation being "Add"). If used as taxonomic information when publishing the service, it can later be discovered by searching for either the service name or these two words ("Product" and "Add").

In a real-world SOA and servicing environment, using only these two words ("Product" or "Add") might not be sufficient. In a larger enterprise, there might be many services that act upon products and that have been published to the service registry with these same two taxonomy entries. As a result, returning a list of many different services from a simple search for "Add" and "Product" would then complicate the service reuse process, rather than enable it.

A more effective approach to classification of services for later discovery and reuse would be to apply a defined taxonomy in which the words and phrases are not only descriptive but also commonly used. Publication of a service would include applying representative and descriptive keyword entries that best describe the service. Even in the largest and diverse enterprise, this approach allows a service to be easily discovered.

The taxonomy should not be restricted to only a single set of words, phrases, and descriptions. While it might be desirable that everyone in the enterprise speaks the same common business language, the reality is that most enterprises have evolved to include different products, lines of business, and organizations, each of which will often have its own derivative business language. Yet, even with these variations, the same basic context is usually common (e.g., a "Product" described by the Product Marketing Group will be similar to an "Item" described by the Engineering organization).

Applied Taxonomy Entries

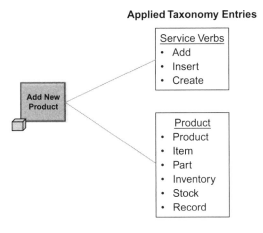

FIGURE 9.2

Taxonomy Entries Applied to the Example Add New Product Service

The application of an enterprise taxonomy is quite powerful for service publications. However, it also can result in complexity if not properly managed. Publishing a service with an overly verbose list of taxonomy entries can be just as ineffective as only classifying the service with one or two entries. If the example Add New Product service were classified with every possible descriptive term and variation, an entry for that service would be returned to many searches where it most likely does not apply (see Figure 9.2). Rather than develop the taxonomy in an ad hoc manner, it should contain entries that describe something of importance to the business and entries that are easily recognized and frequently used.

9.1 FOCUS ON COMMON BUSINESS LANGUAGE FOR DISCOVERY

Development of the enterprise taxonomy requires a base language (spoken and written). For North American and largely English-speaking enterprises, English is the natural choice. For multinational organizations, variations of language can be used. However, with multilanguage taxonomies, there are additional complexities to consider such as character encoding, directionality, and collation sequence.

For each enterprise taxonomy classification, a set of base terms as words or phrases is required. Base terms should be explicit in their context and clearly represent an example of the classification in which they are included (see Figure 9.3). These terms must be stated using the base language and, where appropriate, should be entries within a classification in the singular rather than plural (e.g., "Product" rather than "Products"). However, the names of classifications (the groupings of entries) themselves may optionally be stated in the plural. In rare instances, such as polysemes, it is possible for a base term entry in one classification to also be an entry in another classification. However, this should be avoided.

The taxonomy should also consider multiple classifications. Each classification is a logical or contextual grouping of words or phrases. Most service registries, especially those that are compliant with the UDDI specification,[2] will incorporate a standard set of classifications such as Country and Industry Classifications (sometimes referred to as "value sets"). In addition to these standard taxonomy classifications, a set of enterprise-specific classifications and entries will need to be developed.

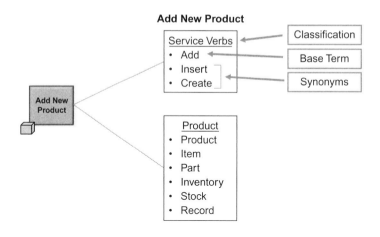

FIGURE 9.3

Example of Taxonomy Classifications and Base Terms

The enterprise canonical model can be exploited for classifications and for the base terms that represent them. Classifications are contextual groupings or categories. Recommended types of taxonomy classifications include service verbs, line of business, application, system, and subject area. Subject area names represent things such as products, locations, people, events, and so on.

For each classification, a base term is required. This base term can be thought of as the word, term, or phrase that best represents the classification to which it will be assigned. Later variations such as synonyms will be derived from the base terms. Base terms can often be derived from the canonical model as the major entity and base class names. Each classification and base term should be reviewed by both business and technology subject matter experts.

In a UDDI-compliant service registry, the classifications are implemented as a "tModel" and a corresponding set of values to represent the base term and any alternatives. Each registry tModel can hold multiple entries. Several UDDI-compliant service registry products also provide the ability to reference and relate tModels as a hierarchy. One registry tModel can refer to other tModels, and so on. A tModel for "Subject Area" might refer to other subordinate tModels for Products, Locations, Parties, Events, Financial Instruments, and so on. Within each of these classifications, a base term and alternative terms describe the category (see Figure 9.4).

When applied to service publications, the registry and tModel-based taxonomy support later service discovery and reuse. As the inventory of discoverable and reusable Web services increases, extending the taxonomy can also increase the effectiveness.

9.2 BROADENING AND EXTENDING THE TAXONOMY

One of the challenges that face every business enterprise is that of everyday, operational language. What is named and recognized as an "Item" by the Product Marketing group might be known as a "Part" to the Engineering organization. Examples like these might seem nonsensical when initially encountered. However, they are formidable obstacles to discovery and reuse. Although the initial

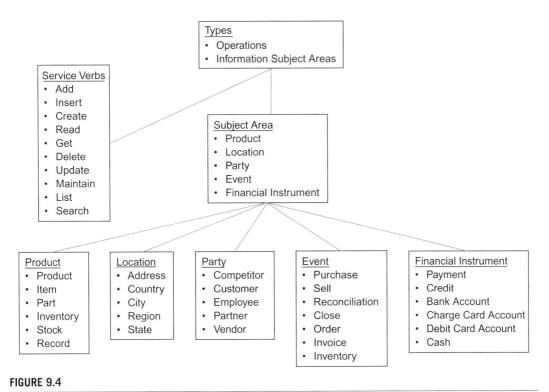

FIGURE 9.4

Example Taxonomy Hierarchy

taxonomy and service registry tModels might be populated with a base term and what appears to be a reasonable selection of alternatives, they might only be recognized by a portion of the enterprise. This is more often the case when the enterprise has multiple lines of business or somewhat autonomous business divisions. If a data service to add products ("Add New Product") were already designed and implemented for the Engineering organization, and a new Add Items service was required by the Product Marketing group, the existing "AddNewProduct" service might not be discovered as potentially reusable if the designer were only searching for "Item."

While it would be highly advantageous that every business organization, every technology organization, and every employee of the enterprise used the same language without variation, it is not a reality. Further, some of the differences in language and terminology used by different areas of the business provide a semantic richness that is valuable and helps to differentiate the enterprise from its competition. Narrowing the number of business language variations can help simplify the taxonomy. However, there is also value in carefully evaluating and including other language variations. Using the earlier example of "Part" and "Item", a service that was classified by both entries would have a higher potential for later discovery.

To resolve semantic impedance and optimize service discovery, synonyms are a recommended approach. A synonym is a language construct that can be thought of as an alternative term, an alias, or an "also known as" term. Using the previous Add New Product service example, the base term might be a "Part" and a valid synonym would be an "Item". Other synonyms could be applied as well and might include entries such as Product, Inventory, Stock, and Record.

Additional examples of synonyms can include more fine-grained entries such as the names of message elements from the service interface (see Figure 9.5). If the Add New Product service interface included a request message with elements for "< ItemID/ >" or "< PartNo/ >", the tag names from these elements would also serve as valuable terms for describing the service publication. The taxonomy entries to classify the service would then include "ItemID" and "PartNo".

So far, the examples of service discovery described the need for a person to search for services. This example is similar to using a Web-based search engine and providing a few search keywords. An architect, designer, or other individual would search the service registry using a variety of key words that map to the taxonomy entries applied to services of interest. The list of services returned from this discovery exercise would then require a deeper validation to determine if they meet the requirements of the new project. If yes, then the service is subject to reuse. If not, then the search would continue, or a new service would be developed.

For a human to interact with the service registry and to search for (discover) services as candidate for reuse, the example taxonomy works well. However, the evolution of SOA and services will also begin to consider more dynamic discovery. That is, where services collaborate with other services and depending upon the characteristics of that interaction, a service might seek out still other services to exploit without human intervention. This new example is sometimes described by an enterprise-to-enterprise collaboration and choreography, where services might begin to seek out and exploit services outside the enterprise. Automated discovery of services using a taxonomy is not a reality today, but it is often stated as a future direction of SOA.

To support this future dynamic lookup and interaction between services, the notion of a taxonomy will require extension beyond that of base terms and synonyms. For an automated service to navigate

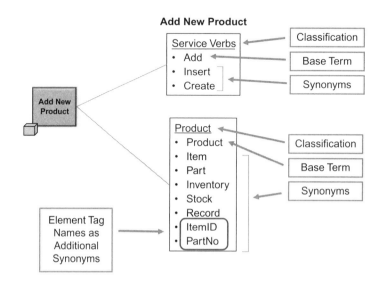

FIGURE 9.5

Example Taxonomy Application with Element Names as Synonyms

among service registries and their published services, the ambiguity of language will need to be resolved. In part, dynamic service collaborations will require a more explicit set of definitions and partners identified in the higher level service definition (both in the BPEL and the WSDLs). Where a service will need to perform service discovery, it will also need to resolve language ambiguity and complexity. This requires a set of semantics that are more robust than a taxonomy with a base term and synonyms. Extending the taxonomy to include antonyms and polysemes provides some potential.

Antonyms would be implemented as another and separate set of taxonomy classifications. Rather than including alternative names or aliases, the antonym classifications would include words and phrases that are explicitly different from the base terms. These opposites can help to narrow the automated service discovery process by excluding services that match to one or more antonyms.

Polysemes are another potential approach to resolve linguistic complexity. A polyseme describes a common word spelling, often with a common pronunciation, but where instances of the words are of different definitions. An example polyseme might be the word "Bank." Although of the same spelling and pronunciation, different applications of the word "Bank" might refer to a financial institution, a building or location of a financial institution, the action of collecting and storing something, a set of technologies (as in a bank of servers), or the shore of a river. While doubtful that a river bank would have a representative service publication in a business context, there might be services for the management and retrieval of information about financial institutions and their physical locations. Distinguishing between these different "Bank"-related services would be simple for a person but might be complicated for an automated discovery process.

While the importance of taxonomy extensions is not of significance today, as SOAs mature and we move toward more dynamic service collaborations and the notion of "semantic services," taxonomy extension will become more important.

9.3 REGISTRY ENTRIES AND DISCOVERY

The technology capabilities of the implemented registry technology will determine what additional taxonomy classifications and entries are supported. For most service registries, taxonomy entries are typically limited to a name-value-pair within a classification. Each entry of the pair would have a base term as the key value and also a corresponding key name. A common example of key values are standard code values or abbreviations. The corresponding key name for each key value is a short descriptive text name (for UDDI, limited to 255 characters). To help avoid misinterpretation or ambiguity, key names should be brief and concise. An example registry taxonomy might include "US States" as a further subtype classification of "Location". The key values for this classification would include state abbreviations such as "AZ", "IL", and "FL", while the names would be "Arizona", "Illinois", and "Florida" (respectively).

UDDI-compliant service registries define the taxonomy as a set of tModel structures. Each structure represents one of the taxonomy classifications and includes one or more key value and key name entries. When a service is published to the registry for later discovery, entries are selected from applicable taxonomy tModels and applied. UDDI-defined taxonomies can be applied to any of the registry entities, including businessEntity, businessService, and bindingTemplate.

The selected tModel entries are referenced within a categoryBag or identifierBag structure associated with each of the applicable UDDI entities. Multiple tModel entries can be applied, which allows a single service publication to be described in multiple ways (see Figure 9.6). A published service to add new products (AddNewProduct) might be described by categoryBag and tModel entries such as "Add", "Create", "Product", "Part", "Item", and so on.

The mechanical process for publishing a service varies with the registry technology product. Suffice to say that most all service registries include a user interface where the service characteristics and the location of the service interface WSDL from the service artifact repository are entered. The user can also search and select from the various taxonomy classifications and terms already defined to the registry, and apply them to each service as appropriate. Some registry products will also include a process by which the service interface WSDL is internally inspected, and the registry harvests and populates much of the required service publication data with the information found in the WSDL.

Regardless of the technology , in order to promote later reuse of a service, the service designer must take on a different perspective. That is, one of a potential service re-user. In this capacity, later discovery of the service might require broader or different business terminology. The designer would then need to carefully select and apply the appropriate business terms (including base terms and synonyms) to the service publication.

```
<businessService serviceKey="http://www.Widget-Example.com/Inventory/AddNewProduct"
           name="AddNewProduct">
  ...
    <categoryBag>

        <keyedReference
           keyName="Add"
           keyValue="Add"
           tModelKey="UDDI:ServiceVerbs"/>

        <keyedReference
           keyName="Create"
           keyValue="Create"
           tModelKey="UDDI:ServiceVerbs"/>

        <keyedReference
           keyName="Product"
           keyValue="Product"
           tModelKey="UDDI:Product"/>
        <keyedReference
           keyName="Part"
           keyValue="Part"
           tModelKey="UDDI:Product"/>

        <keyedReference
           keyName="Item"
           keyValue="Item"
           tModelKey="UDDI:Product"/>

        ...

    </categoryBag>        Subset fragment of example UDDI businessService publication

  ...
</businessService>
```

FIGURE 9.6

UDDI tModel and Service Publication

SUMMARY

One measure of effectiveness for SOA is the degree to which services are reused, that is, where an already defined service is discovered and harvested for use in a project other than the one from which it originated. The SRR is core to this service discovery and reuse process. However, in order for a service to be discovered, it must be described in a manner that allows other designers and architects to find it. An enterprise taxonomy provides this descriptive set of discovery characteristics.

The enterprise taxonomy is a collection of classifications and a set of descriptive word and phrase entries. Classifications can vary and are determined by the enterprise. Some enterprises might define classifications representing service verbs, line of business, application, system, and subject area. Within each of these classifications are further subclassifications and any number of descriptive entries. As an example, a taxonomy classification for "US States" might include entries for each of the US state abbreviations and corresponding state names. Another example might be a classification for service operations. The entries of this classification would include all of the potential operation verbs (e.g., Get, Read, Update, Maintain, Add, Insert, List, Search, etc.).

Synonyms can be used to effectively extend the taxonomy classifications and help to mitigate the complexities of language. For the moderate to large enterprise, what might seem like well-known and common business language actually includes any number of variants. While it would be of value to narrow the number of variations, some variations serve well as synonyms of the taxonomy and provide semantic richness. During publication of a service to the service registry, the application of these classifications and synonyms helps to facilitate later service discovery.

There is also a perspective that more dynamic sets of choreographed service interactions are a future step for SOA. With this model, services are discovered and collaborate in more of an automated manner. For a service to discover (search for) another service to invoke, even within a well-defined set of parameters, will require more explicit discovery and deeper resolution of language. In part, this is an extension of taxonomy, where constructs such as antonyms and polysemes may play a role. This future view of SOA is somewhat beyond the more practical use of services today, but it is often described as "things to come."

REFERENCES

1. Wikipedia contributors, "Taxonomy" (Wikipedia, The Free Encyclopedia, January 10, 2009). <http://en.wikipedia.org/w/index.php?title=Taxonomy&oldid=262704599>

2. "UDDI Version 3.0.2, UDDI Spec Technical Committee Draft" (Copyright © OASIS Open 2002–2004). <http://uddi.org/pubs/uddi_v3.htm> (October 19, 2004).

XML Schema Basics

XML Schema is defined by a set of specifications from the World Wide Web Consortium[1] and is used as a core metadata language to describe and constrain an XML instance such as a message. XML Schemas are requisite to Web services and participate in the definition of the Web service interface "contract." Like WSDL and SOAP, the syntax and encoding of an XML Schema is XML. As with any application of XML, this helps to promote interoperability. It also requires that the XML Schema language syntax complies with the syntactical rules of XML. This includes strict compliance with the open and close tag notation and the attribute-value-pair syntax.

The XML-encoded message is typically "consumed" by the receiving application. Depending on the Message Exchange Pattern (MEP), the source of the message, and the target, this could be either the service (as with receiving a new request message) or a consumer (as with receiving a reply or fault message returned from the service). To consume the XML message, an XML parser and a binding utility are required. This allows the internal object model of the application to consume or produce an XML message (see Figure 10.1). During run-time, this also allows the data value contents of the XML message to be extracted and used by the receiving application.

The XML encoded message and the XML Schema that was created to define and constrain it are typically separate artifacts. Checking that the XML-encoded message complies with XML Schemas requires a piece of technology known as a "parser" and an optional process known as validation. A validating XML Parser will compare the structure, semantics, and content of an XML-encoded message to the declarations and rules of a referenced XML Schema. When an infraction to an XML Schema declaration is encountered during the validation process, a resulting error or fault is raised to the validating application. The validating parser does not implement corrections to the message. There are a very few examples where a validating XML Parser will apply some type of change to the contents of an XML message. The few examples are default values, fixed values, and whitespace facets, which can be defined to an element or an attribute of the message.

Interestingly, there is no stated rule that an XML-encoded instance (e.g., a document, message, or similar) must always have a corresponding XML Schema, nor that a message must be validated with a parser when an XML Schema exists. An XML message could be defined loosely to an application without an XML Schema. However, without the corresponding XML Schema and parser validation, this allows the message and its contents to remain as largely unconstrained, which introduces the potential for anomaly. A design or coding error could easily introduce an invalid message structure or an anomalous data value to be passed between collaborators.

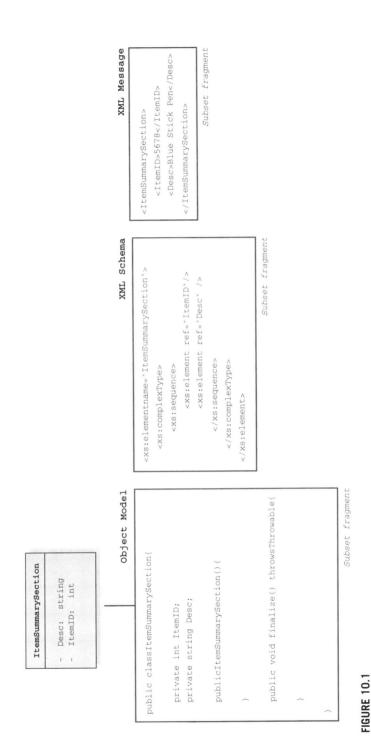

FIGURE 10.1

Consumer, XML Message, and XML Schema

From a service interface design perspective, the potential for error without a referenced XML Schema and validation begs for strict use of XML Schemas and parser validation of every message. Yet, validation is not without overhead. With validation, there are a number of design and architecture trade-offs. Depending upon the complexity and size of the message and its referenced XML Schemas, parser validation can introduce run-time latency. As a result, it is important to consider the use cases under which parser validation is of the most importance. If one of the collaborators (either a consumer or the service) is defined outside the enterprise, as would be the case with a Business-to-Business (B2B) service interaction, there is little ability to force strict compliance with the service interface and contract. In this scenario, parser validation of the incoming messages from the external B2B partner is likely to be of significant importance.

XML Schemas are perhaps one of the most powerful examples of a metadata language. Similar to a programming language, an XML Schema can be complex and difficult to maintain. While the capabilities of XML Schema are many, a general recommendation is to focus on these core declarations:

- element
- attribute
- simpleType
- complexType
- group

Within these basic schema declarations are additional attributes and options that allow for variation and help to describe almost any Web service interfaces and metadata constraints.

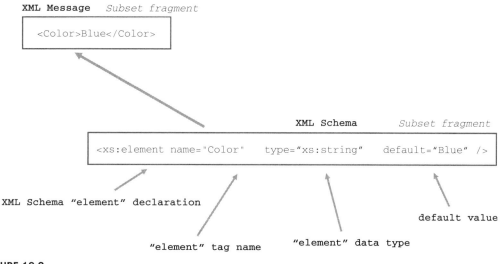

FIGURE 10.2

Example XML Element and the Corresponding XML Schema Declaration

10.1 ELEMENTS

An "element" is a fundamental data container of an XML message. That is, an element can be declared to contain a data value, another element (when defined as a complexType), a combination of a data value and another element, or if allowed to remain empty, nothing at all. In the XML message, an element has a syntactical tag set (open and close tags), and the element tag includes a name. The tag name is defined in the XML Schema (see Figure 10.2). Other XML Schema declarations are then applied to that named element to describe metadata characteristics such as the allowable data type, a default value, or a fixed value.

A default value is used by the validating parser when the corresponding XML message element does not contain any data value. The default value is then substituted by the parser in the object model and passed to the consuming application (see Figure 10.3). However, in this example, the XML message itself is not actually modified to include the default value. Similarly, when a fixed value is defined to an element in the XML Schema, the validating parser will substitute it for an existing value (or for an empty element) and pass it to the consuming application. An element of the message can also be declared in the XML Schema as mandatory or optional (sometimes described as modality), and repeating (known as cardinality). However, these element declarations are specific to elements nested within a structure such as a complexType or a group (which are described in Sections 10.4 and 10.5, respectively).

During parser validation (or binding to the interface), the name of the element, its location in a message, its relationship to other elements in the message hierarchy, and its metadata characteristics such as the data type and length, are used to determine whether the corresponding element in the message and its data value contents meet the expectations of the service interface. This further supports the

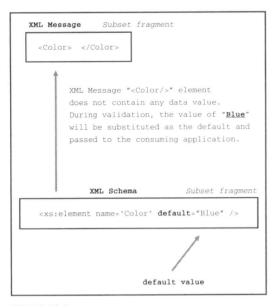 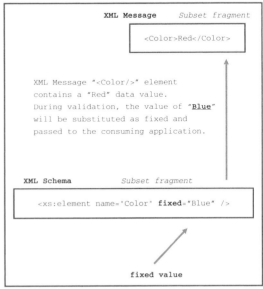

FIGURE 10.3

Example of Element Default Value and Fixed Value

notion of a "contract" to ensure that the message is in compliance with the terms and conditions. The hierarchy of the XML message must be defined (e.g., a single root element, where any other elements are then nested as children and where those elements may also be defined to have child elements, etc.).

The constraints or rules defined by the XML Schema can be very prescriptive, or they can be loosely applied. As an example, an element could be defined with a name but not specify a data type or a default value (see Figure 10.4). With this example, a validating parser would be unable to determine whether a data value of the XML message element was actually numeric, a decimal, a date, a string, or compliant with a specific data type. The validating parser could only determine that the named element was defined to the message and located in the expected position of the message hierarchy. Alternatively, the XML Schemas could include a rigorous set of element declarations, where the named element also had a prescribed data type of integer and a default value of "123" provided back to the parsing application if no value was evident in the message for that element.

The granularity and degree to which XML Schema declarations as rules and constraints are prescriptive is left to the service interface designer. Where XML Schema declarations are more granular and prescriptive, the expectations of compliance between a message and the service interface contract become "tighter." From a data quality perspective, a more prescriptive service interface contract helps to avoid the proliferation of questionable data between service collaborators and their applications. Alternatively, a loose contract allows greater potential for anomaly.

An important consideration for service interface design is the broad impact of data anomalies in a message. With data at rest, a data value anomaly is typically found in a persisted store as a column or field value. The applications that acquire the data value from the data at rest source are then subject to that anomaly. Remediation for this type of anomaly is usually applied directly at the location

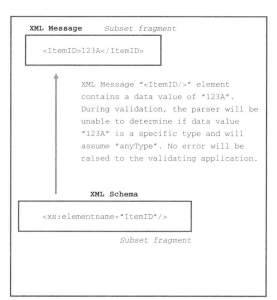
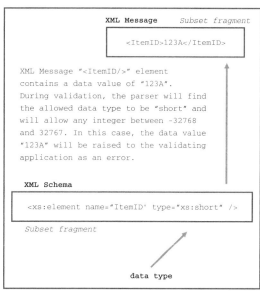

FIGURE 10.4

Prescriptive XML Schema Declarations

of or to the application that maintains the persisted data. Alternatively, an anomalous data value in a message is "in motion." That is, the message and its contained data are moved between the service and potentially many consumers. Once the message data is extracted by the message consumers, it can be persisted locally by those different consumers, or it might be passed on to other collaborators and applications. This scenario can result in a broad proliferation of message-based data anomalies throughout the enterprise. Regardless of whether the service designer or SOA architect has decided that messages will be validated or not, having a well-defined XML Schema with prescriptive element constraints is critical to effective service interface design.

10.2 ATTRIBUTES

Similar to elements, attributes also serve as data containers. While there are several similarities to elements, there are also significant differences. When defined by an XML Schema, and similar to an element declaration, an attribute can have a declared data type, a default value, and a fixed value (see Figure 10.5). The attribute can also be defined as being mandatory or optional. When mandatory, the attribute must appear in the XML message. When optional, the attribute may appear in the message but is not required to appear. An attribute cannot be defined by an XML Schema to exist in a corresponding XML message as a completely standalone container. Rather, an attribute is defined to appear within the context of an element in the XML message. Also, an attribute cannot be defined to repeat by name within the same XML element definition.

As an XML message data container, another area where an attribute varies from an element is in the message instance syntax. When instantiated in the XML message, attributes follow an attribute-value-pair syntax, where the attribute name is defined within the context of an owning element, followed by an equal sign ("="), and then a trailing data value within quotes (see Figure 10.6). However, the syntax for declaring an attribute within the corresponding XML Schema is similar to that of an element. The attribute declaration includes a name, and optionally a data type ("type"), a default value ("default"), a fixed value ("fixed"), and a modality value ("use").

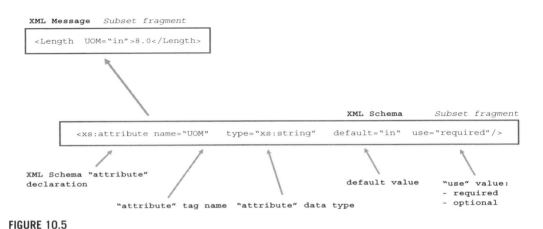

FIGURE 10.5

Example XML Attribute and the Corresponding XML Schema Declaration

One consideration when developing the canonical message design is balancing the amount of metadata content of the XML message to the expected data values held by elements and attributes (see Figure 10.7). This is sometimes referred to as the "tag-to-data ratio."[2] When the overall message size is large, and the number of tag name characters in a message is significantly greater than the amount of actual data, transporting the message across a network or ESB has the potential to introduce latency. Message elements that contain data values require both an open and a close tag, both of which include the tag name. Alternatively, an attribute in the message only includes the attribute tag name, an equal sign, and the data value in quotes, which is significantly less verbose than elements. For extremely large messages, the use of attributes as the prevailing type of data containers (rather than elements) can reduce the overall message size.

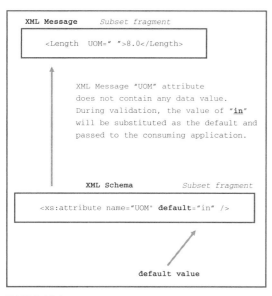
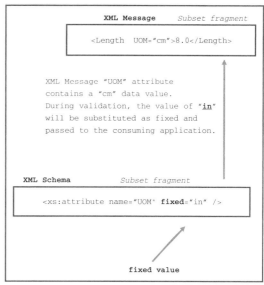

FIGURE 10.6

Example of Attribute Default Value and Fixed Value

XML Message *Subset fragment*
```
<ItemID>5678</ItemID>
<Desc>Blue Stick Pen</Desc>
```
Primarily an "element" model in the XML Message
20 Tag Name character count (metadata)
18 Data Value character count
20:18 Tag-to-Data Ratio

XML Message *Subset fragment*
```
<ItemID Desc="Blue Stick Pen" >5678</ItemID>
```
Primarily an "attribute" model in the XML Message
16 Tag Name character count (metadata)
18 Data Value character count
16:18 Tag-to-Data Ratio

FIGURE 10.7

Comparison of XML Message Elements to Attributes

However, even with the limited verbosity afforded by attributes in a message, the decision to choose between attributes and elements is not simple. A strong recommendation is to use elements as the prevailing type of data container for the content of the message. This is primarily due to the element tags, which also serve as delimiters for over-the-wire message formats, and elements can be defined to repeat by name, whereas attributes cannot.

10.3 SIMPLETYPES

Element and attribute data type declarations can be specified directly within the XML Schemas declaration, with the "type" attribute. The values for a type declaration can be an XML Schema defined data type, a named reference to a user-defined data type (known as a "simpleType"), or a named structure (known as a "complexType"). When a corresponding XML message is then parser validated to the XML Schema, an element or attribute data value will be checked against the declared data type (type attribute value). If the data value does not comply with the type, a parser error will be raised.

The data types that are defined to the XML Schemas language are comprehensive. They include base types, built-in primitive types, and built-in derived types.[3] The types are defined by a hierarchy and descend from the base types down into the derived types. At the top of the hierarchy is "anyType". As implied by the name, a data container declared as "anyType" can hold any value. A structure or "complexType" (e.g., where an element includes other nested elements) is also derived from the "anyType" data type. The XML Schema built-in primitive types cover the most common data types as supported by combinations of object and procedural languages, as well as by many database technologies.

Built-in types include the following:

- string
- duration
- dateTime
- time
- date
- gYearMonth
- gYear
- gMonthDay
- gDay
- gMonth
- boolean
- base64Binary
- float
- decimal
- double
- anyURI
- QName
- NOTATION

Other more fine-grained and further constrained data types are derived from the string and decimal types (known as "built-in derived types"). Examples of built-in derived string types include normalizedString, token, language, name, and so on. Examples of built-in derived decimal types are several numeric types such as integer, nonPositiveInteger, negativeInteger, long, int, short, byte, nonNegativeInteger, and so on. As with the anyType, the allowed data values for data types are somewhat implicit to the name. While the supported built-in and built-in derived types are extensive, XML Schemas also supports custom or user-defined data types.

A user-defined data type further restricts or extends a built-in XML Schema type as a "simpleType" declaration. A simpleType allows the service interface designer to create custom data types that might be specific to the enterprise or that reflect fine-grained data types of the enterprise canonical model. As an example, there might be an enterprise data standard for monetary data values that is applied to database monetary amount columns and fields (see Figure 10.8). Describing and constraining monetary amount values of an XML message requires a simpleType that includes a combination of the "decimal" data type, the total allowed or maximum number of digits, and the number of fractional digits. A user-defined or custom data type could be defined for an enterprise data standard that requires monetary amounts to allow a maximum of nine total numeric digits and two fractional digits (e.g., "9999999.99"). A simpleType could be defined with the XML Schemas supported decimal data type and with constraining facets for totalDigits and fractionDigits. When referenced by name as a type, this example data type can then be applied to any element or attribute as its data type.

XML Schema simpleType declarations can include several types of facets. Facets can be thought of as fine-grained metadata characteristics and constraints that further restrict a data type. Some facets can be applied to several different data types, while others are limited to a domain of similar types. As an example of the latter, the "fractionDigits" facet is useful for a decimal data type but doesn't work

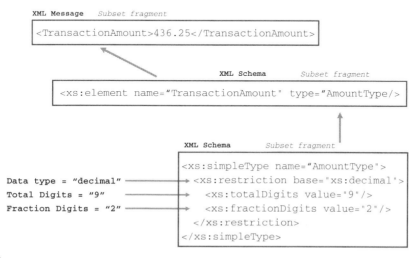

FIGURE 10.8

Example simpleType as a User-Defined Monetary Amount Data Type well for a "negativeInteger" type. In combinations with data types, facets can be used to create user-defined or custom data types. XML Schema facets include the following:

- length
- minLength
- maxLength
- minInclusive
- maxInclusive
- minExclusive
- maxExclusive
- totalDigits
- fractionDigits
- enumeration
- pattern
- whitespace

There are three length-related facets, which are all representative of positional character count. Length-related facets are most useful when applied to string data types and provide an additional length constraint (see Figure 10.9). The "length" facet specifies a fixed length. A value assigned to this facet describes that the data value of a corresponding XML message element or attribute must be of the specific length (similar to a "fixed length"). The "minLength" facet specifies a minimum length. A value assigned to this facet describes that the data value of a corresponding XML message element or attribute must be of at least the specified length (although it may be of a greater length). Alternatively, the "maxLength" facet specifies the maximum possible length of a data value. The minLength and maxLength facets can be combined within a single simpleType declaration to define a character length range.

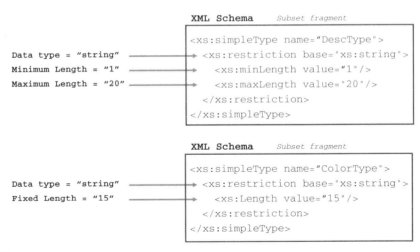

FIGURE 10.9

Example simpleType and Length Facets

Another use of the minLength facet is to specify that a data value is required. An element can be defined to an XML message as being mandatory by setting the XML Schema "minOccurs" attribute value to "1" (or greater). However, the minOccurs declaration only specifies that the element must be present in the XML message. It does not require that the element must also contain a data value (with minOccurs = "1", the element must appear as an element in the message, but it can remain empty of data). If the element also refers to a named simpleType that is defined with a minLength facet value of "1" (or greater), the corresponding XML message element must contain a data value.

Inclusive and exclusive facets provide a method of constraining data held by an element or attribute to a range of values (see Figure 10.10). When applied to a numeric data type, the "minInclusive" facet describes the minimum allowed data value. Alternatively, "maxInclusive" describes the maximum allowed data value. When declared as a pair within the same simpleType, they represent the allowable range of data values. The "minExclusive" and "maxExclusive" facets are similar. The minExclusive facet describes the minimum allowed data value as being greater than the facet declared value. The max-Exclusive facet describes the maximum allowed data value as being less than the facet declared value.

Another facet that is often used for custom or user-defined data types allows the service interface designer to specify a list of allowable data values (known as enumerations). As an example of possible use, "enumeration" values might include a list of predefined status codes, U.S. state names, or U.S. state abbreviations. These enumerations are not limited to codes or abbreviations, and they might also define more contextual values such as allowable text descriptions for color (see Figure 10.11). When parser validated, a corresponding XML message element value will be compared to the list of allowable enumeration values. If the data value does not match one of the values, a parser error is raised. The XML Schemas declared "enumeration" values are also specific to a data type. If the data type for an element is defined as "integer," a set of string or text character values would not be valid as enumerations.

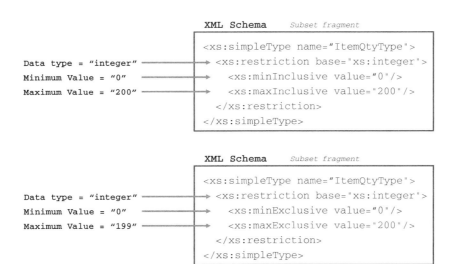

FIGURE 10.10

Example simpleType and Allowable Range Facets

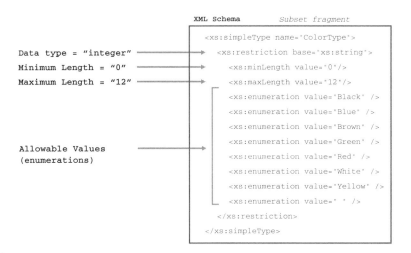

Data type = "integer"

Minimum Length = "0"

Maximum Length = "12"

Allowable Values
(enumerations)

```
XML Schema        Subset fragment
<xs:simpleType name="ColorType">
  <xs:restriction base="xs:string">
    <xs:minLength value="0"/>
    <xs:maxLength value="12"/>
    <xs:enumeration value="Black" />
    <xs:enumeration value="Blue" />
    <xs:enumeration value="Brown" />
    <xs:enumeration value="Green" />
    <xs:enumeration value="Red" />
    <xs:enumeration value="White" />
    <xs:enumeration value="Yellow" />
    <xs:enumeration value=" " />
  </xs:restriction>
</xs:simpleType>
```

FIGURE 10.11

Example simpleType with Enumeration Facets

Another type of facet is a "pattern." Some message data includes embedded formatting. The pattern facet can be applied to a user-defined simpleType to describe and constrain data such as a telephone number or a U.S. Social Security number that might require embedded characters or is more of a presentation format. A common method for describing international telephone numbers is to separate the area code, exchange, and local phone number part with a period character ("."). A U.S. Social Security number is often presented with a hyphen character ("-") between segments (see Figure 10.12). In both examples, a simpleType for a string data type, including a pattern facet, can be used.

XML Schemas provide extensive pattern support and complies with many "Regular Expressions."[4] The regular expression pattern constraint is described by the value of the pattern value.

Another type of facet is "whiteSpace" (see Figure 10.13). Some XML message elements can include a series of words or even a sentence or paragraph as the contained value. A whiteSpace facet allows the validating parser to manipulate whitespace characters that may be included in the data value (including a space, tab, carriage return, or a new line character). There are three possible values for this facet: replace, collapse, or preserve. An example message data value might include two words and a space that separates them (e.g., "< Color > Bright Red < /Color > ", where "Bright Red" is the data value with a space character between the two words). The consumer of the message data might need to suppress the space that separates the two words (e.g., resulting in a data value of "BrightRed", without the space). During parser validation of the message content, the parser can "collapse" the whitespace character.

Alternatively, whitespace characters might be important to the consumer of the message and the data value. An XML Schema with a whiteSpace value of "preserve" will instruct the validating parser to leave whitespace characters to remain within the data value. Another whitespace example occurs when the parser is instructed to replace the whitespace characters of a data value with a different whitespace character.

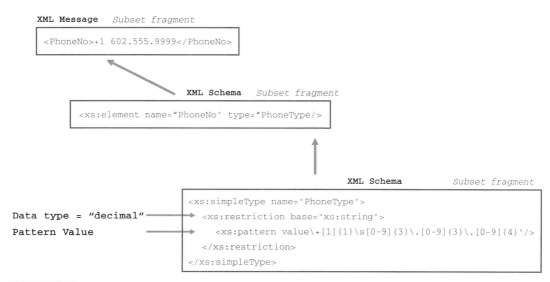

FIGURE 10.12

Example simpleType with Pattern Facets

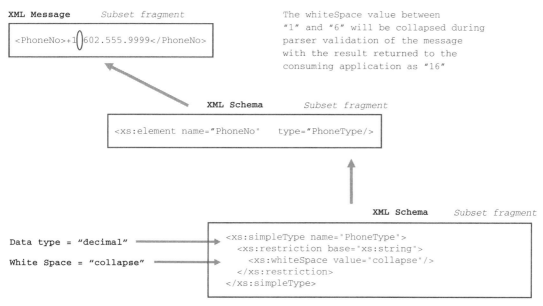

FIGURE 10.13

Example simpleType with Whitespace Facets

The combination of XML Schema simpleTypes and facets allows the service interface designer to develop an extensive array of custom or user-defined data types. The simpleTypes can be tailored to fit the requirements and standards of the enterprise, and can be applied to corresponding XML Schema-defined elements and attributes. When validated, the XML messages and data value contents are then checked against those data types for compliance.

10.4 COMPLEXTYPES

XML supports the notion of a hierarchical structure, where a single root element can have subordinate and nested child elements, and those elements can have their own child elements, sibling elements, and so on. Further, each of the elements can have one or more attributes defined. XML Schemas can include a set of declarations that define and constrain these complex structures known as complexTypes.

Within an XML Schema declared complexType, there are restrictions that can describe how child elements will appear in the message. A compositor is one type of restriction that describes whether one or more nested child elements of a complex type must be defined to a corresponding XML message in a prescribed order, whether they are defined to the message in any order, or whether there are subselections of child elements. XML Schema compositors are of three types:

- sequence
- all
- choice

The XML Schema "sequence" compositor defines a constraint where its contained elements must appear in the XML message in the same order that they are declared to the schema (see Figure 10.14). However, each element may be further defined as mandatory or optional with a "minOccurs" declaration and value. If a child element is defined to a sequence compositor group, and it also has a declared minOccurs attribute with a value of "1" or greater, then that element is considered as mandatory, and it must appear in the corresponding XML message. Alternatively, when the minOccurs attribute value is "0", the element is considered as optional and may or may not appear in the XML message.

Interestingly, the minOccurs attribute and its partner attribute ("maxOccurs") can be valued with any integer. This allows the combination of these two attributes to describe any number of repeating elements within the complexType and sequence (see Figure 10.15). In addition to an integer value, the maxOccurs attribute can also be valued with "*" or "unbounded" as the value. Both of which allow that there is no stated maximum limit to the number of repeating occurrences for that element in the XML message. A common example of the use of repeating elements is a postal address, where the street address lines might repeat from one to several times.

When declared to an XML Schema, the "all" compositor describes that all directly nested child elements of a complexType must appear in the corresponding XML message. They can appear in any order within that group of elements, but they cannot be defined to repeat (only a single instance of each element is allowed to appear in the message). The "choice" compositor describes that one and only one of a nested set of child elements can appear in the corresponding XML message.

A complexType can also include combinations of different compositors and nested elements. However, the compositors, element modality (optional or mandatory using the minOccurs attribute), and the element cardinality (defined by a combination of the minOccurs and maxOccurs attributes) cannot conflict. An

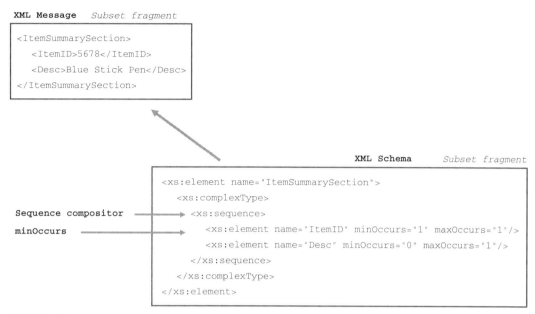

XML Message   *Subset fragment*

```
<ItemSummarySection>
  <ItemID>5678</ItemID>
  <Desc>Blue Stick Pen</Desc>
</ItemSummarySection>
```

XML Schema   *Subset fragment*

```
<xs:element name="ItemSummarySection">
  <xs:complexType>
    <xs:sequence>
      <xs:element name="ItemID" minOccurs="1" maxOccurs="1"/>
      <xs:element name="Desc" minOccurs="0" maxOccurs="1"/>
    </xs:sequence>
  </xs:complexType>
</xs:element>
```

Sequence compositor →
minOccurs →

FIGURE 10.14

Example complexType and Sequence Compositor

XML Message   *Subset fragment*

```
<PostalAddress>
  <StreetAddress>123 Main St</StreetAddress>
  <StreetAddress>Bldg 5, Suite A</StreetAddress>
  <City>Phoenix</City>
  <State>AZ</State>
  <PostalCode>85000</PostalCode>
</PostalAddress>
```

XML Schema   *Subset fragment*

```
<xs:elementname="PostalAddress">
  <xs:complexType>
    <xs:sequence>
      <xs:elementname="StreetAddress" minOccurs="1" maxOccurs="4"/>
      <xs:elementname="City" minOccurs="0" maxOccurs="1"/>
      <xs:elementname="State" minOccurs="0" maxOccurs="1"/>
      <xs:elementname="PostalCode" minOccurs="0" maxOccurs="1"/>
    </xs:sequence>
  </xs:complexType>
</xs:element>
```

Sequence compositor →
maxOccurs = "4" →

FIGURE 10.15

Example complexType with a Repeating Element (Cardinality)

```
                                              XML Schema    Subset fragment
                    <xs:element name="ColorOptions">
                      <xs:complexType>
Sequence compositor         <xs:sequence>
maxOccurs = "2"               <xs:element name="Color" minOccurs="0" maxOccurs="2"/>
Choice compositor             <xs:choice>
                                <xs:element name="Hue"/>
                                <xs:element name="Color"/>
                              </xs:choice>
                            </xs:sequence>
                          </xs:complexType>
                    </xs:element>
```

FIGURE 10.16

Example of Mixed Compositors and Nondeterministic Content Model

example of this type of conflict is known as a nondeterministic content model (see Figure 10.16). In this example, the complexType might include a sequence compositor with an element that is optional but may also repeat up to two times, and a trailing choice compositor that includes two elements, one of which is named identically to the element defined in the sequence compositor. In this example, the parser would not be able to determine which instance of the element meets the compositor constraints of the complexType.

An element can also reference a named complexType. This allows an element to inherit or derive its own structure from that of another separate complexType structure (see Figure 10.17). From a message design perspective, this is sometimes referred to as type abstraction. The XML Schema element declaration would use the "type" attribute, similar to the specification of a data type or reference of a simpleType. A postal address structure is another common example of this technique. A customer might have multiple address types (e.g., Billing Address and a Shipping Address). A service that acquires or "gets" address information for a customer might need to include one or more of the address types in the reply message. Rather than defining each of the address type structures separately in the service interface XML Schema, a single standard address structure can be defined as a named complexType and then referenced by the Billing Address and Shipping Address elements from their type attributes. This provides a high degree of structural consistency to the reply message, and it simplifies the development and maintenance of the service interface schema.

Other forms of complexType inheritance are also possible. As one example, a complexType structure can be extended by the structure of another named and referenced complexType. Also the structural model defined by a named complexType can be used to restrict the structure of another complexType, although in practice a complexType restriction is less frequently used.

10.5 GROUPS

An XML Schema "group" is roughly analogous to a complexType. A group allows for a collection of elements to be referenced and to be inherited as part of a structure (see Figure 10.18). The group also

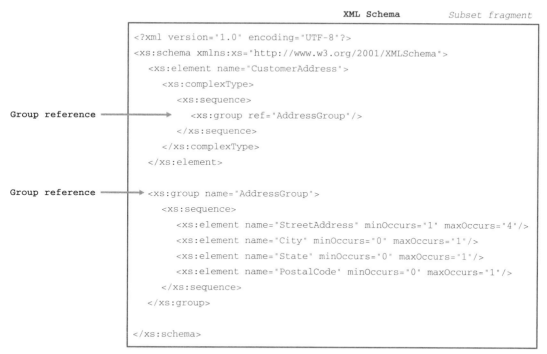

XML Schema   *Subset fragment*

```
Type reference ────►  <xs:element name="BillingAddress" type="AddressType"/>

Type reference ────►  <xs:element name="ShippingAddress" type="AddressType"/>

complexType   ────►  <xs:complexType name="AddressType">
                        <xs:sequence>
                          <xs:element name="StreetAddress" minOccurs="1" maxOccurs="4"/>
                          <xs:element name="City" minOccurs="0" maxOccurs="1"/>
                          <xs:element name="State" minOccurs="0" maxOccurs="1"/>
                          <xs:element name="PostalCode" minOccurs="0" axOccurs="1"/>
                        </xs:sequence>
                      </xs:complexType>
```

FIGURE 10.17

Example complexType That Is Inherited

XML Schema   *Subset fragment*

```
                      <?xml version="1.0" encoding="UTF-8"?>
                      <xs:schema xmlns:xs="http://www.w3.org/2001/XMLSchema">
                        <xs:element name="CustomerAddress">
                          <xs:complexType>
                            <xs:sequence>
Group reference ────►       <xs:group ref="AddressGroup"/>
                            </xs:sequence>
                          </xs:complexType>
                        </xs:element>

Group reference ────► <xs:group name="AddressGroup">
                        <xs:sequence>
                          <xs:element name="StreetAddress" minOccurs="1" maxOccurs="4"/>
                          <xs:element name="City" minOccurs="0" maxOccurs="1"/>
                          <xs:element name="State" minOccurs="0" maxOccurs="1"/>
                          <xs:element name="PostalCode" minOccurs="0" maxOccurs="1"/>
                        </xs:sequence>
                      </xs:group>

                      </xs:schema>
```

FIGURE 10.18

Example Group of Elements

uses compositors to describe and constrain the sequence of elements, and each element can optionally include a minOccurs and maxOccurs attribute to define whether it is optional or mandatory in the XML message instance, or whether it will be allowed to repeat within the defining group of elements. A somewhat conceptual view of XML Schema groups is to think of them as a convenient method for grouping elements that are specifically intended to be referenced and reused as a collection in other areas of a schema. While this is not a singular limitation, it is a reasonable view and use of groups.

The determination of whether an element is mandatory or optional in a corresponding XML message when using a minOccurs attribute value is specific to whether that element will appear in the message. In the case of an element, the minOccurs and maxOccurs attributes can also be used to determine whether an element is allowed to repeat in the message and how many times (attributes cannot be defined to repeat by name within the context of a single owning element). However, this notion of mandatory or optional does not determine whether the element or attribute contains a data value.

If an element is declared to an XML Schema with a minOccurs value greater than "0", then one or more instances of that element (as defined by its open and close tags) must appear in the corresponding XML message (see Figure 10.19). However, those same message element instances are not required to contain any data values. They may in fact, appear in the message, but remain empty of data. Similarly,

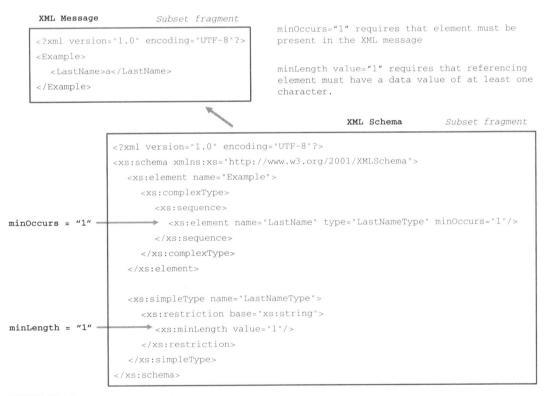

FIGURE 10.19

Example Element with Mandatory Data Value Content

an attribute that is declared to an XML Schema with a "use" attribute value of "required" must have an attribute instance in the corresponding XML message. However, that attribute is not required to contain a data value. When the service interface designer needs to ensure that a message element or attribute also contains a data value, an XML Schema simpleType should be declared with a facet to represent minimum expected content (such as a minLength facet or minInclusive facet or similar).

10.6 NAMESPACES

A namespace can be a difficult and somewhat ambiguous concept to comprehend. In the case of XML Schemas and a corresponding XML message, an XML namespace serves to uniquely identify declarations.[5] That is, an XML declaration such as an element can be declared to participate in a namespace and therefore inherits the namespace as part of its identification and potentially as part of its exposed tag name. The named declarations of an XML message or of an XML Schema are identified by tag names (see Figure 10.20). However, elements with tags such as "< ItemID/ > " and "< Color/ > " might be defined to multiple XML Schemas that are all assembled as part of the service interface. Unfortunately, like named elements and similar declarations can "collide." XML Schema declarations and XML encoded content can be associated with and participate in different namespaces, which helps to avoid collision.

The targetNamespace is also the overall namespace of the schema, and it can be used as a named reference for the schema and its content. Parser validation of an XML message requires that the XML

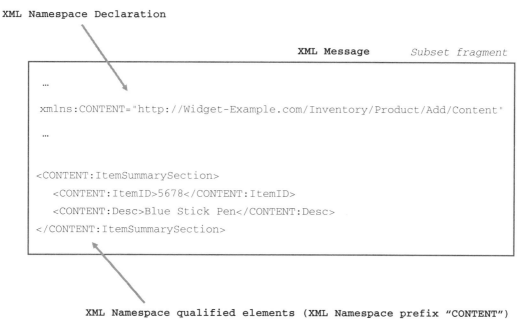

FIGURE 10.20

Example Namespace Prefixed XML Message Elements

message refers to one or more XML Schemas. Further, the element tags of the XML message must map by name and position to the intended structure of the referenced XML Schemas. To check that the message is in compliance, a syntactical reference from the XML message to the XML Schema is required. This reference to the XML Schemas can be declared within the XML message itself as either a "noNamespaceSchemaLocation" or a "schemaLocation" value, or for some parsers, it can be declared externally as a parameter and used during the parsing process. Both types of schema location attributes refer to an XML Schema.

The value of a "noNamespaceSchemaLocation" attribute declaration is used to reference an XML schema that does not have a targetNamespace. Alternatively, the value of a "schemaLocation" attribute references an XML Schema that includes a targetNamespace. Namespaces were previously described in Chapter 7, "The Service Interface—Contract." The difference between a schema with a target namespace and one without a namespace might seem trivial. However, there are important capabilities of both. Reference of the namespace qualified XML Schema from an XML message or instance requires the schemaLocation attribute, with a value pair. The value pair will include the schema name (and possibly a path name) as well as the value of the XML Schema targetNamespace attribute. Alternatively, reference of the unqualified XML Schema (without a targetNamespace) from an XML message or instance requires the noNamespaceSchemaLocation attribute, with a value representing the schema name and an optional directory path.

The schema location reference of the XML message also includes a file name or namespace reference and can be declared without a location or directory path (sometimes referred to as a "relative" location) or with a specified path (sometimes referred to as an "absolute" location). Resolving the location and acquiring a copy of the referenced XML Schema is left to the parser (see Figure 10.21). The file name and location information are known as "parser hints" and are not strictly required by the specification. However, and from experience, a directory path to a named XML Schema file and a namespace are almost always sufficient for the validating parser to find and access the referenced schema.

When the XML Schema has a declared targetNamespace, that namespace name and assigned prefix can also be used to identify specific elements of the XML message that map to and participate in that namespace. As another form of namespace qualification, other more specific namespaces can also be defined to the XML Schema that override the targetNamespace and are applied to qualifying declarations. While namespace participation helps to avoid named object collisions, it also uniquely identifies each namespace-qualified declaration. When the XML Schema does not have a targetNamespace, its declarations are said to participate in no namespace.

This same notion of a namespace can be exploited for reuse. An XML Schema that has a set of element declarations, such as a postal address structure, can then be referenced and reused by other XML Schemas.

10.7 IMPORT, INCLUDE

To invoke reuse of a service interface design, two of the most important XML Schema declarations are those of "import" and "include". These two declarations allow an XML Schema to be referenced and its content reused by other XML Schemas. This capability supports a modular and componentized service interface, with a high degree of reuse across services. Rather than having each service interface defined as a set of unique XML Schema syntax, a service interface can be assembled from among several other more modular XML Schemas.

noNamespaceSchemaLocation reference (referenced XML Schema does NOT have a targetNamespace)

XML Message   *Subset fragment*

```
<?xml version="1.0" encoding="UTF-8"?>
<Example xsi:noNamespaceSchemaLocation="AddNewProductContent.xsd"
         xmlns:xsi="http://www.w3.org/2001/XMLSchema-instance">
  <LastName>Smith</LastName>
</Example>
```

schemaLocation reference (referenced XML Schema has a targetNamespace)

XML Message   *Subset fragment*

```
<?xml version="1.0" encoding="UTF-8"?>
<EXAMPLE:Example
        xsi:schemaLocation="http://Widget-Example.com/Inventory/Product/Add/Content
        AddNewProductContent.xsd"
        xmlns:EXAMPLE="http://Widget-Example.com/Inventory/Product/Add/Content"
        xmlns:xsi="http://www.w3.org/2001/XMLSchema-instance">
  <EXAMPLE:LastName>Smith</EXAMPLE:LastName>
</EXAMPLE:Example>
```

FIGURE 10.21

Schema References from an XML Message Instance

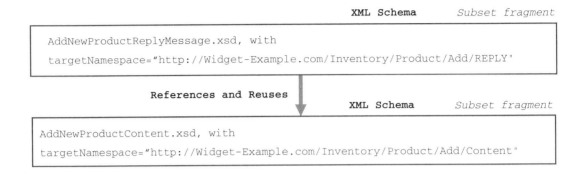

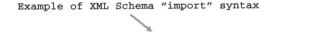

FIGURE 10.22

XML Schema Import Reference

Again, it is important to consider that both referencing and the referenced schemas might have a same named declaration such as an element in each. If the two schemas both have different targetNamespaces, and the like named declarations are qualified to participate in those separate namespaces, a collision should not occur, and each declaration could then be reused in different ways. However, if the two schemas did not have a targetNamespace, the like named declarations would most likely cause a parser error.

An XML Schema "import" is used to create a reference from one XML Schema to another XML Schema where the imported schema has a targetNamespace declared (see Figure 10.22). Alternatively, an XML Schema "include" is used to reference another XML Schema that does not have a target-Namespace (see Figure 10.23). While the advantages of namespace qualification should be obvious by now (avoiding named object collisions), XML Schemas that do not have a targetNamespace can also be of value to service interface designers. When the referencing or parent XML Schema has a targetNamespace, and the referenced or child XML Schema does not have a targetNamespace, the declarations from the included "no namespace" schema are said to be "coerced" into the namespace of the referencing schema.

This supports a powerful interface design pattern known as a proxy. In this case, the XML Schema declarations that do not participate in a targetNamespace could be included by many different XML Schemas. An example where this pattern applies with advantage is a collection of common elements that

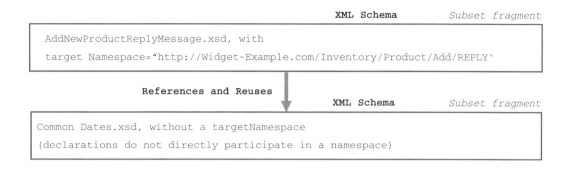

XML Schema   *Subset fragment*

```
AddNewProductReplyMessage.xsd, with

target Namespace="http://Widget-Example.com/Inventory/Product/Add/REPLY"
```

References and Reuses

XML Schema   *Subset fragment*

```
Common Dates.xsd, without a targetNamespace

(declarations do not directly participate in a namespace)
```

Example of XML Schema "include" syntax

XML Schema   *Subset fragment*

```
...

<xs:include schemaLocation="CommonDates.xsd"/>

...
```

FIGURE 10.23

XML Schema Include Reference

can be used in different interface contexts. An element such as a generic "Date" ("< Date/ >") might be referenced and coerced into several different other namespace-qualified XML Schemas to represent a "Created Date" ("< CREATED:Date/ >"), "Last Maintained Date" ("< MAINTAINED:Date/ >"), and "Removed Date" ("< REMOVED:Date/ >"), all of which derive their element definitions from the unqualified and included "Date" element.

The XML Schema import element is also used with the WSDL < types/ > element of the Web service interface. This application of XML Schemas import is little different from that of a namespace-qualified XML Schema to XML Schema import reference. Rather than being an XML Schema to XML Schema import reference, it is a WSDL to XML Schema reference (see Figure 10.24).

XML Schema import and include references allow a service interface to be assembled from separately defined, highly reusable and modular XML Schemas as types of building blocks. This reduces the amount of unique schema syntax that has to be developed and has the added benefit of providing common standards for message structures and definitions.

SUMMARY

The Web service interface relies upon XML Schemas to define the content and context of the XML messages that are passed between service collaborators. The XML Schema language also represents a powerful method of describing the metadata and rules by which XML-encoded messages can be validated. The process of validation requires a validating XML parser and an XML message or similar instance

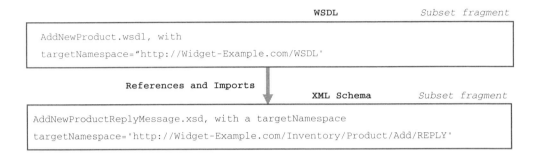

```
                                          WSDL              Subset fragment

   AddNewProduct.wsdl, with
    targetNamespace="http://Widget-Example.com/WSDL"


        References and Imports
                                          XML Schema        Subset fragment

  AddNewProductReplyMessage.xsd, with a targetNamespace
  targetNamespace="http://Widget-Example.com/Inventory/Product/Add/REPLY"
```

Example of WSDL <types/> XML Schema "import" syntax

```
                                          WSDL              Subset fragment

<types>
   <xs:schema xmlns:xs="http://www.w3.org/2001/XMLSchema"
       xmlns:REPLY="http://Widget-Example.com/Inventory/Product/Add/REPLY"
       targetNamespace="http://Widget-Example.com/Inventory/Product/Add/REPLYMESSAGE">

       <xs:import namespace="http://Widget-Example.com/Inventory/Product/Add/REPLY"
                schemaLocation="AddNewProductReplyMessage.xsd"/>
    </xs:schema>
</types>
```

FIGURE 10.24

WSDL to XML Schema Types Reference

with a referenced XML Schema. The parser will evaluate and compare the XML message structure and the data value content to the declarations and constraints of the referenced XML Schema. If an example of noncompliance is encountered, the parser will raise an error to the validating application.

The XML Schemas language is extensive in capability and function. It includes basic data container types (elements and attributes) and allows these declarations to be further described with constraints for data types, default values, and fixed values (among several other constraints). The available set of data types that are defined for the XML Schemas syntax is quite extensive. However, XML Schemas also allow for user-defined types declared as simpleTypes. The simpleType declaration allows a schema-defined data type to be further restricted with facets. In combination, these data types and facets are assembled to represent custom data types that can be applied to elements and attributes of the schema.

The XML messages that move between service collaborators are not limited to simple data containers such as elements. The messages can also include complex structures with various levels of nested substructures, child elements, sibling elements, and repeating elements. These complexTypes are also defined by XML Schemas. Another structural schema declaration is that of a group. While similar to a complexType, a group is specifically targeted for reuse. That is, the elements defined by the group structure are intended to be referenced as a collection by other elements.

Avoiding collisions between like named declarations in the XML message and XML Schemas is critical. If a named declaration is found in multiple XML Schemas, and they are all used in a service interface, there is a potential that a like named reference will fail with a parser error. The participation of these declarations in separate namespaces significantly reduces the potential for error. To participate in a namespace, the declarations (such as element declarations) are "qualified" by name, by prefix, or by inheritance.

XML Schemas also provide the ability for the service interface designer to develop modular component schemas that can be referenced and assembled in different service interface configurations. This capability provides a high degree of reuse and exploits standard definitions across services.

REFERENCES

1. Fallside DC, Walmsley P, eds. XML Schema Part 0: Primer. 2nd ed. (W3C, October 28, 2004). <http://www.w3.org/TR/xmlschema-0/>.

2. Bean J, XML For Data Architects. San Francisco: Morgan Kaufmann; 2003.

3. Biron PV, Malhotra A, eds. XML Schema Part 2: Datatypes. 2nd ed. (W3C, October 28, 2004). <http://www.w3.org/TR/xmlschema-2/>.

4. The Open Group. The Open Group Base Specifications Issue 6 IEEE Std 1003.1, 2004 Edition, Unix, 9. Regular Expressions. (The IEEE and The Open Group, Copyright © 2001-2004). <http://www.opengroup.org/onlinepubs/009695399/basedefs/xbd_chap09.html/>.

5. Bray T, Hollander D, Layman A, Tobin R, eds. Namespaces in XML 1.0. 2nd ed. (W3C, August 16, 2006). <http://www.w3.org/TR/REC-xml-names/>.

XML Schema Design Patterns

11

Design patterns are available for many technologies and languages and can be thought of as repeatable techniques or models. Rather than starting from a clean slate, applying a design pattern allows the service interface designer to reuse and exploit a set of design techniques or best practices. A good design pattern will also allow the architect to further extend, enhance, and evolve the pattern to better fit a particular use case or need. Design patterns are also not exclusive and can be combined. Applying one design pattern does not preclude use of another.

As with the construction of a building, there are many types of patterns that can be applied. Common building design patterns might include access patterns (e.g., entry and exit, hallways, and doors). Other patterns might include location and types of electrical service (e.g., wiring, voltage, and types and locations of outlets). Without these simple and common sense patterns, a building could be built that is poorly designed, prohibitive to occupation, and difficult to modify later. XML Schema design patterns are of a similar analogy but are specific to XML Schemas syntax, schema design, and service interface.

As described in Chapter 10, "XML Schema Basics," the XML Schemas language describes and constrains XML messages created from the Web service interface.[1] XML Schemas also provide a vast number of declarative metadata constraints. The XML Schemas syntax is comprehensive to a degree where there are a number of different approaches to resolving a service interface requirement. Each of these syntactical techniques has advantages and disadvantages. For some, the benefits include reuse, maintainability, and extensibility. For others, even though syntactically correct, the resulting service interface schema can become so complex and irregular that it is also difficult to maintain and largely nonreusable.

Designing a service interface that is complex, prone to error, and not reusable does a disservice to the enterprise. To avoid suboptimal application of XML Schemas syntax, there are a number of effective XML Schema design patterns that can be exploited. Adopting (or adapting) a design pattern also avoids repeated and ad-hoc service interface designs that are specific only to a small subset of services that are difficult to maintain or that are prone to anomaly. Identifying which of the XML Schema design patterns are of potential advantage and then applying them should not be a random service interface design activity. The most effective approach to XML Schema design patterns will compare key capabilities and advantages to the requirements and characteristics of the service interface. As recommendations, the service designer should evaluate and consider patterns with the following characteristics.

- Potential for reuse within a single service interface
- Potential for reuse across services and service interfaces
- Application of enterprise standards (naming, structure, element, and data type standards)
- Potential for future service modification or enhancement and later extension of the service interface
- Service interface simplicity
- Service interface modularity
- Service interface maintainability

The design process described in Chapter 8, "Canonical Message Design," emphasizes a top-down or design to contract approach that begins with an example XML message instance. That example message is then used as the canonical from which the service interface schemas are then created. The service interface schemas can be generated from tooling such as XML Spy (Copyright 2003-2008 Altova GmbH, reprinted with permission of Altova) or can be hand crafted using an XML Schema editor. While tooling generated canonical message schemas are almost always syntactically correct and generally functional, they are also limited to that specific service and service interface. The ability to create and use more modular XML Schemas and syntax requires a set of applicable design patterns. As part of the canonical message design process, the service designer should also look for opportunities to apply these XML Schema design patterns to advantage.

In part, this requires that the service interface designer look for affinity among message structures, elements, and data types. These affinities can be contextual (e.g., grouping all address elements together, grouping all monetary amount elements together, etc.), or they can be driven by enterprise and industry data standards. The canonical message design can then be reorganized into logical or related groupings of message elements, as candidates for potential reuse at other points within the message design (see Figure 11.1). These groupings can also become candidates to separate from the schema as external modular service interface schemas. These separate XML Schemas are then reused by reference and assembly to build other service interfaces.

The grouping of structures and elements by logical affinity requires that the initial message design XML Schemas are also refactored and optimized. Resulting structures and groupings of elements will be moved and repositioned within the service interface XML Schema as complexTypes. Further analysis will determine if these affinity groupings should remain intrinsic to that service interface schema, or if they would be externalized and referenced as separate and modular XML Schemas (either as namespace qualified or no-namespace schemas). A similar approach exists for data types, where an enterprise standard data type is applied to one or more elements or attributes. When declared as global simpleTypes, these data types also become candidates for reuse by reference. For each of the different affinity groups, the application of XML Schema design patterns can further optimize the service interface.

11.1 COMPLEXTYPE PATTERNS

As described in Chapter 10, "XML Schema Basics," an XML Schema declared complexType is most often used to describe a message structure. That is, a complexType describes the hierarchy and nesting of child elements in a message. A complexType also includes further restrictions known as compositors that determine how and in what order nested child elements will appear in the message. The XML

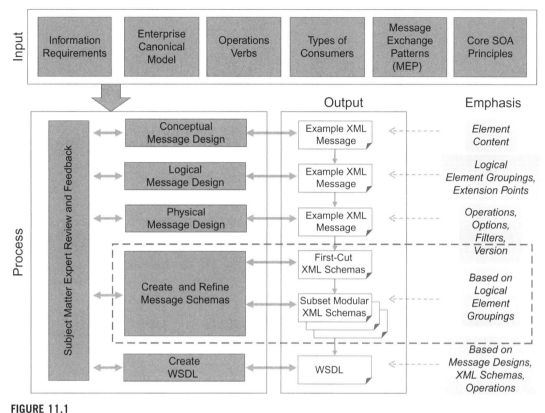

FIGURE 11.1

The Canonical Message Design Process

Schemas complexType syntax allows for a number of variations and techniques to resolve a service interface requirement. While each has extensive capabilities, there are three complexType patterns, most often applied to service interface design.

- Type Abstraction
- Type Extension
- Type Restriction

The Type Abstraction pattern allows an element to be logically abstract and not restricted to acting only as a discrete container for data values. As referenced by its "type" attribute, the abstract element can "inherit" a structural definition from another, separate structure (i.e., a separately named complexType). An approach similar to the Type Abstraction patterns is also sometimes referred to as "Venetian Blind."[2]

As part of the originating element declaration, the "type" attribute will contain a named reference to another separate complexType. The "type" attribute is the same as that described in Chapter 10 and can be used to apply a data type to an element. With the Type Abstraction pattern, the element does

XML Message *Subset fragment*

```
<?xml version="1.0" encoding="UTF-8"?>
<CustomerAddress>
  <BillingAddress>
    <StreetAddress>123 E Main</StreetAddress>
    <City>Phoenix</City>
    <State>AZ</State>
    <PostalCode>85000</PostalCode>
  </BillingAddress>
</CustomerAddress>
```

The element "BillingAddress" inherits its structure from the "AddressType" complexType

XML Schema *Subset fragment*

Type reference

complexType

```
<xs:elementname="BillingAddress" type="AddressType"/>
<xs:complexType name="AddressType">
  <xs:sequence>
    <xs:element name="StreetAddress" minOccurs="1" maxOccurs="4"/>
    <xs:element name="City" minOccurs="0" maxOccurs="1"/>
    <xs:element name="State" minOccurs="0" maxOccurs="1"/>
    <xs:element name="PostalCode" minOccurs="0" axOccurs="1"/>
  </xs:sequence>
</xs:complexType>
```

FIGURE 11.2

complexType—Type Abstraction

not reference a discrete data type to become "strongly typed," but references a complexType for its structure (see Figure 11.2). Later realization of the element in the XML message instance includes the inherited structure of the referenced complexType.

One benefit of the Type Abstraction is reuse. That is, the structural definition of the separate and named complexType can be "reused" (inherited) by one or more referencing elements from their individual type attributes. In addition to reuse, the Type Abstraction pattern can also be applied to promote structural consistency. As examples, the structure defined to the complexType might be representative of an enterprise data standard, such as a Postal Address, an E-Mail Address, a Person Name, and so on. Rather than attempting to independently define these structural standards across many different elements of a service interface or across service interfaces, the structural standard can be defined as a named complexType and then referenced and inherited by elements of these other interfaces.

Using the postal address analogy, an address structure can be defined by a stand-alone complexType, and based upon enterprise standards to include one or more street address lines, a city, state, and postal code. A service and service interface requirement might include exposing multiple customer addresses for the customer's residence, business address, and vacation home address in a reply message. Individual message elements can be declared to the service interface schema for each of these different address types, and then reference the same enterprise standard "Address" structure as a complexType (using their "type" attributes). Each element would then "inherit" the same standard address structure from the complexType, avoiding a separate and potentially disparate set of address structure declarations for each element in the service interface.

Many SOA services will continue to evolve over time, with new requirements that result in additional operations or additional data in the XML messages. When the original service interface must be later maintained and enhanced, the service designer will have to carefully identify which of the structures,

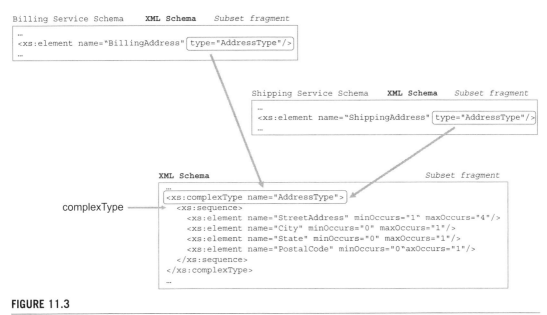

FIGURE 11.3

Type Abstraction—Reference from Multiple Schemas

elements, and types are subject to change. This might include the addition of new elements to an existing structure. If an "Address" structure, such as that previously described, were implemented as separate complexType declarations, each would then require additional modification to remain consistent. If not, a potential for data impedance exists that could negatively impact consumers of the service, the service itself, and the underlying data at rest sources used by the service. Alternatively, a change to the standard "Address" structure would only be applied to that one complexType and then referenced and inherited by the other address type elements. The maintenance of the service interface schema is significantly simplified and with less potential for anomaly.

While the advantages of the Type Abstraction pattern are obvious, there are also complexities and potential disadvantages. The example complexType inheritance is specific and realized by named reference from the elements and their "type" attributes. There may be examples where a later modification of the reusable complexType could cause a rippling impact through multiple services and service interfaces (see Figure 11.3). With the Type Abstraction pattern, a service and service interface change may cause residual object mapping and behavior changes to other consumers of those services. Some of those other service consumers might not be prepared to accept a structural change that started from a common and reusable complexType structure of another and entirely different service interface requirement. The Type Abstraction pattern is still recommended, but caution is advised. The service and service interface designer should consider not only immediate service requirements but also the longer implications of change.

Another complexType pattern involves the extension of an already declared complexType. As implied by the name, the Type Extension pattern allows a new complexType structure to inherit the structure from a named and referenced complexType and combine it with new content such as additional

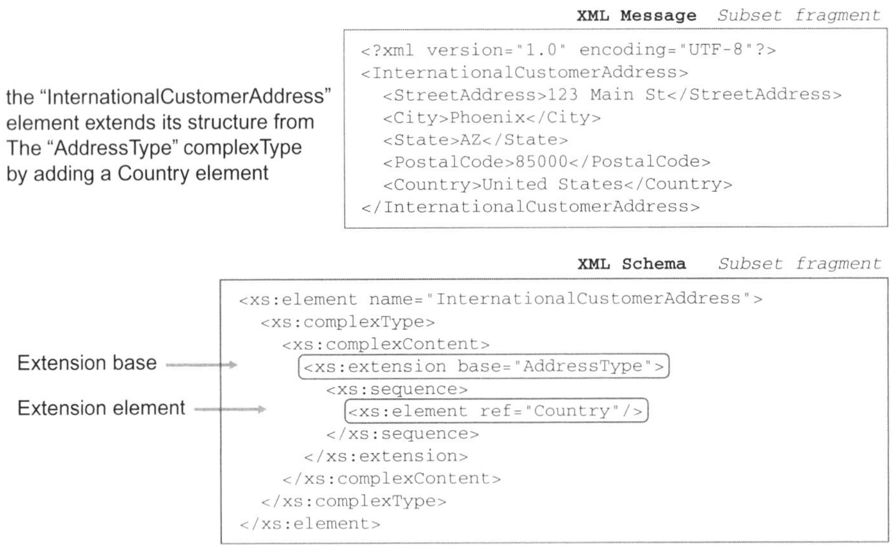

XML Message   *Subset fragment*

```
<?xml version="1.0" encoding="UTF-8"?>
<InternationalCustomerAddress>
  <StreetAddress>123 Main St</StreetAddress>
  <City>Phoenix</City>
  <State>AZ</State>
  <PostalCode>85000</PostalCode>
  <Country>United States</Country>
</InternationalCustomerAddress>
```

the "InternationalCustomerAddress" element extends its structure from The "AddressType" complexType by adding a Country element

XML Schema   *Subset fragment*

```
<xs:element name="InternationalCustomerAddress">
  <xs:complexType>
    <xs:complexContent>
      <xs:extension base="AddressType">
      <xs:sequence>
        <xs:element ref="Country"/>
      </xs:sequence>
      </xs:extension>
    </xs:complexContent>
  </xs:complexType>
</xs:element>
```

Extension base

Extension element

FIGURE 11.4

complexType—Type Extension

elements. That is, the Type Extension pattern inherits an already declared complexType structure and then extends it by adding element declarations.

The syntactical implementation of the Type Extension pattern is somewhat different from the previously described Type Abstraction pattern. Rather than using the "type" attribute of an element declaration to reference a named complexType, the Type Extension pattern uses an element with its own underlying complexType to reference and inherit yet another separate complexType and then to include additional elements. The originating element and its underlying complexType will include an XML Schema "extension" element declaration and its "base" attribute. The value of the "base" attribute refers to the complexType structure that will be inherited and then extended. The originating element and its underlying complexType will also include additional element content that is then combined with the inherited structure.

The postal address analogy can also be used to describe the Type Extension pattern (see Figure 11.4). Based on an enterprise data standard, the typical North American customer's postal address structure will contain one or more street address lines, a city, state, and postal code. However, at a minimum, the address of an international customer will also require a country name (or abbreviation). To resolve this requirement and to still comply with enterprise standards, an International Customer element could be declared that inherits the standard address structure and also extends it by adding a new Country element.

The separate and named extension complexType is not limited to reference by only one complexType and extension base (see Figure 11.5). Other complexType structures can also reference and extend the named complexType by adding elements. The additional elements can also be different from one complexType to another.

The advantage of a Type Extension pattern is that an originating element and underlying complexType structure can inherit the structure of another complexType and extend it with additional elements.

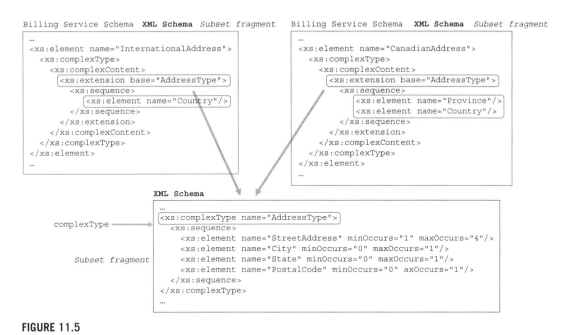

Billing Service Schema **XML Schema** *Subset fragment*

```
...
<xs:element name="InternationalAddress">
  <xs:complexType>
    <xs:complexContent>
      <xs:extension base="AddressType">
        <xs:sequence>
          <xs:element name="Country"/>
        </xs:sequence>
      </xs:extension>
    </xs:complexContent>
  </xs:complexType>
</xs:element>
...
```

Billing Service Schema **XML Schema** *Subset fragment*

```
...
<xs:element name="CanadianAddress">
  <xs:complexType>
    <xs:complexContent>
      <xs:extension base="AddressType">
        <xs:sequence>
          <xs:element name="Province"/>
          <xs:element name="Country"/>
        </xs:sequence>
      </xs:extension>
    </xs:complexContent>
  </xs:complexType>
</xs:element>
...
```

XML Schema

complexType ⟶

Subset fragment

```
...
<xs:complexType name="AddressType">
  <xs:sequence>
    <xs:element name="StreetAddress" minOccurs="1" maxOccurs="4"/>
    <xs:element name="City" minOccurs="0" maxOccurs="1"/>
    <xs:element name="State" minOccurs="0" maxOccurs="1"/>
    <xs:element name="PostalCode" minOccurs="0" axOccurs="1"/>
  </xs:sequence>
</xs:complexType>
...
```

FIGURE 11.5

Type Extension—Reference from Multiple Schemas

As the need for future modifications to the referenced structure arises, those changes are then applied to and inherited by all of the extension base references. This is both a form of reuse by named reference and simplified maintenance.

The Type Restriction pattern is another pattern that inherits and applies the structure of a referenced complexType. The Type Restriction pattern is syntactically similar to the Type Extension pattern, where an element with an underlying complexType references another complexType. Rather than using an extension element from the originating complexType, an XML Schema restriction element and its base attribute are used.

As the pattern name implies, a restriction is also a limitation. With the Type Restriction pattern, the constraints and limitations of the named and referenced complexType are inherited. That is, the structure, elements, and constraints of the referencing complexType cannot violate those of the referenced restriction complexType (see Figure 11.6). As an example, a like named element is defined to both the originating element and to the referenced complexType. However, if the originating complexType element declaration has a minOccurs value of "0" (the element is "optional" in the XML message), and the referenced restriction complexType has a minOccurs value of "1" (the element is "mandatory" in the XML message), the restriction will result in a parser failure. A Type Restriction requires that the originating or referencing complexType structure must comply with (or within) the same declarations and constraints of the referenced complexType.

For most services and service interfaces, a Type Restriction pattern is not as common as either the Type Abstraction or Type Extension patterns. While possible, it tends to be an infrequent occasion when a defined complexType structure is later restricted by reference to a separate restriction schema.

The "CustomerAddress" element structure is restricted. It only allows three of the the Address structure elements.

```
                                        XML Message      Subset fragment
<?xml version="1.0" encoding="UTF-8"?>
<CustomerAddress>
  <StreetAddress>123 Main St</StreetAddress>
  <City>Phoenix</City>
  <PostalCode>85000</PostalCode>
</CustomerAddress>
```

```
                                        XML Schema       Subset fragment
<xs:element name="CustomerAddress">
  <xs:complexType>
    <xs:complexContent>
      <xs:restriction base="AddressType">
        <xs:sequence>
          <xs:element name="StreetAddress" minOccurs="1" maxOccurs="3"/>
          <xs:element name="City" minOccurs="0" maxOccurs="1"/>
          <xs:element name="PostalCode" minOccurs="0" maxOccurs="1"/>
        </xs:sequence>
      </xs:restriction>
    </xs:complexContent>
  </xs:complexType>
</xs:element>
```

Restriction base

Restriction elements

FIGURE 11.6

complexType—Type Restriction

If there is a requirement to modify an existing structure by restriction, a more appropriate recommendation would be to refactor the service interface and XML Schema.

11.2 GLOBAL DECLARATION PATTERNS

As implied by previous XML Schema patterns, there is a need to reference a separate and named complexType. When an XML Schema declaration is a direct child of the overall XML Schema "< schema/ >" element, and those declarations are identified by name, they are considered to be globally declared. In this manner, these declarations can be referenced by name and then applied or inherited by other schema constructs. The structures that were referenced by the previous Type Abstraction, Type Extension, and Type Restriction patterns were all globally declared and named complexTypes.

One of the most common examples of the Global Declaration pattern is where either an XML Schema element or attribute declaration references a separately declared and named global simpleType from which to inherit its data type constraints (see Figure 11.7). For this example, the reference to the "global" simpleType is implemented by a data value of the element's or attribute's "type" declaration. To apply this pattern, the simpleType declaration must have a name and it must be an immediate child of the overall schema element ("< schema/ >"). If the simpleType is declared as a direct child of the corresponding element, rather than of the overall schema element, it is then defined without a name and cannot be referenced and reused by other element declarations. The value of the "type" attribute will refer to the same named global simpleType.

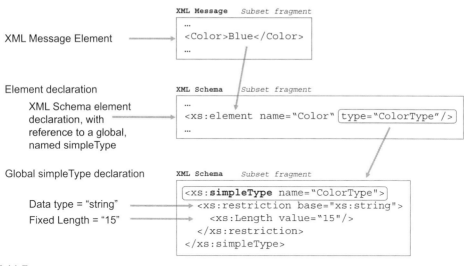

FIGURE 11.7

Reference to a Globally Declared simpleType

Namespaces were described in Chapter 10. Whether the reference to a named global declaration will cross namespaces will also determine whether the reference to the named declaration must be namespace qualified.[3] An example of the Global Declaration pattern is a service interface defined by an assembly of modular XML Schemas, with each of those separate schemas defined with a unique targetNamespace and default namespace. The declarations from within those separate schemas would likely participate in their respective namespaces. If a reference is made from an XML Schema element declaration of a different schema to a globally declared and named element that participates in the targetNamespace of its own XML Schema, the reference may also require a "qualified" name, including a reference to the namespace as a prefix to the tag name.

With the Add New Product service example, the request message XML Schema is largely an assembly of several other reusable XML Schemas. Each of these separate schemas has a unique targetNamespace, and their intrinsic schema declarations all participate in those namespaces. Element references from the top level "AddNewProductRequestMessage" schema are syntactically implemented as data values of the element "ref" attributes, including a namespace qualified prefix (see Figure 11.8). This helps to make the schema more readable, resolves the cross-schema references, and avoids collision between like named elements.

The Global Declaration pattern exhibits a high degree of reuse and utility. Most types of XML Schema declarations can be defined as global declarations and therefore are reusable by named reference (e.g., complexTypes, groups, elements, and simpleTypes). Prolific use of global declarations also simplifies future maintenance of the overall schema and allows for a method of organizing the XML Schema syntax. Since the references to global declarations are by name and not position in the schema, the service interface designer can move and organize groupings of similar global declarations to simplify later schema maintenance. As an example, all of the globally declared elements can be listed together, the global complexTypes together, and simpleTypes together.

```
                                        XML Schema        Subset fragment
                              ...
Reference to other            <xs:element name="Request">
named and globally              <xs:complexType>
declared elements.                <xs:sequence>
                                    <xs:element ref="VERSION:VersionSection"/>
The referenced                      <xs:element ref="OPTIONS:OptionsSection"/>
elements participate                <xs:element ref="OPERATIONS:OperationSection"/>
in other namespaces                 <xs:element ref="CONTENT:ContentSection"/>
and are qualfiied with            </xs:sequence>
name space "prefixes."          </xs:complexType>
                              </xs:element>
                              ...
```

FIGURE 11.8

Namespace Qualified References to Other Globally Defined Elements

---

Example 11.1
Structured Service Interface Schema

```
<?xml version = "1.0" encoding = "UTF-8" ?>
- <xs:schema xmlns:xs = "http://www.w3.org/2001/XMLSchema" elementFormDefault = "qualified"
xmlns = "http://Widget-Example.com/Options" xmlns:OPTIONS = "http://Widget-Example.com/Options"
targetNamespace = "http://Widget-Example.com/Options">
- <!--
=================================
-->
- <!--
Root Element Declarations
-->
- <!--
=================================
-->
- <xs:element name = "OptionsSection">
- <xs:complexType <
- <xs:sequence <
<xs:element ref = "EmptyContainers" minOccurs = "1" maxOccurs = "1"/>
<xs:element ref = "FixedLengthContent" minOccurs = "1" maxOccurs = "1"/>
<xs:element ref = "SynchronizeCorrelationID" minOccurs = "1" maxOccurs = "1"/>
< xs:element ref = "EchoRequestContentInReply" minOccurs = "1" maxOccurs = "1"/>
<xs:element ref = "IncludePre-UpdateImageInReply" minOccurs = "1" maxOccurs = "1"/>
<xs:element ref = "IncludePost-UpdateImageInReply" minOccurs = "1" maxOccurs = "1"/>
<xs:element ref = "IncludeProcessingStatusInReply" minOccurs = "1" maxOccurs = "1"/>
<xs:element ref = "IncludeElementMetadataInReply" minOccurs = "1" maxOccurs = "1"/>
</xs:sequence>
</xs:complexType>
```

```
</xs:element>
- <!--
 = = = = = = = = = = = = = = = = = = = = =
-- >
- <!--
Global Element Declarations
-- >
- <!--
 = = = = = = = = = = = = = = = = = = = = =
-->
<xs:element name = "EmptyContainers" type = "OptionBooleanType"/>
<xs:element name = "FixedLengthContent" type = "OptionBooleanType"/>
<xs:element name = "SynchronizeCorrelationID" type = "OptionBooleanType"/>
<xs:element name = "EchoRequestContentInReply" type = "OptionBooleanType"/>
<xs:element name = "IncludePre-UpdateImageInReply" type = "OptionBooleanType"/>
<xs:element name = "IncludePost-UpdateImageInReply" type = "OptionBooleanType"/>
<xs:element name = "IncludeProcessingStatusInReply" type = "OptionBooleanType"/>
<xs:element name = "IncludeElementMetadataInReply" type = "OptionBooleanType"/>
- <!--
 = = = = = = = = = = = = = = = = = = = = =
-->
- <!--
Global simpleType Restrictions
--<
- <!--
 = = = = = = = = = = = = = = = = = = = = =
-->
- <xs:simpleType name = "OptionBooleanType">
<xs:restriction base = "xs:boolean"/>
</xs:simpleType>
</xs:schema>
```

The example XML Schema (Example 11.1, Structure Service Interface Schema) is a modular subset schema that is referenced by a named import from the higher level "AddNewProduct" service interface schema. The first declaration of the referenced subschema is an "Options Section" element (" < OptionsSection/ > "). This element is by default a global declaration, as it is both specifically named ("OptionsSection") and a direct child declaration of the overall schema element (" < schema/ > "). The "OptionsSection" element also represents a complexType structure. Within the element, eight child elements have also been declared. When the "Options Section" element (" < OptionsSection/ > ") is referenced by name, all of its subordinate elements are also inherited.

For this specific example, each of the eight child elements is also defined by a reference to named and globally declared element declarations. That is, the nested child elements of the "Options Section" element reference the element definitions as named values of the "ref" attribute. Nested child element declarations within a higher-level parent element that also reference other named and globally declared elements are a somewhat common application of the Global Declarations pattern. A similar pattern of global element reference is sometimes described as "Salami Slice."[4]

Advantages of applying the Global Declarations pattern include reuse and simplification of the overall service interface schema. Separately named and global declarations can be reused by named reference from within the schema, as well as from other schemas (when the schema is referenced by an include or an import). Rather than just placing each of the XML Schema declarations at a random or ordinal position within the schema, they can also be grouped by type or some other logical affinity. If this same technique is applied to all service interface XML Schemas, later maintenance and enhancements will be simplified, given that the designer will know to look for groupings of similar global declarations.

While there is no explicit requirement that XML Schema declarations must occur in a particular order, there are several potential techniques to organizing the XML Schema declarations and syntax. One approach is to list all declarations alphabetically by name. This is common with some XML and XML Schema tools. The canonical message design (expressed as an example XML message instance) is used by the tooling to generate an initial draft of XML Schema syntax.

Another approach to organizing the service interface schema is to list XML Schema declarations in the general order of granularity. All named and globally declared complexTypes, groups, elements, and simpleTypes are organized into groups. These groups are then positioned in the service interface schema from the most coarse-grained to the most fine-grained. The most coarse-grained declarations are those that represent structural definitions (e.g., complexTypes and groups). Moderately fine-grained declarations are globally declared elements, and the most fine-grained are simpleTypes. The granularity approach to internally organizing an XML Schema is not perfect, and some complexity can arise for combinations of global and local declarations. Either approach can be effective and will simplify later maintenance of the service interface schemas.

Yet another approach to organizing an XML Schema is to logically position declarations in order, similar to the order of elements in the corresponding XML message (see Figure 11.9). This approach cannot always be strictly applied because the XML Schema declarations might include variations of global element declarations, any of which might serve in the corresponding XML message as the root element. However, it is a more natural approach to organizing an XML Schema. The flow of declarations is generally from top to bottom, which resembles the hierarchical structure of the XML message.

11.3 LOCAL DECLARATION PATTERNS

Alternative to the Global Declarations pattern is the Local Declarations pattern. This pattern is most often applied to complexTypes, elements, and simpleTypes (see Figure 11.10). Rather than defining the service interface with separate global declarations that can be referenced by name, the declarations are defined locally to where they are required. That is, they are nested declarations within other declarations and remain anonymous (without a specific name).

The Local Declarations pattern is a very simple design approach. As the need for a nested complexType, element, or simpleType is encountered during the canonical message design process, it is directly declared. As an example, the Local Declarations pattern could also be applied to a postal address structure. Rather than defining each of the address elements as separate global declarations

Ordered Alphabetically	Ordered by Granularity	Ordered Logically

```
<xs:schema>
...

  <xs:complexTypename="Axxx"/>

  <xs:elementname="Bxxx"/>

  <xs:simpleTypename="Cxxx"/>

  <xs:elementname="Dxxx"/>

  <xs:complexTypename="Exxx"/>

...
</xs:schema>
```

```
<xs:schema>
...

  <xs:complexTypename="Axxx"/>

  <xs:complexTypename="Exxx"/>

  <xs:elementname="Bxxx"/>

  <xs:elementname="Dxxx"/>

  <xs:simpleType name="Cxxx"/>

...
</xs:schema>
```

```
<xs:schema>
...

  <xs:complexTypename="Axxx"/>

  <xs:elementname="Dxxx"/>

  <xs:complexTypename="Exxx"/>

  <xs:elementname="Bxxx"/>

  <xs:simpleTypename="Cxxx"/>

...
</xs:schema>
```

Intrinsic XML Schema declarations are ordered alphabetically by name.

Intrinsic XML Schema declarations are ordered descending by granularity.

Coarse-grained complexType structures are positioned first, followed by moderate grained elements, and then by fine-grained simpleTypes.

Intrinsic XML Schema declarations are ordered in the same general sequence that the corresponding structures and elements will be realized in the XML Message.

FIGURE 11.9

XML Schema Structuring Techniques

Local complexType declaration. The complexType cannot be referenced by name.

Local element declarations. Although named, these elements are specific to the complexType and cannot be referenced by name.

XML Schema   *Subset fragment*

```
...
<xs:element name="Request">
  <xs:complexType>
    <xs:sequence>
      <xs:element name="VersionSection"/>
      <xs:element name="OptionsSection"/>
      <xs:element name="OperationSection"/>
      <xs:element name="ContentSection/>
    </xs:sequence>
  </xs:complexType>
</xs:element>
...
```

Local simpleType declaration. The simpleType cannot be referenced by name.

XML Schema   *Subset fragment*

```
...
<xs:element name="Color">
  <xs:simpleType>
    <xs:restriction base="xs:string">
      <xs:maxLength value="15"/>
    </xs:restriction>
  </xs:simpleType>
</xs:element>
...
```

FIGURE 11.10

Local complexType, Element, and simpleType Declarations

```
<?xml version="1.0" encoding="UTF-8"?>
<xs:schemaxmlns:xs="http://www.w3.org/2001/XMLSchema">
  <xs:elementname="CustomerAddress">
    <xs:complexType>
      <xs:sequence>
        <xs:elementref="BillingAddress"/>
      </xs:sequence>
    </xs:complexType>
  </xs:element>

  <xs:elementname="BillingAddress" type="AddressType"/>

  <xs:complexTypename="AddressType">
    <xs:sequence>
      <xs:elementname="StreetAddress"/>
      <xs:elementname="City" "/>
      <xs:elementname="State"/>
      <xs:elementname="PostalCode"/>
    </xs:sequence>
  </xs:complexType>

</xs:schema>
```

Local element declarations. Although named, these elements are nested within and specific to the complexType declaration and cannot be referenced by name.

FIGURE 11.11

Locally Declared XML Schema Elements

and then referencing them from within the address structure, with the Local Declarations pattern, each of the elements would be explicitly and directly defined within the overall "Address" element.

For a very simple service interface that is not expected to change over time, this can be an effective schema design pattern. The service interface schema will contain fewer syntactical declarations and references. Also, the service interface designer does not have to navigate references to find the global declarations. Rather, each declaration is declared directly where it occurs and within a parent hierarchy (see Figure 11.11). In this model, the XML Schema declarations use an explicit "name" attribute for elements and leaves complexTypes and simpleTypes as nested, "anonymous" declarations. That is, the complexTypes and simpleTypes do not have exposed names.

While the Local Declarations pattern will initially seem to be a simple and intuitive approach for service interface schema design, it has several potential disadvantages. Each of the nested elements, complexTypes, and simpleTypes are exclusively defined to their parent element declarations. That is, they cannot be referenced by name and reused elsewhere in the service interface schema. This means that every time an element or simpleType of the same definition and constraints is needed, it must be repeated as additional syntax. Over time and assuming that some change will occur to the service interface, it is likely that these separate syntactical declarations will evolve to become disparate. Rather than defining an "ItemID" element to the service interface XML Schema once and then referencing that standard definition as needed, separate "ItemID" elements would be defined (see Figure 11.12).

Another disadvantage of the Local Declarations pattern is the inability to apply and enforce enterprise data standards consistently. An example enterprise data standard for all monetary amounts defined as a decimal data type, with seven whole number digits and two fractional digits, can be

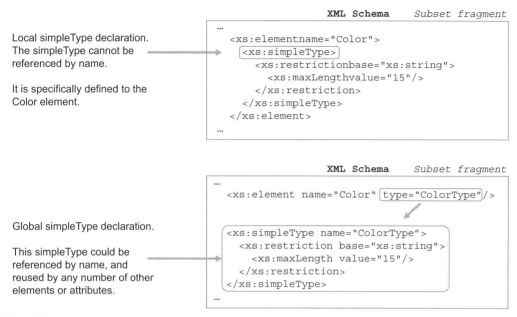

XML Schema   *Subset fragment*

Local simpleType declaration. The simpleType cannot be referenced by name.

It is specifically defined to the Color element.

```
...
<xs:elementname="Color">
  <xs:simpleType>
    <xs:restrictionbase="xs:string">
      <xs:maxLengthvalue="15"/>
    </xs:restriction>
  </xs:simpleType>
</xs:element>
...
```

XML Schema   *Subset fragment*

Global simpleType declaration.

This simpleType could be referenced by name, and reused by any number of other elements or attributes.

```
...
<xs:element name="Color" type="ColorType"/>

<xs:simpleType name="ColorType">
  <xs:restriction base="xs:string">
    <xs:maxLength value="15"/>
  </xs:restriction>
</xs:simpleType>
...
```

FIGURE 11.12

Global vs Local simpleType Declarations

implemented by a simpleType (see Figure 11.13). If defined by a single named and globally declared simpleType, it can then be referenced and consistently reused by any number of element and attribute declarations. Alternatively, if defined locally within each separate element or attribute declaration as a nested and anonymous simpleType, it cannot be referenced and reused. If a Local Declaration pattern is applied to the simpleType, each monetary amount element or attribute that was required to comply with the monetary amount standard would require a replication of the simpleType declaration as its own and separate simpleType definition. As changes to the service interface might be needed over time, the potential for disparity between the separate simpleType declarations increases.

Although it may initially require a more significant service interface design effort, a strong recommendation is to avoid Local Declaration patterns. The Global Declaration patterns are generally more effective.

11.4 REUSABLE SCHEMA PATTERNS

When designing a service interface, there is significant value in modularizing XML Schema declarations that have significant potential for reuse. Reusable Schema patterns allow an XML Schema to be defined as a modular set of schema syntax that is reused by other XML Schemas. With Reusable Schema patterns, the degree of reuse rapidly increases, as does the ability to proliferate enterprise standards as complexType structures, elements, and data types (defined by simpleTypes). The process for designing and developing a service interface is also simplified. The process becomes more of a reference and assembly activity than development.

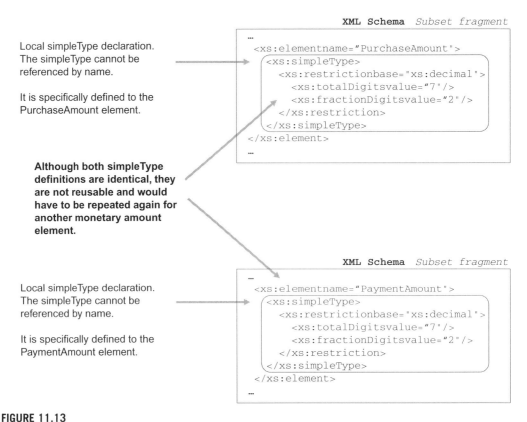

Local simpleType declaration.
The simpleType cannot be
referenced by name.

It is specifically defined to the
PurchaseAmount element.

**Although both simpleType
definitions are identical, they
are not reusable and would
have to be repeated again for
another monetary amount
element.**

Local simpleType declaration.
The simpleType cannot be
referenced by name.

It is specifically defined to the
PaymentAmount element.

FIGURE 11.13

Locally Declared simpleType for Monetary Amount

XML Schemas provide extensive support for the XML Namespaces specification.[5] The application of a targetNamespace and a corresponding default namespace to each XML Schema helps to provide a method of unique identification and to avoid collisions between like-named declarations.

However, an explicit namespace is not required of every XML Schema (e.g., targetNamespace and default namespace). The No-Namespace Schema Reuse pattern exploits the lack of a target Namespace to advantage (see Figure 11.14). Some service interface structures, elements, and data types can have very broad utility across applications and services. Something as simple as a "Date" element ("< Date/ >") that is further constrained by a simpleType to represent an enterprise standard is a common example. Standard "Date" elements could be defined separately within each XML Schema to represent a context specific to those schemas. If each of those "Date" elements participates in the targetNamespace of those schemas, they are separate and unique declarations. If declared globally, they can be reused by named reference. However, the references would in some manner need to be qualified by the namespace.

An alternative is to define an enterprise standard "Date" element to an XML Schema that does not have a target or default namespace. In order to reuse that standard Date element from other schemas,

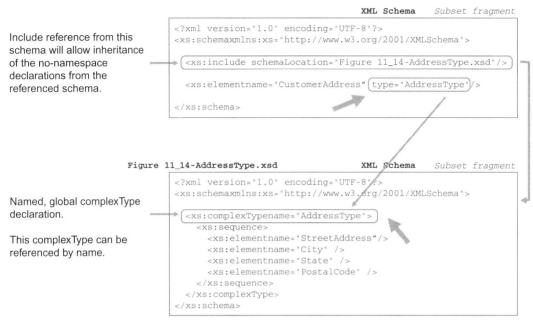

FIGURE 11.14

No-Namespace Schema Reuse Pattern

an XML Schema "include" declaration ("< include/ >") would be required by the referencing schema. When reference is made from the originating and targetNamespace qualified schema to the "Date" element declaration of the no-namespace schemas, it will be "coerced" into the target Namespace of the parent or referencing schema. That is, the referenced "Date" element now participates in the targetNamespace of the referencing schema. A similar pattern is sometime referred to as a "Chameleon."[6]

With the No-Namespace Schema Reuse pattern, the referenced XML Schemas and their intrinsic global declarations can be referenced by name and reused in any number of ways and by any number of other service interface schemas. The referenced no-namespace complexType, element, and simple-Type declarations are coerced into the namespace of the referencing schema (see Figure 11.15). When instantiated form the service interface schemas in the XML message, the namespace of the referencing schema will be inherited and then exposed as part of the element name.

The emphasis of the No-Namespace Schema Reuse pattern is on the broad, utilized reuse of schemas declarations across any number of other namespace-qualified schemas. Yet, coercion of a no-namespace qualified declaration into the namespace of a referencing and targetNamespace-qualified XML Schema is not a limitation. A no-namespace qualified XML Schema declaration could also be referenced by and included in another no-namespace qualified XML Schema (see Figure 11.16). With this example, neither the referencing nor the referenced XML Schemas are namespace qualified. Where this variation of the No-Namespace Schema Reuse pattern can apply is with an assembly of modular schemas into a higher-level parent XML Schema that does not have a defined target or

XML Schema   *Subset fragment*

```
<?xml version="1.0" encoding="UTF-8"?>
<xs:schemaxmlns:xs="http://www.w3.org/2001/XMLSchema"
        targetNamespace="http://Widget-Example.com/Patterns"
        xmlns="http://Widget-Example.com/Patterns"
        xmlns:PATTERN="http://Widget-Example.com/Patterns">
  <xs:include schemaLocation="Figure 11_15-DateType.xsd"/>
  <xs:element name="Transcation">
    <xs:complexType>
      <xs:sequence>
        <xs:element name="TransactionID" />
        <xs:element name="TransactionAmount"/>
        <xs:element ref="Date" />
      </xs:sequence>
    </xs:complexType>
  </xs:element>
</xs:schema>
```

Include reference from this schema will allow inheritance of the no-namespace declarations from the referenced schema.

The element reference for "Date" will coerce the named global element from the included schema into the PATTERN namespace.

Figure 11_15-DateType.xsd   XML Schema   *Subset fragment*

```
<?xml version="1.0" encoding="UTF-8"?>
<xs:schema xmlns:xs="http://www.w3.org/2001/XMLSchema">

      <xs:element name="Date" />

</xs:schema>
```

Named, global element declaration.

This element can be referenced by name.

FIGURE 11.15

Coercion of a No-Namespace Element Declaration

XML Schema   *Subset fragment*

```
...
<xs:include schemaLocation="Figure 11_16-AddressType.xsd"/>
...
<xs:element ref="Country" />
...
```

Namespace Qualified "parent" Schema

Figure 11_16-AddressType.xsd   XML Schema   *Subset fragment*

```
...
<xs:include schemaLocation="Figure 11_16-Country.xsd"/>
...
<xs:element name="Country" type="CountryType" />
...
```

No-Namespace Qualified Schema

Figure 11_16-Country.xsd   XML Schema   *Subset fragment*

```
...
<xs:simpleType name="CountryType">
  <xs:restriction base="xs:string">
    <xs:enumeration value="United States"/>
    <xs:enumeration value="Canada"/>
    <xs:enumeration value="Mexico"/>
  </xs:restriction>
</xs:simpleType>
...
```

No-Namespace Qualified Schema

FIGURE 11.16

No-Namespace XML Schemas Assembled into a Hierarchy

default namespace. The entire no-namespace schema assembly can then be referenced at the highest parent schema level by another namespace qualified schema and coerced into its targetNamespace.

With the No-Namespace Schema Reuse pattern, reference and reuse by a namespace-qualified XML Schema (e.g., with a defined targetNamespace) is sometime referred to as a "Proxy" pattern. The higher-level and namespace-qualified schema acts as a "proxy" over the no-namespace schema. After the no-namespace schema and its referenced declarations are coerced into the namespace of the referencing "Proxy" schema, they can also be referenced by qualified name from additional and higher level references to that namespace-qualified proxy schema. In this example, the No-Namespace Schema Reuse pattern and the Proxy Schema pattern can be applied in combination.

The Namespace Schema Reuse pattern is perhaps the more common pattern for schema reuse (see Figure 11.17). With this pattern, each of the referenced schemas has a defined targetNamespace (and most likely a default namespace). The application of the different namespaces allows the integrity of the schema declarations to be retained, and collisions between like-named declarations are avoided. The XML Schemas syntax for applying the Namespace Schema Reuse pattern requires an "import" declaration ("< import/ >"). Attributes of the schema import declaration include a "namespace" attribute, which is intended to contain a value representing the targetNamespace of the referenced and imported XML Schema.

Of importance are the internal schema declarations of a namespace-qualified schema. When an intrinsic declaration of a namespace-qualified schema such as an element is also qualified by the

FIGURE 11.17

Namespace Schema Reuse Pattern

XML Schema

```
<?xml version="1.0" encoding="UTF-8"?>
<xs:schema xmlns:xs="http://www.w3.org/2001/XMLSchema"
        elementFormDefault="qualified"
        xmlns:OPTIONS="http://Widget-Example.com/Options"
        xmlns="http://Widget-Example.com/Inventory/Product/Add/REQUEST"
        targetNamespace="http://Widget-Example.com/Inventory/Product/Add/REQUEST">
  <xs:import namespace="http://Widget-Example.com/Options"
          schemaLocation="StandardServiceOptions.xsd"/>
  <xs:element name="Request">
    <xs:complex Type>
      <xs:sequence>
        <xs:element ref="OPTIONS:OptionsSection" minOccurs="1" maxOccurs="1"/>
      </xs:sequence>
    </xs:complexType>
  </xs:element>
</xs:schema>
```

StandardServiceOptions.xsd   XML Schema   *Subset fragment*

Namespace Qualified
Schema

```
<?xml version="1.0" encoding="UTF-8"?>
<xs:schema xmlns:xs="http://www.w3.org/2001/XMLSchema"
        elementFormDefault="qualified"
        xmlns="http://Widget-Example.com/Options"
        xmlns:OPTIONS="http://Widget-Example.com/Options"
        targetNamespace="http://Widget-Example.com/Options" >
  <xs:element name="OptionsSection">
  ...
```

FIGURE 11.18

Reference of a Namespace-Qualified Element

schema namespace, reference to that element will require qualification (see Figure 11.18). Even though the element might be simply named as "OptionsSection" ("< element name="OptionsSectio n"/ >"), an external reference to that element would require a qualified name. The most common type of reference includes a namespace prefix that corresponds to the targetNamespace where the element is declared.

Application of Schema Reuse patterns results in the assembly of a service interface schema by referencing other separate XML Schemas. However, as the levels of schema import and include references begin to deepen, they can quickly become confusing. As a result, the intended modularity and reuse are overshadowed by the complexity of the schema assembly. A complex assembly of schemas can also become difficult to manage and maintain. While these patterns provide an effective method for exploiting schema reuse and namespaces, caution is advised. The service interface designer should consider the advantages of schema assembly and reuse, as well as the over application of these patterns.

11.5 SUBSTITUTION GROUP PATTERNS

Another type of XML Schema design pattern helps to resolve the need for polymorphic content in a service interface. In the context of a service interface, polymorphism allows that a somewhat abstract structure can take on different structural forms at different times. For some object-oriented designers,

XML Schema *Subset fragment*

```
...
<xs:elementname="ContactPoint" type="xs:anyType" abstract="true"/>

<xs:elementname="Address" substitutionGroup="ContactPoint">
  <xs:complexType>
    <xs:sequence>
      <xs:elementname="AddressTo"/>
      <xs:elementname="StreetAddress"/>
      <xs:elementname="City"/>
      <xs:elementname="State"/>
      <xs:elementname="PostalCode"/>
    </xs:sequence>
  </xs:complexType>
</xs:element>

<xs:elementname="E-Mail" substitutionGroup="ContactPoint">
  <xs:complexType>
    <xs:sequence>
      <xs:elementname="E-MailAddress"/>
      <xs:elementname="E-MailDomain"/>
    </xs:sequence>
  </xs:complexType>
</xs:element>

<xs:elementname="Telephone" substitutionGroup="ContactPoint">
  <xs:complexType>
    <xs:sequence>
      <xs:elementname="AreaCode"/>
      <xs:elementname="TelephoneNumber"/>
    </xs:sequence>
  </xs:complexType>
</xs:element>
...
```

FIGURE 11.19

substitutionGroup Pattern

polymorphism has a negative reputation. Depending upon the implementation, a polymorphic object class loses its specificity. Rather than dispute the merits of polymorphism across different types of designs and implementatio ns, the application of this pattern to a service interface can be applied to advantage for a narrow set of use cases. XML Schemas supports a declaration known as a "substitution-Group" (see Figure 11.19). This declaration allows a "head" element to be structurally implemented in different ways in the corresponding instance. If the "head" element has the potential to be substituted by different types of structures, its data type should be defined as XML Schema supported "any Type."

Rarely will the substitutionGroup pattern apply to a request or a fault message. Rather, it has some advantageous use to a reply message. The notion of a customer contact point is a reasonable example (see Example 11.2). A reply message might need to include different types of address structures based upon the context of the data at rest sources. If the service exposes a read type operation for customer data, the service interface and supporting behavior might allow a return reply message that contains a preferred contact point as a Postal Address, an E-Mail Address, or a Telephone Number. The service interface schema could include a defined "Contact Point" element (" < ContactPoint/ >"). However, the structure that lies under the Contact Point element might be determined by the customer's contact preferences and could vary from customer to customer. Rather than defining each type of Contact Point by a fixed structure, populating one of the contact points with data in the reply message, and returning all three structures in the reply message, the Contact Point element could be defined as a substitutionGroup. The three types of contact point structures could then be defined to reference and substitute the Contact Point "head" element.

Example 11.2
SubstitutionGroup – Polymorphism Example

```
<?xml version = "1.0" encoding = "UTF-8" ?>
- <xs:schema xmlns:xs = "http://www.w3.org/2001/XMLSchema">
- <xs:element name = "Customer">
- <xs:complexType>
- <xs:sequence>
<xs:element ref = "CustomerID"/>
<xs:element ref = "PreferredContactPoint"/>
</xs:sequence>
</xs:complexType>
</xs:element>
<xs:element name = "CustomerID" type = "xs:integer"/>
- <xs:element name = "PreferredContactPoint">
- <xs:complexType>
- <xs:sequence>
<xs:element ref = "ContactPoint"/>
</xs:sequence>
</xs:complexType>
</xs:element>
<xs:element name = "ContactPoint" type = "xs:anyType" abstract = "true"/>
- <xs:element name = "Address" substitutionGroup = "ContactPoint">
- <xs:complexType>
- <xs:sequence>
<xs:element ref = "AddressTo"/>
<xs:element ref = "StreetAddress"/>
<xs:element ref = "City"/>
<xs:element ref = "State"/>
<xs:element ref = "PostalCode"/>
</xs:sequence>
</xs:complexType>
</xs:element >
<xs:element name = "AddressTo" type = "xs:string"/>
<xs:element name = "StreetAddress" type = "xs:string"/>
<xs:element name = "City" type = "xs:string"/>
<xs:element name = "State" type = "xs:string"/>
```

```
<xs:element name = "PostalCode" type = "xs:string"/>
- <xs:element name = "E-Mail" substitutionGroup = "ContactPoint">
- <xs:complexType>
- <xs:sequence>
<xs:element ref = "E-MailAddress"/>
<xs:element ref = "E-MailDomain"/>
</xs:sequence>
</xs:complexType>
</xs:element>
<xs:element name = "E-MailAddress" type = "xs:string"/>
<xs:element name = "E-MailDomain" type = "xs:string"/>
- <xs:element name = "Telephone" substitutionGroup = "ContactPoint">
- <xs:complexType>
- <xs:sequence>
<xs:element ref = "AreaCode"/>
<xs:element ref = "TelephoneNumber"/>
</xs:sequence>
</xs:complexType>
</xs:element>
<xs:element name = "AreaCode" type = "xs:string"/>
<xs:element name = "TelephoneNumber" type = "xs:string"/>
</xs:schema>
```

The substitutionGroup pattern can help to resolve the need for polymorphic (variable) XML message content. However, there is also a dependency on the consumer of the message to support polymorphism. Some application languages might not provide support for polymorphic message content or for XML Schemas substitutionGroup declarations. Before implementing the Polymorphic schema design pattern, be sure to verify that it is supported.

SUMMARY

XML Schema design patterns are repeatable models that exploit a variety of XML Schemas syntactical capabilities and can be applied to a service interface design. These patterns can simplify the design process and result in significant reuse and compliance with enterprise standards. They can also result in easily maintained and managed service interface schemas.

The types of patterns vary and can include complexType Patterns, Global Declaration Patterns, Local Declaration Patterns, Reusable Schema Patterns, and substitutionGroup Pattern. These patterns can include variations, each with their own advantages and disadvantages. In many cases, they can also be applied in combination to a service interface.

There are three primary types of complexType patterns (e.g., Type Abstraction, Type Extension, and Type Restriction). The Type Abstraction pattern allows an element to inherit the structure of a referenced complexType. The Type Extension pattern inherits the structure of a referenced complexType and then allows for additional elements as extension. The Type Restriction pattern inherits the structure and constraints of a referenced complexType. The restriction ensures that the referencing structure is in compliance with the constraints and limitations of the referenced complexType.

Global declarations allow complexTypes, groups, elements, and simpleTypes (and several other XML Schema declarations) to be declared as children of the overall schema element and have an identifiable name. These declarations can then be referenced by name and reused within the schema or possibly across schemas. Alternatively, Local declarations are defined and encapsulated within other schema declarations. Locally declared complexTypes and simpleTypes do not have a specific name (they are anonymous) and therefore are not able to be referenced and reused. Similarly, local element declarations may have a name but are encapsulated within the scope of other declarations and therefore are not exposed for reference.

Reusable Schema patterns allow XML Schemas to be defined as modular subset schemas. The overall service interface schemas could then be assembled by reference from these modular schemas as building blocks. The service interface design and development effort is greatly simplified, and the schema declarations will exhibit a high degree of reuse. These patterns include No-Namespace and Namespace Schema Reuse patterns. Both are similar in context and allow for reference and assembly of other schemas. However, the No-Namespace pattern is specific to XML Schemas that do not have a declared targetNamespace. Alternatively, the Namespace pattern is specific to XML Schemas with a declared targetNamespace.

The substitutionGroup pattern is a polymorphic pattern. That is, it allows a corresponding XML message element to inherit its structure from other and potentially different structures. Polymorphism is often a topic of controversy, and not all application languages provide support. When polymorphism is a service interface requirement, the substitutionGroup pattern may provide a solution. However, with all XML Schema design patterns, the service designer must ensure that the applicable pattern will provide benefits, and the underlying XML Schema declarations and constraints are supported by the service and consumers of the service.

REFERENCES

1. Walmsley P, eds. XML Schema Part 0: Primer. 2nd ed. (W3C, October 28, 2004). <http://www.w3.org/TR/xmlschema-0/>.

2. Cagle K, Duckett J, et al., Professional XML Schemas. Hoboken, NJ: WROX Press; 2001.

3. Bray T, Hollander D, Layman A, Tobin R, eds. Namespaces in XML 1.0. 2nd ed. (W3C, August 16, 2006). <http://www.w3.org/TR/REC-xml-names/>.

4. Cagle K, Duckett J, et al., *Professional* XML *Schemas*. Hoboken, NJ: WROX Press; 2001.

5. Bray T, Hollander D, Layman A, Tobin R, eds. Namespaces in XML 1.0. 2nd ed. (W3C, August 16, 2006). <http://www.w3.org/TR/REC-xml-names/>.

6. Cagle K, Duckett J, et al., Professional XML Schemas. Hoboken, NJ: WROX Press; 2001.

Schema Assembly and Reuse

12

XML Schemas are not only powerful implementations of metadata rules and constraints, but they are also subject to reuse. The interface schema for an SOA service such as "Add New Product," will define message content that includes supporting product structures, elements, and data types. As a single XML Schema artifact, this schema represents the information context of the service contract that allows consumers to request the service to add products. In addition to the "Add New Product" service, there may be other SOA services such as "Get Product Engineering Data" and "Search Product" that include the same product related message content in their message payloads.

Each of these services will require a service interface that includes an XML Schema. For each of these separate services, the service designer might elect to create separate interface schemas that incorporate and repeat the product context that is required by each of the services (see Figure 12.1). As an example, the "Add New Product", "Get Product Engineering Data", and "Search Product" services would need to include an "Item ID" element ("< ItemID/ > ") defined to each of the service interface schemas. While functional, this approach is also suboptimal. If another, new product-related SOA service such as "Delete Product" was developed, it would also require WSDL and XML Schema, with yet another replication of the same "Item ID" element definition. Over time, the number of other product-related services would most likely increase, and the proliferation of interface definitions would also increase. If at some point a change to the "Item ID" element were required, such as increasing the size from 4 to 5 characters, each of the individual interface schemas would also need to be carefully analyzed, modified, and tested.

As an alternative to this separate schema definition approach, each of the service interfaces could be designed to incorporate an assembly of subordinate schemas (see Figure 12.2). A reusable schema could be defined to include a single "Item ID" element definition and is then referenced and inherited by each of the product-related service interfaces. A later length change to the Item ID element would be implemented in only one standard schema with the change being inherited by all referencing interface schemas. Each of the individual services would still require analysis and testing. However, as a result of reusing the schema, each of the referencing interface schemas would have a consistent Item ID element definition, with consistency across the services. Additional benefits of this reusable schema approach include simplified interface schema maintenance, reduction of one-off metadata definitions, and a reduction in the potential for data anomalies.

235

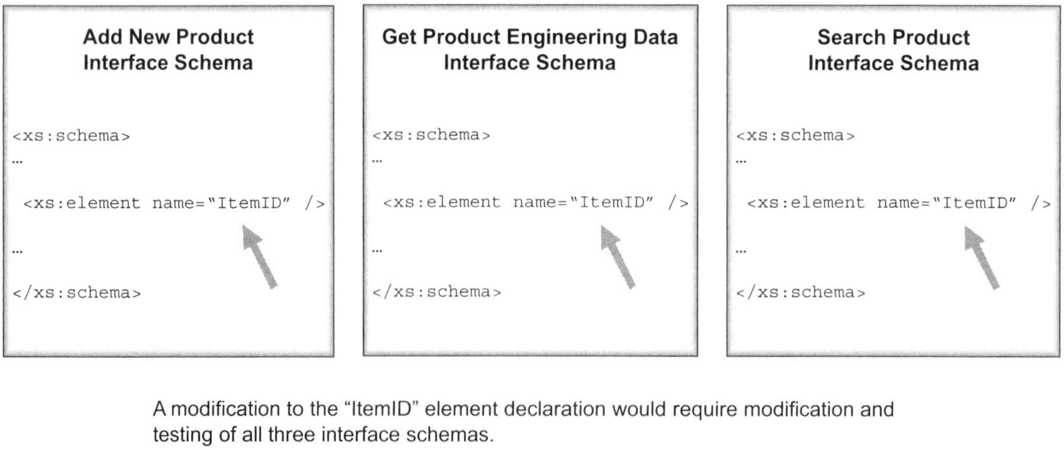

A modification to the "ItemID" element declaration would require modification and testing of all three interface schemas.

FIGURE 12.1

Impact of Change Without Schema Reuse

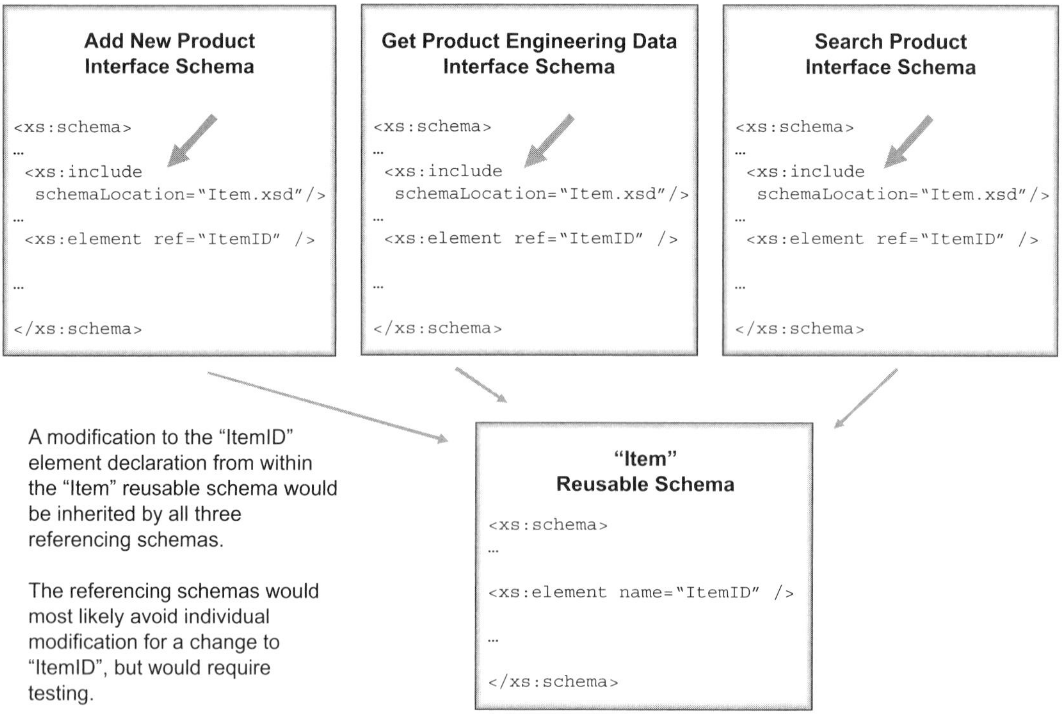

A modification to the "ItemID" element declaration from within the "Item" reusable schema would be inherited by all three referencing schemas.

The referencing schemas would most likely avoid individual modification for a change to "ItemID", but would require testing.

FIGURE 12.2

Impact of Change with Schema Reuse

XML Schema reuse is not limited to a single global element definition. A reusable schema could be defined for element structures (as complexType and group definitions), individual elements, and also data types (as simpleType definitions). However, this ability to define reusable schemas is not without potential complexity. Even though some elements might at first seem to be good candidates to externalize as reusable interface schemas, there are also several important design considerations.

12.1 CONSIDERATIONS FOR SCHEMA REUSE

When developing a canonical message design, a step in the process results in development of initial interface schemas (as discussed in Chapter 8, "Canonical Message Design"). These initial schemas will include the XML Schema declarations for all of the intended message content. They are designed specifically for a single project and possibly to a single service. Similar to the earlier example of numerous "Item ID" element definitions across product-related services, there is a significant potential to design and develop services that replicate the same XML Schema declarations across many services. When this occurs, service interfaces are designed as if new for each service and the cost of development and later interface maintenance increases, rather than decreases.

Alternatively, the Canonical Message Design process (specifically, "Subset Modular XML Schemas") can help to identify schema declarations that if decomposed to separate schemas would present opportunities for reuse (see Figure 12.3). To identify reuse opportunities, the interface designer must consider schema definitions that exhibit some common context, semantics, or functional affinity across services. The potential for interface reuse increases where these affinities are from across the entire enterprise, regardless of the line of business, and where the schema definitions reflect an enterprise standard.

At first glance, the notion of reuse seems to be common sense—just use an XML Schema or a schema declaration more than once. Conceptually, this is correct. However, to effectively reuse an XML Schema, it should have been designed with intent to reuse. Designing a reusable schema also requires several key considerations, such as the following:

- Identifying potential opportunities for service interface reuse
- Interface schema granularity
- Designing the interface schema with intent to reuse

12.1.1 Identifying service interface schema reuse opportunities

The first and most important step is to consider which structures, elements, and types of a service interface are good candidates for reuse. For some services and similar to the earlier "Item ID" example, there will be one or more message structures, elements, or data types that represent a common context across other services. However, not every message element or schema declaration is a good candidate for reuse. Some structures, elements, and data types should intentionally remain specific to a line of business, application area, or functional area.

As one example, a "Get Accounts Receivable Balance" service that extracts and exposes credit lines and accounts receivable balances to consumers might not be appropriate for an Inventory Management functional area. Accounts Receivable information returned by this service might be limited in scope and the financial data might be sensitive, therefore requiring controls over its exposure. Alternatively, a "Get Customer" service would expose customer information such as the Customer

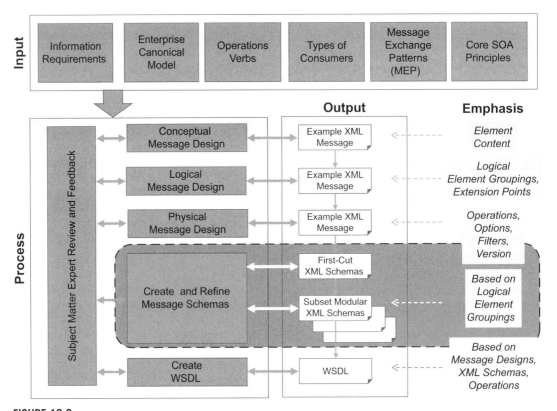

FIGURE 12.3

The Canonical Message Design Process

ID, Customer Contact Information, and Customer Bank Account. This same customer information would be applicable to both Order Entry service consumers and to Accounts Receivable consumers, but not for an Inventory Management process. Similarly, Product information is core to Inventory Management and is also required for Order Processing. However, a "Get Product Data" service might have little value for Accounts Receivable. With each of these different functional areas and servicing examples, there is information that presents a potential for reuse outside of its basic context. Reusable XML Schemas can be designed for each of the cross-functional and common contexts and then reused in other service interface schemas.

Other potential reuse opportunities include those pieces of information that are not limited by any line of business, application, or functional area. Rather, they represent a broadly recognized canonical standard across the entire enterprise. While these "enterprise" reuse opportunities can vary, there are a number of common examples (see Figure 12.4). Reference data and more specifically industry standard code sets, such as Country Code, Currency Code, and Language Code, tend to cross all lines of business and functional areas. These examples are not a limitation, and other enterprise-specific code sets such as status codes, error codes, and processing codes, can also present opportunities for enterprise-level reuse.

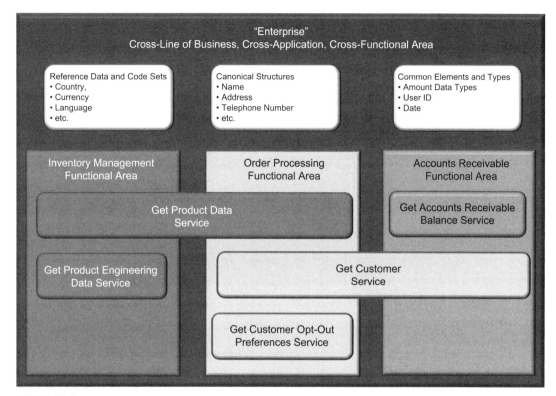

FIGURE 12.4

Types of Reusable Service Context

Another type of enterprise reuse opportunity includes interface and message structures such as a Postal Address, Person Name, and Telephone Number. An enterprise standard Postal Address structure would apply equally well to Customers, Employees, Vendors, Warehouse Locations, Regulatory Agencies, and so on. A standard Person Name structure, including elements such as First, Middle, Last, Prefix, Suffix, Professional Title, Academic Title, Alias, and Pre-Marital Name, would also apply to a Customer, Employee, or Vendor Representative. A standard Telephone Number structure would include the decomposed parts of a telephone number such as Country Code, Area Code, Local Exchange, Local Number, and Private Extension and also apply to any need for telephone number data.

Still other examples of enterprise reuse opportunities can include individual elements and data types. A standard element definition for User ID can be applied as transaction audit information. A standard data type for Monetary Amounts can be applied to financial amount elements, such as an Item Price, Item Cost, Total Order Value, Customer Open Balance, or Customer Credit Line.

Although there are many examples of reuse candidates, some will be unique to a specific enterprise. A standard and reusable XML Schema that defines a Postal Address structure might be a good

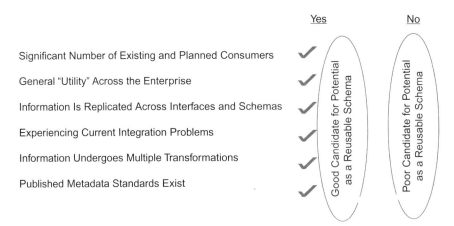

Significant Number of Existing and Planned Consumers

General "Utility" Across the Enterprise

Information Is Replicated Across Interfaces and Schemas

Experiencing Current Integration Problems

Information Undergoes Multiple Transformations

Published Metadata Standards Exist

A higher number of "Yes" responses will generally identify a good schema reuse candidate.

FIGURE 12.5

Criteria for Identifying Candidate Reusable Schemas

candidate for one business enterprise, but possibly not for another. Rather than attempt to describe a list of potential reuse opportunities, another approach is to seek out your own opportunities for reuse and then to examine those structures, elements, and types as reuse candidates. Potential reuse opportunities can be identified from several common scenarios and criteria. One potential source of reuse opportunities can be derived from the list of traditional interfaces between applications. A high number of interfaces that expose data from one data source or one application represents a potential for reuse. In addition to more traditional application interfaces, the service interface designer should look across all of the current and planned SOA services and identify potential reuse candidates with these characteristics (see Figure 12.5):

- A significant number of consumers for a single data source, a single service, or a single application interface

- Obvious "utility" across the entire enterprise

- Information from one service or application that is replicated and again exposed by other services and applications

- Existing integration problems (e.g., mismatched code values between applications and service consumers, different type definitions for a single data element, different names for a single data element, and other data anomalies)

- Elements exposed by one service or application undergo multiple transformation processes between consumers

- Published and well-known enterprise metadata standards

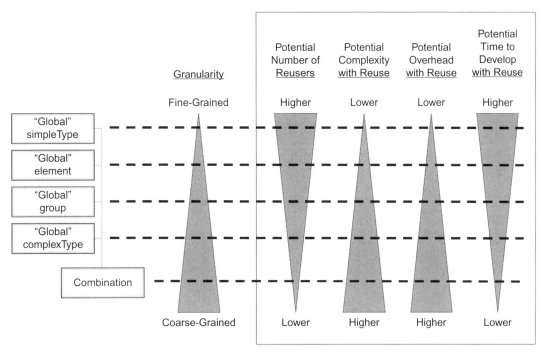

FIGURE 12.6

Reuse Granularity

Once the reuse candidates have been identified, the interface designer must determine which XML Schema Design Patterns will apply to the new, reusable schema.

12.1.2 Interface schema granularity

The granularity of a schema declaration can influence the degree to which a schema will be reused. Schemas that represent common enterprise semantics or context are typically subject to a higher potential for reuse. Similarly, fine-grained schema declarations such as data types (simpleType) and element definitions tend to experience a higher level of reuse (see Figure 12.6). That is, a data type can be applied to many different elements of a service interface and across different services. A schema-defined structure (complexType) also presents an opportunity for reuse. However, as a coarse-grained structure, there may be fewer potential reuse opportunities.

Combining reusable declarations of varying granularity can be very effective within a single and well-defined context. An enterprise standard schema for a Postal Address might include combinations of a complexType structure, along with globally declared elements and simpleTypes. Developing a schema to define a Postal Address structure and also including individual elements for City, State, Postal Code, and Country can be highly effective. However, a schema that includes declarations of mixed granularity and inconsistent scope is less likely to be reused.

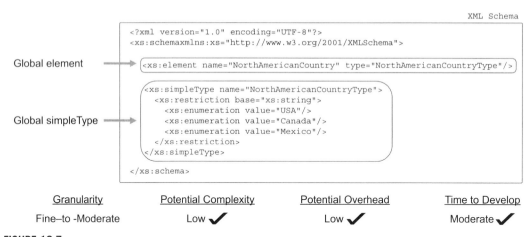

                                                                    XML Schema

Global element ⟶
                    ```xml
                    <?xml version="1.0" encoding="UTF-8"?>
                    <xs:schemaxmlns:xs="http://www.w3.org/2001/XMLSchema">

                    <xs:element name="NorthAmericanCountry" type="NorthAmericanCountryType"/>

                    <xs:simpleType name="NorthAmericanCountryType">
                      <xs:restriction base="xs:string">
                        <xs:enumeration value="USA"/>
                        <xs:enumeration value="Canada"/>
                        <xs:enumeration value="Mexico"/>
                      </xs:restriction>
                    </xs:simpleType>

                    </xs:schema>
                    ```
Global simpleType ⟶

Granularity	Potential Complexity	Potential Overhead	Time to Develop
Fine–to -Moderate	Low ✓	Low ✓	Moderate ✓

FIGURE 12.7

Example Reusable Enterprise Schema

Another consideration is the amount of overhead from potential reuse. A schema that is designed to include a moderate number of elements and data type definitions (simpleType) will have a higher potential for reuse than a schema with an extremely high number of element and data type declarations. If the reusable schema includes a vast number of declarations, the interface designer for a new service might determine that the schema is too heavyweight for reuse. Although subjective, the determination of "heavyweight" reflects the number of declarations or how well an XML Schema parser might or might not optimize across the declarations that are unnecessary (e.g., as potential run-time validation latency).

An enterprise standard schema that represents a common code set is one of the best models to consider (see Figure 12.7). An enterprise standard schema that includes an element and a separate data type (simpleType) for the North American Region with enumeration values of "USA", "Canada", and "Mexico", is moderate to fine-grained, lightweight, easy to reference, and does not include a high number of unrelated declarations that might remain unused. Once the schema is referenced from the overall interface schema, the internal simpleType would be inherited as the referenced "type" value for element or attribute declarations. The interface designer has the option to also inherit the "North American Country" ("< NorthAmericanCountry/ >") element, which also references the same data type.

With this example, the granularity of the reusable North American Country schema is mixed. It would contain both a global simpleType with enumerations and a separate global element declaration. Both of which were available to other referencing schemas as needed. The scope and context of the schema are also consistent (specific to a North American Country element and values), which simplifies later potential for reuse. If the schema were to also include declarations for nonlocation or nongeographic elements such as "Item ID" and "Account Balance", even though they are also standard and reusable elements, they are of completely different contexts and semantics from that of location and geography. This example of inconsistent scope and context complicates the schema and would most likely add element declarations that are "overhead" for potential reusers.

Another example of potential reuse might be an enterprise standard Postal Address structure (see Example 12.1), represented as a complexType declaration. The nested child elements of the address structure (Address Line, City, State, Postal Code, etc.) are also defined in the same schema as separately declared global elements. All of the schema declarations are of the same scope and context (a postal address). However, reusers of the schema have the ability to choose which of the declarations can be used by their interface. The elements can be referenced and reused separate from the structure if needed.

Example 12.1

Example Reusable Postal Address Schema

```
<?xml version="1.0" encoding="UTF-8" ?>
- <xs:schema xmlns:xs="http://www.w3.org/2001/XMLSchema">
<xs:element name="PostalAddress" type = "PostalAddressType"/>
- <xs:complexType name="PostalAddressType">
- <xs:sequence>
<xs:element ref="AddressTo" minOccurs="1" maxOccurs="1" />
<xs:element ref="AddressLine" minOccurs="1" maxOccurs="4" />
<xs:element ref="City" minOccurs="1" maxOccurs="1" />
<xs:element ref="State" minOccurs="1" maxOccurs="1" />
<xs:element ref="County" minOccurs="1" maxOccurs="1" />
<xs:element ref="PostalCode" minOccurs="1" maxOccurs="1" />
<xs:element ref="Country" minOccurs="1" maxOccurs="1" />
</xs:sequence>
</xs:complexType>
<xs:element name="AddressTo" type="AddressLineType" />
<xs:element name="AddressLine" type="AddressLineType" />
<xs:element name="City" />
<xs:element name="State" />
<xs:element name="County" />
<xs:element name="PostalCode" />
<xs:element name="Country" />
- <xs:simpleType name="AddressLineType">
- <xs:restriction base="xs:string">
<xs:maxLength value="40" />
</xs:restriction>
</xs:simpleType>
</xs:schema>
```

Another reusable schema example might represent a combination of several well-defined and standard data type declarations (see Example 12.2). While these types might not be of the same specific context, they are scoped to represent only data types. The example schema does not include structures or elements. This type of schema includes very fine-grained declarations that have broad utility across lines of business, applications, and functional areas. The potential for reuse is high. Alternatively, if the designer had decided to include all possible data types from across the enterprise in this one schema and regardless of context, the potential for reuse by other interface schemas might diminish. That schema could become overly complex and difficult to manage.

Example 12.2
Example Reusable Type Schema

```
<?xml version="1.0" encoding="UTF-8" ?>
- <xs:schema xmlns:xs="http://www.w3.org/2001/XMLSchema">
- <xs:simpleType name="MonetaryAmountType">
- <xs:restriction base="xs:decimal">
<xs:totalDigits value="11" />
<xs:fractionDigits value="2" />
</xs:restriction>
</xs:simpleType>
- <xs:simpleType name="CreditAmountType">
- <xs:restriction base="xs:decimal">
<xs:totalDigits value="11" />
<xs:fractionDigits value= "2" />
<xs:minInclusive value="0.00" />
</xs:restriction>
</xs:simpleType>
- <xs:simpleType name="DebitAmountType">
- <xs:restriction base="xs:decimal">
<xs:totalDigits value="11" />
<xs:fractionDigits value="2" />
<xs:maxInclusive value="0.00" />
</xs:restriction>
</xs:simpleType>
</xs:schema>
```

While there is no single rule or pattern that applies across all potential reuse opportunities, granularity plays a significant role. If the interface schema is designed to represent an abstract set of XML Schema declarations that are not obvious as to intent for reuse, other service interface designers will avoid using it. Alternatively, if the schema appears to be overly coarse-grained, other interface designers will view it as heavyweight and avoid using it. The balance is a subjective but important consideration. Fine-grained schema declarations tend to exhibit a higher degree of potential reuse as a number of reuse instances. Consistency of scope and context for a reusable schema also play a role. Where the schema declarations have an inconsistent scope or they cross over different information contexts, the complexity of using the schema increases. The result is a heavyweight schema that is so complex that it becomes cumbersome to reuse.

12.1.3 Designing the interface schema with intent to reuse

In addition to schema and schema declaration granularity, there are a number of other important design considerations (see Figure 12.8). Although a candidate for schema reuse might have very high potential for reuse, as a separate XML Schema, it must be designed with intent to reuse. That is, the designer of the schema must take the perspective of another service designer that will reuse it later. This simple recommendation can have tremendous impact on the value and quality of the resulting schema. Unfortunately, the current state of development tooling and an emphasis on model-driven development can sometimes produce suboptimal service interface schemas. Later redesign of the service and its interface schemas can require additional and manual refactoring.

A reusable interface schema should be easily discovered by other service interface designers. That is, it must be named and identified to clearly articulate its scope and context. The schema name should avoid ambiguity and be simple, concise, and accurate. When initially evaluating a schema for potential reuse, the interface designer should not have to inspect the internal schema declarations to determine the scope for the schema.

Simplicity also plays a significant role in interface schema reuse. As described in Chapter 11, "XML Schema Design Patterns," the internal structure of XML Schema declarations should be organized for ease of use and for later maintenance. XML Schema declarations should be organized by logical grouping, granularity, or possibly by name. Any of these organizational techniques will work, but they should be applied consistently across all schemas. When the service interface designer inspects the internal XML Schema declarations, those that will be referenced for use in the new interface schema must be obvious and easy to identify. If the designer has to wade through a vast number of randomly placed declarations, the potential for reuse will diminish.

The global declaration pattern (as discussed in Chapter 11) is requisite to reuse. If the reusable XML Schema includes a single complexType structure, and all of the elements nested within the structure are locally declared, reusers of the schema will only be able to reference the top level structure, not any of the individual and nested local elements of the structure. For some reuse scenarios, this will be acceptable. However, there will no doubt be other potential reusers that only require a few of the nested elements, rather than the entire structure. If the interface designer needed only to use the City, State, and Postal Code of a reusable address schema, and the Postal Address structure of the

FIGURE 12.8

Schema Design Considerations for Intended Reuse

schema included only nested "local" element declarations, the potential for reuse diminishes. The recommendation here is to apply the global declaration pattern and avoid local declarations.

Once an interface schema references another schema, there is an implied dependency between them. If a global element declaration of the reusable schema were to change, that change will be inherited by any parent schema that references and inherits that element. This has both benefit and disadvantage. As a benefit, reusable schema definitions are maintained consistently in one place. This avoids proliferation of one-off schema definitions and the potential of data anomalies. As a disadvantage, changes to internal declarations will ripple through the referencing interface schemas regardless of whether those services and service consumers were able to accept the change. A single change to a highly reused schema might result in significant impact across other service interfaces. To avoid this potential problem, the schema designer should assess the potential for change. If the content declarations of the reusable XML Schema are subject to frequent modification, it might not be a good candidate for reuse.

All declarations of a reusable XML Schema should be based upon well-defined metadata standards. The enterprise canonical should serve as the basis for these standards. The intent of the canonical and application across reusable service interface declarations is to help resolve enterprise integration problems. Where data at rest sources behind a service vary from that of the enterprise canonical, the canonical should take precedence. If necessary, a transformation to match the enterprise canonical will be required. Some potential service reusers may not have designed their interface schemas according to the enterprise canonical. When this occurs, the new service and service interface design should be revisited and emphasis placed on alignment with the canonical.

When all design considerations for schema reuse have been resolved, the end product schemas will be well defined and exhibit greater potential for advantage from reuse.

12.2 NAMESPACES

When designing a service interface, a namespace provides a method of identification and scoping for XML Schemas declarations.[1] The concept of a namespace becomes important when considering reuse. The referencing schema must be protected from collisions of like-named global declarations. At the same time, the declarations of the referenced XML Schema should be reusable with little or no restriction as to intended context. As an example, a reusable Postal Address structure should be applicable to different services that contain a customer residence address, a customer shipping address, an employee address, or a vendor returns address in the interface. If a Postal Address structure is defined in a manner where it cannot be reused or where its reuse results in anomalies, then the schema will not be used.

As described in Chapter 11, two important patterns will come into play:

- No-Namespace Schema Reuse Pattern
- Namespace Schema Reuse Pattern

A No-Namespace Schema Reuse Pattern allows the declarations of the schema to not directly participate in a namespace. That is, they are namespace agnostic. When the parent or referencing XML Schema has a defined target namespace ("targetNamespace"), the no-namespace declarations from the referenced schema will be coerced into the namespace of the referencing schema (see Figure 12.9). Alternatively, when the parent or referencing XML Schema is also declared without a target namespace,

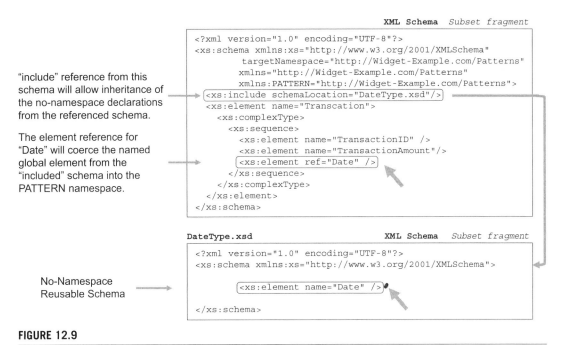

FIGURE 12.9

Reference of a Reusable No-Namespace Schema Element

both the referencing and the referenced XML Schema declarations do not participate in a namespace. The advantage of leaving the reusable XML Schema without a defined namespace is that all global declarations of the schema can be reused by simple, unqualified reference. A global "Date" element ("< Date/ >") can become a participant in the target namespace of any referencing schema.

As a general recommendation, a target namespace and default namespace should always be defined for the top-level service interface schema (such as the base "request", "reply", and "fault" schemas). Subordinate to these top-level interface schemas, the patterns can vary. Application of the Namespace Schema Reuse Pattern results in a reusable XML Schema that has a declared target namespace ("targetNamespace"). This pattern works well when the interface designer believes that there might be some potential for a collision between like-named schema declarations (see Figure 12.10). With this pattern, the target namespace provides a boundary around participating declarations. When a parent interface schema references a reusable schema that also has a declared target namespace, the referenced and inherited schema context is also identified (and to a great degree "protected") by that namespace. The resulting XML message that passes between the consumer and service might also require a namespace prefix to identify the namespaces in which the various structure and elements participate.

The decision to define a reusable XML Schema with or without a targetNamespace can be a difficult one. A high degree of protection against potential collision between like-named declarations is provided by a unique targetNamespace. This approach is also recommended by default (i.e., applying the Namespace Schema Reuse Pattern). Where the service designer is aware of opportunities to reuse

XML Schema

```
<?xml version="1.0" encoding="UTF-8"?>
<xs:schema xmlns:xs="http://www.w3.org/2001/XMLSchema"
           elementFormDefault="qualified"
           xmlns:OPTIONS="http://Widget-Example.com/Options"
           xmlns="http://Widget-Example.com/Inventory/Product/Add/REQUEST"
           targetNamespace="http://Widget-Example.com/Inventory/Product/Add/REQUEST">
  <xs:import namespace="http://Widget-Example.com/Options"
             schemaLocation="StandardServiceOptions.xsd"/>
  <xs:element name="Request">
    <xs:complexType>
      <xs:sequence>
        <xs:element ref="OPTIONS:OptionsSection" minOccurs="1" maxOccurs="1"/>
      </xs:sequence>
    </xs:complexType>
  </xs:element>
</xs:schema>
```

StandardServiceOptions.xsd   **XML Schema** *Subset fragment*

Namespace Qualified
Reusable Schema →

```
<?xml version="1.0" encoding="UTF-8"?>
<xs:schema xmlns:xs="http://www.w3.org/2001/XMLSchema"
           elementFormDefault="qualified"
           xmlns="http://Widget-Example.com/Options"
           xmlns:OPTIONS="http://Widget-Example.com/Options"
           targetNamespace="http://Widget-Example.com/Options" >
  <xs:element name="OptionsSection">
  …
```

FIGURE 12.10

Reference of a Reusable Namespace Schema Element

highly generalized declarations from a no-namespace schema, the no-namespace declarations would be coerced into the targetNamespace or other namespace-qualified reference.

12.3 SCHEMA REUSE BY REFERENCE AND ASSEMBLY

The ability to define reusable interface schemas is part of the XML Schemas specification and syntax.[2] XML Schemas provide several syntactical methods for schema reuse, of which four are commonly applied for service interface design:

- include
- import
- redefine
- any ("wildcard")

The XML Schemas "include" declaration is used to reference a no-namespace schema (see Figure 12.11). The XML Schema "include" declaration will require a schemaLocation attribute with a value that identifies the schema (usually as a schema file name and path). However, the "include" declaration does not allow or support a namespace attribute since the referenced schema does not have a defined target namespace. The referenced global declarations of the "included" XML Schema will

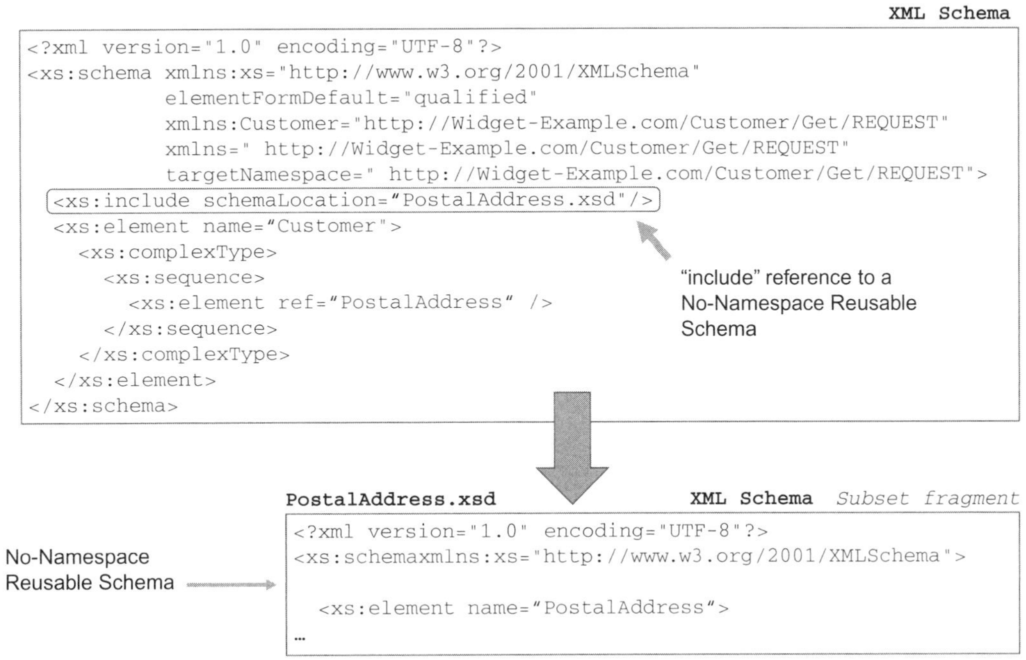

FIGURE 12.11

XML Schema Include Declaration

be coerced into the namespace of the parent or referencing schema, or if referenced from another no-namespace schema, they will not participate in a namespace. The "include" declaration supports the No-Namespace Schema Reuse Pattern, and references to the no-namespace schema do not require a namespace verb or value.

Depending upon the technique used, reference of global declarations that will be instantiated in the XML message can also be defined as qualified or unqualified. This would have little effect on whether the declaration participates in the parent namespace. However, it does affect the tag names of the resulting XML message. A namespace-qualified reference where a namespace prefix has been declared in the parent interface schema will often result in an XML message where the namespace prefix is added to the tag names of the participating message elements (see Figure 12.12). This technique can add to the verbosity of the resulting XML message. However, it clearly identifies which elements participate in which namespaces.

The XML Schemas "import" declaration is used to reference other XML Schemas that have a target namespace. The "import" declaration is required when applying the Namespace Schema Reuse Pattern (see Figure 12.13). The XML Schema "import" declaration will require a schemaLocation attribute with a value that identifies the schema (usually as a schema file name and path) and a namespace attribute with a value that matches the targetNamespace value of the imported schema. Alternative to the "include" declaration, the global declarations defined to a reusable XML Schema with a target namespace will already participate in a namespace. To identify and inherit those declarations, the namespace in which they participate should be included in the reference.

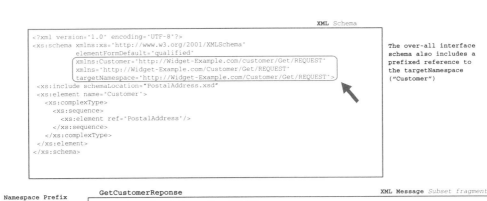

FIGURE 12.12

Namespace Prefixes in the XML Message

Reference of global declarations that will be instantiated in the XML message should be defined as qualified. Namespace-qualified references will include a namespace prefix that refers to the namespace of the imported, reusable XML Schema. As with a namespace-qualified XML message resulting from an "include" reference, this technique increases the verbosity of the resulting XML message (see Figure 12.14).

The XML Schema "redefine" declaration is similar to the "include" declaration. The "redefine" declaration refers to another no-namespace XML Schema (see Figure 12.15). It allows the parent or referencing schema to redefine one or more global declarations of the referenced XML Schema (similar to an override). When used, the XML Schema syntax will also nest the modified (redefined) declarations of the referenced and inherited schema. With service interface design, the "redefine" declaration is rarely used to advantage and can introduce potential for anomaly. One of the important considerations for designing a reusable schema is that it will be based upon well-defined and standard metadata. When the parent schema modifies the declarations of the inherited XML schema, this design consideration is violated. The recommendation is to avoid using the "redefine" declaration.

A more dynamic approach to XML Schema reuse is known as a "wildcard" reference. With this approach, an XML Schema "any" declaration references a namespace. However, the "any" declaration does not inherit a specifically named schema file. The schema file being referenced must have a target namespace that matches the namespace value of the "any" wildcard declaration in the referencing parent schema. The association between the referencing schema and the wildcard schema is done in the XML message instance (see Figure 12.16).

XML Schema

```
<?xml version="1.0" encoding="UTF-8"?>
<xs:schema xmlns:xs="http://www.w3.org/2001/XMLSchema"
           elementFormDefault="qualified"
           xmlns="http://Widget-Example.com/Customer/Get/REQUEST"
           xmlns:Customer="http://Widget-Example.com/Customer/Get/REQUEST"
           xmlns:Address="http://Widget-Example.com/Address"
           targetNamespace="http://Widget-Example.com/Customer/Get/REQUEST">
  <xs:import schemaLocation="PostalAddress.xsd"
            namespace="http://Widget-Example.com/Address" />
  <xs:element name="Customer">
    <xs:complexType>
      <xs:sequence>
        <xs:element ref="Address:PostalAddress" />
      </xs:sequence>
    </xs:complexType>
  </xs:element>
</xs:schema>
```

"import" reference to a
Namespace Reusable Schema.
The "import" namespace value
matches the target namespace
value of the referenced schema.

PostalAddress.xsd   XML Schema   *Subset fragment*

```
<?xml version="1.0" encoding="UTF-8"?>
<xs:schema xmlns:xs="http://www.w3.org/2001/XMLSchema"
           elementFormDefault="qualified"
           xmlns="http://Widget-Example.com/Address"
           xmlns:Address="http://Widget-Example.com/Address"
           targetNamespace="http://Widget-Example.com/Address">

  <xs:element name="PostalAddress">
  ...
```

Namespace
Reusable Schema

FIGURE 12.13

XML Schema Import Declaration

The schemaLocation attribute of the XML message includes a value pair for the namespace as referenced by the "any" wildcard declaration of the parent schema and matching the target namespace of the reusable schema. The declarations from the wildcard schema can then be included and instantiated in the message. This reuse approach is extremely powerful but also subject to risk. The correlation between the originating schema and the wildcard schema is done by namespace matching. Any XML Schema that has a target namespace value that matches the "any" declaration and is available to the parser could suffice. The potential is that multiple and different wildcard schemas could be developed over time, and each with the same target namespace declaration. If the structure, element, and simpleType declarations of those wildcard schemas varied, the XML message would be subject to those differences, and the service consumer might receive unexpected data. In part, a governance process to allocate and assign namespaces and to manage wildcard schema development can help to mitigate the potential risk.

The advantage of a wildcard schema is with future, dynamic extension of an already existing and implemented service. The application of a wildcard schema in this scenario would allow for predefined "extension" areas in the service interface. To avoid anomaly, the service contract would

XML Schema

```
<?xml version="1.0" encoding="UTF-8"?>
<xs:schema xmlns:xs="http://www.w3.org/2001/XMLSchema"
    elementFormDefault="qualified"
    xmlns="http://Widget-Example.com/Customer/Get/REQUEST"
    xmlns:Customer="http://Widget-Example.com/Customer/Get/REQUEST"
    xmlns:Address="http://Widget-Example.com/Address"
    targetNamespace="http://Widget-Example.com/Customer/Get/REQUEST" >
<xs:import schemaLocation="PostalAddress.xsd"
           namespace="http://Widget-Example.com/Address" />
<xs:element name="Customer" >
    <xs:complexType>
    <xs:sequence>
    <xs:element ref="Address:PostalAddress" />
    </xs:sequence>
    </xs:complexType>
    </xs:element>
</xs:schema>
```

The overall interface schema also includes a prefix reference to the targetNamespace ("Address") of the imported XML Schema.

GetCustomerResponse

```
<?xml version="1.0" encoding="UTF-8"?>
<Customer:Customer
    xsi:schemaLocation="http://Widget-Example.com/Customer/Get/REQUEST CustomerPostalAddress.xsd"
    xmlns:Customer="http://Widget-Example.com/Customer/Get/REQUEST"
    xmlns:Address="http://Widget-Example.com/Address"
    xmlns:xsi="http://www.w3.org/2001/XMLSchema-instance" >
    <Address:PostalAddress>
        <Address:AddressTo>John C Doe</Address:AddressTo>
        <Address:AddressLine>123 Main Street</Address:AddressLine>
        <Address:City>Phoenix</Address:City>
        <Address:State>AZ</Address:State>
        <Address:County>Maricopa</Address:County>
        <Address:PostalCode>8500<</Address:PostalCode>
        <Address:Country>USA</Address:Country>
    </Address:PostalAddress>
</Customer:Customer>
```

XML Schema *Subset fragment*

Namespace prefix qualified elements.

Tag names for all elements of the request message that participate in the targetNamespace of the parent schema are qualified with a "Customer" prefix.

Those that participate in the targetNamespace of the imported schema are qualified with an "Address" prefix.

FIGURE 12.14

Namespace Prefixes in the XML Message

XML Schema

```
<?xml version="1.0" encoding="UTF-8"?>
<xs:schema xmlns:xs="http://www.w3.org/2001/XMLSchema"
           elementFormDefault="qualified"
           xmlns="http://Widget-Example.com/Customer/Get/REQUEST"
           xmlns:Customer="http://Widget-Example.com/Customer/Get/REQUEST"
           targetNamespace="http://Widget-Example.com/Customer/Get/REQUEST">
  <xs:redefine schemaLocation="PostalAddress.xsd">
    <xs:simpleType name="AddressLineType">
      <xs:restriction base="AddressLineType">
        <xs:maxLength value="10"/>
      </xs:restriction>
    </xs:simpleType>
  </xs:redefine>
  <xs:element name="Customer">
    <xs:complexType>
      <xs:sequence>
        <xs:element ref="PostalAddress" />
      </xs:sequence>
    </xs:complexType>
  </xs:element>
</xs:schema>
```

"redefine" reference to a Namespace Reusable Schema, with a simpleType declaration that will over-ride the same named simpleType in the referenced schema.

FIGURE 12.15

XML Schema Redefine Declaration

also require a strict and declarative versioning strategy. Depending upon the significance of change between the versions, consumers of a service and service version "A" could be insulated from changes to the same service as implemented in service interface version "B." This technique is most valuable for extension of an interface with new structures and content. However, it does not work as well for modifications to an existing interface contract and resulting XML message structure.

12.4 LIMITATIONS AND COMPLEXITIES

While the ability to reuse schemas and schema content by reference and inheritance are powerful, there are also several disadvantages. One of the most obvious is complexity. A reference can be made from one interface schema to several other schemas (using import and include declarations), and each of those schemas can reference several other schemas, and so on. The result is a highly complex hierarchy of schemas (see Figure 12.17), both at an interface design level and a run-time level (e.g., when parsing or validating an XML message). This example is typical with very fine-grained and small XML Schemas (those that contain only a very limited number of intrinsic declarations). While there is no stated limit to the number of schema references that can be defined, the service interface designer will need to apply a degree of reasonability and weigh the scope and granularity of reusable schemas against manageability. In part, this is related to the "schema granularity" topic described previously.

Another complexity of interface schema reuse is namespace inheritance (see Figure 12.18). Similarly, complex inheritance and class structures also present a problem for some object-oriented applications. In a complex schema reuse hierarchy, a no-namespace qualified schema might exist at a higher level. The

XML Schema

```
<?xml version="1.0" encoding="UTF-8"?>
<xs:schema xmlns:xs="http://www.w3.org/2001/XMLSchema"
           elementFormDefault="qualified"
           xmlns="http://Widget-Example.com/Customer/Get/REQUEST"
           xmlns:Customer="http://Widget-Example.com/Customer/Get/REQUEST"
           xmlns:Address="http://Widget-Example.com/Address"
           targetNamespace="http://Widget-Example.com/Customer/Get/REQUEST">
  <xs:element name="Customer">
    <xs:complexType>
      <xs:sequence>
        <xs:any namespace="http://Widget-Example.com/Address"
                processContents="strict"
                minOccurs="0" maxOccurs="unbounded"/>
      </xs:sequence>
    </xs:complexType>
  </xs:element>
</xs:schema>
```

"wildcard" ("any") reference to a Namespace Reusable Schema.

```
<?xml version="1.0" encoding="UTF-8"?>
<Customer:Customer
    xsi:schemaLocation="http://Widget-Example.com/Customer/Get/REQUEST CustomerAddressWildcard.xsd
                        http://Widget-Example.com/Address PostalAddress.xsd"
    xmlns="http://Widget-Example.com/Customer/Get/REQUEST"
    xmlns:Address="http://Widget-Example.com/Address"
    xmlns:Customer="http://Widget-Example.com/Customer/Get/REQUEST"
    xmlns:xsi="http://www.w3.org/2001/XMLSchema-instance">
  <Address:PostalAddress>
    <Address:AddressTo>John C Doe</Address:AddressTo>
    <Address:AddressLine>123 Main Street</Address:AddressLine>
    <Address:City>Phoenix</Address:City>
    <Address:State>AZ</Address:State>
    <Address:County>Maricopa</Address:County>
    <Address:PostalCode>85000</Address:PostalCode>
    <Address:Country>USA</Address:Country>
  </Address:PostalAddress>
</Customer:Customer>
```

Namespace and Schema Name pair, defined to the XML message. When parser validated, the additional "wildcard" schema will also be used.

The Postal Address structure included in the XML message was defined by the "PostalAddress.xsd" wildcard schema.

FIGURE 12.16

XML Schema Wildcard Reference

no-namespace schema can import another target namespace-qualified, lower-level schema. However, the global declarations of the no-namespace schema cannot participate in the target namespace of the inherited schema. The target namespace of a lower-level, inherited schema cannot be applied to higher-level global declarations. The global declarations that participate in the target namespace of the lower-level schema can be exposed in the resulting XML message, and no-namespace declarations of other even lower-level included schemas can participate. The "view" of namespace application is always upward. That is, a no-namespace declaration of a lower-level inherited schema may participate in the target namespace of the higher-level referencing schema (upward view). However, a higher-level no-namespace qualified declaration cannot be "pulled down" to participate in the target namespace of the lower-level, inherited schema that it references.

Another complexity of schema reuse is collision between like-named declarations (e.g., two separate, global element declarations named as "Date"). While careful application of namespaces can help to avoid these collisions, a possibility of collision still exists. If the target namespace value (as the Universal Resource Identifier [URI]) of two different XML Schemas happens to be identical, then the

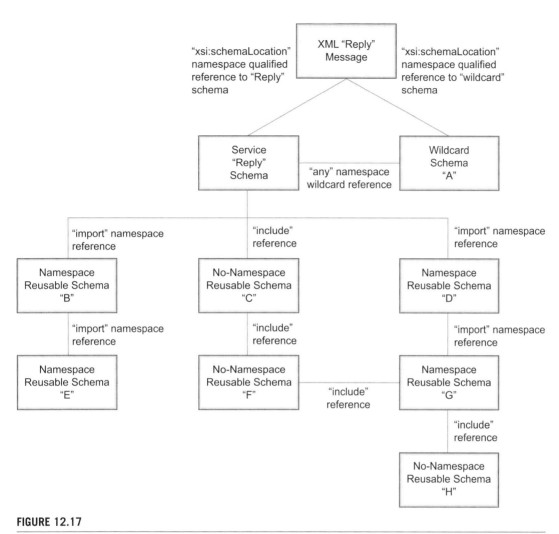

FIGURE 12.17

Complex Schema Reuse Hierarchy

namespaces and schemas themselves will collide when referenced by the same schema, and any participating global declarations are also subject to collision. For this reason, the namespace values for any schema should be carefully managed to avoid duplication.

The assembly of an interface schema from other reusable schemas also requires that the schemas are available and "visible" to the service and to consumers of the service. During the interface binding process, service consumers will need to acquire copies of the Web service WSDL and all referenced XML Schemas. The binding process will then create an object model of the service interface or will map the service interface to the object model of the consumer. If the interface schemas cannot be acquired, the binding process will fail, and the service consumer will not be able to process the

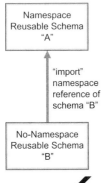
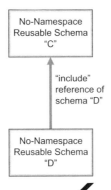
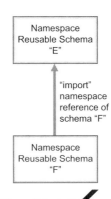
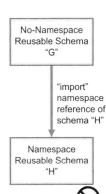

Namespace Reusable Schema "A"	No-Namespace Reusable Schema "C"	Namespace Reusable Schema "E"	No-Namespace Reusable Schema "G"
↑ "import" namespace reference of schema "B"	↑ "include" reference of schema "D"	↑ "import" namespace reference of schema "F"	↓ "import" namespace reference of schema "H"
No-Namespace Reusable Schema "B"	No-Namespace Reusable Schema "D"	Namespace Reusable Schema "F"	Namespace Reusable Schema "H"

"Upward View" ✔
Global declarations of the "include" referenced No-Namespace schema "B" can be coerced into and participate in the targetNamespace of the top-level Namespace schema "A".

"Upward View" ✔
Neither the global declarations of the "include" referenced No-Namespace schema "D" nor the global declarations of the top-level No-Namespace schema "C" participate in a namespace.

"Upward View" ✔
Global declarations of the "import" referenced Namespace schema "F" will participate in their own targetNamespace, while global declarations of the top-level Namespace schema "E" will participate in their own targetNamespace.

"Downward View" 🚫
The "import" reference from a No-Namespace schema to a Namespace schema is valid. Global declarations of the "import" referenced Namespace schema "H" will participate in their own targetNamespace.

However, global declarations of the top-level No-Namespace schema "G" remain without a namespace and cannot participate in the targetNamespace of the "import" referenced schema "H".

FIGURE 12.18

Namespace Inheritance

request or reply messages. Managing service interface WSDL and XML Schema artifacts is not to be taken lightly. Even the simplest assembly of interface artifacts can be complicated by versioning and also by wildcard schemas. The service designer must verify support for versioning and also for wildcard schema references if they are to be implemented. The recommendation is to implement a service artifact repository and a set of design-time and bind-time governance processes for service artifacts.

SUMMARY

The ability to reuse XML Schemas as a form of reference and assembly is a powerful service interface capability. Protecting the integrity of those schemas with namespaces is also important. However, there are powerful schema reuse examples where schemas without a target namespace can be inherited and applied in many different contexts.

The patterns and techniques most often applied to schema reuse include no-namespace schemas (referenced by the XML Schema "include" and "redefine" declarations), namespace-qualified schemas (referenced by the XML Schema "import" declaration), and wildcard schemas (referenced by the XML

Schema "any" declaration). Each of these techniques has advantages and disadvantages. As a general recommendation, the service interface designer should avoid the XML Schema "redefine" declaration.

Critical to the application of any interface schema reuse is ensuring that the reusable schemas were designed and developed with intent to reuse. There are several important design considerations to resolve when designing a new, reusable schema. The designer must ensure that the schema is of appropriate granularity, has a consistent scope, is reasonably static (not subject to frequent change), is identified in a way that is discoverable, is simple and easy to use, exploits the "global declarations" pattern, and is based upon well-defined metadata standards. Where the designer has resolved these considerations, the resulting XML Schema will have a higher potential for effective reuse.

As with any technology, the service and interface designer should have a reasonable degree of expertise with XML Schemas. The XML Schemas syntax is extensive, and there are often a number of different approaches to defining a schema-based interface. Validating and testing the interface schemas is also important. An effective XML Schema-based Web service interface will have been tested and proven before it is deployed.

REFERENCES

1. Bray T, Hollander D, Layman A, Tobin R, eds. "Namespaces in XML 1.0. 2nd ed." (W3C, August 16, 2006). <http://www.w3.org/TR/REC-xml-names/>.

2. Fallside DC, Walmsley P, eds. "XML Schema Part 0: Primer. 2nd ed." (W3C, October 28, 2004). <http://www.w3.org/TR/xmlschema-0/>.

The Interface and Change

13

All things change. This simple statement describes the most complex concept for any SOA—change. A simple service to read the Item database and return details to the consumer for a particular item will no doubt change over time. The change might be adding a new element to the item database and returning it in the reply message. Or it might be a complete restructuring to the data and as a result the message. Each of these scenarios and any number of other variations represent the types of change that a service will undergo over time.

Once a Web service (or any type of service) has been designed, developed, tested, published, and deployed, it is then also available to consumers. Consumers will search for services (i.e., "discover" or "find"), and when found, the consumer will then "bind" to the service interface. The process of binding associates the service consumer to the service interface and messages and is analogous to signing a contract. By virtue of publishing the service interface and making it available, the service commits to supporting the defined service interface, service operations, message formats, and supported messaging protocols. Similarly, when service consumers "bind" to a service interface, they commit to sending request messages in the stated format to the exposed endpoints on the ESB and using the supported protocols. Between the service, the consumers, and the service interface, a contract for collaboration has been defined.

This concept of a contract that is largely based upon the service interface is fundamental to SOA. It removes ambiguity and potential anomaly from consumer and service interactions. It also constrains or limits the scope and context of messages that are exchanged. However, when changes occur to the service that would in some manner be exposed to consumers, this contract can be broken.

The terms and conditions implied in this interface contract are important because the message structures and message content are used to either build or map the consumer's object model. The structure, location, naming, and the metadata characteristics of the message are reflected by the internal processing of the service consumer. If something in a request message has changed, and the consumer is unaware of that change, the service will reject the request and return a fault message. Similarly, if something has changed in the reply message, and the consumer is unaware of it, the message will not be deemed as consumable, or an error will be raised. To keep the SOA up and running, to avoid unnecessary and ongoing code changes, where possible, service consumers must be insulated from change.

The significance of a change is what determines whether the consumer can be protected from it or not. There are numerous types of change that will occur naturally and over time to a service. A simple change, such as adding a new element to the response message, can have significant impact. However, if the new message element were optional, the potential for impact to consumers might be somewhat reduced. Examples of change with less significant potential for impact to consumers include the following:

- Add a new service operation.
- Add a new, optional element to either the request or reply message.
- Change an element of either the request or the reply message, from mandatory to optional.
- Remove simpleType constraints from any element (remove type restrictions).

The preceding examples are still of potential impact and should not be ignored or taken lightly during service interface design. Rather, the service interface designer should anticipate that every service will undergo some type of change and include patterns and techniques to help mitigate the potential impact on consumers.

Other types of change are of greater significance, and, unfortunately, service consumers will most likely incur some type of impact if they do not rebind to the new or revised service interface. These types of changes will require structure, content, type, or behavioral modifications, and potentially a refactoring of the consumer's underlying object model. Following are a few examples of significant change:

- Add a new mandatory element to either the request or reply message.
- Modify an element's type or type constraints (change to a simpleType or its facets).
- Modify the placement of an element (move an element from one location in the message to another).
- Change an optional message element to mandatory.
- Delete an element from either the request or the reply message.

For any of the previous "significant" service interface changes, the consumer will at minimum be required to rebind to the new or revised service interface, and most likely will also have to modify its internal object model and behavior. Anticipating change is something that can help to reduce potential impact on and optimize the design and development investment for already deployed and bound service consumers.

Change management for Web services has been struggled with for many years, and it is an area that introduces more complexity than should be expected. This is not to say that Web services cannot change over time or that there isn't a solution. Rather, the challenge is in mitigating the impact from change to service consumers. Some practitioners will rely entirely upon the SOA and Web service design tooling to manage change. The approach often taken here is to just design, build, and deploy a new version of the service whenever a change occurs. Existing service consumers remain bound to their current version of the service, and new service consumers will have their own versions of the service. While this approach initially seems to make sense, it is fraught with complexity and potential cost. Each new service deployment will be a "one-off" from the original with significant potential to introduce disparity and anomaly. Further, each deployment of a service into the SOA infrastructure includes cost. Each of these services requires additional management, monitoring, maintenance, and governance.

13.1 **SCHEMA EXTENSION**

An experienced service designer will adopt the position that a service interface will always require future modification. Determining exactly when those changes might occur and the degree of significance is not easy, but the designer can make an optimistic assumption that one or more changes will be of minimal significance, such as adding a new, optional element to the reply message. For these less impactful types of change, the service designer can prebuild extension areas into the service interface and resulting message structures.

This technique is not quite the same as that of more traditional and procedural languages such as COBOL (Common Business Oriented Language), where "FILLER" elements are defined to preallocate a fixed length of space in a structure. With XML and as supported by XML Schemas, the service designer can incorporate an optional extension element that is also a complexType structure. Additional and nested structures and elements can be defined subordinate to the extension element at a later time (see Figure 13.1).

This extension element approach still has some limitations. Depending upon the binding process, an optional element can still be prescriptively defined to the consumer's object model. On receipt of a reply message, the consumer would correctly process when the optional extension element is present in the message or not. However, if the element contains additional and subordinate structures and elements, processing becomes more complex. To avoid anomaly, and when present in a message, the consumer's object model would have to ignore any nested content of an optional extension element. This approach can be somewhat limiting, but it does help to mitigate the potential for impact to the consumer. The value of this technique is exploited when the consumer's object model has been refactored to ignore the optional element and its subordinate content. As new, optional elements are added to the message, the consumer can ignore those changes.

The use of XML Schemas to define and constrain a Web service interface provides additional advantages. Not only can the service interface be designed to include a predefined and optional extension

```
01  Item-Details.
      05  Item-ID            PIC X(4).
      05  Desc               PIC X(20).
      05  Version            PIC 9(3).
      05  Length             PIC X(10).
      05  Color              PIC X(12).
      05  Diameter           PIC X(12).
      05  Weight             PIC X(10).
      05  Extension-Area     PIC X(30).

      05  Filler Redefines Extension-Area.
         10  Version.
            15    MajorVerNo    PIC 9(2).
            15    MinorVerNo    PIC 9(2).
         10  Base-Packaging-Unit   PIC X(6).
         10  Bulk-Packaging-Unit   PIC X(6).
```

FIGURE 13.1

COBOL "Filler"

element but the underlying and subordinate structure and element content of the extension can also be defined to evolve somewhat dynamically. This is accomplished by defining a schema "wildcard" to the optional extension element.[1]

A "wildcard" allows additional and variable structural content to be incorporated at the point of implementation in the service interface. The schema declaration is known as an "any" wildcard declaration. The schema wildcard "any" declaration allows another separate schema to be referenced and defined as additional content of the message. The "any" declaration allows the service designer to reference a namespace (in this sense, a namespace representing another separate schema) that matches the targetNamespace of the current schema, an explicitly declared namespace (specified by namespace URI as the name), a local namespace, or another namespace that does not match the targetNamespace of the current schema (no-namespace schemas can also be referenced with this option). The wildcard pattern is also somewhat of an indirect namespace association pattern, where the primary XML Schema references a separate wildcard schema (see Figure 13.2).

In addition to identifying the namespace of the separate wildcard schema, the XML Schema "any" declaration provides an attribute-defined parameter to determine whether the constraints of the wildcard schema will be strictly applied or not. The "processContents" attribute of the "any" declaration instructs the validating XML parser to strictly apply the referenced schema constraints (with a processContents value of "strict"), to loosely apply the constraints (with a processContents value of "lax"), or to ignore the wildcard schema (with a processContents value of "skip").

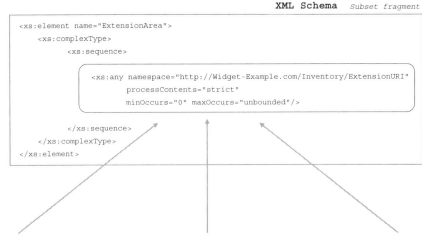

XML Schema *Subset fragment*

```
<xs:element name="ExtensionArea">
    <xs:complexType>
        <xs:sequence>
            <xs:any namespace="http://Widget-Example.com/Inventory/ExtensionURI"
                    processContents="strict"
                    minOccurs="0" maxOccurs="unbounded"/>
        </xs:sequence>
    </xs:complexType>
</xs:element>
```

In this example, the "**namespace**" attribute value matches the targetNamespace URI value of the parent schema.

In this example, the "**processContents**" attribute value is set to "strict", which will instruct the validating XML parser to strictly test against and apply the XML Schema constraints of the "wildcard" schema.

In this example, the wildcard content is set to optional ("**minOccurs**" attribute value of "0"), and an unlimited number of occurrences are allowed ("**maxOccurs**" attribute value of "unbounded").

FIGURE 13.2

Example XML Schema Wildcard Syntax

The determination of which additional wildcard schema will be applied to the service interface and resulting XML message is also determined by contract. That is, the service interface specifies which namespace-qualified schemas are allowed to define the subordinate structures and content of the wildcard extension. Additional parameters determine how strictly these additional schema structures will be enforced when the message is parser validated. The consumer also plays a role in the definition of the contract. The consumer of the service will specify which namespace and namespace-qualified XML Schema (of those that are allowed by the service interface) will be used.

When the service is initially deployed, the optional extension element of the service interface message does not include any additional content. At a future point, the service is enhanced, and the optional extension point might then include a new element. The originally bound consumers of the service can ignore the optional extension element and are unaware of the underlying content. New consumers that are "aware" of a separate wildcard schema will make an association between the service interface, the message, and the wildcard schema using the schemaLocation attribute of the XML message. The schema location attribute will contain a pair of values to represent the namespace of the wildcard schema and its file name (a directory path is optional but recommended).

Prior to implementation, these new consumers will bind to both the original service interface and the identified wildcard schema. The previously bound consumers will not include the additional wildcard namespace reference in their schemaLocation attribute values, and as a result, they will be "unaware" and unaffected by the additional element from the new schema (see Figure 13.3). In this case, the new element will not be exposed in the message. This allows previously bound service consumers and new service consumers to invoke the same service and process messages with and without the additional wildcard content as appropriate to their understanding of the contract.

As described, the wildcard schema pattern to extend a service interface is quite powerful. It can also be complex. The service designer must ensure that the interface content model is still deterministic. That is, the interface should not include schema declarations that are in conflict, or where the validating XML parser cannot determine which element is next in the corresponding XML message. To avoid these potential problems and to optimize the wildcard pattern, the service designer should follow a set of simple best practices:

- Ensure that XML Schemas "any" wildcards are supported by the environment, parsers, and binding utilities.
- Position the extension element at the end of the element set for the message.
- Define the extension element to the primary interface schema as an optional complexType.
- Specify the wildcard "any" declaration "namespace" attribute with an explicit namespace value.
- Specify the wildcard "any" declaration "processContents" attribute with a value of "strict".
- Test the wildcard extension.

Positioning an optional extension element at a specific location in the message plays a significant role (see Figure 13.4). When the extension element has been located at the end of the message, consumers of the message will have increased ability to ignore any additional content. During the XML Parser validation process, the consumer can elect to stop parsing with the last element of the XML message that maps to the lowest-level termination point of the object model. If the extension element is placed somewhere before the last element, some consumers may encounter difficulty in processing

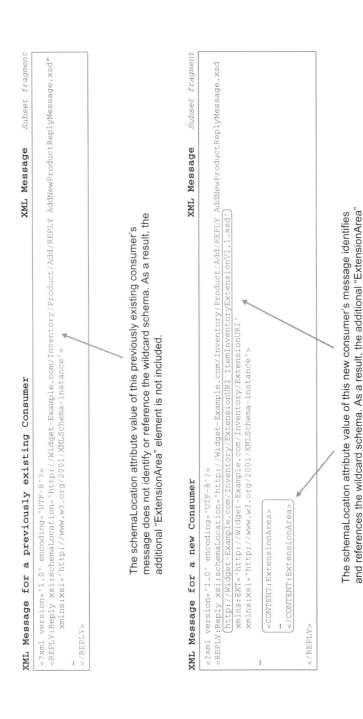

XML Message for a previously existing Consumer   XML Message   *Subset fragment*

```
<?xml version="1.0" encoding="UTF-8"?>
<REPLY:Reply xsi:schemaLocation="http://Widget-Example.com/Inventory/Product/Add/REPLY AddNewProductReplyMessage.xsd"
    xmlns:xsi="http://www.w3.org/2001/XMLSchema-instance">
..
</REPLY>
```

The schemaLocation attribute value of this previously existing consumer's message does not identify or reference the wildcard schema. As a result, the additional "ExtensionArea" element is not included.

XML Message for a new Consumer   XML Message   *Subset fragment*

```
<?xml version="1.0" encoding="UTF-8"?>
<REPLY:Reply xsi:schemaLocation="http://Widget-Example.com/Inventory/Product/Add/REPLY AddNewProductReplyMessage.xsd
    http://Widget-Example.com/Inventory/ExtensionURI ItemInventoryExtensionV1.1.xsd"
    xmlns:EXT="http://Widget-Example.com/Inventory/ExtensionURI"
    xmlns:xsi="http://www.w3.org/2001/XMLSchema-instance">
..
    <CONTENT:ExtensionArea>
    ..
    </CONTENT:ExtensionArea>
..
</REPLY>
```

The schemaLocation attribute value of this new consumer's message identifies and references the wildcard schema. As a result, the additional "ExtensionArea" element is included.

FIGURE 13.3

Existing and New Service Consumers with a Wildcard

```
XML Message with an extension area                    XML Message   Subset fragment
<?xml version="1.0" encoding="UTF-8"?>
<REQUEST:Request
   xsi:schemaLocation="http://Widget-Example.com/Inventory/Product/Add/REPLY AddNewProductReplyMessage.xsd
                       http://Widget-Example.com/Inventory/ExtensionURI ItemInventoryExtensionV1.1.xsd"
           xmlns:REQUEST="http://Widget-Example.com/Inventory/Product/Add/REQUEST"
           xmlns:CONTENT="http://Widget-Example.com/Inventory/Product/Add/Content"
           xmlns:EXT="http://Widget-Example.com/Inventory/ExtensionURI"
           xmlns:xsi="http://www.w3.org/2001/XMLSchema-instance">

   <CONTENT:ItemDetailSection>
     <CONTENT:ItemID>5678</CONTENT:ItemID>
     <CONTENT:Desc>Blue Stick Pen</CONTENT:Desc>
     <CONTENT:Version>2</CONTENT:Version>
     <CONTENT:Length>8.0 in</CONTENT:Length>
     <CONTENT:Color>Blue</CONTENT:Color>
     <CONTENT:Diameter>0.25 in</CONTENT:Diameter>
     <CONTENT:Weight>1.5 oz</CONTENT:Weight>
   </CONTENT:ItemDetailSection>                        ┌─────────────────────────────────┐
                                                       │ The Extension Area of the message │
   <CONTENT:ItemExtendedSection>                       │ (in this example, an element named│
     <CONTENT:ExtensionArea/>  ◄─────────────────────  │ as "<ExtensionArea/>") is defined │
   </CONTENT:ItemExtendedSection>                      │ near the end of the message.      │
                                                       └─────────────────────────────────┘
   </CONTENT:ContentSection>
</REQUEST:Request>
```

FIGURE 13.4

Position the Extension Element at the End of the XML Message Structure

the elements that trail after the extension. This is often the case with a structured and procedural language such as COBOL, where the elements of a file definition have been statically mapped one for one to the elements of a message. If an unexpected element occurs somewhere between the boundaries of the file definition element grouping, an error may result.

The service designer should define the extension element as an optional complexType structure. The extension element will be defined by a globally declared and named complexType element with a minOccurs value of "0". To allow for multiple occurrences of the wildcard schema reference, the extension element should also include a maxOccurs value of "unbounded", which will allow for any number of occurrences (see Figure 13.5).

As a recommendation, the service designer should define the wildcard schema with an explicit targetNamespace value. Avoid matching of namespaces across schemas where possible (this will prohibit reuse) and avoid using an open "##other" namespace value. The value of the referenced wildcard schema namespace will also be declared as its internal targetNamespace value. The referencing XML Schemas will identify the wildcard schema as an explicit namespace value of the "namespace" attribute for the "any" declaration. The XML message will also include the namespace value along with the name of the wildcard schema as a value of the schemaLocation attribute.

While this is somewhat limiting, it also simplifies that pattern and adds a degree of referential consistency. Service consumers that include the additional extension content in their XML message processing will need to include a reference to the wildcard schema as a schemaLocation value that matches the targetNamespace of the wildcard extension schema (see Figure 13.6). This approach will also avoid having multiple unmanaged and potentially disparate wildcard schemas being defined with the same targetNamespace.

XML Schema *Subset fragment*

```
<xs:element name="ExtensionArea">
  <xs:complexType>
    <xs:sequence>

      <xs:any namespace="http://Widget-Example.com/Inventory/ExtensionURI"
              processContents="strict"
              minOccurs="0" maxOccurs="unbounded" />

    </xs:sequence>
  </xs:complexType>
</xs:element>
```

In this example, the wildcard content is set to optional ("**minOccurs** " attribute value of "0"), and an unlimited number of occurrences are allowed ("**maxOccurs**" attribute value of "unbounded").

FIGURE 13.5

Optional Extension Element

XML Message with an Extension Area   XML Message *Subset fragment*

```
<?xml version="1.0" encoding="UTF-8"?>
<REQUEST:Request
  xsi:schemaLocation="http://Widget-Example.com/Inventory/Product/Add/REPLY AddNewProductReplyMessage.xsd
                      http://Widget-Example.com/Inventory/ExtensionURI ItemInventoryExtensionV1.1.xsd"
          xmlns:EXT="http://Widget-Example.com/Inventory/ExtensionURI"
          xmlns:xsi="http://www.w3.org/2001/XMLSchema-instance">
...
</REQUEST:Request>
```

XML Schema with Reference to "any" Wildcard Schema   XML Schema *Subset fragment*

```
<?xml version="1.0" encoding="UTF-8"?>
<xs:schema xmlns:xs="http://www.w3.org/2001/XMLSchema"
           elementFormDefault="qualified"
           xmlns="http://Widget-Example.com/Inventory/Product/Add/Content"
           xmlns:EXT="http://Widget-Example.com/Inventory/ExtensionURI"
           targetNamespace="http://Widget-Example.com/Inventory/Product/Add/Content" >
...
 <xs:element name="ExtensionArea">
    <xs:complexType>
      <xs:sequence>
        <xs:any namespace="http://Widget-Example.com/Inventory/ExtensionURI"
          processContents="strict"
          minOccurs="0" maxOccurs="unbounded"/>
      </xs:sequence>
    </xs:complexType>
 </xs:element>
...
</xs:schema>
```

The namespace value of the "any" wildcard refernce is the same as that specified in the consumer's message.

FIGURE 13.6

Consistent Namespace Values Across Schemas and Messages

XML Schema *Subset fragment*

```
<xs:element name="ExtensionArea">
  <xs:complexType>
    <xs:sequence>

      <xs:any namespace="http://Widget-Example.com/Inventory/ExtensionURI"
              processContents="strict"
              minOccurs="0" maxOccurs="unbounded" />

    </xs:sequence>
  </xs:complexType>
</xs:element>
```

In this example, the "**processContents**" attribute value is set to "strict", which will instruct the validating XML Parser to strictly test against and apply the XML Schema constraints of the "wildcard" schema.

FIGURE 13.7

Wildcard Schema "processContents" value

The service designer should also specify the processContents attribute value of the schema "any" wildcard declaration as "strict" (see Figure 13.7). When validating the message, this ensures a higher degree of compliance with the service interface contract. It will also result in a higher quality message, with a lower potential for data anomaly. If the processContents attribute value is set to "lax", the validating parser will ignore checking the message for schema content that it cannot identify and apply. If the processContents attribute value is set to "skip", the validating parser will not evaluate the extension of the XML message for compliance to any schema definition. The only check will be to ensure that the content of the message at that point was well-formed.

The service designer should also carefully test the schema "any" wildcard extension. The association among the primary service interface schema, the wildcard extension schema, and XML message are critical. There may be technical complexities or infrastructure nuances that will need to be resolved. At a minimum, testing will need to include unit testing, integration testing, validation testing, and regression testing (to ensure previously existing consumers remain unaffected by the additional extension message content). Tools such as XML Spy (Copyright 2003-2008 Altova GmbH, reprinted with permission of Altova) can be used to simplify initial unit testing and parser validation (see Figure 13.8). The example message, including the appropriate namespace and wildcard schema references, can be used as an initial test of the service interface design. The service designer can easily verify that the example message parses and validates and that the reference to the additional wildcard extension is resolved.

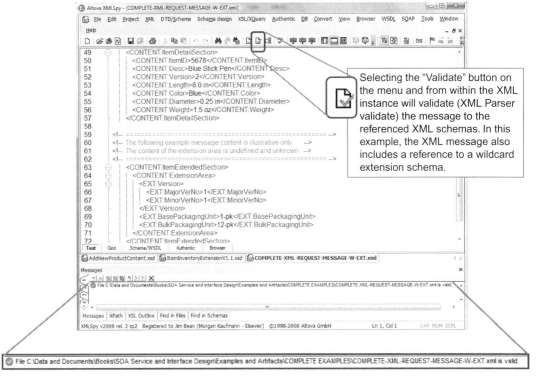

FIGURE 13.8

Using XML Spy to Test a Service Interface and Message Extension Design (Copyright 2003-2008 Altova GmbH, reprinted with permission of Altova)

The schema wildcard pattern provides a dynamic and an optimized approach to extending a service interface and message. For interface changes with a low degree of significance, the wildcard pattern can also be optimized to mitigate impact to previously bound consumers. New consumers that are aware of the changes can incorporate the appropriate references and, as a result, process the additional content. However, all consumers should have visibility of the service and service interface version that they are processing.

13.2 SCHEMA VERSIONING

The point in time "state" of a service and its interface are often referred to as a version. Versions can be specified by any number of different identifiers and values. The most common of which is a numeric declaration typically including two parts: 1) the major version and 2) the revision or minor version. A best practice approach to version identification is to align major versions to significant changes, the value of which is numeric and increments from a value of "1" as the initially deployed

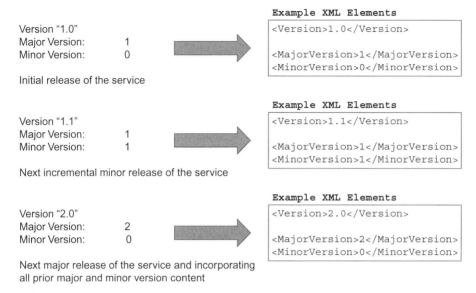

Version "1.0"
Major Version: 1
Minor Version: 0

Initial release of the service

```
Example XML Elements
<Version>1.0</Version>

<MajorVersion>1</MajorVersion>
<MinorVersion>0</MinorVersion>
```

Version "1.1"
Major Version: 1
Minor Version: 1

Next incremental minor release of the service

```
Example XML Elements
<Version>1.1</Version>

<MajorVersion>1</MajorVersion>
<MinorVersion>1</MinorVersion>
```

Version "2.0"
Major Version: 2
Minor Version: 0

Next major release of the service and incorporating all prior major and minor version content

```
Example XML Elements
<Version>2.0</Version>

<MajorVersion>2</MajorVersion>
<MinorVersion>0</MinorVersion>
```

FIGURE 13.9

Version Identification

state of the service (see Figure 13.9). The minor version is also a numeric value but incrementing from "0". For example:

- A version of "1.0" would represent the first implemented state of a service.
- A version of "1.1" would represent a follow-on release of the same service, with a minor modification.
- A version of "2.0" would represent a follow-on and significant release of the same service.

A service version of "1.0" would represent the very first release of a service into the SOA. This version of the service would include an extension point (as an extension element) and a wildcard schema reference. However, the extension would at this point remain empty and not exposed to consumers. As the service evolves and changes are made, the value of the version would reflect the significance of those changes by incrementing of the version. Where a change is minor and previously existing and bound consumers are less likely to be impacted, the minor version number would be incremented. The extension element would be available to new service consumers that are "aware" of the change, and the extension element would likely contain additional content as defined by the referenced "any" wildcard schema. These changes could continue over time with a new and separate wildcard schema being progressively defined for each change and inheriting the previous wildcard content. At some point, a major change might occur where all service consumers would be impacted (something like deleting a mandatory element from a request message). In this case, the major version number would be incremented with a value of "2", and the minor version would reset to "0" (e.g., "2.0"). All consumers of the service would need to be notified, and they would need to revisit their internal object models and internal behavior, and at minimum rebind to the new version "2.0" service

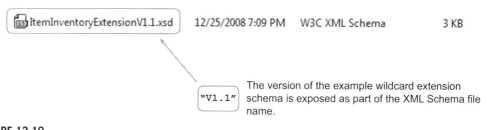

FIGURE 13.10

Exposing the Version in the File Name

interface. Service version identification is generally user defined (as in "enterprise defined"). There is no single, specific standard regarding SOA or Web services versioning.

In addition to version identification, the next challenge is where to specify and expose the service version. A general recommendation is to expose the version as part of the service interface. The rationale being that all service consumers should have bound to the interface in order to successfully invoke the service. However, there is no single or agreed upon approach to placement of the version. Some practitioners recommend placing the version as part of the service interface file name, while others recommend adding the version number to the targetNamespace value of the service interface schema. There are several possibilities and each has advantages and disadvantages.

- Add the version to the service interface schema file name.
- Add the version to the targetNamespace URI value.
- Add the version to an "annotation" within the service interface schema.
- Add the version to the schema "version" attribute.
- Add the version as internal content of the interface, resulting in an XML message element and value.

For some SOA implementations, exposing the version to the interface file name can be an effective approach (e.g., the XML Schema artifact name used for the file management system) (see Figure 13.10). However, changing the file name can also introduce potential impact to service consumers. That impact should be less for those services that are bound during design-time (often referred to as "static" binding). However, for those that invoke a run-time binding such as a choreography (using dynamic binding), changing the file name may cause problems. Exposing the version as part of the external file name for wildcard schemas is an effective approach and is cautiously recommended. This will help to correlate wildcard schemas with consumer messages. Exposing the version as part of the external file name for other types of schemas is not generally recommended for all schemas. However, adding the version to the file name of a wildcard extension schema is recommended. This allows that multiple and incremental minor versions can be defined by separate wildcard schemas. The determination of "which" wildcard schema to apply is resolved as a combination of design-time version identification for consumers.

Adding the version to the data value of a targetNamespace is possibly the most recommended approach by other industry practitioners. This technique requires that the namespace URI value used for the service interface schema targetNamespace will include the version number. When this approach is used, the version number is usually appended to the end of the URI string. However, this is a somewhat coarse-grained technique, and it will impact most consumers of the service. Including

XML Schema *Subset fragment*

```
<?xml version="1.0" encoding="UTF-8"?>
<xs:schema xmlns:xs="http://www.w3.org/2001/XMLSchema"
           elementFormDefault="qualified"
           xmlns="http://Widget-Example.com/Inventory/ExtensionURI/v1.1"
           xmlns:EXT="http://Widget-Example.com/Inventory/ExtensionURI/v1.1"
           targetNamespace="http://Widget-Example.com/Inventory/ExtensionURI/v1.1">
...
</xs:schema>
```

"v1.1"   The version of the example wildcard extension
schema is exposed as part of the namespace URI
value and, in this example, has been assigned to:

- Default namespace (xmlns="")
- Qualified namespace (xmlns:EXT="")
- targetNamespace (targetNamespace="")

FIGURE 13.11

Exposing the Version in the TargetNamespace

a new and incremented version number in an existing schema will result in different binding models between previous and new service consumers, and it can result in anomalous references between subordinate "included" schemas (those with no namespace). If a reusable schema that is referenced by many service interfaces is versioned in this manner, it will cause a ripple of changes across all of those higher-level import namespace references.

For this reason, I do not recommend using the namespace URI as the primary vehicle for exposing the entire service version (both major and minor version identification). Rather, I cautiously recommend including only the "major" version in the targetNamespace URI. This follows the previous approach to version identification and granularity. A major version should be used to identify significant change that requires service consumers to rebind. The minor version should be exposed in a different and separate manner (see Figure 13.11).

As the definition of a service interface, XML Schemas also provide an additional annotation capability. Annotations are XML Schemas declarations that can be added to any XML Schema definition. Annotations have two child types, and each has a somewhat different intent. The documentation annotation element is largely that—documentation. It is primarily intended for human consumption. Alternatively, the "appinfo" child element is consumable by both humans and in some cases by validating XML Parsers. The content of an appinfo element can be identified and extracted during parser validation and exposed to the parsing application. This schema capability can be used to include the version number of the service. Using schema annotations to expose the service version can be effective (see Figure 13.12). However, not all validating parsers will expose the appinfo content. Also, the appinfo declarations of an annotation are largely unconstrained. That is, they must be well-formed, but they do not have explicit rules that govern the number of occurrences, the data types, and so on. The

XML Schema *Subset fragment*

```
<?xml version="1.0" encoding="UTF-8"?>
<xs:schema xmlns:xs="http://www.w3.org/2001/XMLSchema"
           elementFormDefault="qualified"
           xmlns="http://Widget-Example.com/Inventory/ExtensionURI"
           xmlns:EXT="http://Widget-Example.com/Inventory/ExtensionURI"
           targetNamespace="http://Widget-Example.com/Inventory/ExtensionURI">

  <xs:annotation>
    <xs:appinfo>
      <xs:element name="MajorVerNo" default="1"/>
      <xs:element name="MinorVerNo" default="1"/>
    </xs:appinfo>
  </xs:annotation>

...
</xs:schema>
```

 The version of the example wildcard extension schema is exposed as elements defined within an XML Schema "annotation" and in this case, as "appinfo" elements.

FIGURE 13.12

Exposing the Version in a Schema Annotation

XML Schema *Subset fragment*

```
<?xml version="1.0" encoding="UTF-8"?>
<xs:schema xmlns:xs="http://www.w3.org/2001/XMLSchema"
           elementFormDefault="qualified"
           xmlns="http://Widget-Example.com/Inventory/ExtensionURI/v1.1"
           xmlns:EXT="http://Widget-Example.com/Inventory/ExtensionURI/v1.1"
           targetNamespace="http://Widget-Example.com/Inventory/ExtensionURI/v1.1"
           version="1.1" >
...
</xs:schema>
```

 The version of the example wildcard extension schema is exposed as an XML Schema "version" attribute value.

This is generally not an effective technique as the "version" attribute of the root schema element is not parsed as content.

FIGURE 13.13

Exposing the Version Using the Schema Root Element "version" Attribute

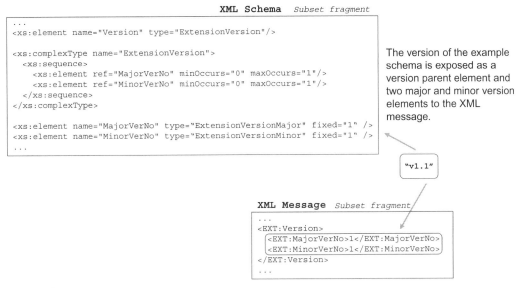

FIGURE 13.14

Exposing the Version as Element Content of the Schema and Message

recommendation here is to encourage use of annotations as a form of documentation but not as a technology consumable "appinfo" method of exposing the version.

Another approach to versioning is to expose the service version as a data value of the XML Schema "version" attribute (see Figure 13.13). Another capability of XML Schemas syntax is the ability to optionally declare a version attribute to the root element of an XML Schema. Unfortunately, the XML Schemas specification does not provide any metadata facilities to constrain and govern content of the schema version attribute. Similar to an annotation, there is no method of defining the data type of the schema version attribute. For this reason, using the schema version attribute to expose the service version is not recommended.

Another approach to versioning is to include and expose the version (both major and minor) within the service interface and resulting message as element content (see Figure 13.14). Some practitioners will argue against this approach. The rationale is that any consumer as well as the service will require additional behavior (logic) to populate, manage, consume, and interpret the version from the message body as information content. This is a correct and valid concern. Any consumer of the message will require some set of behaviors to consume and interpret the version from the message. However, it is also the most powerful approach. If this versioning behavior were externalized and exposed as a reusable object or utility type of service, it would only need to be developed and maintained in one place and would be broadly used (reused) across the enterprise and SOA.

Further, the reference and assembly of subordinate schemas to represent the overall service interface could correlate versions across all referenced schemas. Evolution and change of the service interface over time also applies to reusable subschemas. Each of these subschemas will also experience some degree of change. The ability to effectively version and correlate versions when assembling into

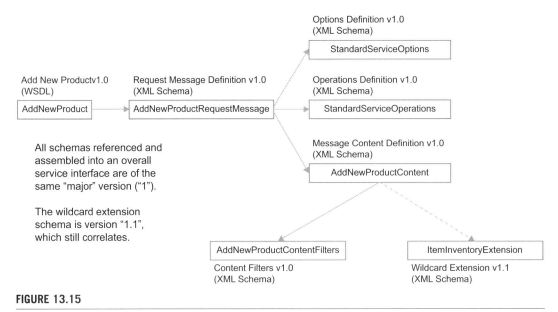

FIGURE 13.15

Correlation of Major and Minor Version Across Schemas

a larger service interface becomes critical. Having a set of common and shared behaviors to manage these versions at a schema and XML message level (via XML Parser validation) provides a tremendous advantage. This approach would help to avoid anomalies and to ensure that all service consumers will bind to the correct version of the service interface.

Where this approach is applied, the versioning behavior should look to correlate the major version. The major version number must be identical across all service interface schemas for a service and should also reflect the current version (change state) of the service itself. Minor versions can vary within the same major version (see Figure 13.5). If those schemas were designed to only reflect insignificant changes, service consumers should have a reduced potential for impact or anomaly.

The versioning patterns and techniques previously described can also be used in combination. However, the service designer should carefully evaluate the advantages and disadvantages of each. For some situations, combining versioning approaches can add more complexity, rather than reduce it. The service designer should also define an overall framework for change management. Just because a technical approach to versioning seems to work, it may not always be effective. For some services, the rate of change can be significant. A single service might encounter a need to change and add new content 10, 20, or more times over its life. Even when each of these changes is of minimal significance and impact to consumers, there is a level of reasonability. Having to design, maintain, test, and redeploy a high number of minor version changes can result in complexity and cost. Alternatively, a change management framework might prescribe that a maximum of 5 or 10 minor versions are allowed for any service. At some defined threshold, it may make more sense to introduce a new major version increment that incorporates all of the previous minor version changes.

Another important and technical consideration for change management is the ability of the SOA infrastructure to support "change in place," which is the ability to include a new minor version change, create a

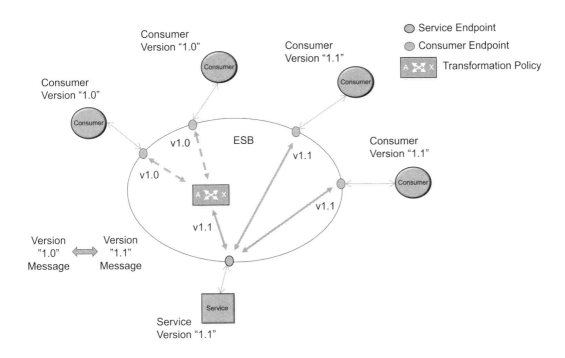

The graphic representing an ESB is not intended to represent a "token ring" or any other network topology.

FIGURE 13.16

ESB Message Transformation Between Versions

new extension schema as a wildcard, and deploy it to the SOA without impact. This is sometimes referred to as "hot" or "active" deployment. In this case, the originating service is not removed from the architecture and generally remains available during the change. Where the SOA infrastructure supports "change in place," previously existing and bound consumers should notice minimal run-time impact.

13.3 CHANGE AND CAPABILITIES OF THE ESB AND WSM

While there is no single approach to SOA and Web services versioning, there are some capabilities of the SOA infrastructure that can help. Some SOA technologies such as the Enterprise Service Bus (ESB) can support message transformation. ESB-enabled transformation is most often used to help resolve data impedance between different message structures and encodings. However, a similar approach to versioning can be applied (see Figure 13.16). The ESB could be configured to transform version "1.0" messages from one consumer to a version "1.1" format that might be supported as the current version of a service. Similarly, the return reply message could be transformed from the version "1.1" of the service response back to version "1.0" as expected by that consumer. This ESB capability can help to resolve some change management and versioning challenges, but it is not without some complexity. For the ESB to perform a bidirectional transformation as described with the specific

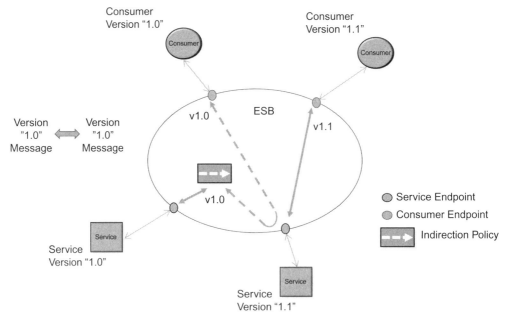

FIGURE 13.17

WSM Policy-Based Indirection

purpose of resolving versioning, it must be "aware" of the version being requested by each consumer and also of the version supported by a service at a defined endpoint on the bus. This is not a trivial activity, and it relies upon some method of exposing the service version in the message. Similarly, it requires that the approach to versioning is managed not by services or the service contract (as in the service interface) but by an enabling SOA technology capability. This might have dependencies into the operational deployment of SOA in the enterprise.

Another approach is to exploit Web Services Management (WSM). For change management and versioning, WSM allows "policies" to be defined and then applied to endpoints on the ESB. These policies are then triggered when an event is encountered, such as the receipt of a message (see Figure 13.17). As with the ESB approach to change management, WSM and the policy must be aware of the version and have a well-defined policy action that can be applied. Also similar to the ESB approach, this will usually result in a message transformation. Another possible WSM policy action might be to redirect a message of different versions to separate endpoints for processing. This is sometimes referred to as "indirection." A single service endpoint is exposed to all consumers of the service regardless of version. The WSM policy would detect the version of the messages and then redirect the messages to their appropriate endpoints, where they would be processed by the different versions of the service. Each version of the service would be deployed to a different endpoint on the ESB.

Redirecting the messages based upon version and the applied indirection policy can in some scenarios help to insulate consumers from version changes. However, the difference between significant and insignificant change still applies. This is also better applied as a temporary versioning and change management solution. Replication of services as new versions is generally an anti-pattern and not recommended.

SUMMARY

Almost all services will, at some point, go through change. For many services, there will be several changes. Some change will be less significant than others and, if properly designed, the service interface can help to mitigate the impact of those changes. More significant change such as adding a new mandatory element or deleting an element from the service interface are more impactful and may require deeper refactoring of the service and its consumers.

The service interface plays a significant role in not only allowing for change but anticipating change. The service designer can prebuild extension points into the service interface and the resulting messages. These extensions do not have to be exposed to all consumers and can be more dynamic and based upon the version of the service being invoked. For Web services, the XML Schema definitions for the service interface allow a "wildcard" capability that can be exploited to advantage. However, use of wildcards requires an understanding of the XML Schemas "any" syntax and XML namespaces, infrastructure support, and thorough testing of the versioned services.

Versioning does not resolve all change management complexities. Rather, it describes the "change state" of a service. Unfortunately, there isn't a single, agreed upon approach to version identification or how a version should be exposed. There are several different techniques, each with advantages and disadvantages. As one recommendation, the version should in some manner be defined by the external file name for the schema artifact or by the internal element content of the message. Another technique is to include the version as part of the namespace URI value.

One important design consideration is to distinguish between significant and less significant types of change. Significant changes to a service and its interface should be reflected by a "major" version. This is the most impactful to all consumers of the service and will likely require refactoring of the consumer's object models and behavior, and thorough testing. Less significant changes should be identified by a "minor" version. A less significant change should reduce the potential impact to already existing and bound consumers of the service but will still require validation and testing.

The SOA infrastructure can also help to implement methods of resolving different versions of a service. The ESB can implement forms of message transformation between versions. WSM can apply indirection policies to an endpoint and then redirect messages to the appropriate service versions. However, these SOA technical capabilities will also require visibility of the service versions that have been deployed and of the versions being requested.

Regardless of the chosen technique, the service designer will need to develop a change management framework to not only resolve issues of versioning but also to apply prescriptive practices and standards. All change and all versions that reflect change must be implemented in a consistent manner with minimal impact to consumers (where possible), must be optimized to avoid proliferation of one-off services, and must be tested to ensure the framework is operational and effective.

REFERENCE

1. Thompson HS, Beech D, Maloney M, Mendelsohn N, eds. "XML Schema Part 1: Structures 2nd ed." (W3C, October 28, 2004). <http://www.w3.org/TR/xmlschema-1/>

Service Operations and Overloading

14

The scope of an SOA service is largely determined by a combination of the information (data) that is either manipulated by the service or returned to a requesting consumer in the response message, and the operations that act upon that information. The information exchanged between a consumer and service is contained in the message as content. The operations of a service are instructional. That is, the operation instructs a service as to what behavior to invoke.

Service operations are described as a combination of verb, object, and an optional modifier. The verb describes the intended action or behavior. The object is an abbreviated name or description of the data, or the message context. An optional modifier can also be included and generally refers to the object. Examples of operations described in the form of "verb – modifier – object" are given in Table 14.1.

Operations are behaviors or some representation of a process that resolve functional requirements for a service. They are defined by the service and determined during service design. The service operations are then exposed to consumers after the service is implemented. To provide consistency and avoid later creation of redundant operations, the operation verbs should be defined by an enterprise standard. The operation verbs are usually aligned with the type of service. Some operations will apply to the access or manipulation of data. Other operations might be more specific to business processes and activities. Services can be classified by three general types:

- Data services
- Utility services
- Functional service

Underlying most service interactions is some form of data-related activity. These data-centric activities are resolved by one or more data services. Most data service operations will access, manipulate, or act upon data from one or more "data at rest" sources. The most common data service operations are analogous to the data manipulation activities of a database and are often described by the acronym CRUD, which refers to Create, Read, Update, and Delete data manipulation activities. With the advent of SOA and servicing, the core CRUD activities have also evolved to include an additional set of extensions such as "Correlate" (for correlation of updates across multiple data at rest sources), "List" (to read and return a list of instances or records in a reply), "Check" (to check for duplicates), or "Query" (allowing a consumer to specify an ad hoc query string).

279

Table 14.1 Example Service Operation Verbs and Objects

Service Operation	Verb (describes an action or behavior)	Modifier (further modifies or describes the object)	Object (the "thing" upon which the operation will act)
AddNewProduct	Add	New	Product
ValidateMessage	Validate		Message
CheckDuplicateItem	Check	Duplicate	Item
AddItem	Add		Item

It is important to note that some types of services and service operations can introduce complexity or potential risk. One example is a "Query" operation where consumers are allowed to specify a query string as text in the request message. While this can be a powerful functional service capability (especially for data services), it can also open a number of security vulnerabilities such as SQL injection. Security is a critical consideration for any SOA, and the service designer should consult with appropriate subject matter experts as part of the service design process.

Utility services are another type of service. Utility services can be more technical or mechanical. That is, utility services perform some sets of activities that are enabled by a technology utility or application. Rarely would a utility service include operations to represent business functionality or processes. An example of a utility service is a validating XML Parser. A common requirement of an SOA is to ensure that the structure and content of a message correctly maps to and complies with the service interface schema. When the interface schema is declared using XML Schemas (as would be the case with a Web service), the validating parser will interrogate the XML message and compare it with the metadata, rules, and constraints of the interface schema.

A validating XML Parser is not a data service (i.e., an XML parser doesn't really access or manipulate data at rest sources), and it doesn't expose business functionality or behavior. Rather, the validating XML Parser accepts whatever XML message it is sent and compares it with a referenced or otherwise provided XML Schema. When exposed as a utility service, the validating XML Parser can be invoked by almost any requester, whether a service consumer or another service. Utility services are not limited to the XML Parser example, and there are others such as data replication services, data movement services, and encryption and decryption services.

The operations of a utility service tend to be very narrow and specific to the technology that underlies the service. Examples of utility service operations and verbs might include "Validate" (as with the validating XML Parser example), "Replicate" (which will replicate or copy a specified set of data), and "Move" (which will move a specified set of data from one location to another).

Functional services involve some form of business behavior. Functional services are also sometimes known as business services. The rationale is that a functional service will enable some type of business function, process, activity, or similar behavior. Functional services can be designed as very narrow and fine-grained, or as higher-level service orchestrations. In either case, the functional service exposes operations that make sense to the business (see Table 14.2). Examples of functional service operations can include "Compute" (as a somewhat mathematical behavior to compute or calculate a result), "Perform" (performing a function, process, or activity), and "Send" and "Receive" (which sends information or a notification of processing such as a token).

Table 14.2 Service Types and Service Operation Verbs

Data Service Operations (CRUD)	
Action	**Common Verbs (use only one from the list)**
Create	Add, Create, Insert, Maintain
Read	Get, Read, Retrieve, Select
Update	Update, Modify, Change, Maintain
Delete	Delete, Remove, Kill, Eliminate

Data Service Operations ("Extended" CRUD)	
Action	**Common Verbs (use only one from the list)**
Check	Check, Check Exists, Check Duplicates
Correlate	Correlate, Synchronize
List	List, Set
Metadata	Info, About, Metadata
Ad Hoc Query	Query, Select
Search	Search, Find, Seek

Utility Service Operations	
Action	**Common Verbs (use only one from the list)**
Validate	Validate, Verify, Parse
Replicate	Copy, Replicate
Move	Move, Transport, Relocate

Functional Service Operations (Business Services)	
Action	**Common Verbs (use only one from the list)**
Perform	Execute, Invoke, Perform, Process
Compute	Derive, Calculate, Compute
Send	Transmit, Message, Alert, Send (usually referring to a message or processing token)
Receive	Consume, Respond, Receive (usually referring to a message or processing token)

Regardless of the service type or the intended service behavior, the verbs that describe a service operation should be derived from a single enterprise standard. This will help to avoid duplication and inconsistency. As an example, it would be disadvantageous to create a service that exposed an operation for "AddNewProduct", while another and different service was also created with an operation

Product Service Operations
AddNewProduct   (Create)
GetProductData   (Read)
UpdateProductData   (Update)
DeleteProductData   (Delete)

Product
Service

One Service with Four Operations
"One-to-Many"

FIGURE 14.1

Coarse-Grained Service with Multiple Operations

for "CreateNewProduct". Assuming the behavior of both services and their operations were roughly analogous, the redundancy is costly, service reuse is ignored, and there may be the potential for contention or even anomaly at the underlying data at rest source. Defining and complying with a single enterprise standard for operations verbs will help to avoid this problem.

14.1 SERVICE GRANULARITY

Service operations play a significant role in the determination of service granularity. The notion of service granularity can be viewed from different perspectives. One is simply the degree to which a service is decomposable. With this perspective, a coarse-grained service is more of an orchestration that interacts with other fine-grained services. Alternatively, a fine-grained service is not as decomposable as other more fine-grained services. A fine-grained service is the lowest possible set of deployed and encapsulated service behavior.

Another alternative method of describing service granularity is by the number and type of operations that are exposed. Using the example of a single deployed data service, multiple CRUD operations could be defined and exposed to consumers (see Figure 14.1). That is, the example data service might be specific to the context of a "Product", and includes four separate operations to "Add" a new product (an operation verb that is analogous to "Create"), "Get" product data (an operation verb that is analogous to "Read"), "Update" existing product data, and "Delete" product data. Exposing all four basic CRUD operations from a single service qualifies this service as coarse-grained, and the relationship of services to operations becomes one-to-many. The possible behaviors to affect a product are all contained in one service, and consumers would have to specify which of the operations of that service is required.

Alternative to the example of a coarse-grained service, each of the same CRUD operations could be applied to individual and separate "Product" services (see Figure 14.2). In this case, each of the individual services is considered as fine-grained and is limited only to the single operation that each exposes and supports. With a coarse-grained service, consumers would request a particular operation from a single service. The relationship of services to operations becomes one-to-one.

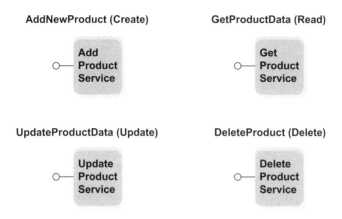

Four Services, Each with a Separate Operation
"One-to-One"

FIGURE 14.2

Fine-Grained Services with Each Supporting a Single Operation

The design decisions for choosing to develop coarse-grained or fine-grained services are not well defined. There are both technical and practical considerations. Some SOA architects and Web service designers might prefer to design a single coarse-grained service with multiple operations with the rationale of being able to more rapidly develop and deploy the service. Another rationale might be a view toward the overall SOA cost. Deploying and managing a single service in the SOA will often have a lower operational cost than deploying many fine-grained services.

Alternatively, service granularity design decisions might be heavily influenced by the potential for reuse (fine-grained services will usually exhibit a higher potential for reuse) and the mitigation of impact to consumers from future changes. When a fine-grained service that only exposes a single operation undergoes modification, only those consumers that have bound to the service interface are subject to potential impact from the changes. The consumers of the other services are typically not subject to these changes.

Another consideration for service granularity is related to optimization. Data services will almost always invoke some underlying set of data at rest behaviors. That is, an "AddNewProduct" operation will insert new data into the Product database. A relational database analogy fits well with this scenario. Over time, several factors can negatively impact the performance of the underlying database, which then extends back to the service. Example factors might include things such as the number and frequency of requests for data, the types of operations that are performed (e.g., read vs. update), the amount of data returned, and the volatility of the data.

Within the database management system are access paths that are defined by a plan and help the database to navigate to the data of interest for requesters. When performance begins to degrade, these access paths become one of the most important areas of interest for tuning and correction. A database analyst (DBA) will evaluate performance issues and often refer to the access paths to determine if there are problems and opportunities for optimization. The optimization exercise might include deep analysis of the access paths, including research into indexes, joins, SQL optimizer choices, and so on Although the specific implementation and syntax can vary from database to database, the analysis is usually enabled by an "Explain", "Explain Plan", or similar statement and utility.

When the primary accessors of the data are fine-grained services, each may have their own, unique plan (as a set of access paths). The DBA can quickly identify which of the services is incurring latency, identify the access paths being used, and take action that in many cases can be localized to that database and service. When the services are more coarse-grained and include numerous requests from varied consumers and for any number of different operations, the ability to identify the root cause and then optimize can become complex (see Figure 14.3).

The advantages between coarse-grained and fine-grained services are not clear-cut. There are other trade-offs to consider, as well. The cost of designing and managing separate and individual fine-grained services can be excessive. This is an example where the expertise of the SOA architect comes into play. The SOA architect can solicit assistance from other business and technology subject matter experts to carefully assess and balance trade-offs and provide the appropriate design guidance to the service designer.

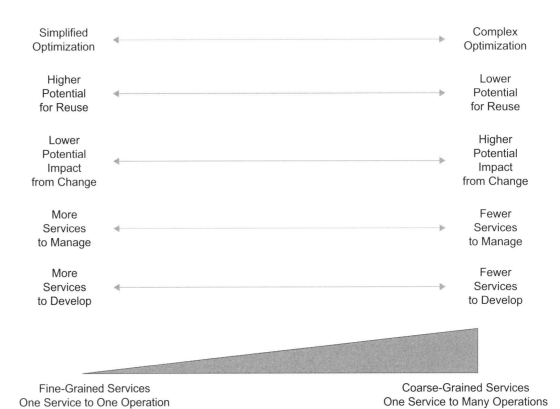

FIGURE 14.3

Balancing Coarse-Grained and Fine-Grained Services

14.2 SCOPING OF SERVICE OPERATIONS

Data services almost always rely upon CRUD and extended CRUD operations. Looking beyond these simple operations are the resulting actions taken on the data at rest sources that support the data services. A "Create" operation (as in "Add" a new row of data to the database) will result in one or more database "inserts." However, the scope of data for a data service is not always analogous to a single row in a single database table. Some data services will access or manipulate a set of related data (multiple rows) that might also be persisted across several tables and possibly across multiple databases (see Figure 14.4). For the latter example, a data service with federated query capabilities and update correlation is required. The previous product data analogy is more simplistic. A somewhat more complex model is that of customer data. A Customer data service with a "GetCustomerData" operation might return a set of customer data that crosses several tables of the implemented customer data model. The service would navigate and join across the various Customer tables and return a complex result set, or, if an update operation were used, the service would manipulate data that are persisted in several different tables. The complexity of the data model then extends into the complexity of the service behavior.

When the scope of the service crosses multiple data at rest tables or data sources, the integrity of the request must be maintained. That is, if there are referential constraints between data at rest source tables, the service must include the elements that represent the content of those relationships in the message. The operations that act upon the related data at rest tables and sources must be resolved as a consistent unit of work. As one example, if the service were to delete a record from the Customer Master table, it might also need to delete corresponding Customer Address data. If the Customer Master was deleted, but the corresponding Customer Address remained in place for that same customer, the database would become inconsistent. If the relationships between these tables were also managed by referential integrity constraints at the database level, the service would need to correlate its operations and supporting behavior with those constraints.

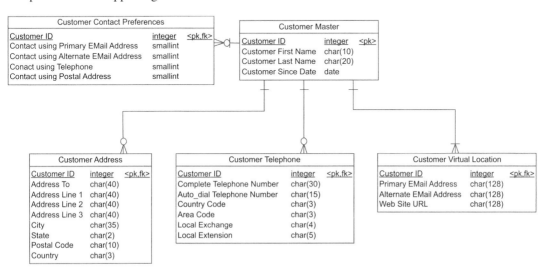

FIGURE 14.4

Example Customer Data Model

Where a Customer service might be more coarse-grained, multiple operations are exposed to access and manipulate customer data. These example service operations might include "AddNewCustomer", "ModifyCustomerData", and "DeleteCustomer". In this case, one Customer service exposes four separate operations. In addition to the noted Customer data service, there might be any number of other services as well as more traditional applications that also access the same data at rest Customer data. This scenario presents a potential database optimization and management problem.

Different consumers, each with types of data queries, access and update actions to the Customer database to further complicate service optimization. This can result in contention between different consumers, all requesting the same data. If any of the requests include other than "Read" operations, database locking and lock escalation can result. To avoid these types of problems, the DBA will look to create different indexes and more optimized tablespace and page sizes. Narrowing the scope of a service to a set of similar operations or even a single operation that can be analyzed and managed by the DBA is known as "moderate service scope" and is a design advantage.

To help avoid data access and performance problems, the service designer can "balance" the operations of the service. For some services, a fine-grained and single-operation per service design pattern is optimal. For others, there are combinations of service operations that exhibit affinity across data at rest actions. At the database level, "insert" and "update" actions will both result in a lock of the affected table or row. The database management system will verify that appropriate rules and constraints are applied to each of the data elements before the insert or update actions are completed (such as, verifying that the data values match the column data types and mandatory columns have data values). Rather than separating these two types of database actions different separate services and operations, it might be more advantageous to design a single "MaintainCustomer" service that exposes both "Add" (Create) and "Update" operations.

A similar synergy exists among "Read", "List", and "Search" operations. All three of these operations will "read" data from an underlying data at rest source, and the most obvious differences are in the volume of data returned. A "Read" operation will typically return requested data for a single record, row, or "read" unit of work. The "List" and "Search" operations can return data for one or more records, rows, as a unit of work. Here again, the service designer might design a single "GetCustomer" service that exposes three read operations ("Get", "List", and "Search").

Other types of data service operations such as "Delete" and "Query" are unique in the action that takes place and will usually warrant the development of individual and separate services. A request to a delete service and operation will usually apply to an entire unit of work. Other than the identifier or primary key, rarely are other elements required in the request message. A query operation is highly variable and dynamic. The scope and context of a query service and operation are generally left to the consumer. The consumer will request an ad hoc query string that is similar to a SQL query and predicate (see Figure 14.5).

With a fine-grained service that exposes only one service operation, there is the potential for many separate services where each will in some manner access the same data at rest sources. This adds to the overall operational and management cost of the SOA. Alternatively, a coarse-grained service with all possible operations is difficult to troubleshoot and optimize. A coarse-grained service is also subject to more frequent modifications and, therefore, has a higher potential to impact all consumers of the service. Alternatively, a moderate-grained service will balance and optimize across similar operations (see Figure 14.6). These synergies between service operations can help the service designer determine whether a service should be defined by a common set of service operations (moderate grained), a single

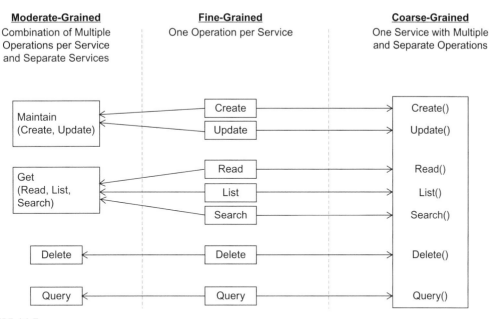

FIGURE 14.5

Synergies Between Service Operations and Service Scope

operation per single service (narrow or "fine-grained" scope), or a single service that exposes all possible operations (broad or "coarse-grained" scope).

Rarely is a single approach to operations and service granularity applicable across the entire SOA. Rather, an optimized SOA will contain an inventory of services that have different scope and granularity. This allows the services as well as underlying "data at rest" sources to be optimized and managed.

14.3 OPERATIONS OVERLOADING

Another approach to designing service operations is overloading, which refers to the use of declarative data values intrinsic to the service interface that describe consumer requested actions. With operations overloading, only a single service operation is exposed by a service (see Figure 14.7). However, the service will have been designed to support multiple operations with supporting internal behavior. The single exposed operation is really a façade that allows consumers to request and submit different operations of the service by instantiating a corresponding data value in the request message. These operation values become part of the message payload and must then be extracted and evaluated by the service to determine what action has been requested.

For simplicity, we'll return to the product service example where an "Add" and an "Update" operation are supported. However, the service only exposes a single Web service "Maintain" operation to consumers. Consumers can then specify which of the two supported operations are requested by including a data value in the request message that is sent to the service.

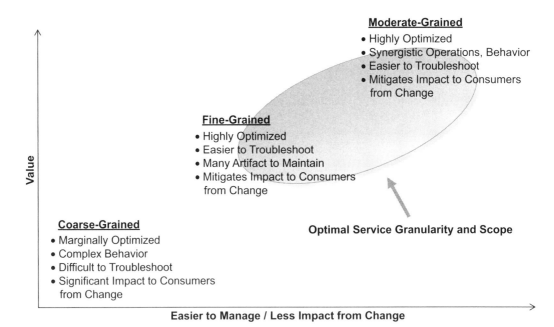

FIGURE 14.6

Balancing Service Operations Granularity and Service Scope

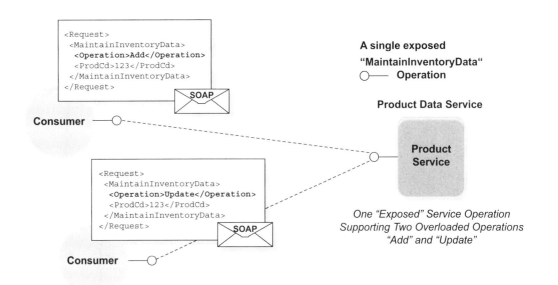

FIGURE 14.7

Operations Overloading

The service contract and interface cannot be violated, and all service consumers are still required to comply with the structure, data types, and constraints of the service interface (see Figure 14.8). In this case, the service would have been designed to allow for the two possible service operation types as data values of the request message. Further, each of the two values would have required an enumeration value in the request message interface schema. Consumers would need to insert the appropriate operation type as a data value in the "Operation" element ("< Operation/ >"). Requisite to this design approach is a strong emphasis on standard operation verbs. Other operations such as "Create", "Insert", "Modify", and so on would not be allowed.

The benefits of operations overloading are that new operations can be added with little or no impact to previously existing service consumers. Where new operations are required and assuming the element content of the request message remains unchanged, previous consumers of the service have little risk of impact. The service interface would need to allow for the new overloaded operation data value, and the service would need to map the appropriate message content with the new operation.

If the service has also been designed as either fine-grained or moderate-grained, then management and optimization of the service are simplified. Although not entirely the same, overloading is somewhat similar to the design pattern of "document-literal," where explicit operations and parameters are avoided (as with RPC-style services). When the operations are overloaded, they become part of the message context, rather than an explicit operation signature. Again, the intent is to mitigate the impact of change to previously existing service consumers.

Operations overloading can also have several disadvantages. Similar to the reasons why overloading of parameters or variables with programming languages is considered an anti-pattern, operations overloading is implicit and ambiguous. That is, the operations data values are not explicitly exposed by the Web service. Rather, the overloaded operations are encapsulated in the message payload and exposed only through the service interface schema. Designers of consumer applications will need to

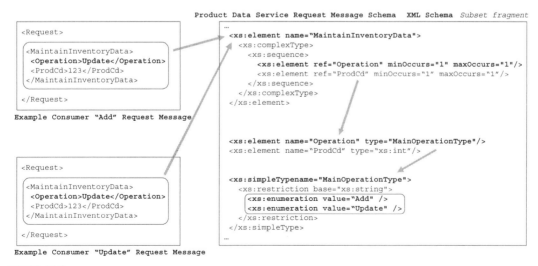

FIGURE 14.8

Request Message Operation Enumerations

inspect the service interface schemas and as a result, explicitly design their applications to instantiate the operation values that correspond to the expected behavior of the service. If not, there is a potential for violation of the service contract and resulting anomaly.

Another disadvantage of overloaded service operations is the association of message context and elements. When operations are explicit and exposed by the Web service as an operation and port, the Web service WSDL will have mapped to the expected interface schemas. This simplifies the service contract and makes it explicit. Alternatively, where only a single Web service operation is exposed and the service supports overloaded operations, only a single interface XML Schema is defined. The service interface designer will have to carefully define the schema constraints of each intrinsic element to match according to the expected behavior for allowed operations. If overloaded operations are allowed for both "Get" (i.e., "Read") and also "Add" (i.e., "Create"), there can be significant differences in the element content that is required of the request message. A "Get" operation might only require an identifier or key element, while the "Add" operation will require that all mandatory elements for that record, row, or unit of work have been included. The XML Schema language is powerful but lacks the ability to conditionally cross-correlate element constraints. This means that the differences between message content and elements cannot be conditionally determined from the operation data value. When service consumers are being developed and bound to the service interface, this can result in anomalies.

As an additional disadvantage, the service object model and behavior can become quite complex. Unlike explicit and exposed Web service operations, where the service interface is mapped to the object model of the service, the service must interrogate each request message and unmarshal the message content and data values to determine whether a requested operation is valid. In a simple sense, this means that the service must accept any request message (whether correct or not), extract the content, and determine if the requested operation is supported. This requires more complex processing by the service even before the service can resolve a request or, in the case of an unsupported operation, before the service can return a fault to the consumer.

Operations overloading can be a powerful service interface design technique. However, overloading should only be applied to a limited number of use cases and only when the service operations are clearly defined, the scope of the service is moderate to narrow, and the service behavior is relatively static. Even then, the operations values must be clearly defined and enumerated in the service interface schema. Any violation of the service contract should result in a fault being returned to the consumer. Further, the service interface schemas must be carefully designed with well-defined constraints.

SUMMARY

The scope of an SOA service is largely determined by a combination of the information (data) that is either manipulated by a service or returned to a requesting consumer in the response message and the operations that act upon that information. The service operations are described as a combination of verb, modifier, and object, where the verb is the action or behavior, the modifier further describes or characterizes the object, and the object is an abbreviated name or description of the data.

The three primary types of services include data services, utility services, and functional services. The operations for each type of service should be defined by a standard set of verbs. These verbs can be uniquely defined for each enterprise, but they should be consistently defined across the enterprise. The most common verbs used to describe service operations are those related to data services and are known as CRUD (Create, Read, Update, Delete). These verbs also refer to fundamental behaviors that can be applied to data. As services have evolved, the notion of CRUD has also been expanded to include other operations verbs as well (such as "List", "Query", and so on).

Other types of services also require a standard set of operations verbs. A utility service might include "Validate", "Replicate", or "Move" operations. Functional services (also known as Business Services) are often higher-level orchestrations or combinations and represent some type of business function, activity, or process. Two of the more common business service verbs include "Perform" and "Compute".

The scope of a service and its relationship to supported operations are critical design considerations. A coarse-grained service will expose multiple operations to consumers. Alternatively, a fine-grained service only includes a single operation. This service is very narrow in scope and only resolves and responds to one specific requested action. An alternative is to identify affinities between operations and to balance the resulting service granularity. A moderate-grained service will expose multiple operations but only those that have functional or data-related synergy. As an example, a single service that exposed both "Add" and "Update" operations would be of moderate grain.

Coarse-grained services that combine all possible CRUD operations are difficult to manage and optimize. The underlying data at rest SQL bindings, database plans, and packages are difficult to evaluate and refine. Balancing the scope and granularity of a service by combining similar service operations can be of significant value from a database perspective. Optimization of the service as well as analysis for problem solving is simplified.

Another design technique allows for overloading service operations as elements and data values of the request message payload. This can be a powerful design pattern that helps to insulate existing consumers from change, when additional and new operations are added to a service. However, it also has disadvantages. Operations overloading can result in complex and difficult-to-maintain services. Service consumers must become aware of allowed operations (which are encapsulated by the service interface) and the explicit data values that represent those service verbs. Although operations overloading can be applied to advantage for some use cases, strong caution is advised.

Selective Data Fragmentation

15

When designing a new service, one of the first steps is to collect and validate functional service requirements. Functional requirements include the requisite "information requirements" representing data context and the service operations as "operations verbs." The data elements that resolve the information requirements and represent the data context then become part of the initial canonical message design. For functional and data services, the requirements and list of resolving data elements can be quite comprehensive. This collection of data elements has the potential to include all of the elements, columns, and fields from underlying data at rest sources (see Figure 15.1).

For some SOA architects and service designers, it might initially seem advantageous to include a list of all possible data elements in the canonical message structure for that servicing context. This simplifies the early requirements and analysis design steps, and the result would be a service that can deliver all possible information content from the implemented data sources. This approach is overly data centric and, unfortunately, does not include a more practical and optimized view of service design.

While the critical importance of data and metadata to a servicing paradigm should be clear, there is also a more practical balancing of nonfunctional requirements and consumer considerations that come into play. For example, a fully functional service that delivers every possible customer data element to consumers might initially seem to be of significant value. However, if that same service took several minutes to acquire the data and return the response over the SOA to the requesting consumer, it would become impractical and very likely not survive to become reusable.

Nonfunctional requirements such as performance, scalability, capacity, and availability need careful consideration with any service design. As implied by the name "nonfunctional," these requirements are rarely a directly stated need of the enterprise business community. Rather, they describe the expected or target technical qualities of the SOA and serve to further the effectiveness of a service and optimize its deployment. The result can become critical to the business response to SOA. Where a service might provide every possible data element and operation, the ability to meet performance expectations can be offsetting.

A service that has been designed to require that every possible data element of a reply must be accepted and processed by all consumers is also likely to never reach a point where it becomes a candidate for reuse. There are several design alternatives to help simplify the scoping of data and use by consumers. One approach is to group, segment, and correlate sets of data elements with the operations exposed by the service. This can be an effective approach. However, it also broadens the overall scope

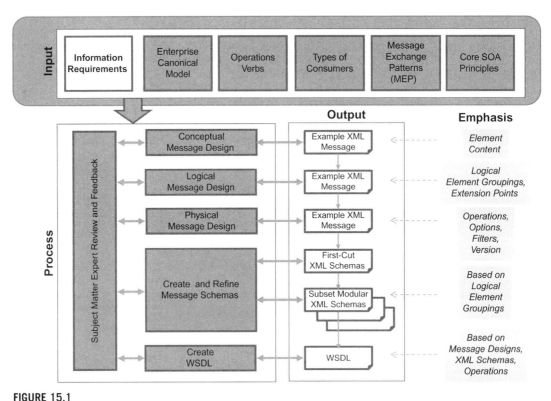

FIGURE 15.1

Canonical Message Process Input

of the service to extend the consumer and service object models. Further, some service consumers may be historic or legacy and may have limitations for SOAP and XML message processing. While it is becoming less of an issue as technologies evolve, the latter is common for some procedural languages such as COBOL.

Another effective approach to resolving the service scope and consumer requirements is more practical (see Figure 15.2). In this case, the service designer should look across the technology and assess the number and types of potential service consumers. Many service consumers will only require a subset of the message element content (i.e., a subset of the data elements returned by the service).

When combined with nonfunctional requirements such as performance, a design constraint can quickly arise where the service contract between consumers and the service needs to be somewhat negotiable. Rather than forcing all possible consumers of the service to accept and process an overly verbose message, including data elements that they might not require, this can be offset with consumer requested collections of data elements. These collections or groupings of data elements are often described as "fragments" of data, in that they represent and contain a subset of the data element content from a service response.

When the selective data fragmentation approach has been implemented in the service design, the service interface will include a set of "Filter" elements. Service consumers can select which sets of

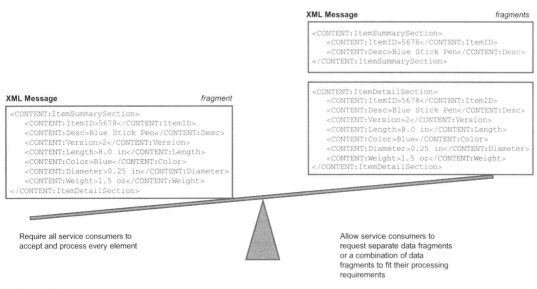

XML Message   *fragments*

```
<CONTENT:ItemSummarySection>
    <CONTENT:ItemID>5678</CONTENT:ItemID>
    <CONTENT:Desc>Blue Stick Pen</CONTENT:Desc>
</CONTENT:ItemSummarySection>
```

```
<CONTENT:ItemDetailSection>
    <CONTENT:ItemID>5678</CONTENT:ItemID>
    <CONTENT:Desc>Blue Stick Pen</CONTENT:Desc>
    <CONTENT:Version>2</CONTENT:Version>
    <CONTENT:Length>8.0 in</CONTENT:Length>
    <CONTENT:Color>Blue</CONTENT:Color>
    <CONTENT:Diameter>0.25 in</CONTENT:Diameter>
    <CONTENT:Weight>1.5 oz</CONTENT:Weight>
</CONTENT:ItemDetailSection>
```

XML Message   *fragment*

```
<CONTENT:ItemSummarySection>
    <CONTENT:ItemID>5678</CONTENT:ItemID>
    <CONTENT:Desc>Blue Stick Pen</CONTENT:Desc>
    <CONTENT:Version>2</CONTENT:Version>
    <CONTENT:Length>8.0 in</CONTENT:Length>
    <CONTENT:Color>Blue</CONTENT:Color>
    <CONTENT:Diameter>0.25 in</CONTENT:Diameter>
    <CONTENT:Weight>1.5 oz</CONTENT:Weight>
</CONTENT:ItemDetailSection>
```

Require all service consumers to accept and process every element

Allow service consumers to request separate data fragments or a combination of data fragments to fit their processing requirements

FIGURE 15.2

Balancing Between All Possible Data Elements and Selective Data Fragments

data elements they will require by setting the value of a request message filter to true (similar to "on"). The service will then interrogate the request message, map the requested filters to the service object model, process the request, and return only those data elements that were requested.

The described analogy implies a request-reply Message Exchange Pattern (MEP). When combined with a "Read" type of operation, this is perhaps the most common example of selective data fragmentation (see Figure 15.3). However, it is not a limitation. Depending upon the information requirements, operations, and data context for the service, selective data fragmentation could be applied with equal effectiveness to other service types and operations.

A more effective service design approach is to start with the larger and overall superset of elements that resolve known functional requirements and then further group elements into subsets according to some observable affinity (as per Chapter 8, "Canonical Message Design"). If we consider that the list of elements from a service reply message is the data portion of the service scope and context, then the subset element groupings are "fragments" of that superset list.

Rationale for grouping some elements together can be contextual, based upon some common set of requirements across consumers, or nonfunctional affinity. Contextual affinity is some common sense relationship or dependency between the elements in a contextual grouping. These contextual groupings will often exhibit some common sense similarity and semantics. A few common examples include the following:

- Postal Address Elements
  - Address To
  - Street Address lines
  - City
  - State

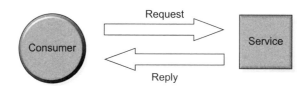

XML Request Message   *fragment*

```
<ItemFilterSection>
    <IncludeItemSummary>true</IncludeItemSummary>
    <IncludeItemDetail>true</IncludeItemDetail>
    <IncludeItemExtendedSection>true</IncludeItemExtendedSection>
</ItemFilterSection>
```

XML Reply Message   *fragment*

```
<ItemSummarySection>
    <ItemID>5678</ItemID>
    <Desc>Blue Stick Pen</Desc>
</ItemSummarySection>
```

XML Reply Message   *fragment*

```
<ItemDetailSection>
    <ItemID>5678</ItemID>
    <Desc>Blue Stick Pen</Desc>
    <Version>2</Version>
    <Length>8.0 in</Length>
    <Color>Blue</Color>
    <Diameter>0.25 in</Diameter>
    <Weight>1.5 oz</Weight>
</ItemDetailSection>
```

Allow service consumers to request
separate data fragments or a
combination of data fragments to fit
their processing requirements

FIGURE 15.3

Request-Reply MEP and Selective Data Fragmentation

- ❐ Postal Code
- ❐ Country
- ▪ Product Dimension Elements
  - ❐ Product Weight
  - ❐ Product Diameter
  - ❐ Product Length
  - ❐ Product Height
  - ❐ Product Width
- ▪ Person Name Elements
  - ❐ Name Prefix
  - ❐ First Name
  - ❐ Middle Name
  - ❐ Last Name
  - ❐ Name Suffix
  - ❐ Name Title

While the example element groupings will fit most business scenarios and requirements, they are still grouped in a somewhat experiential manner. A more appropriate source of business affinity would exploit the classes and data entities of the enterprise canonical.

The determination of most appropriate element groupings to meet subset consumer requirements is largely determined by analysis. The initial information requirements for the service will serve as the overall information scope or data context for the service. The service designer will then seek out both known and potential service consumers to evaluate their individual current servicing requirements as well as future or expected requirements. These element groupings required by different consumer types will often include collections of data fragments that were determined by contextual affinity.

For these groupings, consumers specify which subsets of elements or selected collections of element groupings they require in a reply message, or the elements on which the operations will be applied. This allows consumers to meet their unique processing requirements, while avoiding the overhead and complexity of those elements from the service that are not needed. Consumers will specify the elements of interest with filters being declared in the request message sent to the service. Using a product service analogy, several contextual groupings of elements might include the following:

- Product Identifier Elements
  - Product Identifier
  - Product Engineering Drawing Number
- Product Description Elements
  - Product Name
  - Product Description
- Product Dimension Elements
  - Product Weight
  - Product Diameter
  - Product Length
  - Product Height
  - Product Width

There might be three different classes of Product service consumers. The originating and primary consumers of the service would require all possible elements, crossing the three element groups (e.g., Product Identifier, Product Description, and Product Dimensions). The set of data elements in the reply message for these consumers would likely need to include all possible elements. Alternatively, there might be two other classes of Product service consumers. One set of consumers might only require the Product Identifier elements. The other type of service consumer might require both the Product Identifier elements and the Product Description elements. Rather than forcing all three types of service consumers to request, receive, and process a reply message with the superset of all possible elements, regardless of whether they are needed or not, the three data fragments could be defined to the reply message of the service interface and three request message filters could be defined (with one for each data fragment). Each type of Product service consumer would set the filter to "true" for those data fragments it requires in the request message (see Figure 15.4).

The last approach to element grouping as data fragments is based upon nonfunctional requirements, of which, performance is often the most common. Nonfunctional performance-related requirements might require a subsecond response time from request to reply, or there might be a limit on the overall message size. In this case, the previously defined contextual and consumer-driven data fragments might be further decomposed.

Continuing with a Product service, the Product Description element might include a significant amount of text that is unnecessary for some consumers. However, the Product Name might be a simple, concise, text name of 40 characters in length or less. A significant number of service consumers might require the Product Name, but a limited few would require the full text of the Product Description

XML Request Message *fragment*

```
<ItemFilterSection>
    <IncludeItemSummary>true</IncludeItemSummary>
    <IncludeItemDetail>true</IncludeItemDetail>
    <IncludeItemExtendedSection>true</IncludeItemExtendedSection>
</ItemFilterSection>
```

Service consumers can selectively request a subset of the message
content by setting a filter value to "true".
A data fragment is returned for each "true" filter.
Combinations of filters and fragments can be requested.

FIGURE 15.4

Product Service Consumer with Three Selective Data Fragments

element. In this example, the service designer might move the Product Name to the Product Identifier data fragment, leaving the Product Description Element to remain in a separate standalone data fragment. In this manner, consumers would be able to specify in the request message to the service which of the elements were of interest:

- Product Identifier Elements
  - Product Identifier
  - Product Engineering Drawing Number
  - Product Name
- Product Description Element
  - Product Description
- Product Dimension Elements
  - Product Weight
  - Product Diameter
  - Product Length
  - Product Height
  - Product Width

For each grouping and regardless of the rationale, the service designer should consider whether the data fragment and its mix of participating data elements are optional or mandatory. Mandatory groupings of elements have some rigid or strict dependency, often determined by the underlying data sources, and are requisite to resolve a service request. These groupings of elements are required in every service interaction and reply message and are not selectively determined by the consumer. Optional elements may or may not be instantiated in the reply message. Similar to the nullable columns of an implemented database, these elements are loosely constrained by the service interface contract. However, interface schema-defined metadata constraints such as data types will still apply (see Figure 15.5).

From the perspective of canonical message design, elements are positioned in the message and grouped under a parent element. When indented, these nested data fragments help to provide a visual prototype of the canonical message design and support later service interface design steps where service interface schemas are created. The parent message element for each data fragment is specified in the service interface schema as a complex type (e.g., "complexType"). The elements that are positioned as children and participate in a grouping may be defined as individual elements (similar to data containers), or they may be deeper nested parent elements with nested child elements. The maximum

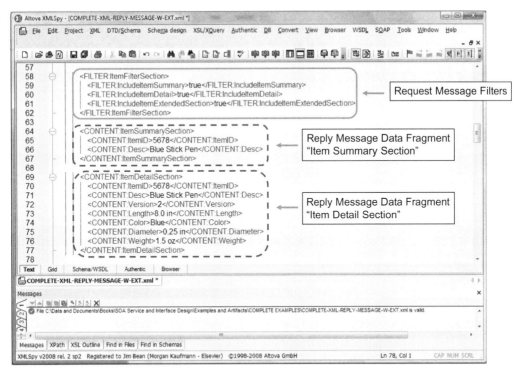

FIGURE 15.5

Canonical Message Design with Data Fragments (Copyright 2003-2008 Altova GmbH, reprinted with permission of Altova)

depth to which elements are nested is not a constraint of either the service interface or the XML Schema that describes it. Rather, it is a design technique that attempts to optimize the overall message structure and the location of elements.

Some service designers may rely upon a more traditional data modeling approach to designing the message and service interface, where the keys and foreign keys that support navigation of the underlying relational data sources are included as element content of the message (see Figure 15.6). However, it is important to remember that data in motion (as with messages) is not identical to data at rest. The structure of a message (data in motion) is a hierarchy and complies with the structural and encoding rules of XML. While a more relational approach to message design might initially seem as intuitive, it can complicate the hierarchical nature of XML and the supporting object models of both consumers and services.

While there are some synergies between data models and relational implementations to the content of a service message, it is critical that SOA architects and service designers recognize that a relational architecture is not synonymous with that of a message hierarchy. Groupings of message elements should not be restricted exclusively to a data model or to the tables, columns, and relationships of the underlying data at rest sources. Strictly enforcing this relational analogy on a canonical message design can quickly become an anti-pattern and result in a less than effective service interface. Including

XML Reply Message   *fragment*   **Relational Data Model**

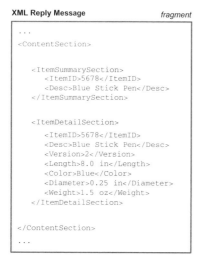
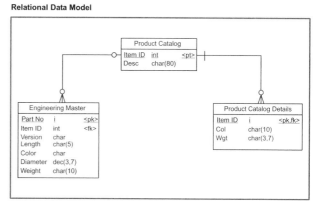

FIGURE 15.6

XML Message Hierarchy vs. Relational Data Model

navigational elements representing relationships or foreign keys in the service message tends to result in overly verbose and complex messages that are difficult for an object-oriented consumer to map, navigate, and resolve, and can also significantly add to network latency. These more data-driven and database-driven techniques can

- Add to the overall message size
- Complicate navigation of the XML-encoded and hierarchical message
- Complicate unmarshaling of the data values from the message
- Complicate mapping of the message structure to the object model of the consumer and service

Alternatively, the service message is usually an implicit unit of work. The elements of the message are included in that unit of work and, when combined with the service operations, represent the scope of the service. Some services will act upon or return multiple records or units of work. This is often common with a "List" type of operation and service. With a "List" reply message that contains multiple instances of data (similar to the notion of records), each record is defined by a parent element structure and is considered as a logical unit of work. With this scenario, each record will require appropriate data identifiers but only within the given context.

As implied previously, not all service consumers will require the same set of data from a reply message. Some will require the superset collection of elements, while others may require subset variations. Anticipating these needs and working to structure and organize the canonical message design become critical to the service interface design process. Interestingly, the initial canonical message design can include subset groupings of element content that overlap. That is, one data fragment of the message (grouping of elements) may contain several individual elements that are also defined to other data fragments of the message.

The repeated data fragments are overlapping but are not redundant. This is an area where the Global Declaration pattern plays a role (Chapter 11, "XML Schema Design Patterns"). Each of the individual

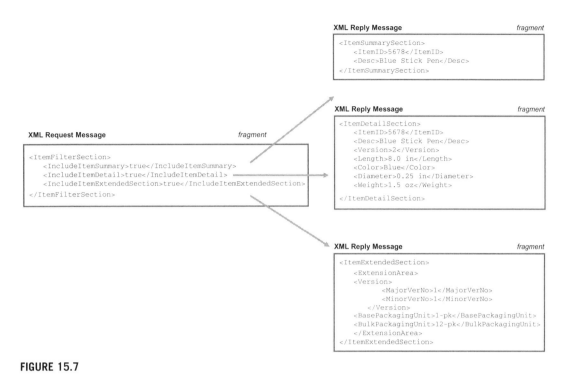

FIGURE 15.7

Item Summary and Item Details

elements can be defined separately to the service interface schema. These global elements can then be referenced and reused in data fragments as logical assemblies. An element representing an Item Description ("< Desc/ >") can be defined globally once to the service interface, yet referenced by name and reused in both an Item Summary data fragment ("< ItemSummarySection/ >") and an Item Detail data fragment ("< ItemDetailSection/ >"). Extension elements can also be defined by a data fragment and a filter. However, when requested by a consumer, the reply message will require a namespace-qualified reference to the "wildcard" schema to support schema validation (see Figure 15.7).

For each data fragment, a corresponding "filter" is then added to the canonical message design and resulting service interface schema. When a consumer requires a set of data fragments, the filters for those fragments would be set to "true." Upon receiving the request message, the service would need to interpret the filter elements, map the requested filters to data fragment structures, acquire the requisite data from the underlying data at rest sources, instantiate the data elements of those structures in the reply message, and respond to the consumer with a reply message.

15.1 AVOIDING A COMPLEX OR NON-DETERMINISTIC CONTENT MODEL

When following the message design process as described in Chapter 8, "Canonical Message Design," a critical step is the logical grouping of elements according to some affinity. The affinity might be contextual and result from data element groupings and relationships of the enterprise canonical model. Using the "Add New Product" service example, exposing all possible product and engineering item data elements in a single reply can promote consistency. However, when the number of message elements is significant (sometimes referred to as an overly "verbose" message), it can be unreasonable for those consumers that might only need a limited few of the elements from the total set. The problem is in determining how to balance between a service that exposes a large superset of elements with the creation of several smaller services that each expose a subset of the same element content.

In the example where a large superset of data elements is provided in the reply, the service and service interface design process is somewhat simplified. In this scenario, it is usually easier to identify the data of interest and collect all possible elements to resolve the functional (information) requirements. For the example where separate sets of elements are defined by individual services, there is a tremendous amount of overlap and potential for divergence from any standard. This can result in increased integration problems and operational costs.

The most extreme design approach would allow for ad-hoc consumer requests, where any service consumer could request any possible set of data elements in a reply message. This is sometimes abstractly described as a non-deterministic content model. The model is so open and unconstrained or managed that any request is accepted and the service is then responsible for resolving it.

For some servicing use cases, this type of open and unconstrained data access can be of value, but the question of a loosely coupled, reusable servicing paradigm versus direct, data at rest access arises. If the types of consumers and their requests will be highly varied and nonstandard, this might be a scenario where SOA and servicing are not the best technology solution. The use of native SQL and XQuery against the underlying data at rest sources might be a better choice.

However, most enterprise servicing scenarios are the opposite. Aligning on some degree of standardization and to avoid continuing the enterprise integration problem take precedence. Most consumers require some common subset of data from a given data subject area. Where these subsets of data elements are predefined as data fragments and allowing the consumer to select those elements with request filters is an optimized approach.

With predefined data fragments and filters, the service object model and behavior is optimized. There is no abstract or nondeterministic behavior required. Further, the implementation of data fragments and supporting request message filters provides a significant degree of flexibility to consumers. Those consumers that either do not require or might not be able to effectively process all data element content from the service can limit their scope of processing without affecting the needs of other consumers for the same service.

SUMMARY

Data fragmentation is a canonical message and service interface design approach that balances between the scope of information requirements and supporting data elements of the service with individual processing needs of different consumers. Rather than forcing all consumers of a service to always accept and process every element of the message or service response, the consumers can select which of the elements as data fragments (groups of elements) that they require.

Consumers specify the required data fragments in the request message using filters. Filters are simple XML elements that have an allowable value of "true" (i.e., "on" or "yes") and "false" (i.e., "off" or "no"). Each filter is mapped one-to-one with a data fragment (collection of data elements defined to a parent, complex type element) of the message. For each data fragment that is required by a service consumer, the value of the filter is set to "true" in the request message. Upon receiving the request message, the service unmarshals the filter elements and data values from the message, maps the request values to the service and data access object model, processes the request and acquires the data from the data at rest sources, and returns only the requested data elements in the reply message.

Rather than allowing abstract and unconstrained requests, an effective service will have predefined the allowable data fragments and filters to the service interface and supporting service behavior. This allows that the service interaction is highly optimized for both consumers and the service. Where there are extreme requirements to support ad-hoc data requests, services can be designed, but this may not be an optimal approach. For these scenarios, the SOA architect and service designer must carefully evaluate the variability of use cases and then determine if direct data at rest access with technology such as SQL or XQuery might be more appropriate.

Update Transactions

16

The most well-defined and understood SOA interaction pattern is a simple read-only, request-reply. The request-reply interaction mimics human conversation, and a read-only CRUD operation is far simpler than an update. The service consumer submits a request for information, and the service carries out the activities necessary to identify, acquire, and return data elements in a reply that meets the request. The simple read-only, request-reply pattern is also the most common across SOA implementations, as well as being the most limited (see Figure 16.1). As implied by the read-only operation, there is no capability to enable the other CRUD operations of Create, Update, and Delete.

An alternative to a read-only service is update. With an update service, the CRUD operations of Create, Update, and Delete are implemented. The granularity of the service and number of exposed operations will determine whether the operations are exposed by a single coarse-grained service or across several fine-grained services.

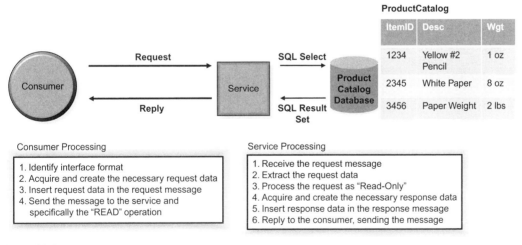

FIGURE 16.1

Simple Read-Only, Request-Reply

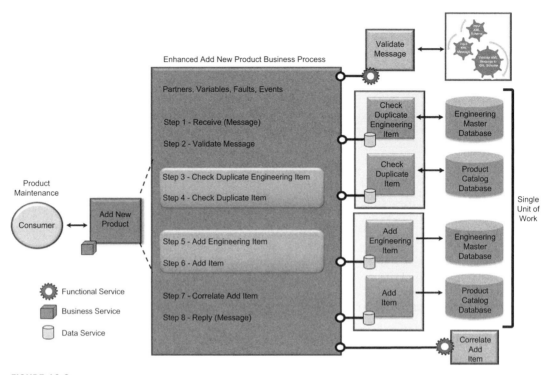

FIGURE 16.2

Single Unit of Work

As described in Chapter 5, "Data Services," a data service can access one or possibly many differ-ent data at rest sources for a single consumer-to-data service request. When the service has resolved to a single data source, that interaction will also ensure that update requests have been resolved at the implemented database. With a service that crosses multiple data sources, there is an implicit requirement to correlate update operations across each and to ensure that the update request was treated as a single and complete "unit of work." That is, a single consumer request for update might require multiple and subordinate requests to other fine-grained data services or to multiple data at rest sources (see Figure 16.2). If any of the subordinate update requests were unsuccessful, the entire originating request should be considered as unsuccessful, and all implemented data is rolled back to the original state.

Another important consideration of an update service and operation is managing multiple and com-peting update requests to the same data at rest implementations. There may be two or more consumers that are requesting an update of the same information. While each of these requests is valid, they must be applied independently and result in a consistent and expected state. The typical database is capable of managing and resolving these types of multiple and competing updates (see Figure 16.3).

However, the detached and loosely coupled nature of SOA and Web services adds another layer of complexity to updates. In part, this complexity is related to the SOA loose-coupling principle. The interactions between a consumer and service are not rigid. Nor do they maintain a stateful interaction.

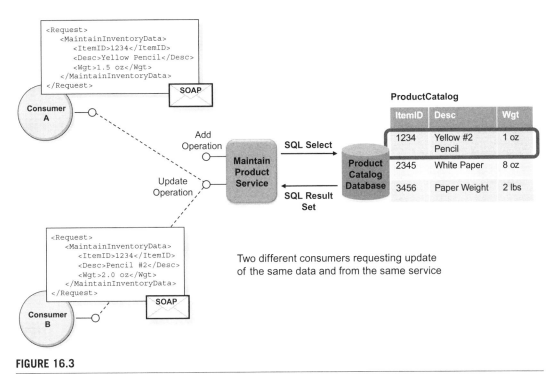

FIGURE 16.3

Update Complexity of an Enterprise Class SOA

Rather, they interact in a more detached manner using messages. The consumer requests some operation of the service, and the service then resolves the request or, on error, produces a fault.

16.1 UPDATE TRANSACTIONS AND STATE

A consumer request for update assumes that prior to beginning the update and also after the update, the data are in a consistent and expected state. That is, when the originating update is requested, the consumer has either read that same data (if already existing) or has a pre-add image of the data (if the data is new). There should not be any pending or partially resolved updates to the data from other consumers or service interactions that would produce an end result other than expected (see Figure 16.4).

The typical service will have abstracted and insulated consumers from the data at rest implementation and database management technologies. In many cases, the consumer request for update will be resolved by a coarse-grained data service that crosses multiple data at rest sources. In this example, the data are federated. It may be implemented by multiple and different types of database management systems, each with its own implemented view of the information.

With a federated data implementation where there are multiple data at rest sources, a single update request will result in multiple and more fine-grained updates. These updates will target each implemented data source. However, the total set of all the more fine-grained transactions represents a complete

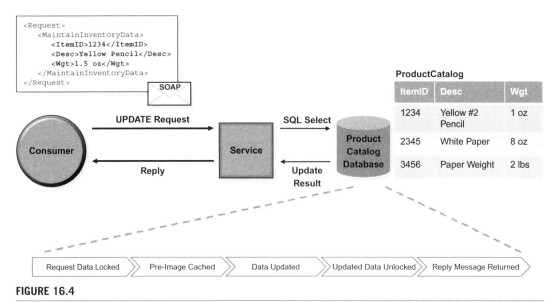

FIGURE 16.4

Consistent State of Data at Rest

unit of work. If any single request fails, then all of them must be abandoned, and each of the data at rest sources must be returned to its pre-update state (see Figure 16.5). Assuming a request-reply Message Exchange Pattern (MEP), a fault is also returned to the originating consumer.

To determine whether any of the more fine-grained update requests have failed, a correlation ID is assigned to each transaction and a process to match and compare the updates and to ensure that all were successful is required. The correlation process can be designed and implemented for each service. However, this can be a complicated process, and the recommended approach is to use a commercial technology such as a federated query processor or an information integration server.

If the update service requires a set of separate transactions to update federated data at rest sources, and the decision is to develop the correlation process, it will have to be managed as part of the service behavior or possibly by the BPEL.[1] In this case, it becomes important to create a correlation ID for each of the transactions, representing the complete unit of work. As part of the BPEL orchestrated service, an additional set of service behavior will be required to match and compare correlation IDs from each of the subordinate update transactions to ensure that the complete set of updates was successful (see Figure 16.6). The service interface will need to include an "option" element in the request message, allowing the consumer to request correlation across updates (e.g., "< SynchronizeCorrelationID/ >").

For an internally developed service, the success or failure of the update request at each of the implemented data at rest sources must be determined. When the data source is a relational database, the update status can be described by the SQL State, SQL Status, or a similar SQL error code.[2] Some database technologies have implemented extensions to the X/Open specification, while others have implemented more proprietary mechanisms for reporting SQL State. A SQL State value of "00000" is considered as a successful operation (or possibly "00" depending on the specific database communication interface). While there are a number of possible SQL State codes, for purposes of correlation, anything other than "00000" should be considered as unsuccessful.

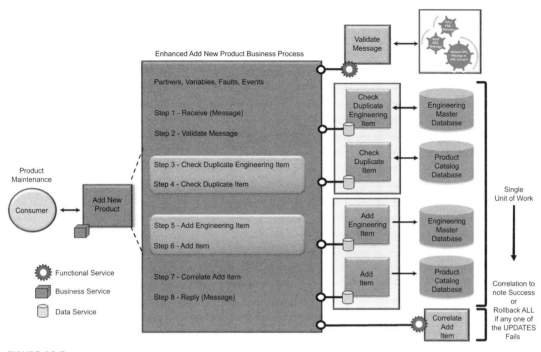

FIGURE 16.5

Unit of Work—All Updates Succeed or All Updates Fail

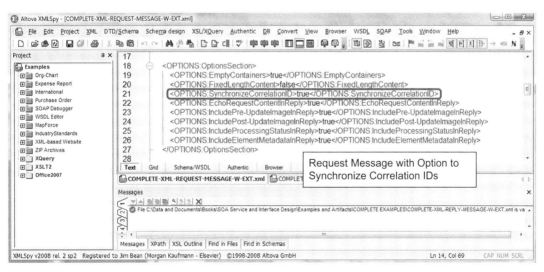

FIGURE 16.6

Request Message with Option to Synchronize Correlation IDs (Copyright 2003-2008 Altova GmbH, reprinted with permission of Altova)

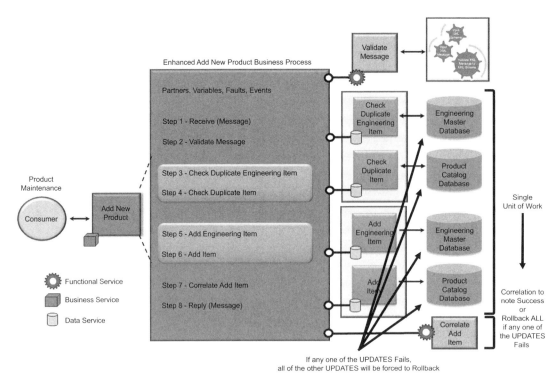

FIGURE 16.7

Rollback to Original State

If any of the federated update requests returns a SQL State other than "00000", then the entire update request as a logical unit of work should be considered unsuccessful. In this case, any of the individual updates that might have been successful will need to be rolled back to their prior state (see Figure 16.7). That is, the completed updates must be removed, and the data returned to its pre-update image.

Some service consumers will require notification of update success or update failure. This can be resolved by designing an "option" in the request message to instruct the service to return the SQL State values for each of the data sources (see Figure 16.8). The service will then also need to perform the requested behavior. This is a user-defined option and might include an element such as "< IncludeProcessingStatusInReply/ >".

Update correlation is complex at best. Each of the federated update requests to the individual data at rest sources will be largely independent. This helps to ensure compliance with the SOA loose-coupling principle. Depending upon the implemented database technologies, each of these update requests will also result in the target data being "locked" from update by other services and applications. In part, this helps to preserve data consistency. When the update has been successfully completed, the locks are released, and the data now becomes available for other updates. If an error condition has resulted, the data is restored to its pre-update state (known as a "rollback"), and the locks are released.

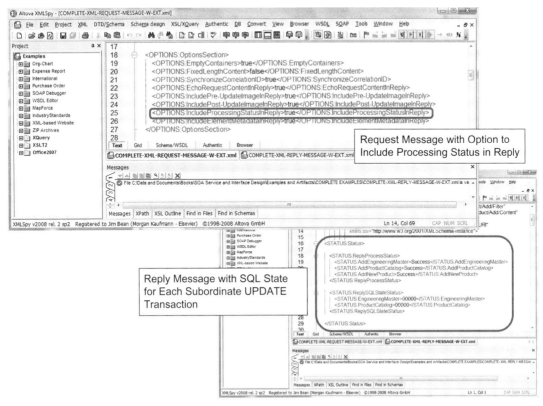

FIGURE 16.8

Request Message with Option to Return Processing Status Values (Copyright 2003-2008 Altova GmbH, reprinted with permission of Altova)

An additional complexity can result with correlation processing across federated updates. If one of the federated update requests is successful, the resulting data reflects the expected state and are then available for other updates. If another of the federated updates fails with an error and is rolled back, the entire correlated set of transactions must be rolled back. However, if another separate update request has been successfully applied to the first federated data source, a rollback to its original state is not possible. The data will then be in an inconsistent state across the data at rest sources. This situation is the primary rationale for using a commercial technology to manage the federated updates. Most federated query engines will manage multiple levels of locks, correlate across the federated update requests, and prohibit updates to any of the individual data sources until the final determination of the correlation has been made.

When there are multiple update requests for the same information (e.g., multiple service consumers and applications), these competing requests must be managed (see Figure 16.9). Even with a single, non-federated data at rest source, the data must remain in a consistent and expected state. Competing updates have to be prioritized and queued, locks taken, and pre-update and post-update images retained to allow for potential rollback. The database is generally expected to handle these contentious update requests.

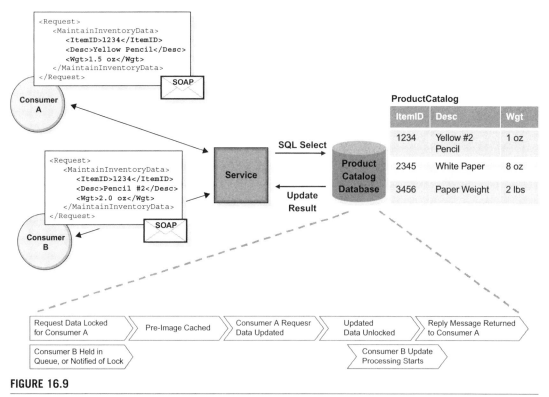

FIGURE 16.9

Multiple Update Requests for the Same Data

Another scenario occurs when consumers request a read operation of data that are locked and in the process of being updated. Many database technologies can be configured to allow dirty reads. This is where the pending update has not yet completed, and the data are locked, but consumers are allowed to read the data. Scenarios vary, but some databases can be set to allow a dirty read that represents the intended end state of the data post-update. The risk of a dirty read with a pending post-image of the data is if a rollback occurs. The consumer reading the data will have assumed that the update occurred and that post-update image of the data may not reflect the pre-update image resulting from the rollback. Other potential options are to only allow the consumers to read a pre-update image of the data even though the pending update will result in a change.

Although competing read and update requests are common for a database technology, the notion of separate and loosely coupled services adds some complexity. Database locks are typically held for the duration of the transaction. If the update is complex or there is a potential for latency, the data can be locked for an unreasonable period of time. Further complicating the scenario is when the data is an image of the intended update, but the database rolls back to the pre-update image. If other consumers are allowed to read the data that is also subject to long-running and in-process updates (dirty reads), a higher number of consumer reads will revert to the pre-update image of the data. This can result in business processing of data that is not current and may not be in a consistent state.

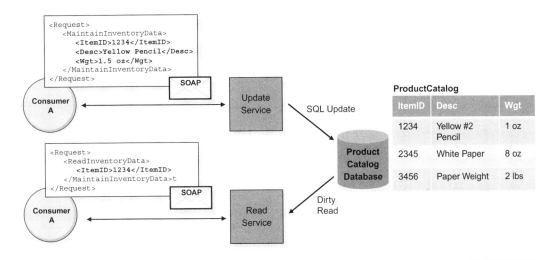

```
<Request>
   <MaintainInventoryData>
      <ItemID>1234</ItemID>
      <Desc>Yellow Pencil</Desc>
      <Wgt>1.5 oz</Wgt>
   </MaintainInventoryData>
</Request>
```

```
<Request>
   <ReadInventoryData>
      <ItemID>1234</ItemID>
   </MaintainInventoryData>t
</Request>
```

ProductCatalog

ItemID	Desc	Wgt
1234	Yellow #2 Pencil	1 oz
2345	White Paper	8 oz
3456	Paper Weight	2 lbs

Potential Types of Dirty Read Processing
1. Consumer B, Read request is locked from Read and "Data is Locked" Error or "Timeout" is returned. Consumer B has option to retry the Read request.
2. Consumer B, Read request is resolved by a reply with a pre-update image of requested data before update by Consumer A.
3. Consumer B, Read Request is resolved by a reply with a pending post-update image of requested data "assuming" update by Consumer A is successful. However, if Consumer A update rolls back, reply to Consumer B may be inconsistent.

FIGURE 16.10

Dirty Read Processing

Alternatively, the data source may be configured to restrict dirty reads (see Figure 16.10). In this example, a request to read data that is also in process of update will either move to a wait queue until the data are unlocked, or it will result in a locked data SQL State code being returned. Some database implementations will queue the read request until the pending update is complete and the lock is released, or until a time-to-live threshold is reached with a read fault being returned (as with a timeout). Either scenario works but can result in some processing latency or errors being returned to the requesting consumer. If the consumer is resolving an online request, significant delays in acquiring the requested data can impact response time for that application.

Where a rollback is required, it is best to let the implemented database manage the rollback to release any locks. Forcing rollbacks can be complicated and generally requires what is known as a compensating transaction.

16.2 REQUEST-REPLY MESSAGE EXCHANGE PATTERNS

The request-reply Message Exchange Pattern (MEP) is the most common across an SOA. It is also the most effective for single unit of work updates. The consumer will provide the data elements in the request message that are necessary to complete the intended update. The service will respond to the consumer with a reply message noting that the update request was successful or a fault to note that there was some error in processing.

Where the update is federated across multiple data at rest sources, it is likely that some service consumers will require deeper information in the reply message. This requirement may be to resolve complex update behavior for a coarse-grained data service, or it may support some legacy behavior of the originating consumer. It may be advantageous to optionally include detailed status reporting such as SQL State for each of the underlying data at rest sources. It might also be of value to optionally include a pre-update image of the data read from the database (just before the update process was started) and a post-update image of the data (after the update was completed) in the reply message. Some consumers might also require a copy of their original request data to be returned, which allows for a comparison to the post-update image.

Rather than build these complex and deep interactions into every request message as mandatory for every service consumer, a more effective design practice is to implement request message options. Each of these options would be set by the consumer as needed (e.g., using a boolean value of "true" or "false" as appropriate). The names for each of these request message elements (e.g., element tag names) are defined by the service designer and should be intuitive to any potential consumer of the service. Corresponding service behavior for each option would then be required, as well. Several request options to consider in the service interface design can include the following:

- SynchronizeCorrelationID
- EchoRequestContentInReply
- IncludePre-UpdateImageInReply
- IncludePost-UpdateImageInReply
- IncludeProcessingStatusInReply

A request-reply MEP is also required for compensating transactions. A compensating transaction allows the consumer to direct a service to force a rollback of updated data to a previous state. This requires that the service performing the update must have returned a pre-image (before the update) and a post-image (after the update) of the data in the reply message. After the update, the end state of the data is logically moved to the consumer. The consumer then takes on the responsibility of determining whether the resulting post-image of the data is acceptable and the update should remain in place, or if a rollback should be forced. If a rollback is forced by the consumer, the pre-image of the data must be submitted in the follow-on request message for update to the service.

From a service and service interface design perspective, these become requirements that manifest as the combination of "options," including pre-update and post-update element content being included in both the request message and the reply message (see Figure 16.11). Where the consumer may force a rollback, the corresponding options of the request message will need to be set to "true". These elements are defined by the service designer and would reflect tags names similar to "< IncludePre-UpdateImageInReply/ >" and "< IncludePost-UpdateImageInReply/ >".

This model is most often used with either an internally developed coarse-grained data service that will federate across data sources, or with traditional or legacy consumers with complex and tightly coupled update behavior. This model also disallows the database management system to be exploited for its natural rollback processing. Rather, the rollback of an update is logical and implemented by the consumer's behavior as a second or follow-on request message for update with elements representing the image or state of the data prior to the most recent update.

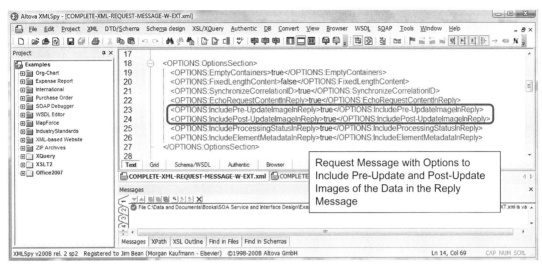

FIGURE 16.11

Request Message with Pre-Update Image and Post-Update Image Options (Copyright 2003-2008 Altova GmbH, reprinted with permission of Altova)

This is also a complex and imperfect model. It is further complicated by locking and unlocking of the data at the underlying data at rest sources. When these locks are released, there is a risk that other update requests for the same data may be processed before a follow-on compensating rollback can be requested. The service could be designed to include more extensive locking behavior where locks are held and transferred to the consumer. However, this approach also violates the loose-coupling principle. The consumer and service would be tightly coupled with the underlying data at rest sources.

The recommended design approach is to identify update processing status, update correlation, and unit of work transaction management options and elements that meet specific processing requirements for the service. Each of these requirements should be carefully evaluated to determine if an effective design alternative or a commercial solution exists. A federated query engine or information integration server is often the better choice over internal development of the same capabilities. Also, updates, locking, and state management for data are better left to the implemented database technology.

16.3 COMPLEXITIES OF FIRE AND FORGET FOR UPDATES

While a request-reply MEP is the most common and recommended interaction for an update, there may be sufficient rationale to warrant a fire-and-forget update. Where the update is particularly complex or where there is a specific requirement for performance and limit of latency (i.e., a long-running transaction), an asynchronous fire-and-forget pattern may be required.

The value of a request-reply MEP is that the consumer has an opportunity to evaluate a reply message and determine whether to continue with intended processing or to take an alternative processing path. A fault response from the service or inability of the service to successfully complete a requested update is a common example of the latter. As an alternative to a request-reply interaction, with an asynchronous fire-and-forget pattern, the consumer can request the update but is then disconnected from the service interaction. In most cases, the consuming application will have to "assume" that the requested update was successful. Not receiving a reply message leaves the success of the requested service operation in question and may have an adverse effect on other continued processing. Generally, the recommendation is not to use an asynchronous fire-and-forget pattern for update processing. However, there may be some situations such as a mass update of multiple "records" or a complex update that will affect numerous databases and tables in which the processing time may run considerably longer than would be acceptable for an online consumer and request-reply.

One important design consideration for an asynchronous fire-and-forget update service is the unit of work granularity. If the service will be expected to process updates for numerous records, it may be of value to set frequent commit points. This allows the underlying data at rest sources to be frequently updated and to release locks on the data. Other read or update requests can then process without contention or time-out while waiting for access to locked data. Alternatively, it might be important that the unit of work is coarse-grained for logical consistency. In this case, the entire set of updates, regardless of whether it includes multiple records or only a single record, is treated as a whole. The risk with a coarse-grained unit of work is that the data may be locked for an unreasonable period of time during processing, and other consumers will be prohibited from access.

If a consumer submits an update to an asynchronous fire-and-forget service and a failure to update results, there is additional complexity. The original and requesting consumer may have assumed that processing the updates would be successful and based additional or later process behavior on that assumption. This may also be true of other consumers. The data may be rolled back to its pre-update state and cause residual faults for those other consumers.

One effective use of the asynchronous fire-and-forget pattern for updates is with a composite or "stacked" MEP (see Figure 16.12). With this pattern, the consumer might require a series of high volume update requests. Due to other nonfunctional requirements such as performance, the consumer also needs to disconnect from the update request and continue with other processing. However, the consumer also requires a high degree of data integrity and relies upon successful updates. To help resolve this complex servicing scenario, multiple MEPs can be combined or stacked.

The publish-subscribe pattern allows consumers to subscribe to a service, a message queue, a similar concept known as a topic, or to a set of servicing behaviors. Once the service has completed its processing and resolved the request, it then publishes pertinent data and notifies the subscribing consumers. This allows the service consumers to later "pick up" their processing information.

A subscribed consumer can submit an asynchronous fire-and-forget request message for update to a service and disconnect from that direct interaction. Once the subscribing consumers are notified that the service has completed processing, they can also interrogate the resulting information to determine if the updates were successful, or a fault occurred and the updates were rolled back. Based upon the result, the consumer can continue with other processing.

While a request-reply pattern is generally recommended, there can be complex processing scenarios that warrant an alternative. For update processing, an asynchronous fire-and-forget MEP can only imply potential for success. This lack of a cohesive response introduces risk. However, the asynchronous fire-and-forget pattern can be combined into a composite or stacked pattern, where the updates are appropriately managed and the consumer requirements are met.

1. Consumer "subscribes" to service and operation.
2. Consumer submits asynchronous "fire-and-forget" request to update service.
3. Consumer is "disconnected" from the interaction and can continue with other processing if needed.
4. Update service processes the request and formulates a reply message.
5. Update service "publishes" notification to subscribing consumer of success or failure.
6. Consumer can base additional processing on the notification and whether the update process was success or failure.

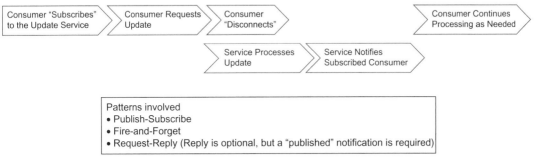

FIGURE 16.12

Stacked Pattern for Long-Running and Disconnected Processing

SUMMARY

The most common and effective pattern for updates is a simple read-only, request-reply. This pattern allows consumers to not only request the update of data but also to verify whether the update request was successful or a fault occurred. Any update must leave the data in a consistent state. When a fault occurs, the data must be rolled back to a state that reflects its pre-update image. Rollback of data to a prior state is best left to the implemented database technology.

There are several design complexities for update servicing. The first is to consider that most enterprise servicing scenarios will involve multiple consumers, services, and applications, all of which may request a read or update of the same data from the same underlying data at rest sources. This can result in complex database locking, competing requests for access to the same data, and the potential for time-outs. The service designer will need to carefully consider the requirements for the update service and evaluate the impact across the enterprise. The result may include consideration for dirty reads, or other alternatives.

Another complexity is with the number and type of underlying data at rest sources that are the target of an update request. Federated updates across multiple data sources must be correlated. The entire set of updates must be treated as a single unit of work. If one update fails, then the other updates must be rolled back. If all updates are successful, then the entire update transaction is successful.

Another complexity is the granularity for the unit of work. If the update request involves a high volume of data where multiple records are intended for update, it may be of value to define several commit points. This allows the data to be incrementally updated at the data at rest sources and to release those records for access by other consumers. If the unit of work is more coarse-grained, and the commit point is not taken until all of the data is updated, then the data will remain locked and other consumers requesting access to the same data can incur time-outs.

While a request-reply MEP is the recommended and most common, it may not effectively resolve high-volume update requests where the consumer cannot wait until completion (e.g., a long-running and disconnected transaction). In this example, an asynchronous fire-and-forget pattern could be combined with (e.g., "stacked") other patterns such as publish-subscribe. This allows the consumer to disconnect from potentially long-running service behaviors and yet to still get a notification of update success or failure.

REFERENCES

1. Jordan D, Evdemon J. chairs "Web Services Business Process Execution Language Version 2.0, OASIS Standard" (April 11, 2007). <http://docs.oasis-open.org/wsbpel/2.0/OS/wsbpel-v2.0-OS.html/>.

2. *X/Open CAE Specification, Data Management: Structured Query Language (SQL), Version 2*, X/Open Document Number: C449 (Reading, UK: X/Open Company Ltd.).

Fixed-Length Transactions

17

As described in previous chapters, the interactions between SOA consumers and services are enabled by messaging. For Web services, the service interface, including WSDL and XML Schemas, defines the structure and allowable content for those messages. XML provides a generally platform-agnostic method for encoding message content and is the de-facto standard for messaging.[1]

Current state technologies such as Java have deep rooted support for XML and provide the ability to create XML messages, as well as navigate and read XML message content. However, Java is not the only development platform, and Web services is not the only service type supported by SOA. Traditional or "legacy" applications such as COBOL programs also have potential to act as both SOA consumers and SOA services.[2] While most organizations would prefer to adopt the most current SOA and messaging technologies, the historic investment in legacy applications is often significant. Many of these applications are fully functional and used in production, so it would be economically disadvantageous to ignore or abandon them.

In recent years, many technology vendors have also recognized the importance of SOA and have included support for XML messaging with their development tools and compilers for technologies such as COBOL and relational database products. The type and degree of XML support varies, but most COBOL compilers now include an XML Parser or XML API to help marshal and unmarshal data from XML messages. Similarly, many relational database technologies now have extensions to store XML content as complete XML document instances or as more fragmented parts of an XML document. Many of these database products can also expose persisted relational data as XML tagged data elements. These simple XML capabilities help to preserve the past investment in legacy applications.

However, even when considering these added XML capabilities, there are also a number of complexities and limitations. For example, many COBOL programs might also interact with other COBOL programs. These interactions are often exposed as positional or fixed-length interfaces. If a legacy COBOL application is refactored to now produce and consume XML content (assuming XML capabilities are available as described previously), when passing that data along to other traditional applications, the repurposing of data content from XML to a more positional format can be difficult. Depending upon the technology, the COBOL program might require additional formatting logic to left- or right- justify the data, add missing characters to "fill out" each element to a specific length, and even perform "type casting" to move a data value of one data type to another.

COBOL File Definition

```
05  Reply.
    10    Item-ID            PIC X(10)  NOT NULL.
    10    Item-Description   PIC X(25).
```

COBOL Positional File Format

| | | | |Item-ID| | | | | | |Item-Description| | | | | |

FIGURE 17.1

COBOL String Data Value

The most common types of formatting complexities and impedance that occur between legacy applications such as COBOL and more SOA, XML, and messaging-centric technologies such as Java include the following:

- Positional data values with fixed length vs. data that is encapsulated between XML open and close tags
- Missing data elements (such as "optional" elements defined to the XML message)
- Legacy data type support and types supported by XML and XML Schemas

Traditional technologies such as COBOL tend to work well with fixed data structures. Within these structures, data values begin and end at specified positions. If the relevant part of the data value is fewer characters or positions than allowed, the remaining positions are filled with characters of the appropriate type. As an example, a string data value (e.g., "PIC X(10)" to COBOL) defined as 10 characters in length, containing a value of "1234", and representing an "Item ID" consumes 10 positions in the COBOL file definition (see Figure 17.1). As long as the COBOL elements were type specified and initialized on start, the remaining positions would be suffixed with allowable type-specific characters such as spaces.

Alternatively, an element defined to an XML message for the same data value of "1234" would be positioned within an XML open tag and a close tag (see Figure 17.2). With the XML message and unless there were an interface schema-declared length or minLength constraint, the default length of the XML element is variable and fits the length of the data value that it contains. The length of the "Item ID" data value would be four positions and nothing more.

Some XML Parsers and compiler extensions will allow a COBOL program to map between named XML elements and internally defined COBOL elements. Differences in data value length may be accounted for with additional type-specific characters being added by the XML Parser to fill in any missing positions of the length. An alternative would be to design the service interface with an XML Schema facet for each XML message element as a minimum length constraint. When the service consumer binds to the service interface schema or when validating the message to a schema, the minimum length value

COBOL File Definition

```
05  Reply.
    10      Item-ID              PIC X(4)  NOT NULL.
    10      Item-Description     PIC X(25).
```

XML Message

```
<SOAP-ENV:Envelope xmlns:SOAP-ENV="http://schemas.xm
                   xmlns:SOAP-ENC="http://schemas.xm
                   xmlns:xsi="http://www.w3.org/2001/XMLSchema-instance"
                   xmlns:xs="http://www.w3.org/2001/XMLSchema">
   <SOAP-ENV:Body>
     <Reply xmlns:m="http://Widget-Example.com/Inventory">
      <ItemID>1234</ItemID>
        <ItemDescription>Yellow #2 Pencil</ItemDescription>
     </Reply>
   </SOAP-ENV:Body>
</SOAP-ENV:Envelope>
```

```
<ItemID>1234</ItemID>
```

FIGURE 17.2

XML String Data Value

would help to ensure that the data value for each defined reply message element was of the expected length. In addition to the minimum length facet of the service interface schema, a maximum length facet would help to avoid data values that exceeded the expected length. With this approach, COBOL consumers will incur far less complexity in trying to determine if the data value received is within the prescribed length definition.

Another possible technique is to include a length constraint in the interface schema. However, this would specifically fix the data value length. Rather than forcing all service consumers to accept a fixed-length data value, these design techniques can be further extended to allow legacy service consumers (COBOL or similar) to specify a fixed element length as "options" in the request message to the service (see Figure 17.3). With this technique, the consumer will set a request message option such as "< FixedLe ngthContent/ >" to "true" or "false" as required. Note that neither the example request option nor any other recommended canonical message design option is defined to or required by any Web service standard. Rather, the option element is user defined and would also require corresponding service behavior (logic) to resolve the request. If implemented as part of the service behavior, the data values in the reply message from the service would be set to the "minimum" length as defined by the service interface schema.

A similar complexity encountered by legacy service consumers is that of missing data elements. Most fixed-position data structures, such as those defined to a COBOL file definition, prescribe that each element of a structure occurs in a specific order based upon the defined length of the element, at a fixed position. XML is more flexible and dynamic. Where a message element is defined to the service interface as optional, the XML element tag does not have to be included in the reply message

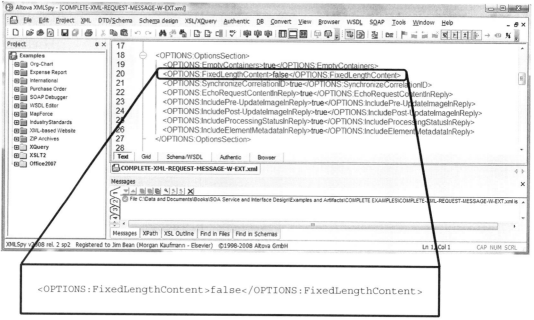

FIGURE 17.3

Request Message Option for Fixed-Length Data Values (Copyright 2003-2008 Altova GmbH, reprinted with permission of Altova)

if there is no data value found. In this example, the reply message elements are only those that are mandatory or where an optional element has a data value. Missing elements can throw off the more statically defined structure of a legacy consumer and result in potential errors.

This scenario can be resolved with another request message option. Legacy consumers can request that all message elements, including optional elements, are returned in a reply message, regardless of whether they contain data values or not (see Figure 17.4). The service consumer would set an "< EmptyContainers/ >" request message element to "true." As with the "< FixedLengthContent/ >" request message element, this option is user defined. It is not defined by or required by Web service standards. The corresponding service behavior to include all elements in a reply message would also need to be developed.

Another potential complexity incurred by legacy service consumers is that of mismatched data types. Unless constrained by a referenced XML Schema, all data values encoded as XML are defined as "characters."[3] The value space and lexical space of these characters include almost any possible Unicode character or value.[4] For a consumer that is not aware of a corresponding XML Schema or is not bound to a type definition for the message, the elements of a raw and unvalidated XML message will appear as "string" characters (see Figure 17.5).

For numeric or other type-constrained content, this can result in anomalies. To avoid type mismatch, the data type for each element and constraining facets that might be applicable must be mapped to the internal element type system of the legacy consumer. This may limit the data types that can be applied to message elements. To resolve this requirement, the data types must be common or converted to those

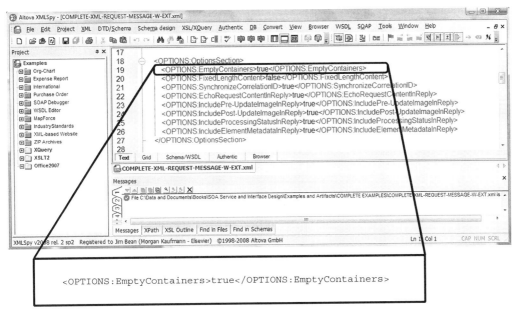

FIGURE 17.4

Request Message Option for Empty – Optional Elements (Copyright 2003-2008 Altova GmbH, reprinted with permission of Altova)

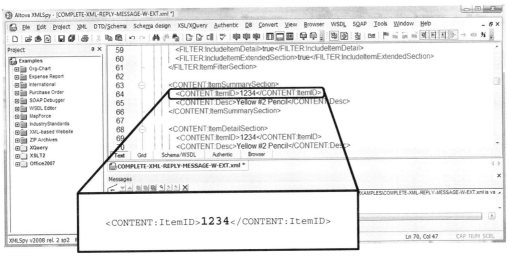

FIGURE 17.5

Unconstrained Data Value of an XML Message (Copyright 2003-2008 Altova GmbH, reprinted with permission of Altova)

of consumers, the service, underlying data at rest sources, XML, and XML Schemas. The service interface designer will be required to match across the various type systems. The potential for mismatched data types is another reason for a well-defined service interface, with XML Schemas that describe and constrain XML message structures and content.

In an enterprise where there is a significant amount of investment in legacy applications, the service designer is encouraged to consider the complexities of these legacy technologies. Where appropriate, the described design techniques can help to continue exploiting those legacy applications and simplify their processing.

SUMMARY

The traditional enterprise will have a significant investment in historic or "legacy" applications. Many of these applications are fully functional, contain extensive business logic, and are part of the production technology set. Abandoning or disinvesting in these applications without due diligence can be of significant economic disadvantage.

The technology that supports these applications can include procedural languages such as COBOL. In view of SOA and Web services, there have been numerous extensions and enhancements to these more traditional technologies, including XML Parsers and similar capabilities, and there also continue to be a number of complexities. The most common include positional and fixed-length data structures, optional element processing, and data type mismatches.

There are service and service interface design techniques that can help mitigate these legacy applications to the SOA as service consumers. Message options and corresponding service behavior can be developed, allowing legacy consumers to request that all data values are set to a minimum length, and all optional and empty elements are required in the reply message. The service designer will also need to evaluate supported data types between consumers, the service, underlying data at rest sources, XML, and XML Schemas.

REFERENCES

1. Bray T, Paoli J, Sperberg-McQueen CM, Maler E, Yergeau F, eds. Extensible Markup Language (XML) 1.0. 4th ed. W3C Recommendation. (W3C, August 16, 2006). <http://www.w3.org/TR/2006/REC-xml-20060816/>.

2. Common Business Oriented Language – COBOL, ANSI X3.23-1985, Information Technology Industry Council (National Committee for Information Technology Standards), INCITS/ISO/IEC 1989–2002, Information Technology - Programming Languages - COBOL.

3. Bray T, Paoli J, Sperberg-McQueen CM, Maler E, Yergeau F, eds. Extensible Markup Language (XML) 1.0. 4th ed. W3C Recommendation. (W3C, August 16, 2006). <http://www.w3.org/TR/2006/REC-xml-20060816/>.

4. The Unicode Consortium. *The Unicode Standard, Version 5.1.0, defined by: The Unicode Standard, Version 5.0.* Boston: Addison-Wesley; 2007 <http://www.unicode.org/versions/Unicode5.1.0/>.

Document Literal Interfaces

The SOA loose-coupling principle becomes a critical consideration for the service interface design. The exchange of messages to represent and comply with the service interface is a fundamental servicing approach. However, within those messages, there are different structural designs that comply with the loose-coupling principle and those that are in violation. The two most common structural forms for a message are RPC style and document literal.

An RPC-style message structure and operations represent a parameter and data-driven approach. The RPC style is perhaps the most simple to design and understand as it is analogous to parameter passing between applications. When a consumer sends a request message to a service, it will specify the operation (usually defined by a URL for the service) and will also include the parameters as elements and data values. Each parameter is also located in the message in a specified order. One or more parameters are mapped to the operations of the service; when provided in a request message, the parameters act as modifiers or additional criteria for the requested service operation.

If the service exposed a "Get" (e.g., read) operation, the parameters for that operation will most likely include the identification, selection, or filtering data required by the service to seek out and return the data of interest. This process is not unlike that of a SQL query over a single table or view. A SQL "select" statement is also a read-only operation that will include the columns of interest and the table where the table is located.

With the SQL query, the columns of interest follow the "select" verb and are typically listed in the order that the data will be returned. The select statement and specified columns are also similar to the element content of a reply message. The "from" clause identifies the table where the columns can be found. The SQL "where" clause describes conditional information that can also be thought of as a filter over the data, or in the case of a service interface, the request message element content (see Figure 18.1).

With the RPC-style interface, the service can be thought of as similar to the table or source of the requested information. The service operation is roughly analogous to the SQL select statement. That is, "select" is analogous to a "Get" operation (with "get" as an alternative name for a CRUD "Read" operation). The parameters of the RPC-style operation are similar to the SQL where clause and represent filtering data (see Figure 18.2). A service operation of "GetInventoryData Request(ItemID)" would imply the ability to seek out Item and Inventory information from one or more data at rest sources that matched the Item ID data value provided by the consumer in the request message. This style of interaction is quite common and has been successfully applied for many different types of application interactions.

325

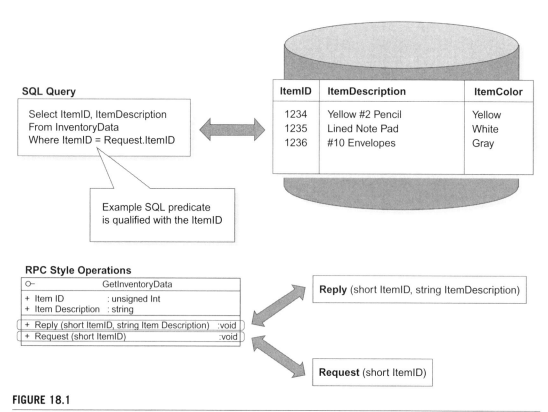

FIGURE 18.1

SQL Query Compared to an RPC-Style Operation

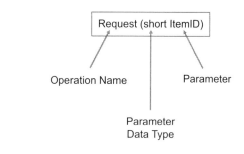

FIGURE 18.2

RPC-Style Operation

If the service is coarse-grained and exposes multiple operations, each of those operations will have its own set of parameters. The parameters are specific to the successful interaction of the consumer with the service for that operation (see Figure 18.3). However, the parameters are not required to be unique. That is, the parameters defined to one operation might also be defined to another different

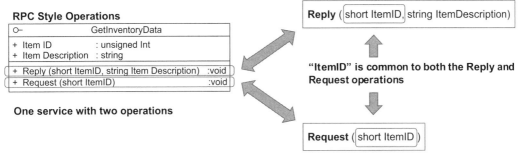

FIGURE 18.3

A Service with Multiple RPC-Style Operations

RPC Style Operations

O–   GetInventoryData
+ Item ID   : unsigned Int
+ Item Description   : string
+ Reply (short ItemID, string Item Description)   : void
+ Request (short ItemID)   : void

FIGURE 18.4

UML Class Diagram with RPC-Style Operations

operation. As an example, a coarse-grained service that exposes both a "Request" operation and a "Reply" operation will have its own list of defined parameters. Consumers of the service will be expected to provide the data values for those parameters in the request message. However, one or more of the parameter elements for one operation might also be defined to the other operation.

RPC-style operations are also simple to represent using the Unified Modeling Language (UML).[1] A common example is that of a UML class diagram, where the class might represent the context of a service (see Figure 18.4). The data elements available to and defined by the class are described as attributes, and they are located in the attribute compartment. The operations of the class can be defined to the operations compartment and can also include the parameters for each operation.

From the perspective of interface design, RPC-style operations are exposed in the message as a parent operation element, defined by a complex type or parent element and including the parameters as child elements. The parent operation element is named to match the operation exposed by the service. Another common example of RPC-style message elements is that the data types are often specified in the message along with their corresponding elements as attribute data (see Figure 18.5).

As evidenced by the examples, an RPC-style operation and supporting service interface is simple to design, easy to understand, and can be expressed or described using diagram techniques such as UML. Unfortunately, there are also disadvantages to the RPC-style service interface. The RPC-style operation and implementation as an interface design approach is also tightly coupled. That is, the combination of parameters and data types for an explicitly defined operation is analogous to a signature. This is sometimes referred to as an operation signature or a method signature.

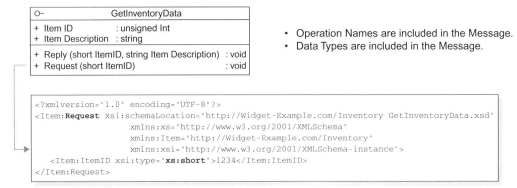

FIGURE 18.5

Example RPC-Style Request Message

Consumers that explicitly bind to the service interface, operation, and parameters are unlikely to be insulated from any future change. If the earlier example of a "Get" operation were to include a new parameter, the service consumers already using the service and operation, and providing the Item ID element would have resulting impact. These previously existing consumers would have to change their internal object models and rebind to the new, modified interface.

Other types of operations and parameter changes could also cause the need for refactoring or rebinding. Something as simple as a reordering of parameters for an operation could have the potential for impact. Also, a data type change or an abstraction of the data type could introduce impact to existing service consumers (as with an integer type being recast as a long integer). The potential for impact from change is significant. A service interface that has been designed according to best practices will have resolved the SOA loose-coupling principle with an alternative operations and interface style.

Rather than exchanging discretely defined operations, parameters, and elements, the document literal style focuses on exchanging a message context. As implied by the name, messages represent more of a "document" than a parameter list. A common analogy is that of a paper order form.

A customer might go into a storefront business and order 12 dozen pencils. If the order is placed on a paper order form, the order taker will capture the customer information, item being ordered, the quantity, and a notation of cash payment. As an initial part of the process, the order taker would also provide a copy of the order form back to the customer as a receipt. This order form is a document. It contains the request information, and the returned copy of the form is analogous to a reply message. Captured on the document are the important and critical elements of the order.

If the storefront later modified its order form to also include a credit card number element, it would not affect previous customers who have always paid with cash and who continue to pay with cash. The document represents the order context, and the interaction between original customer and the storefront remains unaffected by the change.

From a service interface perspective, the document literal style of operations does not include the operation as a named element. Using a request example, the message contains an overall request message element and any number of nested child elements. The overall parent element is not specific or explicit to any operation that is exposed by the service. Rather, the document style message could

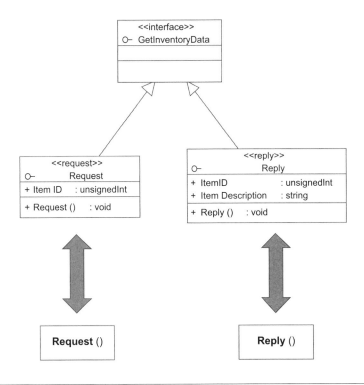

FIGURE 18.6

UML Class Diagram with Document Literal Style Operations

apply to any of the operations for that service. Further, the child elements do not include a declarative data type within the message. The document literal style of interface relies upon the interface schema (e.g., XML Schema) to describe the elements and data types.

The document literal style interface can also be represented by a UML diagram. There are several techniques for modeling this type of service interface. One of the most common techniques is to diagram the interface as a class model (similar to the earlier RPC-style UML diagram). As an alternative to the RPC-style diagram, a document literal operation does not include a fully defined parameter list. Rather, the elements required for the operation are defined as attributes to the classes (see Figure 18.6).

From the perspective of interface design, Document Literal Style operations are implied by the service interaction and operation URL. The parent element of the message is a complex type, but does not explicitly reference an operation. The child elements of the parent element are defined by the interface schema and do not include explicit typing in the message (see Figure 18.7).

Changes to service operations and to the service interface can be positioned as wildcard elements (defined by a wildcard schema) or as optional and additional child elements of the message. This allows previous consumers of the service to generally avoid remapping their object models and rebinding. Note that even the document literal style of interface is completely devoid of impact from change. There may be changes of significance such as adding a new mandatory request message element that would impact previous consumers of the service.

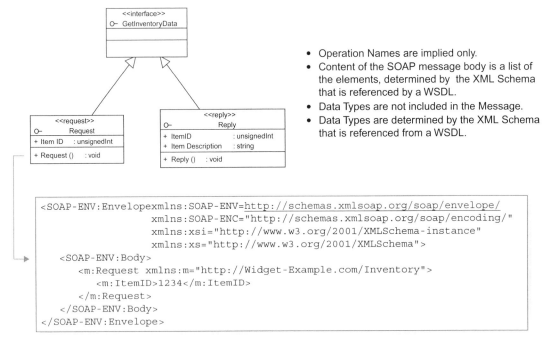

FIGURE 18.7

Example Document Literal Style Request Message

SUMMARY

While the RPC style of service operations and interfaces is well-known and simple, it also has potential disadvantages to the service interface. Consumers that are bound to an RPC-style interface are more likely to be negatively impacted by change. If the service were modified to include a new parameter element for the RPC-style operation, it is highly likely that existing consumers of that service and operation would also require a refactoring of the object model and a rebinding to the service interface.

An alternative to the RPC style is the document literal style of operation and interface. With the document literal style, the service interface defines a document context. The resulting messages are not structured around discretely defined message elements and message-specified data types but appear in more of a document context. The document literal style of service operations and interface design is the more effective and recommended design approach.

REFERENCE

1. Unified Modeling Language\(OMG UML). Infrastructure, Version 2.2 (OMG, February 4, 2009). <http://www. omg.org/docs/formal/09-02-04.pdf/>.

Performance Analysis and Optimization Techniques

Web services receive significant criticism regarding performance, and, as a result, optimizing SOA and Web services is a critical design activity. Unfortunately, some of the criticism is deserved. The notion of a "Web service" is largely defined by a set of artifacts that comply with industry specifications and standards, including XML, XML Schemas, WSDL, and SOAP. All of the artifacts are encoded using XML, which is admittedly verbose as a result of the extensive tagging that is included in the message instance and carried across the wire. Alternative to XML, other types of encoding used for information exchange between consumers and services are binary. That is, these alternate encodings have a condensed over-the-wire form, and either apply a positionally mapped format or a highly abbreviated and simplified form of tagging for messages.

There are offsetting arguments and obvious value from using Web services over alternative service types that are less technology agnostic. The most obvious argument for Web services is interoperability. For the moderate- to large-scale enterprise, the underlying technologies that represent consumer and service behavior can be many. Example technologies might include Java, .NET, COBOL, and any number of others. Relying on a set of well-defined Web service standards provides a high degree of interoperability, rather than mediating and transforming between these varied technologies. While the advantages of standards compliant and highly interoperable consumers and services are fundamental to SOA, the interoperability argument begins to lose support if the performance characteristics of the service interaction are poor. Being able to more easily integrate and onboard new consumers and gaining advantage from reusable services is a moot point when the business process exhibits significant latency.

Yet the performance and optimization challenge is not limited to Web services, XML, and SOAP. There are multiple performance factors to consider, with the most obvious including the following:

- Complexity of consumer and service behavior
- Performance of the ESB or message backbone
- Security
- Complexity and size of the message

Each of these performance factors can influence or affect overall SOA performance. However, none of these factors should be ignored or de-emphasized. In some manner, each can also negatively or positively influence the others. While the emphasis of this book is on the service interface, all of these performance-related topics warrant discussion.

19.1 COMPLEXITY OF CONSUMER AND SERVICE BEHAVIOR

The complexity of the consumer and service behavior (e.g., "business logic") is perhaps the most common area of potential optimization. The application code that defines and supports business logic is either generated from developer tooling or handcrafted by the developer. In either case, there are limitations and deficiencies to consider. While not always the case, application logic that is entirely generated from tooling has need for review and optimization. Often, there are opportunities for improvement of simple concepts such as declaration of variables, looping, and conditional branching, as well as more mechanical activities such as memory recovery and thread management. Even when the overriding emphasis is on model driven development, tooling and machine-generated code, applying follow-on optimization is a strong recommendation. When the development of code is more driven by human expertise, the emphasis should be on coding standards and best practices with an eye toward optimization. Code reviews by experienced developers are an obvious solution. Good coding practices with code reviews and consideration for performance optimization will go a long way toward optimizing performance.

19.2 PERFORMANCE OF THE ENTERPRISE SERVICES BUS OR MESSAGE BACKBONE

The core technology capability of an SOA is the Enterprise Service Bus (ESB) or a similar network and messaging backbone. As an SOA infrastructure component, the ESB is the carrier for all consumer and service interactions. It is also a potential bottleneck. When defining the SOA strategy and in addition to other nonfunctional requirements (NFRs), the SOA architect must take into consideration several influencing criteria of performance:

- Capacity
- Scale
- Frequency of messaging interaction
- Complexity and frequency of ESB-enabled message transformations

Capacity is typically represented as the maximum number of messages or a byte count that can be transported between consumers and service endpoints. In this sense, capacity is analogous to maximum throughput. Capacity can also be influenced by or augmented with the other ESB performance criteria as well. Scale is a time-based influence for the growth characteristics of capacity. Over time ᵈ as new consumers and services onboard to the SOA, increases in capacity are usually required. ᴼA architect must develop a reasonable forecast of growth and increased movement to the SOA ᵇᵃt growth as scale to influence capacity.

ᶜy of messaging interactions reflects the number of messages that move between con- ᵥices for a given period of time. A high frequency of messaging interactions will usu- ery fine-grained service interactions. When the average number of interactions between an originating consumer and the services required to resolve a simple business process exceed a range of three to five, the application can be perceived as "chatty," and the SOA architect should revisit the service granularity to look for optimization opportunities such as aggregating the fine-grained services as an orchestration.

Note that this description is specific to an originating consumer and not to a high-level business service that might interact with many fine-grained and subordinate services. When the messaging interaction between an originating consumer and services is chatty, the ESB can become over-taxed. In this example, the ESB may have to manage and mediate between a significant number of messaging interactions in order to complete a single business process. With capacity, scale, and frequency, the SOA architect must consider not only discrete measures but also peaks or thresholds and averages.

In previous chapters, an underlying theme has been use of a canonical model. When a significant number of SOA collaborators agree upon not only the interface contract but also on the context and semantics of the information contained in those messages, there are fewer message transformations. A higher number of transformations have significant impact on performance. The effect of transformations on performance is further impacted when they are also complex transformations. Simple movement of data values from one element to another is impactful on performance but not as much when a translation of the data value must also occur. Even when service collaborators cannot fully implement a canonicalized message as a whole, there is significant performance advantage when portions of the message have been canonicalized. For these parts of the message and where all of the service collaborators have adopted the canonical, transformation is rarely required.

Another potential consideration is to augment the ESB with an accelerator. An accelerator is an XML processor, XML transformation engine, or gateway that has been implemented as a specialized infrastructure technology (most often as an SOA hardware appliance or edge device). An accelerator has been optimized for performance. One or more accelerators can be added to the SOA infrastructure as a method of offloading XML and transformation processing from the ESB. This can help to reduce processing latency and improve the overall performance of the ESB.

19.3 SECURITY

For almost all SOA services, there will be some degree of security. Security requirements are generally based upon business or functional requirements and may be driven by regulatory compliance. Simply put, most data require protection. Security requirements can include encryption of data at rest or data in motion (encrypted in the message), authentication of service consumers to ensure they are recognized, authorization to determine what operations and activities are allowed, and protection against potential vulnerabilities. All SOA and Web service interface designs must carefully consider security requirements. This can include seeking out the assistance of security specialists. The methods for protecting information are many and extend well beyond the scope of this book. However, there are implications to performance.

One of the most common security-related performance impacts is encryption. To encrypt a message, the service consumer will invoke an encryption algorithm or a standard encryption utility. The process of encryption is largely a set of complex mathematical operations, and depending upon the amount of data to be encrypted, can be performance intensive. Once the request message is received by the service, it is then decrypted. As with encryption, this is also a complex process. The recommendation here is not to avoid or ignore security requirements. Rather it is to anticipate them, recognize their importance to a successful SOA and set of consumer-to-service interactions, and account for the performance impact as one part of the overall design process.

Another security topic is that of vulnerabilities. There are an almost unlimited number of creative ways to invade the technology space of a business enterprise and to gain access to information. Some can be as simple as intercepting an XML-encoded message that has not been encrypted. This is particularly dangerous with XML since the element tags are carried along with the data values in the message. Where a binary encoding might be less obvious to a human, a clear text data value such as a Credit Card Number that is also enclosed by an open and close tag becomes painfully obvious (e.g., "< CreditCardNumber >1234-5678-9012-3456< /CreditCardNumber >").

While a powerful service interface and design technique, exposing an "ad hoc query" operation such as "Query" or "Select", or allowing for a consumer provided SQL Query string in a request message can exploit a number of vulnerabilities. One of the more common is known as SQL Injection, where a SQL query of a data at rest source can either manipulate database security openings or can introduce a circular query that causes the processor to reach a maximum threshold, stalls the database or service, and directly impacts performance. The recommendation here is not to ignore appropriate design techniques but to carefully evaluate their function and value, and seek out security subject matter expertise.

19.4 COMPLEXITY AND SIZE OF THE MESSAGE

Message size is possibly the most common area of concern for Web services. With the additional tags of an XML-encoded message being carried across the wire, message size is an obvious candidate for performance optimization. There are no specific limits to message size found in any of the Web service specifications. While there are industry and practitioner observations, there are also no specific limits posed as a single and recognized best practice.

There are general rules of thumb, however. From a practical perspective, an XML-encoded request or reply message that begins to approach 100 KB in size, might be a candidate for evaluation. A message that begins to approach 500 KB in size warrants a review and should be subject to optimization. A message that exceeds 1 MB in size warrants potential concern (see Figure 19.1). However, it is important to note that a message of 1 MB might in some scenarios be a valid and acceptable message

As a simple analogy, smaller XML messages can usually be processed quicker and more efficiently than larger messages. Raw message size measured as character count is an important indicator of potential Web service message optimization. However, it is not the only indicator. Other performance-related XML-encoded message optimization opportunities are related to the complexity of the message.

19.4.1 Uniform structure

The processing of a SOAP and XML-encoded Web services message includes several steps. The creator of the message must take a set of data values and semantics and serialize them as XML-encoded content (also known as marshaling). The most common approach takes an object model used to represent the internal behavior of the message creator, maps it to the structure of the message, and then creates the message. These steps are also analogous to the service interface binding process. The consumer of a service

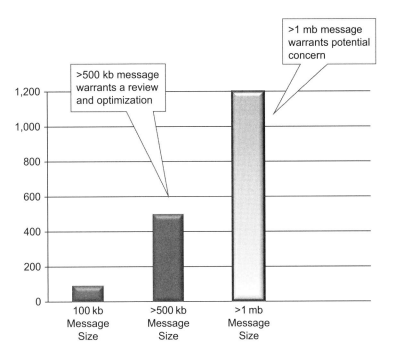

FIGURE 19.1

General Rules for Message Size

will need to bind to the service interface. If the Message Exchange Pattern (MEP) is request-reply, the consumer will need to bind to the request message type, reply message type, and potentially to a fault (assuming SOAP as the encoding scheme).

The interface represents the contract for collaboration with the service. The XML Schema of the service interface defines the structure, content, and typing of the XML-encoded message, and WSDL defines the overall service interface, including the service operations, encodings, and the location of the service. There are utility technologies to help with this process, and it is usually a design-time activity that occurs infrequently. However, the run-time consumption of message data can be quite complex.

After the consumer creates the request message and sends it to the endpoint location for the service, the ESB will route the message to the service for that exposed operation. On receipt of the message, the service will need to extract the message data and apply it to its internal behavior (potentially defined by another and different object model). This process of extracting the message content is known as deserialization or unmarshaling. Again, there are technology utilities and even language-specific frameworks to help simplify the process. However, navigating the message structure to find the data values and to also map them to the object model can be a tedious and process intensive effort.

If the message is composed of a simple and sequential list of elements, processing is significantly simplified. A "flat" message structure would allow the consumer of the message to just process one element after another, extracting the data values as it went along. However, rarely are messages simple,

XML Fragment

```
<PostalAddress>
  <AddressTo>John M. Doe</AddressTo>
  <StreetAddress>123 E Main St.</StreetAddress>
  <StreetAddress>Suite ABC</StreetAddress>
  <City>Phoenix</City>
  <State>AZ</State>
  <PostalCode>85999</PostalCode>
</PostalAddress>
```

Address elements of the message are
grouped according to an obvious and
logical affinity

XML Fragment

```
<AddressTo>John M. Doe</AddressTo>

<StreetAddressLines>
  <StreetAddress>123 E Main St.</StreetAddress>
  <StreetAddressSuite>
    <Suite>Suite ABC</Suite>
  </StreetAddressSuite>
</StreetAddressLines>

<PostalAddress>
  <City>Phoenix</City>
  <State>AZ</State>
  <PostalCode>85999</PostalCode>
</PostalAddress>
```

Address elements of the message are not
logically grouped and are candidates for
optimization

FIGURE 19.2

Affinity Grouping of Postal Address Elements

sequential, or flat. Most message structures will include any number of nested substructures and elements. Each of these structures and elements can also contain their own substructures and elements. Some elements can also repeat as "siblings" under the same parent element. Repeating elements then adds a more horizontal aspect to navigating the message.

As we learned in Chapter 7, "The Service Interface—Contract," XML messages are hierarchies. That is, an XML message has a single root element and then descends through child elements, structures, substructures, and so on. XML Parsers provide the mechanical technology to walk through the XML message hierarchy and to obtain the data values from individual elements. As previously described, navigating a simple, sequential, and flat XML structure is quite simple, and an XML Parser will generally perform quite well with this type of message.

As a parser encounters nested elements and substructures, performance begins to degrade. The notion of a hierarchy is also similar to the root system of a tree. There can be many branches to the root system that all extend below ground. Walking down one path of an XML message structure (similar to following one root system), and then having to back up and start down another path requires complex processing. When these different paths are reasonably consistent, the negative impact to processing the message is less. This is known as a uniform structure. When message paths are significantly irregular, there is increased negative impact to message processing. These navigational irregularities are known as a nonuniform structure.

As a design technique, designing the canonical message should include consideration for uniform structure. While a completely flat XML message structure would be a rarity, the designer should strive to optimize the canonical message design and reduce the number of irregular substructures. Elements that exhibit close affinity should be grouped together at the same level within a parent element structure. As an example, a set of elements for Address To, Street Address, City, State, and Postal Code, are most likely components of an address and could be grouped under a single, parent Postal Address element (see Figure 19.2).

A reasonably uniform structure is not specifically a flat structure. Nesting and grouping of XML elements is both an intended capability of XML and an effective approach to canonical message design. A message structure that has reasonable and uniform degrees of nesting allow the message consumer to navigate the message content quickly in order to reach the data of interest. Reasonable message uniformity is measured in two primary dimensions:

- Message depth
- Message width

The "depth" of a message refers to the overall length of the message and can be expressed as the total count of individual elements. If the message were visualized or modeled as an indented list of elements, the "width" of the message equates to the horizontal span of elements from the leftmost to the rightmost nested element.

19.4.2 **Navigation and data graphs**

The rationale for designing a uniform message structure is that most XML Parsers will navigate an XML message structure as top-down and left-to-right. All of the message elements of the message, including parent element complexTypes, are defined as "nodes" by the parser. Depending upon the type of XML parser, the structure of the document is exposed as the organized set of element nodes. The set of nodes can be exposed as in a memory model and roughly analogous to the natural tree root structure of the message (as with a DOM [Document Object Model] parser), or where individual nodes are events raised to the consuming application (as with a SAX [Simple API for XML] or StAX [Streaming API for XML] parser) as a series of events.

Choice of parser type can also impact performance. The DOM parser builds a tree model of the element nodes in memory. The building of the model can take considerable processing time and consume significant memory resources. However, the navigation after the model is created can often provide more capabilities to the consuming application. The SAX parser does not build an extensive in-memory model, and navigates the XML message in a serial manner. Each node is raised as an event to the processing application. The application can choose to consume the data and information for that node or to continue processing. A SAX parsing process is typically much more efficient than a DOM parsing process. However, the ability of the consuming application to navigate the XML message is more complex.

With any of these parsers, the consuming application must in some manner navigate through the various nodes (or events), extract the data of interest, and continue processing. When there is a requirement for recursion, where a consuming application needs to revisit a previous message node or event, or where the message structure is largely irregular, navigation can become complex. The consuming application may be required to manage a set of pointers for already processed nodes. When the message structure is more uniform with fewer structural or element nesting irregularities, an XML parser and consuming application will perform better.

A simple method for conceptualizing the uniformity of an XML message structure is to visualize it as a data graph. Unfortunately, there are currently no developer tools that provide this navigational data graph capability for XML messages and service interfaces. However, many XML editors such as XML Spy (Copyright 2003-2008 Altova GmbH, reprinted with permission of Altova) will apply a logical indent of nested elements and structures (see Figure 19.3). An indented canonical message sample provides a reasonable visual representation, where the message designer can imagine walking through the hierarchy of the message as a consumer. Uniformity can be estimated by visualizing a vertical line

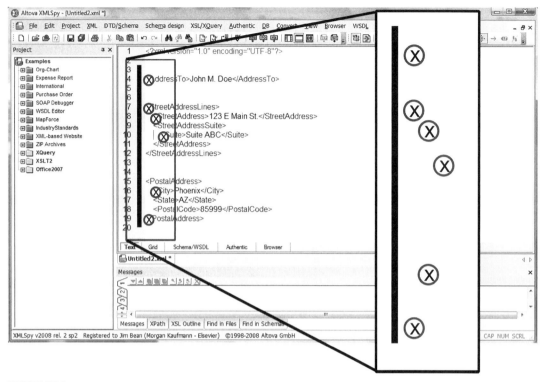

FIGURE 19.3

Visualization of a Navigational Data Graph (Copyright 2003-2008 Altova GmbH, reprinted with permission of Altova)

drawn from top to bottom of the XML message. Data points can be imagined as the left angle bracket for each XML element open tag. The elements that would left-align to the imagined line are uniform. If the line were to move toward the right, other groups of nested elements would also left-align.

However, significant degrees of variance in the depth of nesting between the various groups implies a nonuniform structure. A model where each group of indented elements (as data points) is assigned a value and incremented from "1 to n" defines the horizontal element spread. If each of the assigned values were used to compute a standard deviation or similar measure of delta, a higher number would imply a nonuniform structure (see Figure 19.4).

An optimal message structure for navigation and processing would have all of the elements left aligned to a vertical line running from the first indented child element under the root element of the message to the bottom of the message. However, this type of flat message structure is rarely the case. Most canonical message designs will naturally have varied examples of nested elements and structures and will have exploited the natural affinities and groupings of elements. The recommended optimization technique for a uniform message structure is to determine when there are a significant number of variations between nested elements and structures. The message structure can be reviewed, and where appropriate, elements can be regrouped.

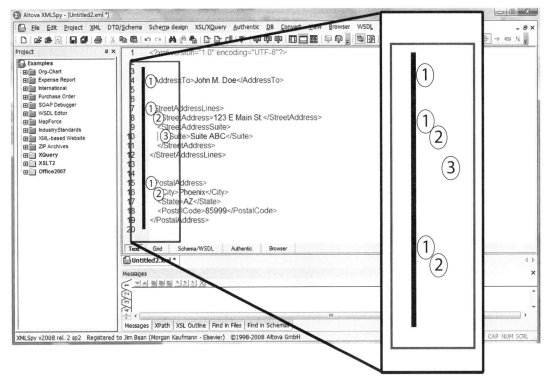

FIGURE 19.4

Conceptualization of a Navigational Data Graph (Copyright 2003-2008 Altova GmbH, reprinted with permission of Altova)

19.4.3 Depth of nesting

An influencing characteristic of an XML message is the maximum depth to which an element can be nested. The XML specification[1] does not include a specified maximum limit for the levels of element nesting.

Unfortunately, some message designers have taken an explicit relational data modeling approach to message design, and the resulting structures often include significant irregularities and very deep nesting. Attempting to force a relational data model with numerous key relationships is not a recommended practice. There are some synergies between canonical message design and relational modeling, but caution is advised. The XML message is a physical artifact that will be created and consumed by consumers and services. This message is a hierarchy and is navigated during processing as a hierarchy. Forcing a more relational model over that hierarchy and resulting navigation can be significantly and negatively impactful to message processing.

While there is no stated limit as to depth of nesting, there are general rules of thumb. From a practical perspective, when an XML-encoded request or reply message with a maximum depth of nested elements begins to approach 10 levels of indentation, the message might be a candidate for evaluation

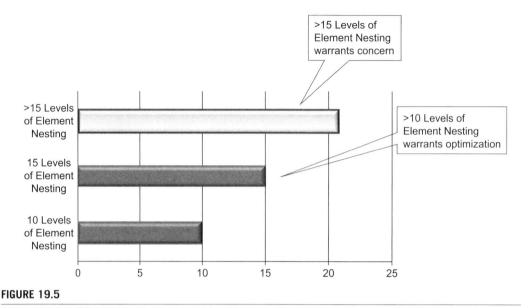

FIGURE 19.5

General Rules of Thumb for Maximum Depth of Element Nesting

and redesign. Where the depth of nesting is between 10 and 15 levels of indentation, the message design warrants a review and should be subject to optimization. A message that exceeds 15 levels of nesting warrants concern (see Figure 19.5).

A simpler canonical message design that optimizes the hierarchy of XML and has applied a reasonable depth of element nesting will be easier to process by a consuming application.

19.4.4 Verbosity

Another of the common Web service and XML-related criticisms is verbosity of the message resulting from tagging. Where a raw XML-encoded message is sent over the wire, each of the element tags can take considerable space as character positions of the overall message size. However, one of the benefits of XML is the ability to define semantically rich and descriptive open and close tag names. These names help to describe the intended contents of each element. Tag names can also be derived from a canonical model. In either case, the tags are carried along with the data values over the wire and contribute to the overall message size.

There is no stated maximum tag name length found in the XML specification.[2] The application of a tag naming standard with a maximum tag name length can help reduce the message size and still exploit the value of user-defined and descriptive tagging.

Defining an XML tag name standard and including a tag name length limit is arbitrary. A standard for one enterprise could vary significantly from that of another. General recommendations would be to align with the tag names of the enterprise canonical model. The messages that support Business-to-Business (B2B) servicing partners and any applied industry vocabularies are also important considerations. While some service designers might take a more extreme approach to tag name standards and rely heavily on abbreviations and acronyms to shorten tag name length, this is not a general recommendation.

XML Fragment

```
<ProcessingStatusIndicatorCode>0</ProcessingStatusIndicatorCode>
```
Tag Name Length = 29   Data Value Length = 1

The element tag name is 29 characters in length.

The data value of the element is 1 character in length.

The "Tag-to-Data Ratio" for this one element is 29:1.

Although this is only a single element example, this XML
fragment is considered to be "metadata heavy."

FIGURE 19.6

Tag-to-Data Ratio and a Metadata Heavy Message

User-defined tag names are one of the most obvious advantages of XML-encoded messages. Applying tag names that are descriptive and concise is an advantage. Abbreviations and acronyms should be used as part of the tag name but only when they are well-known and agreed upon across the enterprise.

Another method technique for evaluating the size of an XML-encoded message is to compare the number of tag name characters to the characters used for data values, as an average across the entire message. A common approach is to use an empirical "tag-to-data ratio" measure.[3] In many scenarios, data values will vary in length within a single element. A sampling of data or an expected average length as the number of characters will suffice. When the tag name character usage is significantly greater than the data value character usage, the message is thought to be metadata heavy. A message that carries far more tag data than an actual data value might be a better candidate as a binary-encoded message than an XML-encoded message, or it should be combined with other message data to optimize the total character count of the message payload (see Figure 19.6).

Alternative message encodings will usually not include tag names or additional metadata in the over-the-wire message format. These non-XML-encoding schemas can often be processed more efficiently than a larger and more verbose XML-encoded message. In those scenarios where the participants of a servicing collaboration are well-defined, static, within the same application boundary, and there is no expectation to add other consumers at some future point, an alternative message encoding scheme, such as binary encoding, might be warranted.

19.4.5 Abstract vs. specific cardinality

The concept of repeating XML elements is known as cardinality. As described in Chapter 10, "XML Schema Basics," an interface schema (e.g., an XML Schema) can be defined to allow XML message elements to repeat by name. When the XML Schema includes an XML element declaration with a "maxOccurs" attribute value greater than "1", that named element can appear in the corresponding XML message one or more times.

This capability allows for a flexible message structure where the number of occurrences for a specifically named element might vary between the records or rows of a data at rest source. A commonly recognized example is that of the street address lines for a postal address (see Figure 19.7). A postal

FIGURE 19.7

Postal Address Schema with Repeating Street Address Elements (Copyright 2003-2008 Altova GmbH, reprinted with permission of Altova)

address might require one street address line and as many as four or more address lines in addition to other elements such as the City, State, and Postal Code (other elements might also be necessary for an international postal address).

Where the interface schema allows for multiple occurring elements, there are two possible options for the XML Schema "maxOccurs" attribute value (see Figure 19.8). The maxOccurs value could be set with a discrete value such as "4", or it can be limitless with a value of "unbounded" or "*". Given the potential for an unknown number or a future increase in the number of occurrences, an unbounded value for a repeating message element might initially seem as the most flexible and best possible choice for all scenarios. However, an unbounded maxOccurs value can require some message consumers to fully navigate all of the sibling nodes for that repeating element. If the consumer is unmarshaling to an array, the maximum array boundaries are generally fixed, and an unknown number of repeating element data may result in an anomaly when the array bounds are exceeded.

Where possible, an "absolute" maxOccurs value will simplify processing and allow the message consumer to determine the maximum array size at bind-time. With the postal address example, a

The maximum cardinality is set to "unbounded" (relative). This can present complexity or some consuming applications or where an array is used to hold the repeating elements.

```
<xs:element ref="StreetAddress" maxOccurs="unbounded"/>
```

```
<xs:element ref="StreetAddress" maxOccurs="4"/>
```

The maximum cardinality is set to "4" (absolute). The message structure is still flexible and can expand to accommodate up to a maximum of four address lines.

FIGURE 19.8

Cardinality and the XML Schema maxOccurs Value (Copyright 2003-2008 Altova GmbH, reprinted with permission of Altova)

maximum cardinality of four can be declared, and where the minOccurs attribute value is set to "1", this would allow a number of street address elements in the message to occur from one to four times.

19.4.6 To validate or not to validate

In addition to parsing the XML-encoded message, another type of XML processing is validation. The service interface contract for a Web service includes one or more XML Schemas to define and constrain the structure and content of the corresponding XML message. These XML Schemas can represent metadata rules such as placement and nesting of elements' structural definitions, cardinality constraints, data types, and constraining facets. Compliance with the Web service interface contract requires that the creator of any message must have applied the constraints of the corresponding interface schemas, and any consumer of the message can expect that the structure and content will comply with the interface.

The parser validation process compares the XML-encoded message to the corresponding service interface schemas. Where an infraction or example of noncompliance with the interface schemas is encountered during the validation process, an error is raised to the parsing application. Most validation errors are either structural (an element found in an unexpected area of the message, a mandatory element missing, a multiple occurring element not matching the cardinality constraints, etc.), or a data anomaly (mismatch of a data value with the declared data type, a missing data value that is mandatory, noncompliance with a facet such as the length, and so on).

For most SOA servicing scenarios, compliance with the service interface contract occurs during the binding process, where the internal object model and behavior of the application (consumer or service) is mapped to the interface definition. For internal enterprise applications where compliance with the service interface contract is governed as mandatory, the binding process significantly reduces the potential for a message to be inconsistent with the interface definition. These consumers and services will rarely introduce a data anomaly in the XML message. The rationale is that internal, enterprise servicing participants are typically "trusted" participants.

Depending on the size and complexity of the message and the granularity of the interface XML Schemas, validation can be a complex process and can introduce significant run-time latency. For this reason, many enterprises have opted to validate only during development and testing but not in production.

However, a challenge arises with untrusted servicing participants. With many SOAs, some consumers and services may exist external to the enterprise. They may be partner or other commercial applications that are developed, owned, and maintained by some external organization (Business-to-Business [B2B]). Even when a significant degree of due diligence has been performed, the control of those servicing interactions may be suspect. These external, B2B types of interactions should be subject to schema validation. When a message is received by the enterprise and prior to consumption, it should be validated to the service interface schema. This will help to avoid potential data anomalies.

The ability to dynamically extend a message is another powerful capability of XML and XML Schemas. With Schema "wildcard" extensions, future requirements for additional and optional data elements can in most cases be resolved with a wildcard extension. However, to effectively process a wildcard schema extension, validation of the XML-encoded message with the primary service interface schemas and the additional wildcard schema is again a requirement. The same processing impact from validation will be evident at run-time. This is a strong consideration for the SOA architect and interface designer. The benefits and advantages of interface schema wildcards are significant, but the run-time performance impacts may offset the value.

To optimize compliance with the service interface contract and to avoid potential data anomalies, validation of XML-encoded messages is recommended. However, the SOA architect and service designer will need to carefully evaluate whether the benefits of validation will exceed the run-time performance impacts, and whether validation in production might be selectively applied.

SUMMARY

Achieving an acceptable level of performance for any SOA and servicing interaction is critical to success. Although SOA promotes the benefits of interoperability, reuse, and rapid development, poor performance will spell disaster. The SOA architect and service designer must include strong consideration for performance, capacity, and scale in the design process.

Evaluating and optimizing SOA and Web service performance is not a trivial exercise. There are several contributing factors, and each can significantly affect the overall performance of the SOA. Consideration should be given to the complexity of the internal consumer and service behavior, the ESB, security requirements, and design of the message.

Internal complexity of consumer and service behavior requires a combination of skilled designers and developers, and compliance with standards and best practices. Code reviews and including a view toward performance are strongly recommended.

Careful selection of an ESB technology is also requisite. The ESB is the primary SOA technology capability and component. If the ESB does not have sufficient capacity or it cannot scale to meet demand, latency will result. Selecting the ESB should include consideration for point in time performance requirements, as well as longer term growth and trending. In some scenarios, the addition of an accelerator to help resolve performance impacts of XML processing and transformations may be warranted. Accelerators are technologies that have been optimized for specialized processing such as XML validation and XML message transformation.

Ensuring security of the SOA, service interactions, messages, and data are critical. There are many approaches to securing an SOA or Web service, and many will require additional or specialized processing such as encryption and decryption. The performance impact of resolving security requirements can be significant. However, this is an area where compromise may not be acceptable. Security is often an overriding requirement. The SOA architect and service designer should carefully weigh the potential impacts of security-related processing and look to optimize accordingly.

The complexity and size of a message is possibly the most obvious and easily optimized area of an SOA. Processing of a simple, reasonably sized, and uniformly structured message will almost always be more efficient than processing a message that is complex, large, and irregularly structured.

XML-encoded messages tend to be verbose. This is largely due to the element open and close tags that accompany the data of the message in the over-the-wire format. User-defined tagging is a benefit of XML that aids in interoperability and adds a degree of semantics to message data. For canonical message designs, the general recommendation is to exploit the element tag names of the enterprise canonical model. However, excessive tag name length when compared to the amount of data carried in a message can offset the value of tagging. A tag name standard with a length limitation can help, when the message is overly verbose as a result of tag names. In some scenarios, the use of XML-encoded messages can be replaced with a more binary style of message. However, this should be strictly limited to participants of a servicing collaboration that are well-defined, static, and within the same application boundary, and there is no expectation to add other consumers at some future point.

Validation of XML-encoded messages is another potential area of performance impact. Yet, validation can help to ensure compliance with the service interface contract and also avoidance of data anomalies in the message. When validation of XML messages is found to be a significantly contributing factor to overall Web services run-time performance, the SOA architect may choose to validate only during development and testing of services, and when the consumer or service is an untrusted participant, as in a B2B interaction.

REFERENCES

1. Bray T, Paoli J, Sperberg-McQueen CM, Maler E, Yergeau F, eds. *Extensible Markup Language (XML)* 1.0 (Fourth edition.). (W3C, August 16, 2006). <http://www.w3.org/TR/REC-xml/>.

2. Bray T, Paoli J, Sperberg-McQueen CM, Maler E, Yergeau F, eds. *Extensible Markup Language (XML)* 1.0 (Fourth edition). (W3C, August 16, 2006). Edited in place 29 September 2006. <http://www.w3.org/TR/REC-xml/>.

3. Bean J. *XML for Data Architects*. San Francisco: Morgan Kaufmann; 2003.

Error Definition and Handling

20

Including error handling in the interface is a fundamental activity for any application design. All architects, designers, and developers recognize that applications encounter exceptions and errors. Some errors are minor and represent a warning, others are recoverable or can be remediated "in process," while others are significant and potentially damaging. An SOA or Web service has these same requirements to handle errors. However, the principles of interoperability and loose coupling can also result in somewhat more complex error-handling scenarios.

As a reflection of the interoperability principles, a well-designed SOA will allow for and support consumers and services that are developed using varied technologies. That is, consumers and services might be developed using traditional technologies such as COBOL, or they might be Java, .NET, or other technologies. The challenge is that these myriad technologies can also have different methods for handling errors. SOA and Web services can help to resolve these interoperability challenges by relying upon Web services related standards such as SOAP, WSDL, XML, and XML Schemas.

Each of the various technology components also has some type of exception-handling or error-handling capability. Yet, the granularity, format, and content of these errors might be very different. There might be an object class that allows an application to "throw" an error, and another object class that catches them on the receiver side of the interaction. Some of these errors might be derived from a cryptic set of code values, while others might include verbose and human-readable error messages.

A relational database might return a SQL State code of "00000" to report a successful query. In this example, a SQL State code beginning with "00" might report a successful database operation, a code of "01" might be a warning, and "02" might be an error. More granular error codes might be used to extend the remaining three positions of the SQL State code. Other database technologies might report an error as a SQLCA value for SQLCODE.[1]

Application technologies such as COBOL might produce runtime errors of "S0C7" when the application attempts to perform a numeric operation on character data or when a working storage field has failed to be initialized before moving data. In still other examples, the application developer may have created a proprietary set of error codes that are specific only to the behavior of that application. All of these different errors and codes can mean something of importance to the receiver. However, differences in error codes and the level of detail can be significant.

347

When developing canonical message designs, there are three possible message types (depending upon the intended Message Exchange Pattern [MEP]):

1. The request message, which is also the "input" message of WSDL
2. The reply message, which is also the "output" message of WSDL
3. A fault message, which maps to a "fault" message declaration of WSDL

WSDL and more importantly SOAP provide a standards-based method of reporting errors. The SOAP 1.1 envelope allows for an optional "fault" ("< Fault/ >") element as a child of the SOAP body that is intended for error reporting. If a fault is encountered and is reported as part of a SOAP message, it must be the only child element of the SOAP "Body", and it can occur only once in that particular message.

There are a few child elements of the fault element that can provide additional detail, such as a fault code ("< faultcode/ >"), "fault string" ("< faultstring/ >"), fault actor ("< faultactor/ > "), and a "detail" element ("< detail/ > ") for reporting application-specific error information.[2]

The SOAP "< faultcode/ >" is a mandatory element of the SOAP "< Fault/ >" element and describes the type of fault. There are four defined types available from the SOAP 1.1 specification (see Table 20.1). A fault code value of "Client" notes that the fault originated with the sender of the message. A fault code of "MustUnderstand" describes an error with a SOAP header instruction. A fault code of "Server" defines an error where the receiver could not process the message. However, when the "Server" fault is returned to the original sender of the message, the message can be sent again by the requester (similar to a retry). A fault code of "VersionMismatch" occurs when the receiver of the message expected a different SOAP envelope version than was received.

The fault string ("< faultstring/ >") is also a mandatory element of the SOAP "< Fault/ >" element. The fault string should describe the fault in text and is intended to be read by a person. The text value of the fault string element is user-defined. The fault actor ("< faultactor/ >") is optional and can be used when the fault code value is "MustUnderstand". The fault actor is a location or address of the actor where the fault occurred. A SOAP envelope can contain an optional header element ("< SOAP:Header/ >"), which can also include information such as addressing or intermediaries defined as actors. An actor is typically defined by a URI or similar network or ESB location. When a designated intermediary does not process the SOAP message as intended, the fault actor element can contain the location of that intermediary.

The detail element ("< detail/ >") is also optional and can contain further nesting of child elements. The elements under the detail element are user defined. Most often, the content of the detail

Table 20.1 SOAP 1.1 Fault Code Values

Error Value	Error Description Info
Client	The sender of the message was the source of the fault.
MustUnderstand	A header instruction was not able to be processed.
Server	The receiver of the message was either the source of the fault, or the message could not be processed.
VersionMismatch	The SOAP version was not expected by the receiver.

element is used to carry application-specific or nonstandard error information. Examples might include application processing status codes, database return codes, and network error codes.

SOAP 1.2 has changed the SOAP fault element ("< Fault/ >") somewhat by including elements for code ("< Code/ >"), reason ("< Reason/ >"), node ("< Node/ >"), role ("< Role/ >"), and detail ("< Detail/ >").[3] The fault element is still a SOAP 1.2 standard. The code element is analogous to the SOAP 1.1 fault code element in that it describes the types of faults. With SOAP 1.2, there are now five provided code values for the code element (see Table 20.2).

The code element ("< Code/ >") is similar to the SOAP 1.1 fault code element ("< faultcode/ >"). The code element describes the type of error, but with a nested child element. Different from SOAP 1.1, the SOAP 1.2 code element can contain two nested child elements. The value element ("< Value/ >") is mandatory and contains the fault code. However, as noted by Table 20.2, SOAP 1.2 Code Values, there are five possible codes, and they are slightly different from the SOAP 1.1 fault codes. The subcode element ("< Subcode/ >") is an optional element and the other nested child of the code element. The subcode element can also have its own nested child elements, including another set of nested value and subcode elements.

SOAP 1.2 also contains a mandatory reason element ("< Reason/ >"). The reason element is roughly analogous to the SOAP 1.1 fault string ("< faultstring/ >"). It provides a descriptive text explanation for the fault. The reason element also carries a nested child element for the text explanation ("< Text/ >"). The text element can repeat (occur multiple times) as a child of the reason element.

The node element ("< Node/ >") is an optional SOAP 1.2 element. The node element is similar to the SOAP 1.1 fault actor element ("< faultactor/ >"). The node element is intended to hold a URI that represents the identifier for the node where the fault occurred. The role element ("< Role/ >") refers to the node element and describes the role of the fault node. The detail element ("< Detail/ >") allows for application or user-defined content that further describes the fault. The content of the detail element can include a text string, or it can include nested child elements. The detail element is analogous to the SOAP 1.1 detail element (see Figure 20.1).

The SOAP envelope is quite intuitive, and most SOAP processors will expose the fault information to a language-specific class to extract the content of the envelope (including SOAP faults) and to unmarshal the fault content (see Figure 20.2). The Java language provides a SOAP Fault interface class ("SOAPFault") with methods to set the fault element values and to extract data from the elements.[4]

A common challenge is to fully apply the SOAP specification and fault elements. Many legacy applications will have implemented their own proprietary error reporting schemes. During the canonical

Table 20.2 SOAP 1.2 Code Values

Error Value	Error Description Info
DataEncodingUnknown	The SOAP header or body included content with an unsupported encoding.
MustUnderstand	A header instruction was not able to be processed.
Receiver	The receiver of the message was either the source of the fault, or the message could not be processed.
Sender	The sender of the message was the source of the fault.
VersionMismatch	The SOAP version was not expected by the receiver.

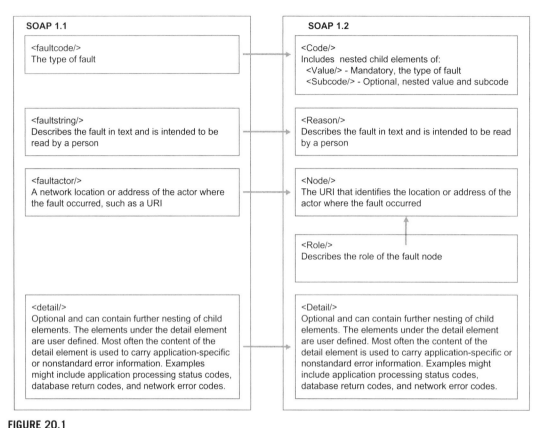

FIGURE 20.1

Comparing SOAP 1.1 and SOAP 1.2 Fault Elements

message design process, the service designer should map those proprietary errors to the appropriate SOAP fault codes ("< Code/ >"). Additional error detail can then be nested as child elements of the detail element ("< Detail/ >").

SUMMARY

Resolving error handling is a fundamental activity for any application design. All architects, designers, and developers recognize that applications encounter exceptions and errors. Some errors are minor and represent a warning, others are recoverable or can be remediated "in process," while others are significant and potentially damaging. An SOA or Web service has these same requirements to handle errors.

SOAP helps to provide a consistent and interoperable method for describing faults. The SOAP fault element structure includes elements for describing the fault type, a descriptive text reason, the location of the fault, and an area where proprietary or user-defined fault data can be included. SOAP processors and language-specific technologies provide APIs and classes over the SOAP fault content to help create and unmarshal fault data.

```
<SOAP-ENV:Envelope xmlns:SOAP-ENV="http://schemas.xmlsoap.org/soap/envelope/"
                               xmlns:SOAP-ENC="http://schemas.xmlsoap.org/soap/encoding/"
                               xmlns:xsi="http://www.w3.org/2001/XMLSchema-instance"
                               xmlns:xsd="http://www.w3.org/2001/XMLSchema">
 <SOAP-ENV:Header>
   <m:Header xmlns:m="http://Widget-Example.com/Product/Header"
                      role="http://Widget-Example.com/Inventory/Header/Actor/AddItem"
                      mustUnderstand="1"/>
 </SOAP-ENV:Header>

 <SOAP-ENV:Body>
   <m:Fault xmlns:m="http://Widget-Example.com/Fault">
     <m:Code>
       <m:Value>Receiver</m:Value>
       <m:Subcode>
          <m:Value></m:Value>
       </m:Subcode>
     </m:Code>

     <m:Reason>
       <m:Text>Data Service was unable find the requested ItemID</m:Text>
     </m:Reason>

     <m:Node></m:Node>

     <m:Role></m:Role>

     <m:Detail>
       <m:ItemIDFault>5678</m:ItemIDFault>
       <m:SQLStatus>02000</m:SQLStatus>
       <m:FaultType>No Data</m:FaultType>
       <m:FaultDesc>ItemID Not Found</m:FaultDesc>
     </m:Detail>
   </m:Fault>
 </SOAP-ENV:Body>
</SOAP-ENV:Envelope>
```

FIGURE 20.2

Example SOAP Fault

Including a canonical message design for faults is critical to the service interface contract. This representation of a potential error will result in a more effective service interaction.

REFERENCES

1. *X/Open CAE Specification, Data Management: Structured Query Language (SQL), Version 2*, X/Open Document Number: C449. (Reading, UK: X/Open Company Ltd).

2. Box D, Ehnebuske D, Kakivaya G, Layman A, Mendelsohn N, Nielsen HF, Thatte S, Winer D, eds. *Simple Object Access Protocol (SOAP) 1.1.* (W3C Note, May 8, 2000). <http://www.w3.org/TR/2000/NOTE-SOAP-20000508/>.

3. Mitra N, Lafon Y, eds. *SOAP Version 1.2 Part 0: Primer.* 2nd ed. (W3C, April 27, 2007). <http://www.w3.org/TR/soap12-part0/>.

4. Java2 Platform Enterprise Edition, *J2EE v1.4, SOAPFault Class.* (Sun Microsystems, Inc., 2003). <http://java.sun.com/j2ee/1.4/docs/api/javax/xml/soap/SOAPFault.html>.

Glossary and Abbreviations

A1

Attribute A type of container used by XML. An XML attribute requires a tag-value-pair format, where a single named tag is followed by an equal sign and a data value between quote delimiters.

B2B (Business-to-Business) A type of servicing interaction where the consumer or the service is an external entity such as another business enterprise.

BAM (Business Activity Monitoring) A technology that monitors the SOA infrastructure and reports activities and events. Although there are many different BAM technology products and offerings, most will include some form of monitoring or instrumentation that is attached to the ESB and extends out into the network at large. BAM technologies will also include a reporting mechanism (usually visual) that allows key subject matter experts to define measures they consider important to their enterprise and to then monitor against these measures.

Begin Tag See Open Tag

BPEL (Business Process Execution Language) A specification for a type of service artifact that serves as the description of a coarse-grained service such as an orchestration, and including one or more fine-grained and subordinate service interactions.

BPM (Business Process Management) A model for interaction where sets of services are referenced as a complete business process. BPM can generally support orchestrations and, in some cases, choreographies.

Canonical A common representation or standard. An enterprise canonical model describes a standard expression for enterprise data and processes. That is, the enterprise canonical is a model for the common information that can be reused across the enterprise.

Choreography A set of interactions between participating services. However, the scope of interaction can be broader than an orchestration and might include SOA services that are defined outside of the enterprise. In this case, the choreography drives a set of steps between collaborators, and they may invoke other services or functionality that is unknown to the original consumer. There may also be a more dynamic assembly of services and service interactions that reflect variations in response from the various SOA services involved as part of the process.

353

Close Tag The closing or ending tag for an XML element.

Complex Type A type of element that includes or encapsulates other elements within, as with a structure. A parent element is sometimes referred to as a complex type. Interestingly, a parent element can also include data values of its own in addition to encapsulated child elements. This is referred to as "mixed content."

Consumer A technology or capability that in some manner interacts with, requests, consumes, and exploits services.

Contract An agreement between consumers and services. For Web services, the contract is generally defined by the service interface as a combination of WSDL and one or more XML Schemas. Policies (i.e., WSM policies or security policies) can also become part of the contract.

Data at Rest Data that are persisted. Usually data are at rest when persisted in a database or file management system.

Data in Motion Data that are inserted into a message and are then moved or transported between service providers and consumers.

Element A type of container used by XML. An element includes a begin tag and an end tag, with the data value located between. An empty XML element can use a shorthand notation.

End Tag See Close Tag.

ESB (Enterprise Service Bus) The backbone technology that supports an SOA. As implied by the name, the ESB is a "bus." That is, the bus is a technology capability that includes the network, transport, and delivery of messages and content, and supporting communication protocols (collectively referred to as the "service bus").

Extension Point A predefined location of a canonical message design that allows for later extension (usually as additional element content) and realized as part of the service interface.

Fire-and-Forget An asynchronous message exchange pattern. Also known as "one-way." A consumer submits a request to a service but does not expect a reply.

KPI (Key Performance Indicator) A metric and measure that is of critical importance to an enterprise. KPIs can be of different types and reflect the things of interest to the enterprise as a whole, a line of business, a geographic area, a market, a customer segment, and so on.

MEP (Message Exchange Pattern) A pattern that describes the interaction between service collaborators. A MEP can represent the directional movement of messages between consumers and services.

Metadata Often described as "data about data." Metadata can be defined at a more granular level as structural, descriptive, semantic, and typed characteristics of data.

NFR (Nonfunctional Requirement) A technical requirement of services, applications, systems, or similar enabling technology solutions. Nonfunctional requirements describe the "qualities" of a system. There can be many different NFRs, but the most common include performance, availability, capacity, scale, recoverability, security, usability, productivity, extensibility, flexibility, interoperability, and security.

Open Tag The beginning or opening tag for an XML element.

Orchestration An orchestration is a set of service interactions that are well defined, with clearly identified steps (often ordered steps) that invoke a set of known services with known interactions.

The rationale for the name "orchestration" is that the overall process is generally led as with an orchestra led by a conductor. Every participant in the orchestration knows their role and their interactions, and they take their lead from the BPM engine and the script representing the steps of the business process.

Over the Wire The electronically digitized and encoded data that travels over a network of some type.

Publish-Subscribe A collaboration model, similar to a Message Exchange Pattern (MEP), where consumers "subscribe" to a service, topic, or similar. Following a service interaction or event, a notification or data resulting from that event is then published to the subscribing consumers.

Request-Reply The most common type of Message Exchange Pattern (MEP), which is also known as synchronous or two-way. The consumer request is expressed in the payload of a message and is sent to a service. A corresponding service response is expressed in a reply message and returned to the originating consumer.

Service Some form of encapsulated technology or behavior that is exposed to consumers to resolve a request.

Simple Type A type of XML Schema declaration that is atomic. An XML Schema element declaration is often considered as a simple type. However, XML Schemas also provide a "simpleType" declaration that is most often used to define data types.

SLA (Service Level Agreement) An agreement between servicing participants (consumers and services) as to the level of service that will be provided. Often an SLA will reflect one or more measures of a nonfunctional requirement such as performance, availability, capacity, and scale.

SOAP (Simple Object Access Protocol) A type of message encoding framework and messaging protocol that uses an envelope analogy.

Tag A declarative delimiter for XML-encoded documents and messages. Depending upon the XML declaration or container type, the tag has a specific format and a name.

Tag-to-Data Ratio A comparison of the XML-encoded tag name length as a character count to a reasonable sampling or example of the data values for those elements. A tag-to-data ratio that is significantly higher for tag count is said to be "metadata heavy."

UDDI (Universal Description Discovery and Integration) An industry standard and model for service registries.

Uniform Structure A message structure that is simple and, to a large degree, vertical or linear when conceptualized as a data graph.

Wildcard A technique that can be implemented by XML Schemas "any" declarations and referenced by a namespace pair from an XML document. The intent of a wildcard is to dynamically extend a message, while hiding the extension from consumers that do not require it.

WSDL (Web Services Description Language) The overall technical interface specification. It serves as not only the definition of the interface, but it also contains technical information such as the allowable operations for a service and its endpoint address.

WSM (Web Services Management) A technology that works with the ESB to describe, manage, and apply policies, as well as trap events (usually at endpoints). WSM technologies will either take action directly or to instruct the ESB to take action. The emphasis of WSM is on the definition and the application of what are often described as policies. Policies are sets of behavior that can be defined to resolve a number of different activities

XML (Extensible Markup Language) The prevailing message encoding form for SOA consumers and services.

XSD (XML Schema Definition Language) XML Schemas are in themselves almost a metadata language. That is, an XSD can describe the structure, types, and even some rules for the content of an XML message.

Important Web Services and Related Specifications

A2

XML-Extensible Markup Language
http://www.w3.org/TR/2006/REC-xml11-20060816/
W3C-Worldwide Web Consortium
"Extensible Markup Language (XML) 1.1 (Second Edition)"
W3C Recommendation 16 August 2006, edited in place 29 September 2006

XML Namespaces
http://www.w3.org/TR/2006/REC-xml-names11-20060816/
W3C-Worldwide Web Consortium
"Namespaces in XML 1.1 (Second Edition)"
W3C Recommendation 16 August 2006

XML Schemas-Part 0, Primer
http://www.w3.org/TR/xmlschema-0/
W3C-Worldwide Web Consortium
"XML Schema Part 0: Primer Second Edition"
W3C Recommendation 28 October 2004

XML Schemas-Part 1, Structures
http://www.w3.org/TR/xmlschema-1/
W3C-Worldwide Web Consortium
"XML Schema Part 1: Structures Second Edition"
W3C Recommendation 28 October 2004

XML Schemas-Part 2, Datatypes
http://www.w3.org/TR/xmlschema-2/
W3C-Worldwide Web Consortium
"XML Schema Part 2: Datatypes Second Edition"
W3C Recommendation 28 October 2004

WSDL-Web Services Description Language-Part 0, Primer
http://www.w3.org/TR/2007/PR-wsdl20-primer-20070523/
W3C-Worldwide Web Consortium

"Web Services Description Language (WSDL) Version 2.0 Part 0: Primer"
W3C Proposed Recommendation 23 May 2007

WSDL-Web Services Description Language-Part 1, Core Language
http://www.w3.org/TR/2007/PR-wsdl20-20070523/
W3C-Worldwide Web Consortium
"Web Services Description Language (WSDL) Version 2.0 Part 1: Core Language"
W3C Proposed Recommendation 23 May 2007

WSDL-Web Services Description Language
http://www.w3.org/TR/2001/NOTE-wsdl-20010315
W3C-Worldwide Web Consortium
"Web Services Description Language (WSDL) Version 1.1"
W3C Note 15 March 2001

SOAP-Simple Object Access Protocol-Part 0, Primer
http://www.w3.org/TR/2007/REC-soap12-part0-20070427/
W3C-Worldwide Web Consortium
"SOAP Version 1.2 Part 0: Primer (Second Edition)"
W3C Recommendation 27 April 2007

SOAP-Simple Object Access Protocol-Part 1, Messaging Framework
http://www.w3.org/TR/2007/REC-soap12-part1-20070427/
W3C-Worldwide Web Consortium
"SOAP Version 1.2 Part 1: Messaging Framework (Second Edition)"
W3C Recommendation 27 April 2007

WS-CDL-Web Services Choreography Definition Language-Overview
http://www.w3.org/TR/2004/WD-ws-chor-model-20040324/
W3C-Worldwide Web Consortium
"WS Choreography Model Overview"
W3C Working Draft 24 March 2004

WS-CDL-Web Services Choreography Definition Language-Primer
http://www.w3.org/TR/2006/WD-ws-cdl-10-primer-20060619/
W3C-Worldwide Web Consortium
"Web Services Choreography Description Language: Primer"
W3C Working Draft 19 June 2006

WS-CDL-Web Services Choreography Definition Language-Language
http://www.w3.org/TR/2005/CR-ws-cdl-10-20051109/
W3C-Worldwide Web Consortium
"Web Services Choreography Description Language Version 1.0"
W3C Candidate Recommendation 9 November 2005

BPEL-Business Process Execution Language
http://docs.oasis-open.org/wsbpel/2.0/OS/wsbpel-v2.0-OS.html
OASIS

"Web Services Business Process Execution Language Version 2.0"
OASIS Standard 11 April 2007

UDDI-Universal Description, Discovery, Integration
http://www.oasis-open.org/committees/uddi-spec/doc/spec/v3/uddi-v3.0.2-20041019.htm
OASIS

"UDDI Version 3.0.2 UDDI Spec Technical Committee Draft, Dated 20041019"
WS-I Basic Profile v1.1 Second Edition
http://www.ws-i.org/Profiles/BasicProfile-1.1.html
WS-I.org
"WS-I Basic Profile v1.1 Final Material"
Dated 2006-04-10

WS-I Basic Profile v1.2
http://www.ws-i.org/Profiles/BasicProfile-1_2(WGAD).html
WS-I.org
"WS-I Basic Profile Version 1.2"
Dated 2007-10-24

WS-I Basic Profile 2.0
http://www.ws-i.org/Profiles/BasicProfile-2_0(WGD).html
WS-I.org
"WS-I Basic Profile Version 2.0"
Dated 2007-10-25

References and Bibliography

A3

Chapter 1
SOA—A Common Sense Definition

1. IBM. *Technology Options for Application Integration and Extended Enterprise Patterns*. Redbooks Paper; 2004:10.

2. Bean J. SOA from A-to-Z. (Presented at DAMA International and Wilshire Metadata conference, Boston, 2007):8.

3. Bray T, Paoli J, Sperberg-McQueen CM, Maler E, Yergeau F, eds. Extensible Markup Language (XML) 1.0 (Fourth Edition) W3C Recommendation. (W3C, August 16, 2006). <http://www.w3.org/TR/2006/REC-xml-20060816/>.

4. The Unicode Consortium. *The Unicode Standard, Version 5.1.0*. Boston: Addison-Wesley; 2007 <http://www.unicode.org/versions/Unicode5.1.0/> (ISBN 0-321-48091-0, as amended by Unicode 5.1.0).

5. UDDI Version 3.0.2, UDDI Spec Technical Committee Draft (Copyright © OASIS Open 2002–2004). <http://uddi.org/pubs/uddi_v3.htm/> (October 19, 2004).

6. Booth D, Liu CK, eds. Web Services Description Language (WSDL) Version 2.0 Part 0: Primer (W3C, W3C Recommendation, June 26, 2007). <http://www.w3.org/TR/wsdl20-primer/>.

7. Fallside DC, Walmsley P, eds. XML Schema Part 0: Primer Second Edition (W3C, W3C Recommendation, October 28, 2004). <http://www.w3.org/TR/xmlschema-0/>.

8. Jordan D, Evdemon J, chairs. Web Services Business Process Execution Language Version 2.0, OASIS Standard (Oasis, April 11, 2007). <http://docs.oasis-open.org/wsbpel/2.0/OS/wsbpel-v2.0-OS.html/>.

Chapter 2
Core SOA Principles

1. Christensen E, Curbera F, Meredith G, Weerawarana S, eds. Web Services Description Language (WSDL) 1.1 (W3C, March 15, 2001). <http://www.w3.org/TR/wsdl/>.

2. Fallside DC, Walmsley P. XML Schema Part 0: Primer Second Edition (W3C, October 28, 2004). <http://www.w3.org/TR/xmlschema-0/>.

3. Jendrock E, Ball J, Carson, D, Evans I, Fordin S, Haase K. Java EE 5 Tutorial, Binding XML Schemas, Part No: 819-3669-10, Table 17-2 (Sun Microsystems Inc., September 2007). <http://java.sun.com/javaee/5/docs/tutorial/doc/bnazq.html/>.

4. Ballinger K, Ehnebuske D, Gudgin M, Nottingham M, Yendluri P. Basic Profile Version 1.0 (Web Services Interoperability Organization, April 16, 2004). <http://www.ws-i.org/Profiles/BasicProfile-1.0-2004-04-16.html/>.

Chapter 3
Web Services and Other Service Types and Styles

1. Christensen E, Curbera F, Meredith G, Weerawarana S, eds. Web Services Description Language (WSDL) 1.1 (W3C, March 15, 2001). <http://www.w3.org/TR/wsdl/>.

2. Chinnici R, Moreau JJ, Ryman A, Weerawarana S, eds. Web Services Description Language (WSDL) Version 2.0 Part 1: Core Language (W3C, June 26, 2007). <http://www.w3.org/TR/wsdl20/>.

3. Fallside DC, Walmsley P, eds. XML Schema Part 0: Primer Second Edition (W3C, October 28, 2004). <http://www.w3.org/TR/xmlschema-0/>.

4. Bray T, Paoli J, Sperberg-McQueen CM, Maler E, Yergeau F, eds. Extensible Markup Language (XML) 1.0 (Fourth Edition). (W3C, September 29, 2006). <http://www.w3.org/TR/REC-xml/>.

5. Mitra N, Lafon Y, eds. SOAP Version 1.2 Part 0: Primer (Second Edition). (W3C, April 27, 2007). <http://www.w3.org/TR/soap12-part0/>.

6. Fielding RT. Architectural Styles and the Design of Network-Based Software Architectures (University of California, Irvine, Dissertation, 2000). <http://www.ics.uci.edu/~fielding/pubs/dissertation/top.htm/>.

7. Fielding RT. Architectural Styles and the Design of Network-based Software Architectures, Section 5.1.5, "Uniform Interface" (University of California, Irvine, Dissertation, 2000). <http://www.ics.uci.edu/~fielding/pubs/dissertation/top.htm/>.

8. Fielding RT. Architectural Styles and the Design of Network-based Software Architectures, Section 5.1.5, "Uniform Interface" (University of California, Irvine, Dissertation, 2000). <http://www.ics.uci.edu/~fielding/pubs/dissertation/top.htm/>.

Chapter 4
Data, the Missing Link

1. Jordan D., Evdemon J. chairs, Web Services Business Process Execution Language Version 2.0, OASIS Standard (April 11, 2007). <http://docs.oasis-open.org/wsbpel/2.0/OS/wsbpel-v2.0-OS.html/>.

Chapter 5
Data Services

1. Jordan D, Evdemon J. chairs, Web Services Business Process Execution Language Version 2.0, OASIS Standard (April 11, 2007). <http://docs.oasis-open.org/wsbpel/2.0/OS/wsbpel-v2.0-OS.html/>.

2. Mitra N, Lafon Y, eds. "SOAP Version 1.2 Part 0: Primer (Second Edition)" (W3C, April 27, 2007). <http://www.w3.org/TR/soap12-part0/>.

3. Java2 Platform Enterprise Edition, J2EE v1.4, SOAPMessage Class, Copyright 2003 Sun Microsystems, Inc. <http://java.sun.com/j2ee/1.4/docs/api/javax/xml/soap/SOAPMessage.html/>.

4. *X/Open CAE Specification, Data Management: Structured Query Language (SQL)*, Version 2, X/Open Document Number: C449 (Reading, UK: X/Open Company Ltd.).

5. DB2 Version 9 Database for Linux, Unix and Windows, Declaring the SQLCA for Error Handling, © IBM Corporation 1993, 2008. <http://publib.boulder.ibm.com/infocenter/db2luw/v9/index.jsp?topic=/com.ibm.db2.udb.apdv.embed.doc/doc/t0004664.htm/>.

6. DB2 Universal Database, Handling an SQLException under the DB2 Universal JDBC Driver, © IBM Corporation 1993, 2006. <http://publib.boulder.ibm.com/infocenter/db2luw/v8/index.jsp?topic=/com.ibm.db2.udb.doc/ad/tjvjcerr.htm/>.

7. "The Java Tutorials, Creating Complete JDBC Applications, Retrieving Exceptions" (Sun Microsystems, Inc., 1995-2008). <http://java.sun.com/docs/books/tutorial/>.

8. MSDN Microsoft Developer Network. NET Framework Developer Center, SqlException Class, © 2008 Microsoft Corporation. <http://msdn.microsoft.com/en-us/library/system.data.sqlclient.sqlexception.aspx/>.

Chapter 6
Transformation to Resolve Data Impedance

1. Kay M, ed. "XSL Transformations (XSLT) Version 2.0," (W3C, January 23, 2007). <http://www.w3.org/TR/xslt20/>.

2. Chamberlin D, Berglund A, Boag S, et al., eds. "XML Path Language (XPath) Version 2.0" (W3C, January 23, 2007). <http://www.w3.org/TR/xpath20/>.

Chapter 7
The Service Interface—Contract

1. Chinnici R, Moreau J-J, Ryman A, Weerawarana S, eds. "Web Services Description Language (WSDL) Version 2.0 Part 1: Core Language" (W3C, June 26, 2007). <http://www.w3.org/TR/wsdl20/>.

2. Christensen E, Curbera F, Meredith G, Weerawarana S, eds. "Web Services Description Language (WSDL) 1.1" (W3C, March 15, 2001). <http://www.w3.org/TR/wsdl/>.

3. Fallside CF, Walmsley P, eds. "XML Schema Part 0: Primer Second Edition" (W3C, October 28, 2004). <http://www.w3.org/TR/xmlschema-0/>.

4. Bray T, Paoli J, Sperberg-McQueen CM, Maler E, Yergeau F, eds. "Extensible Markup Language (XML) 1.0 (Fourth Edition)." (W3C, August 16, 2006, edited in place September 29, 2006). <http://www.w3.org/TR/REC-xml/>.

5. Mitra N, Lafon Y, eds. "SOAP Version 1.2 Part 0: Primer (Second Edition)" (W3C, April 27, 2007). <http://www.w3.org/TR/soap12-part0/>.

6. Bray T, Hollander D, Layman A, Tobin R, eds. "Namespaces in XML 1.0 (Second Edition)." (W3C, August 16, 2006). <http://www.w3.org/TR/REC-xml-names/>.

7. The Unicode Consortium. *The Unicode Standard, Version 5.1.0, defined by: The Unicode Standard, Version 5.0 as amended by Unicode 5.1.0*. Boston: Addison-Wesley; 2007. <http://www.unicode.org/versions/Unicode5.1.0/>.

Chapter 8
Canonical Message Design

1. Mitra N, Lafon Y, eds. "SOAP Version 1.2 Part 0: Primer (Second Edition)." (W3C, April 27, 2007). <http://www.w3.org/TR/soap12-part0/>.

2. Chinnici R, Moreau JJ, Ryman A, Weerawarana S, eds. "Web Services Description Language (WSDL) Version 2.0 Part 1: Core Language" (W3C, June 26, 2007). <http://www.w3.org/TR/wsdl20/>.

3. Mitra N, Lafon Y, eds. "SOAP Version 1.2 Part 0: Primer (Second Edition)." (W3C, April 27, 2007). <http://www.w3.org/TR/soap12-part0/>.

Chapter 9
The Enterprise Taxonomy

1. Wikipedia contributors, "Taxonomy." (Wikipedia, The Free Encyclopedia, January 10, 2009). <http://en.wikipedia.org/w/index.php?title=Taxonomy&oldid=262704599>.

2. "UDDI Version 3.0.2, UDDI Spec Technical Committee Draft" (Copyright © OASIS Open 2002-2004). <http://uddi.org/pubs/uddi_v3.htm (October 19, 2004)>.

Chapter 10
XML Schema Basics

1. Fallside DC, Walmsley P, eds. XML Schema Part 0: Primer Second Edition. (W3C, October 28, 2004). <http://www.w3.org/TR/xmlschema-0/>.

2. Bean J, *XML For Data Architects*. (San Francisco: Morgan Kaufmann; 2003).

3. Biron PV, Malhotra A, eds. XML Schema Part 2: Datatypes Second Edition. (W3C, October 28, 2004). <http://www.w3.org/TR/xmlschema-2/>.

4. The Open Group. The Open Group Base Specifications Issue 6 IEEE Std 1003.1, 2004 Edition, Unix, 9. Regular Expressions. (The IEEE and The Open Group, Copyright © 2001-2004). <http://www.opengroup.org/onlinepubs/009695399/basedefs/xbd_chap09.html/>.

5. Bray T, Hollander D, Layman A, Tobin R, eds. Namespaces in XML 1.0 (Second Edition). (W3C, August 16, 2006). <http://www.w3.org/TR/REC-xml-names/>.

Chapter 11
XML Schema Design Patterns

1. Fallside DC, Walmsley P, eds. XML Schema Part 0: Primer Second Edition. (W3C, October 28, 2004). <http://www.w3.org/TR/xmlschema-0/>.

2. Cagle K, Duckett J, et al., *Professional XML Schemas*. Hoboken, NJ: WROX Press; 2001.

3. Bray T, Hollander D, Layman A, Tobin R, eds. Namespaces in XML 1.0 (Second Edition). (W3C, August 16, 2006). <http://www.w3.org/TR/REC-xml-names/>.

4. Cagle K, Duckett J, et al., *Professional XML Schemas*. Hoboken, NJ: WROX Press; 2001.

5. Bray T, Hollander D, Layman A, Tobin R, eds. Namespaces in XML 1.0 (Second Edition). (W3C, August 16, 2006). <http://www.w3.org/TR/REC-xml-names/>.

6. Cagle K, Duckett J, et al., *Professional XML Schemas*. Hoboken, NJ: WROX Press; 2001.

Chapter 12
Schema Reuse and Assembly

1. Bray T, Hollander D, Layman A, Tobin R, eds. "Namespaces in XML 1.0 (second edition)," (W3C, August 16, 2006). <http://www.w3.org/TR/REC-xml-names/>.

2. Fallside DC, Walmsley P, eds. "XML Schema Part 0: Primer Second Edition" (W3C, October 28, 2004). <http://www.w3.org/TR/xmlschema-0/>.

Chapter 13
The Interface and Change

1. Thompson HS, Beech D, Maloney M, Mendelsohn N, eds. "XML Schema Part 1: Structures Second Edition," (W3C, October 28, 2004). <http://www.w3.org/TR/xmlschema-1/>.

ʾer 16
ʾransactions

ʾemon J. chairs "Web Services Business Process Execution Language Version 2.0, OASIS Standard," ıl 11, 2007). <http://docs.oasis-open.org/wsbpel/2.0/OS/wsbpel-v2.0-OS.html/>

2. *X/Open CAE Specification, Data Management: Structured Query Language (SQL), Version 2*, X/Open Document Number: C449 (Reading, UK: X/Open Company Ltd.).

Chapter 17
Fixed-Length Transactions

1. Bray T, Paoli J, Sperberg-McQueen CM, Maler E, Yergeau F, eds. Extensible Markup Language (XML) 1.0 (Fourth Edition) W3C Recommendation. (W3C, August 16, 2006). <http://www.w3.org/TR/2006/REC-xml-20060816/>.

2. Common Business Oriented Language – COBOL, ANSI X3.23-1985, Information Technology Industry Council (National Committee for Information Technology Standards), INCITS/ISO/IEC 1989–2002, Information Technology - Programming Languages - COBOL.

3. Bray T, Paoli J, Sperberg-McQueen CM, Maler E, Yergeau F, eds. Extensible Markup Language (XML) 1.0 (Fourth Edition) W3C Recommendation. (W3C, August 16, 2006). <http://www.w3.org/TR/2006/REC-xml-20060816/>.

4. The Unicode Consortium. *The Unicode Standard, Version 5.1.0, defined by: The Unicode Standard, Version 5.0*. Boston: Addison-Wesley; 2007 <http://www.unicode.org/versions/Unicode5.1.0/>.

Chapter 18
Document Literal Interfaces

1. Unified Modeling Language (OMG UML). Infrastructure, Version 2.2, (OMG, February 4, 2009). <http://www.omg.org/docs/formal/09-02-04.pdf/>.

Chapter 19
Performance Analysis and Optimization Techniques

1. Bray T, Paoli J, Sperberg-McQueen CM, Maler E, Yergeau F, eds. Extensible Markup Language (XML) 1.0 (Fourth Edition). (W3C, August 16, 2006). <http://www.w3.org/TR/REC-xml/>.

2. Bray T, Paoli J, Sperberg-McQueen CM, Maler E, Yergeau F, eds. Extensible Markup Language (XML) 1.0 (Fourth Edition). (W3C, August 16, 2006). Edited in place 29 September 2006. <http://www.w3.org/TR/REC-xml/>.

3. Bean J, *XML for Data Architects*. (San Francisco: Morgan Kaufmann; 2003).

Chapter 20
Error Definition and Handling

1. *X/Open CAE Specification, Data Management: Structured Query Language (SQL), Version 2*, X/Open Document Number: C449 (Reading, UK: X/Open Company Ltd).

2. Box D, Ehnebuske D, Kakivaya G, Layman A, Mendelsohn N, Nielsen HF, Thatte S, Winer D, eds. Simple Object Access Protocol (SOAP) 1.1. (W3C Note, May 8, 2000). <http://www.w3.org/TR/2000/NOTE-SOAP-20000508/>.

3. Mitra N, Lafon Y, eds. SOAP Version 1.2 Part 0: Primer (Second Edition). (W3C, April 27, 2007). <http://www.w3.org/TR/soap12-part0/>.

4. Java2 Platform Enterprise Edition, J2EE v1.4, SOAPFault Class. (Sun Microsystems, Inc., 2003). <http://java.sun.com/j2ee/1.4/docs/api/javax/xml/soap/SOAPFault.html/>.

Index

A

"Absolute" location, 204
Abstract vs. specific cardinality, 341–3
Abstraction, 120–2
Accelerator, 333, 345
"Ad hoc query" operation, 334
"Add Item" data services, 68, 77, 81
Add New Product BPEL Process, 70
Add New Product Sequence Diagram, 75, 83
Add New Product service, 67, 68, 69, 79, 80, 82, 90, 177, 179, 219, 235, 281, 283
Aggregate on-hand inventory service, 120
Aggregation, 117–20
"All" compositor, 198
Altova, 103, 123
"anyType", 192, 193
"appinfo" element, 271, 273
Application-to-Application (A2A), 4, 53
Attributes, in XML message, 190–2
  and elements, comparison of, 191

B

Benefits of SOA, 23
Bind-time governance, 39–40
Built-in derived types, 192, 193
Built-in primitive types, 192
Business Activity Monitoring (BAM), 18–19
Business agility, 3
Business Process Execution Language (BPEL), 17, 22, 55, 69, 73, 130, 308
Business Process Management (BPM), 15–18, 22, 69
Business services, 280
Business-to-Business (B2B), 18, 53, 102
Business-to-Consumer (B2C), 53

C

Canonical message design, 143–5, 213, 222, 237, 238
  bottom-up design approach, 149
  with data fragments, 299
  hierarchical message, 145–9
  model-driven interface design, 171–2
  top-down approach, 149–50
    conceptual message design, 153–5, 159
    design requirements, 150–3

logical message design, 155–8
message schemas, creating and refining, 168–70
physical message design, 158–68
WSDL creation, 170–1
Canonical metadata, for element, 100
Canonical model, 8, 98, 101, 172
  and data source impedance, 99
  and database mappings, 92
  Request and Reply mapped to, 101
  XML reply message based on, 93
  XML request message based on, 92
Cardinality, 154, 188, 199, 341
Chameleon, 227
Check Duplicate Item service, 68, 76, 77, 80, 81
Child element, 27, 133, 139, 147, 148
Choice compositor, 198
Choreography, 18
Closed loop SOA, 21–3
Coarse-grained service, 67, 286
COBOL (Common Business Oriented Language), 32–3, 261, 265, 319, 320, 348
  string data value, 320
  vs. XML format, 33
Code element, 349
Compensating transaction, 313, 314
Complex hierarchy of schemas, 253, 255
ComplexType patterns, 198–200, 201, 212–18
Composite data service, 67, 97, 109
Compositors, 198, 212
Conceptual message design, 153–5, 156, 159
Consumer, XML message, and XML Schema, 186
Consumer and service, 5–7, 332
Contextual affinity, 295
Core SOA principles, 25
  discoverability, 37
  governance, 37–9
    bind-time governance, 39–40
    design-time governance, 39
    run-time governance, 40–1
  interoperability, 32–4
  loose coupling, 25–32
  reusability, 34–7
COTS (Commercial Off The Shelf applications), 77
Country and Industry Classifications, 177

367